FIERY JOE

FIERY JOE

THE MAVERICK WHO LIT UP THE WEST

KATHLEEN CARLISLE

WITH EILEEN FORRIETER

University of Regina Press

Printed and bound in Canada at Marquis. The text of this book is printed on 100% post-consumer recycled paper with earth-friendly vegetable-based inks.

Cover: Duncan Campbell, University of Regina Press
Text design: John van der Woude, JVDW Designs
Copy editor: Kirsten Craven
Proofreader: Kristine Douaud
Indexer: Patricia Furdek
Cover art: "Tangled Wires" by aon168 / iStock Photo

Library and Archives Canada Cataloguing in Publication

Carlisle, Kathleen, author
Fiery Joe : the maverick who lit up the west / Kathleen Carlisle with Eileen Forrieter.

Includes bibliographical references and index. Issued in print and electronic formats. ISBN 978-0-88977-485-8 (softcover).—ISBN 978-0-88977-486-5 (PDF).—ISBN 978-0-88977-487-2 (HTML)

1. Phelps, Joseph Lee, 1899-1983. 2. Politicians—Saskatchewan—Biography.
3. Saskatchewan—Politics and government—20th century.
4. Saskatchewan—Biography. I. Forrieter, Eileen, author II. Title.

FC3525.1.P54C37 2017 971.24'02092 C2017-900251-1 C2017-900252-X

10 9 8 7 6 5 4 3 2 1

U OF R PRESS

University of Regina Press, University of Regina
Regina, Saskatchewan, Canada, S4S 0A2
tel: (306) 585-4758 fax: (306) 585-4699
web: www.uofrpress.ca

We acknowledge the support of the Canada Council for the Arts for our publishing program. We acknowledge the financial support of the Government of Canada. / Nous reconnaissons l'appui financier du gouvernement du Canada. This publication was made possible through Creative Saskatchewan's Creative Industries Production Grant Program.

Canada Council for the Arts Conseil des Arts du Canada Canada creative SASKATCHEWAN

In memory of Ella Little, who understood the historical significance of her father's unique brand of dirigisme, social democratic ideals, and entrepreneurial spirit.

CONTENTS

FOREWORD

At the turn of the twentieth century, Saskatchewan often was a lonely place, dominated by vast farmlands and buffeted by an unpredictable climate. For the thousands of settlers who came to Saskatchewan to build new lives, the seemingly endless prairie took great courage to homestead. It also took something else—the capacity to dream, and dream "big." Joe Phelps personified these characteristics. His contribution to building Saskatchewan and Canada is an important demonstration of what big dreams can achieve.

Joe Phelps came of age during a time of great adversity. He arrived in Saskatchewan from Ontario in 1909 to join his father, who had come earlier in pursuit of new opportunities. Unpredictable weather, stormy grain markets, and large distances posed constant challenges to the hopes of the Phelps family and to the residents of the province. While Joe's older brother fought in the First World War and his father fell into a period of depression, the younger Phelps took on the responsibility of operating a farm and the numerous associated challenges.

He also quickly came to understand the fragility of what was, then, a one-commodity provincial economy. That fragility was further underlined by the impact of the Great Depression of 1929. It was this Great Depression that fuelled Joe Phelps's belief that unbridled free enterprise and unrestrained capitalism exacerbated the economic devastation by their inability to deal fairly with the unconscionable and rising levels of economic and social inequity. Thus, he grew to strongly believe that government and local co-operative initiatives, led by ordinary citizens, would produce the economic diversification necessary to lessen the province's economic dependency on the wheat economy, while also implementing important and positive reforms to the capitalist system.

All of this led Joe Phelps to seek a new political approach to remedy the situation. He found that message of hope in the founding of the Co-operative Commonwealth Federation (CCF) in 1932. Attracted and motivated by the powerful oratory of building the so-called New Jerusalem, as articulated by Tommy Douglas and other social-democratic activists, the CCF's ideas began to resonate throughout western Canada and, in particular, within Saskatchewan.

Few were more passionate or committed to the ideals of the CCF than Joe Phelps. He envisioned this new Prairie movement as the political vehicle to build a more just, more diversified, and more plentiful province. Thus, it was inevitable that Joe Phelps would enter elective political life. He became one of the most fiery and compelling advocates for the goals of the CCF. In 1938, he won political office as the CCF member for Saltcoats. And, when Douglas and his team swept into government in 1944, Joe Phelps became a senior member of that first Douglas Cabinet. He brought with him his philosophical commitment to social democracy, his perpetual optimism, and his "can do" work ethic. This was a perfect fit with the new Douglas Government, and was precisely what a challenged Saskatchewan needed.

The first Douglas term of office saw the enactment of numerous and transformative social and economic reforms. It was a blizzard of activity. Rural electrification, public hospitalization insurance, which later led to public medicare, and a blossoming of new Crown corporations to stimulate economic growth to defeat the worst impacts of the depression were some of the hallmarks of that first Douglas term.

These large and ambitious ideas required energetic and committed activists if they were to become reality. In his new role as Minister of Natural Resources and Industrial Development, armed with a persistent belief in the merits of public ownership of the means of production, Joe Phelps fit the needs of the new task perfectly. With unsurpassed enthusiasm, Joe Phelps introduced many innovative economic initiatives. Crown corporations, such as SaskPower, were organized to become vehicles for economic and social development. The Crown corporations generated wealth and employment, and provided much-needed services to the people of Saskatchewan. They also demonstrated an alternative to private, for-profit corporations. Moreover, new public corporations were created to diversify the economy by processing primary products into consumer goods.

But unbridled hope and optimism collided with harsh economic and fiscal reality. Investments in enterprises such as a brick plant, a shoe factory, a box factory, and a woollen mill failed to make a profit. The failure of theses ambitious businesses highlighted the reality of limited human resources and manufacturing experience, small markets, large distances, and the ironclad rules of the market economy in which these enterprises had to operate. Moreover, critics successfully argued that ideology and unrealistic ambitions had trumped methodical decision making and the recognition that Canada based its economic growth on private enterprise.

Thus, the philosophy of the social democractic movement of the 1944 election met vociferous economic and political opposition. The Douglas Government and Joe Phelps came under sustained and serious criticism of their policies and their refusal to acknowledge the overarching disciplines of the free-enterprise market economy.

The 1948 general provincial election was fought, in large measure, on the merits of these many bold, new initiatives of economic diversification. The optimism of 1944 was swept away by a return to the traditional voting patterns in Joe Phelps's constituency. And 1948 saw the defeat of Joe Phelps in the Saltcoats constituency. The controversies surrounding the numerous and complex commercial and financial undertakings ensured that Joe Phelps's re-election campaign would be unsuccessful.

Looking back at this moment in Saskatchewan history, few would doubt that it represented a remarkable period of renewal, experimentation, and optimism. In large measure, much credit is to be assigned to the principled, exuberant, and persuasive personality exhibited by Joe Phelps inside and outside Cabinet. Even after his electoral defeat, his reform agenda and undying optimism never left him. Thus, his accomplishments are not to be underestimated. His contributions assisted ordinary Saskatchewan people to maintain their hope and to eventually see the province recover from the ravages of the Great Depression and the World Wars.

Although Joe Phelps's time in elective office was short, his contribution to Saskatchewan remains timeless. His commitment to the people of Saskatchewan and his social democratic principles, his constant enthusiasm, and his never-ending capacity to "dream the big dreams" are demonstrated by his achievements.

Moreover, Joe Phelps's contributions to civil society did not end with his electoral defeat. He continued the pursuit of his ideals as a fierce voice for farmers as president of the Saskatchewan Farmers Union. Moreover, his dedication to respecting, understanding, and preserving the history of our shared Prairie destiny led to the foundation and growth of the Western Development Museum of Saskatchewan.

Kathleen Carlisle has eloquently and thoroughly explored the life and accomplishments of Joe Phelps. By understanding more about this "maverick dreamer," his ideals, vision, and principles, we also learn a lot more about the great province of Saskatchewan.

—Roy J. Romanow, April 20, 2016

ACKNOWLEDGEMENTS

This book was in the making for over a decade and many people contributed to the process along the way.

First, a tribute to my co-author, Eileen Forrieter. Although ours was not a collaboration in the usual sense, her contribution to *Fiery Joe* is such that "authorship" is the necessary and fitting acknowledgement. Ms. Forrieter spent several years researching Joe Phelps's political career, culminating in her master's thesis, "Joseph Lee Phelps: An Impulsive Radical" (2005). She freely shared her research with me and granted permission to include excerpts directly from her thesis. These excerpts are found throughout parts I and II, and more specifically in chapters 3, 4, 5, and 12. The addition of her fine work added the depth and breadth of research that was required to produce a balanced and comprehensive historical biography of Joe Phelps. Sadly, Ms. Forrieter died suddenly on March 18, 2015, and so did not live to see the completion of the book. I am tremendously grateful for her careful scholarship and her generosity, and I am honoured to share authorship with her on this project.

I would like to extend my thanks to Roberta Mitchell Coulter for her wise critique of an early manuscript, expert editing, and suggestions for improvement, and most recently for the arduous process of reducing the size of the manuscript prior to publication. I would also like to thank University of Regina Press, especially Karen May Clark, acquisitions editor, and Bruce Walsh, director and publisher, for their publishing and marketing acumen and expertise, as well as senior editor Donna Grant and copy editor Kirsten Craven.

I am also grateful to Dr. Bill Brennan, who acted as thesis supervisor for Eileen Forrieter's work noted above. His appraisal of an early draft of the manuscript was essential to completing this book.

Stuart Thiesson, a long-time farm activist and executive secretary of the Saskatchewan Farmers Union for many years, was also a tremendous help. Stuart's knowledge of the voluntary farm movement was essential to documenting Phelps's involvement in the movement. Thanks also to Chris Hansen, Bruce Dodds, and Herbert Schulz for their excellent suggestions. All provided valuable input, particularly in the chapters related to agriculture, and I am grateful.

Thank you to Douglas Charrett of Prince Albert, who completed an initial manuscript titled "The Life and Times of Fiery Joe Phelps" in 2003, and to Larry Shaak of Moose Jaw, who conducted an extensive series of interviews with many of Joe Phelps's colleagues and associates from his years in government, the farm movement, and in British Columbia, as well as many of Joe's family members at the same time. Thanks also to Lois Simmie, who provided input on Douglas Charrett's early manuscript. Kathryn Nogue provided suggestions and proofreading, and Dr. Stuart Houston provided feedback early in the process. Thanks also to my partner, Garry Walsh, who has been a tremendous help throughout the project.

Finally, thank you to Dr. David Goranson, who along with his mother, Ella Little, initiated this book and whose Phelpsian persistence and tenacity ensured that it reached completion.

INTRODUCTION

Joseph Lee Phelps has been described as a "human dynamo."[1] He was unequivocally a man of action. His outspoken voice echoes in archival documents and the recollections of those who lived and worked with him. Deemed by his colleagues in government and the farm movement to be "volcanic," "charismatic," and "fiery," Phelps propelled himself into leadership roles where he could effect genuine change unhampered. Never reluctant to express his frustration with those who did not share his enthusiasm and drive, or who could not keep up, he left behind a compelling, and at times controversial, legacy. Indeed, many consider Phelps to be one of Saskatchewan's most memorable and colourful political figures.[2]

Saskatchewan has been one of the most politically progressive of Canada's provinces, introducing many innovative policies, including universal health care.[3] In July 1944, the Co-operative Commonwealth Federation took office in Saskatchewan, forming North America's first social democratic government. Led by Tommy Douglas, it advocated sweeping reforms that would dramatically alter the social, economic, and political landscape of the province. To implement the CCF plan, Premier Douglas turned not only to outside experts but also to those who had proven their mettle in provincial farm and labour movements, like Joe Phelps, who as Minister of Natural Resources and Industrial Development would become a key member of his team. Phelps's indefatigable work ethic, courage, and ideological commitment to the ideals of the party made him the perfect fit for this challenging post. Indeed, Phelps initiated many of the significant changes brought about by the Douglas Government in Saskatchewan. Impatient with the status quo, his propensity for quick, decisive action meant he often forged ahead with blatant disregard for conventional bureaucratic procedures, earning the respect and admiration of many, cautious skepticism from those who favoured a more conventional approach, and outright disdain from those who opposed his ideas. Not surprisingly, some historians have not looked favourably on Phelps's rather unconventional approach. His involvement in the province's early attempts to diversify Saskatchewan's economy garnered mixed reviews. Some of Phelps's early forays into businesses such as a shoe factory have been ridiculed and dismissed as misguided ventures, but his efforts to establish publicly owned and administered businesses were important in the ongoing struggle to diversify Saskatchewan's economy through added-value agricultural enterprises. Joe Phelps played a prominent role in the Douglas Government's ability to turn, as Gregory Marchildon has put it, "a relatively isolated and poverty-stricken province into Canada's most important social laboratory."[4] The public ownership of utilities and the building of a modern infrastructure, in which Crown corporations played a major role, were ground-breaking initiatives led by Phelps; they have been instrumental in the long-term stability of the province ever since.

Similarly, Phelps's prominent role in Saskatchewan's agrarian history is particularly salient to the current agricultural situation, including the disintegration of the family farm and the futile struggle to protect the Canadian Wheat Board. Herbert Schulz, grassroots organizer for the Manitoba Farmers Union (MFU) and author of *Betrayal: Prairie Agricultural Politics in the Fifties*, argues that decisions taken since Phelps's time have resulted in the current circumstances in Canadian agriculture. Phelps and Herbert's father, Jake Schulz (who together were known as the "Terrible Twins" during their heyday as grassroots farm organizers), predicted that these decisions would lead to fewer farms, impossible debt loads, and "neo-feudal" control of agricultural processing, arguing, "The yeoman farmer who opened the West and built the community is being reduced to a serf. If vertical integration of agriculture continues he will end up as a hired man on his own land working for subsidized, non-resident investors."[5] Phelps's minority report for the Saskatchewan Royal Commission on Agriculture and Rural Life in 1958 stands as the most complete and mature expression of his views on agriculture and farm organization, and is a poignant and timely reminder of what might have been had his advice been heeded.

Championing causes that were not always widely embraced or popular, often with considerable personal sacrifice, was difficult and at times disappointing for Phelps. His energy and vision earned him positions as director of the United Farmers of Canada (Saskatchewan section) (UFC), charter member of the CCF, Minister of Natural Resources in the first social democratic government in North America, first president of the Saskatchewan Farmers Union (SFU), chairman of the Interprovincial Farm Union Council, a member of the Saskatchewan Royal Commission on Agriculture and Rural Life, and a place in the Saskatchewan Agricultural Hall of Fame. The two decades of his life that he spent collecting and restoring vintage machinery and establishing the province's Western Development Museum remain with Saskatchewan people and provide concrete documentation of the ingenuity and monumental changes in Saskatchewan's material culture over the course of the twentieth century.

Phelps's ability to advance important projects rapidly and efficiently, to organize and mobilize people at the grassroots level, to reconcile competing claims or interests when necessary, to resist or embrace compromise when required, gauging goals against obstacles and at the same time satisfying high ethical and ideological standards in a practical way, distinguish him as one of Saskatchewan's great pioneers.[6] He lived an exciting life, and he excited many people along the way.[7]

Much of the impetus for Phelps's involvement in social movements originates in the circumstances of his upbringing and the values he learned growing up on a farm. By many accounts he was a farmer through and through—a fact demonstrated by his resourcefulness and practicality. He always had coveralls handy wherever he went (in the trunk of his car, and in baggage when travelling by air), which he was quick to don should someone happen to need a hand. The smell of the horse liniment he used to soothe his aching muscles was often evident,[8] as were his characteristic expressions: "By jingles, Nellie!" he'd exclaim, banging his hand down brusquely on the nearest solid object when he spoke about something that inspired him.

Joe Phelps left his mark on this province in the improvement of rural life, the political culture of Saskatchewan people, and the preservation of history. He was an important voice in the province; a man who lit up Saskatchewan in so many ways. This is his story.

PART I

PRELUDE TO POWER

1899–1944

CHAPTER 1

LAND OF OPPORTUNITY

In the fall of 1908, nine-year-old Joe Phelps was riding high in the cupola of a red caboose, a guest of the crew of the train that would take his family halfway across Canada. He was going to join his father, big brother, and sister on their homestead in Saskatchewan, a place that had held his father's attention almost exclusively for three years.[1] Even when his father returned to Ontario for the winter, his dreams remained in the West, a land of freedom, boundless potential, and adventure. Young Joe was travelling with his mother, his younger brother, Don, and sisters Eva and Lulu to join the rest of the family in a one-room, twelve-by-sixteen-foot shack. Theirs was the first train to travel the new line from Saskatoon to Wilkie; the rest of the family had come down through the Battlefords, travelling by Red River cart on a rutted track.[2] Joseph Phelps was the second son and third of six children born to George Phelps and Caroline Phelps at Thurlow, Ontario, on August 12, 1899.[3]

As he looked out from the caboose, Joe saw miles of prairie grass, interrupted by sparse scrub brush and the occasional shallow coulee. Though the land had recently been divided into a checkerboard of townships, each consisting of thirty-six square miles of farmland, each divided into quarter sections of 160 acres, the order imposed had not yet made its physical impression on the land. In each township, two quarters had been set aside for the Hudson's Bay Company (HBC) and two for schools, while odd-numbered quarters were kept for the Crown or the railways, and even-numbered quarters were intended for homesteaders.[4] With the nearest neighbours several miles away, the Phelps family would have spent many lonely evenings on the homestead.

Four years earlier, George Phelps and his wife Caroline (Carrie) made the decision that they and their six children would leave their farm at Tweed near Belleville, Ontario, and move to the new frontier, as George's Irish Protestant family had done in the early 1800s when they left Massachusetts and moved to Brantford.[5] Enthusiastic about the cheap land and the potential he saw on the Saskatchewan prairie, George had obtained entry for the homestead on May 25, 1905, the year Saskatchewan became a province.[6] He chose land just north of Wilkie and travelled to Saskatchewan that fall to begin breaking the prairie.[7] Before he returned to Ontario the first winter, he had cultivated forty acres of prairie grass to sow to wheat the following spring. He spent most of the next two years at the homestead, farming.

A year before young Joe made the journey, in the fall of 1907, George and his two eldest children, Fred and Etta, travelled to Saskatchewan with the first of three railway cars of settlers' effects: household items, farm equipment, and even livestock. They also brought planed oak lumber from the trees that grew on their Ontario farm, laying it flat a foot thick on the floor of the railway freight car and packing their other belongings on top. The oak eventually became flooring in the house that remains to this day on the homestead.

The Phelps family homestead, Wilkie, Saskatchewan, date unknown. Permission granted by the Phelps family estate.

THE LAST BEST WEST

Promotional efforts by the Immigration Branch of Canada's Department of the Interior portraying the West as a land of opportunity—"the Last Best West"—had convinced George and thousands of others to move west. In 1905, over nineteen thousand new homesteads were taken out.[8] Pamphlets described "a healthy climate guaranteed to be free of malaria," hot prairie summers that were "delightfully invigorating," and winters that were "cold but dry and not unpleasant."[9] The spirit of adventure and the promise of a better life, along with the offer of 160 acres of land for a ten-dollar registration fee, provided enough incentive to make the move. In exchange, they were required to build habitable houses, prepare twenty-five acres of land for seeding, and live on the land for three years.

By the spring of 1909, George had complied with all of the homestead requirements and had also disposed of his property in Ontario. By this time, the Phelps homestead had 120 acres cropped, six horses, eleven cattle, and two hogs. George had also built a twenty-eight-foot-square sod barn, four hundred rods of fence, a frame granary, and a well. Together with the house, these assets were valued at $620, with no mortgages or transfers against the property.[10] His financial situation would not always be as promising, and George's optimism would be severely tempered by the hardships to come—the short growing season, low rainfall, and long winters, along with economic instability and uncertainty.

Farm women worked equally hard in those days, without electricity and running water. Carrie looked after all the domestic chores, including curing much of the family's meat in a smokehouse constructed of scraps of leftover lumber, as well as sewing, knitting, and caring for the six children. But this work was not enough to satisfy the former schoolteacher. She set up the first Ladies' Aid of the Narrow Lake district and was its president for a number of years, arranging quilting bees and other activities. Many pioneer families could not afford health care, and often a doctor was not available, so Carrie also acted as midwife and nurse for the area, and was frequently the first to be called to tend an illness or birth.[11]

Although there are very few references to Joe's religious inclinations, his mother apparently had a strict regime of religious instruction, and as a young man Joe aspired to the ministry, which perhaps would later contribute to the appeal of the social gospel message in the CCF's ideology.[12]

Joe attended Starview School in Wilkie for a time and played baseball for the Narrow Lake Britons at local sports days and on Sundays in the early 1920s, and became the team's manager in 1926. Saturday nights were spent at dances, and the affable Joe found himself in demand for square dance calling.

The matched team of driving horses brought from Ontario took the family to town for supplies and visiting, and worked long hours alongside the men in the fields. Joe repaid the horses with devotion and treated them with kindness. He remained a respected horseman throughout his life and was often called upon to judge horses and plowing matches, sliding easily from the role of politician to horseman. As Joe's son Bruce recalled of his father: "No one ever dared abuse a horse in front of my dad! In the field he would stop after every round and give the horses a rest. He also made sure they were wiped down and well fed at the end of the day.... He certainly respected them."[13]

Described as a land of opportunity, the West was essentially a colony of eastern Canada. Since 1885, there had been a slow but steady influx of Central Canadian, English, European, and American immigrants. At the turn of the century, the government of Canada had increased its promotional efforts to encourage settlement, and the pace accelerated. The first to feel the impact of the expansion westward were the First Nations. To facilitate future development and unrestricted access to the land and resources, the Canadian government had moved quickly to negotiate treaties to extinguish Aboriginal title to land suitable for farming before Saskatchewan became a province in 1905.[14] Conservative Prime Minister John A. Macdonald was then free to institute his National Policy's three pillars: settling the West to produce grain and raw materials and provide markets for eastern business; building a transcontinental railway to transport settlers and manufactured goods to and raw materials from the West; and establishing a tariff wall to protect eastern manufacturers from foreign competition. The steady stream of settlers turned into a flood, increasing the province's population from around thirty thousand in 1885 to over 640,000 by 1916.[15] It was a captive market that only eastern Canada would be able to service, and over the next century Prairie farmers would engage in an arduous struggle to alter the colonial status of their region.

When the Phelps family arrived in Saskatchewan, farmers had already begun to fight for reforms. They had little control over many farm-related matters, especially grain prices, freight rates, and machinery costs. As a growing sense of antagonism toward the big grain companies emerged, many farmers turned to political action. Settlers brought with them diverse views and experiences, including a familiarity with farm organizations, trade unions, and a variety of socialist and other political traditions. There was some inequality amongst them—land quality varied, and some settlers brought more resources with them than others—but for the most part, farmers were a relatively homogeneous economic class. And although they were from diverse cultural backgrounds, they were bound together not only by the relative "classlessness" of the new frontier but also by their common experience of forging a living on it. The economy of the fledgling province was based exclusively on one commodity, wheat, and unpredictable weather made the single cash crop economy very risky. Many farmers became debtors, borrowing money in the hope of earning more in the future.

Farm groups such as the Patrons of Industry had been formed as early as 1891 to address issues related to the sale, movement, and price of grain, and the excessive freight rates and tariffs imposed.[16] In 1897, the Canadian Pacific Railway (CPR) ordered that wheat delivery must go through grain elevators. Farmers who had been loading grain directly into boxcars suspected monopoly price fixing, and future problems with the weighing and grading of their grain. When the 1901 bumper crop overloaded the elevator system,[17] farmers joined together to protest, forming the Territorial Grain Growers' Association, which became the Saskatchewan Grain Growers' Association (SGGA) in 1905.[18] Their first victory gave farmers the right to order railway cars on the same terms as the elevator companies, and reinforced their belief in the benefits of collective action. The SGGA boasted 1,300 branches and a membership of twenty-eight thousand by 1916.

THE CO-OPERATIVE SPIRIT

In such a demanding and unforgiving environment, settlers had to work together. Co-operative effort was the only effective political and social strategy. Besides, they were lonely. It was common for people to participate in work bees and share their resources. Often families joined together to purchase a railcar load of supplies such as flour, twine, coal, and feed. This practice soon led to the formation of local co-operatives in small towns across the Prairies.

In 1911, the SGGA convinced the Scott Liberal government to pass legislation to form the Saskatchewan Co-operative Elevator Company, creating an elevator system owned and operated by farmers with substantial support from the government. Two years later, the government passed the Agricultural Co-operative Associations Act, which helped farmers set up local co-operatives to purchase farm supplies at lower prices, and established a Co-operative Organization Branch within the Department of Agriculture. The co-operative movement began to shape the unique political and social consciousness that was emerging in Saskatchewan.[19]

As a young farmer, Joe Phelps began to take an active interest in farm politics, attending SGGA meetings with Alex Cotter, secretary of the Narrow Lake local. By 1916, seventeen-year-old Joe was elected a district director of the SGGA.[20] Discussion of local trading association issues, such as buying carloads of coal, twine, or other supplies, dominated SGGA meetings. But Joe had much bigger things on his mind:

> I was grumbling to Alex on the way home about why we could not find something else to discuss except what to buy. Alex thought I had a good point. The last meeting I attended they were still talking about what to buy and when to buy and I was getting more disgusted all the time. I was 18 then, and was standing toward the rear of the room with my arm along a ledge. All at once I decided to give them a good jolt and go home. I walked out into the center of the room and tied into them. I can remember standing in the middle of the floor swinging my arms. That was the last meeting I attended, although I retained my membership for another year or two.[21]

This incident would become typical of Phelps's involvement in politics. He had little patience for bureaucratic procedures and organizations that focused on the mundane. He did not hesitate to "give a good jolt" when he felt a situation required it, and his ability as a forceful and flamboyant orator continued to develop throughout his career, with "the charisma to stir even the most passive souls with a sense of indignation—and hope."[22]

"TOUGH SLEDDING"

Soon after the First World War broke out, Joe's older brother Fred enlisted and left the farm to serve overseas. Joe called the hard times that followed "tough sledding." To support the war effort, farmers were encouraged to increase production with government loans to farmers and their of-age sons to start or augment herds. George Phelps arranged for the maximum line of credit for both himself and his two eldest boys, and they went into beef cattle in a big way. They seeded all the cultivated land they had in 1918, but they soon felt the wrath of the elements, losing most of the seed to an early frost. The same year, they bought two railcar loads of breeding heifers and one carload of feeders at a cost of $87 each, with loans for two-thirds of the money from the government and one-third from the bank. Unfortunately, the bottom dropped out of the beef cattle market, making the cattle worth a fraction of their initial cost. The Phelpses kept the cattle for two years, waiting for a market, paying up to twenty-five cents each for oat sheaves, which had to be shipped in during the winter of 1918. The cattle were eventually taken to Winnipeg for sale, and George netted only about $43 a head for the three-year-olds.[23]

This experience remained permanently seared in Joe's mind, and the adversity and stress took its toll on the Phelps family. George suffered from severe depression and was hospitalized in Prince Albert. Pressures from the unpredictable weather and unstable farm economy, combined with the isolation and hardship of daily living, were resulting in an increasingly widespread incidence of mental breakdown among Prairie farmers. Mental illness was a source of shame at that time and so was rarely spoken of, but in small communities neighbours knew each other's hardships. Although just in his mid-teens, with his brother Fred overseas, Joe was the oldest boy in the family. Of necessity, his formal education stopped at grade six as he took on the responsibility of managing the farm and looking after the family.[24] When George returned from the hospital, his condition did not completely stabilize, and Joe continued to shoulder the bulk of the load, supporting the family both financially and emotionally. He took advantage of a free construction and repair course with the Narrow Lake Telephone Company, and in his late teens found long-term employment there to supplement the family's farm income.

The rural telephone system was expanding, and Joe would remain with the company for the next twenty-two years.[25]

When Fred returned from the war, he married and moved to a farm of his own, but he had been profoundly wounded. The horrific carnage of the First World War changed the generation of young men who returned to Saskatchewan and the rest of Canada, and their massive suffering and sacrifice affected Joe deeply. He came to share the anti-imperialist views advocated by J. S. Woodsworth and others in a new political movement that would emerge in the early 1930s. Along with unstable grain and livestock prices and myriad related problems, this motivated Joe and other farmers in similar circumstances to seek political solutions.

Joe turned to political action naturally: his father was a strong Liberal and had faith in men like William Motherwell, founding president of the SGGA. Joe later recalled that his father had always been sympathetic to the Grain Growers and had been a fairly active member, but at this point farmers had many reasons to be dissatisfied with the conservative SGGA.[26] Some felt that its leadership and the government overlapped too much. William Motherwell, co-founder and first president of the Territorial Grain Growers Association, served as Minister of Agriculture from 1905 to 1918. George Langley, who entered the Cabinet in 1912, and Charles Dunning, who followed in 1916 and became premier in 1922, had both been active in the SGGA. J. A. Maharg, another SGGA president, also joined the government as agriculture minister. Farmer dissatisfaction with the SGGA led to the appearance of a rival farmers' organization, the Farmers' Union of Canada (FUC), founded in December 1921 at Ituna.[27] Little wonder that when an Alberta man named Harris held a meeting in the Narrow Lake School to introduce the FUC and its plan to unite farmers to fight for a better deal, young Joe was tremendously impressed. Eight people were needed to form an FUC lodge in their own region. When Alex Cotter, the secretary of the Grain Growers' local, joined the seven people present at the first meeting, the first Wilkie area Farmers' Union local was formed.[28] Phelps, who considered the SGGA too staid, became one of the FUC's first members.[29] He later said, "When I heard their program and knew what they were after, I darned quick switched over.... I just left the Grain Growers because they were too old-fashioned for me altogether. I wanted to go faster than they were prepared to go."[30] By 1924, the FUC had ten thousand members.

HUMANITY FIRST

Joe's social conscience and socialist beliefs had their roots in this period. The adversity and hardship he faced as a young farmer struggling with economic uncertainty, dependent on countless factors beyond his control; leaving school early and taking on added responsibility after his father's illness; and seeing the effects of the war on his friends and family led him to champion the cause of others who were experiencing similar hardships and ignited in him a desire to create a kinder and more compassionate society. He would work toward building a society in which wealth was distributed more equitably through an array of programs that ensured people's basic needs were met and made their lives more secure. "Humanity first," the fundamental premise that was later put forward in the Regina Manifesto in 1933, held great appeal and cemented his commitment to the socialist movement.

It is not that Phelps wanted a free lunch for himself or anyone else. In fact, he expected almost slavish devotion to duty from himself, his family, and almost everyone else he came into contact with. Without his incredible ambition and drive and uncompromising work ethic, he would not have accomplished so much. Eiling Kramer, former CCF Member of the Legislative Assembly (MLA) for the Battlefords, remembers him as "impetuous and impatient, driving himself relentlessly at any task or project he undertook. His answer, when asked when a job should be finished was, 'How about the day before yesterday?'"[31] Daughter-in-law Muriel Phelps, who with Joe's son Lee later farmed the Wilkie homestead when Joe left to enter politics, recalled his concern when he learned the hired men were not working on Saturday nights. The hired men had a saying when they referred to Joe: "Six days shall ye rip and tear. The seventh day ye shall repair."[32] His work ethic served him well as he juggled his work as a telephone lineman, farmer, and budding farm activist throughout the next two decades.

CHAPTER 2

A NEW POLITICAL LANDSCAPE

Young Joe Phelps had learned first-hand that Saskatchewan's one-dimensional economy was risky and unstable. As a farmer, he was not only vulnerable to the weather but was also at the mercy of the grain companies and high tariffs. Improved commodity prices, due in large part to federal wartime legislation passed in 1917, had taken the grain trade out of the hands of private traders and placed wheat prices under the control of an early version of the Canadian Wheat Board. Farmers began receiving a fixed price on delivery of grain and a final payment on grain sold during the crop year. In 1919, No. 1 Northern wheat was selling at $2.63 a bushel, significantly higher than before the federal government had taken control of the buying and selling of grain.[1] When the war ended and the legislation was lifted, wheat trading returned to the private sector. This coincided with a postwar slump in demand, and prices fell drastically, strengthening the farmers' belief in the need for a monopoly marketing system.

The FUC, realizing that the federal government was not willing to change the tariff structure or revive the Wheat Board, began advocating the formation of a central commodity pool to which farmers could sell their grain. Conflict emerged over how the commodity pool should be organized, and tensions were high as farm organizations struggled with how best to serve the interests of the farmer.[2] The radical FUC supported a 100 per cent compulsory pool, which meant that as soon as a certain percentage of farmers had contracted to the pool, legislation would compel all farmers to sell to it.[3] Thus, the entire wheat crop of the province would be pooled, greatly strengthening the selling position of the wheat pool on the world market. Other farm groups, like the SGGA, advocated a contract pool in which farmers decided on a voluntary basis whether to participate.

Phelps joined in the crusade for compulsory grain pooling, convinced that this would ensure that all farmers would receive the same price for the same grade of wheat and thus stabilize the marketplace. Phelps was among many who had become disillusioned with the SGGA, whose membership dropped from 33,445 in 1919 to 15,661 in 1923. Phelps and others representing the FUC went on the road promoting compulsory pooling of wheat, and many recall the lively Saturday morning meetings at the Burgess Café in North Battleford, where farmers would come to discuss their problems.

There were other groups involved in the fight. The Canadian Council of Agriculture (an early forerunner of the Canadian Federation of Agriculture) attempted to set up a voluntary contract pool in 1920 in which the farmers would commit to five-year contracts, but the attempt was abandoned when it concluded it would not be successful in achieving a 60 per cent sign-up.[4] Its failure was likely due to rivalry between organizations.

In December 1921, the FUC launched a campaign to sign up farmers for a five-year compulsory pooling contract, but SGGA refused to co-operate with its new rival.[5] The rivalry between the two organizations became increasingly divisive, but despite their differences they met in 1923 to discuss the formation of a contract wheat pool, and Premier Dunning managed to convince the two organizations to work together.[6] The Saskatchewan Co-operative Elevator Company, operating since 1911, also supported the plan.

In the summer of 1923, the campaign to get farmers to sign up for the Saskatchewan Wheat Pool (SWP) was launched. To be successful, they needed to have at least 50 per cent of the province's wheat acreage under contract.[7] Aaron Sapiro, a California lawyer and gifted orator, was invited to western Canada to "promote unity among interested farm groups."[8] By mid-September, they had fallen short of the target that would enable them to market the 1923 crop; however, by June 1924, the Saskatchewan Co-operative Wheat Producers (which later became the

Saskatchewan Wheat Pool) had signed up enough members to begin pooling.[9] During the same period, contract pools were being formed in Alberta and Manitoba, and the three provinces jointly set up the Central Selling Agency in 1924. The pool contracted existing elevator companies to handle the grain and began acquiring elevators of its own in 1924. Within a year, it had accumulated eighty-nine line elevators.[10]

Phelps remained active in the Farmers' Union at the local and district (District 12) levels throughout the early and mid-twenties. At the annual meeting of the Narrow Lake Lodge of the Farmers' Union held on December 2, 1925, he was elected president for the coming year.[11] By this time, the executives and most members of the SGGA and FUC realized that the existence of two rival farmers' organizations was weakening both of them. Although there was tension between them, they agreed to collaborate, opting for co-operation rather than competition.

On July 15, 1926, Phelps attended the joint convention in Saskatoon to merge the SGGA and FUC into the United Farmers of Canada, Saskatchewan Section, with counterparts in Alberta and Ontario.[12] As a founding member of the UFC, Phelps was involved in its activities in the Narrow Lake and Wilkie areas. When farmers met in 1926 to establish the UFC at Narrow Lake, they appointed Phelps chairman.

After the merger, the pool purchased the 451 elevators that had been part of the Saskatchewan Co-operative Elevator Company, and 55 per cent of the wheat in the province was sold through the pool in 1926.[13] The Wheat Pool had no problem obtaining credit, and farmers began receiving initial, interim, and final payments for their wheat. Between 1924 and 1928, farmers had better returns selling to the pool than to line elevators.

BOOM

Wheat pooling was not the only new development on the Prairies during the 1920s. Value-added processing of agricultural products was beginning, with companies like Quaker Oats and Robin Hood milling locally produced grain, and a number of small abattoirs in operation. By the late 1920s, packing houses and creameries were expanding, and some new industries such as fur farming and sodium sulphate refining started up. Imperial Oil built a refinery in Regina, and in 1928 General Motors opened a small auto assembly plant in Regina. There were also expansions to schools and hospitals, as well as new highway construction. In addition, the co-operative movement grew, including the creation of the Saskatchewan Livestock Pool, a Poultry Producers Co-op, and a Seed Growers Co-operative, and the expansion of the co-op creameries, grazing associations, and many local consumer co-operatives.[14]

Life was changing. Automobiles were beginning to replace the horse and buggy, and farms were less isolated.[15] Many rural homes now had a telephone. Although most farms still did not have running water or electricity, battery-operated radios brought news from the outside world, along with programs like Jack Benny, Charly McCarthy, and Saturday night hockey.[16] Silent motion pictures showed rural folk a wider world, and local baseball and hockey tournaments provided recreation and comradery. The one-way seeder and tiller and the first small gasoline tractors improved productivity, and by 1926 the first combines appeared. Farm sizes were beginning to increase; more than two-thirds of Saskatchewan's population still lived on the land by the end of the decade, and at least 85 per cent of the population was dependent on agriculture.[17] Farmers' perennial problems related to the production, sale, and transportation of their crops persisted.

Phelps remained keenly involved in farmers' affairs throughout the late twenties, serving as president of the Narrow Lake Lodge in 1927 and 1928,[18] and attending a UFC convention in Saskatoon in 1928. At the second annual United Farmers' picnic in July 1929, Phelps introduced and thanked the two speakers, Mrs. Pearl Johnson, president of the Women's Section of the UFC, and J. S. Woodsworth, Independent Labour Party Member of Parliament for Winnipeg. He had been invited to Saskatchewan to spread his socialist ideas to farmers eager to hear about other solutions to their problems,[19] and, again, Phelps was involved in this endeavour: "We [the UFC] got Mr. Woodsworth here...for ten days and paid his fare up from Winnipeg....And he took those ten meetings. Well, it was just like lighting a prairie fire. From then on it really went."[20] Woodsworth was an important influence on Joe Phelps in the late 1920s. Joe was impressed and inspired not only by Woodsworth's oratorical skills but also by his commitment to socialist ideals and his stance on the war.

At the United Farmers' District 12 convention held at Wilkie in 1929, Joe was the unanimous choice as director. This convention was considered "the most successful yet held in District 12" and "a great deal of credit [was] due to the executive and the Director J. Phelps."[21] Phelps remained active in the UFC at both the local and district levels, holding the position of director of District 12 until 1930. He gave financial reports, chaired meetings, reported on conventions, helped to form a Junior Lodge at Narrow Lake, served on the Junior Committee of the Narrow Lake Lodge of the UFC, and participated in debates.[22] One such debate was entitled: "Resolved: That the nationalization of land is in the best interests of the people of Saskatchewan." Phelps and his partner debated for the affirmative, but the local paper did not divulge the results.[23] Given his increasingly socialist orientation, it seems likely that Phelps would have enjoyed making a strong and convincing argument in favour of nationalization. At the 1930 annual convention, Phelps was again commended for his laudable job as director of District 12. The *Wilkie Press* noted, "High tribute was paid to the efficient and conscientious work done by Director J. L. Phelps, who had repeatedly taken a firm stand in the interests of those he had chosen to represent."[24] Through his involvement in the UFC, Phelps came to work closely with and admire George H. Williams, an Ituna farmer who was the president of the UFC from 1929 to 1932, leader of the Farmer-Labour Party from 1934 to 1935, and president and leader of the CCF from 1935 to 1941. He came to know Frank Eliason as well, who served as secretary of the Farmer-Labour Party from 1932 to 1935. Phelps also became involved in the debate as to whether the UFC should become directly involved in politics, a question that divided the membership for some years, with the more radical members favouring political involvement and the more conservative opposing it. By 1929, adverse economic conditions propelled them toward political action.[25]

BUST

The collapse of the stock market in October 1929 sent the world economy into a tailspin and signalled the beginning of the decade-long Great Depression. International trade in commodities such as wheat and lumber fell precipitously. Many mines, mills, and factories closed. Tens of thousands of Canadians would be thrown out of work. By the spring of 1933, one and a half million Canadians, more than 10 per cent of the national population, were on relief. Of all the provinces, Saskatchewan was hit the hardest. World prices for wheat collapsed, and drought, dust storms, and grasshopper plagues devastated the farming community. Without crops, farmers were unable to earn even the dismal incomes offered by the lower commodity prices. In these desperate circumstances, farmers increasingly turned to new and radical ideas to find solutions.

The UFC continued to lobby on behalf of farmers and began to call for radical changes to the economic system. Although they rejected political action in 1930, their program called for "the abolition of the present competitive system of manufacture and democratic operation of public utilities and natural resources."[26] Initially, Phelps was among those opposed to entering the political arena, noting that many had joined the movement because it was a nonpolitical organization. He favoured the kind of farm unity that had been achieved during the formation of the pool, and felt that if they entered the political arena in support of one political party, it could cause division among the membership and harm the pool movement. For the most part, those who strongly supported a compulsory grain pool were opposed to political action,[27] while those on the extreme left continued to favour it, openly advocating support of groups such as the Communist Party. By this time, many right-wing members also favoured involvement through more moderate political parties.

In some districts, including District 12, farmers also briefly toyed with the idea of secession of the Prairie provinces from Canada. After a farmers' meeting in Wilkie passed a resolution to discuss this "Charter of Liberty," District 12 decided to hold a series of mass meetings to advocate its adoption.[28] Other farm leaders from Major, Biggar, Kerrobert, and Wilkie decided to campaign actively for signatures and donations and instructed the secretary to forward copies of the charter to Prime Minister Ramsay MacDonald of Great Britain and Prime Minister R. B. Bennett of Canada.[29] Phelps, along with other prominent UFC leaders such as G. Bickerton, believed that adopting this charter would force the federal government to act.

> This "Charter of Liberty" is an ultimatum to the federal government, and failing the assurance of immediate and sufficient action we shall organize at once for the political conquest of this province, along with other such provinces as will join us,

> for the purpose of forming a co-operative commonwealth within the British Empire, trading directly with Great Britain and other countries on a free trade and barter basis.[30]

Looking back on this action, Phelps said,

> We were pretty radical. We were determined. Radical, no, I don't like to use that term myself. But in the eyes of a lot of people we were regarded as being radical simply because we were ahead of them. We were beyond their thinking. After a while I got so I realized it and so you have to handle it a little differently and take things a little more easy, I guess. I wanted to get it done in a hurry about that time.[31]

During the winter of 1930–1931, many large meetings of farmers discussed secession, but the movement waned. At the February 1931 annual UFC convention, the secession movement died when George Williams, the retiring president of the UFC, strenuously opposed it.

By 1930, Phelps was serving on the board of directors of the UFC. At the board meeting that year, he moved that the committee draw up a resolution on public health to be recommended at the annual convention.[32] The resolution was carried, and the public health resolution became part of UFC policy.[33] Heated debate continued to surround the issue of direct political action. At the 1930 UFC convention, Walter Wiggins and L. P. McNamee, both former FUC members, moved and seconded a resolution favouring direct political action. Phelps opposed the resolution and maintained, "We have built this organization at too great an expense to the farm men and women of Saskatchewan to take the risk of wrecking it on a political rock, and I believe that will be the danger if we take the move. I believe we should take political action individually or through other means, but not through this organization." He added that many in the organization "are very set in their ways and politically would drop out of the organization.... I am afraid this will split us open on every side."[34] Wiggins and McNamee and former progressives like John Wellbelove and Mrs. A. Hollis argued in favour of the amendment, and, after a lengthy debate, 305 votes out of 470 were cast for its adoption. This was a clear majority, but fell just nine votes short of the two-thirds required for such a constitutional change. As a result, some members broke away and formed the more radical Farmers Political Association to contest the 1930 election.

A similar debate was taking place within the labour movement in Saskatchewan and across Canada. As the new industrial unionists began to advocate political action, many of the more traditional craft unionists continued to shy away from politics, considering it divisive, distracting, and futile. They preferred to concentrate on "bread-and-butter" issues, such as obtaining wage increases or better working conditions for their membership, simply rewarding their friends and punishing their enemies with their votes.[35]

RADICAL THOUGHTS

Further to the left, the communist-affiliated Farmers' Unity League (FUL) appeared in rural Saskatchewan in the early thirties. Interested in what it had to say, Joe Phelps and George Williams attended a FUL meeting in December 1930.[36]

FUL used a variety of strategies, including farm auction boycotts, to draw attention to the plight of farmers. FUL members flooded farm foreclosure sales, making ridiculously low bids as articles came up for sale. By common agreement, no one else would bid, and the low-priced articles would then be given back to the farmer, who was then free of his obligations. (This strategy surfaced again during the farm crisis of the 1980s and 1990s, when farmers used farm boycott auctions in an attempt to gain public awareness and support.) FUL also called for immediate farm debt cancellation, a halt to farm foreclosures and evictions, tax boycotts, and a $1,000 guaranteed annual income for all farmers.

Phelps rejected FUL's more militant approach. He agreed with the farm auction boycott strategy, but he felt the remainder of its program was cluttered with too many immediate demands and did not place enough emphasis on long-term economic solutions:

> It was a worthy approach to get people to recognize their position but what I was more concerned about was to get them to recognize why they were in that position, and what some of the things were that they had to do to get out permanently,

> and not as a stop-gap, and that was where we seemed to part ways so far as the Farmers' Unity League was concerned.[37]

Economic reform, Phelps felt, would only come about if farmers were able to influence the government through the democratic process.

FUL members worked both within and outside of organizations such as the UFC. The fact that they were communists did not faze Phelps. He respected their significant contribution to the farm movement. During a 1970 interview with Saskatchewan archives staff, Phelps drew a comparison between the rank-and-file membership of FUL and the CCF:

> The membership in the Farmers' Unity League were much more students of economics. They had done their homework...they knew their stuff better. They were better debaters. If you were up against one of those fellows, if you were going to cross swords with them, or oppose them, you'd better have your homework done, or they would floor you—no question about that. They were more capable and seemed to have a clear understanding of things.[38]

Reflecting on the influence of FUL activists on the other organizations and political parties at the time, Phelps added,

> No one ever wants to underestimate the contributions that they made.... They were a tremendous influence and I think it was an influence for the good, on the rank and file membership. They were ahead of their time, sure, just like we have people today who are ahead of their time and are advocating things that the majority won't accept, but that is always good for society; that's how we make progress.[39]

Phelps also reflected on the personal characteristics of some of the individuals involved in the more radical farm organizations:

> They were genuinely concerned. There was never any doubt in my mind that those men were not out for publicity or for a personal reason at all. They were dedicated to getting

> some changes made in the economic system, particularly as it affected farmers here in the West. I didn't agree with the methods they used sometimes, or the particular route they took to get to a stated objective, but there was no doubt that they sowed the seeds that resulted, for example, in the Wheat Pool. They were the ones that helped to break the trail to have the Wheat Pool before the Wheat Board. I mean the Wheat Pool that Sapiro helped us to bring into being. They were all for it.[40]

At a February 1931 UFC board meeting, which Phelps attended, alliances with FUL were discussed. The board decided that because of FUL's affiliation with the Communist Party of Canada, no elected UFC officer would act as an official or organizer of FUL.

Saskatchewan's agricultural economy continued to deteriorate, and UFC President George Williams appealed directly to Prime Minister Bennett concerning the plight of Saskatchewan farmers. When he received no response, political action seemed inevitable. While some UFC district conventions were reluctant to take this step, others were eager to do so. By December 1930, the District 12 UFC convention had passed a motion in favour of political action. It also elected George Bickerton of Neola as director of District 12, replacing Phelps, who was retiring as director but remained as alternate director, a position he held for several years.[41]

By 1931, an overwhelming majority of the UFC membership were in favour of political action, even those who, like Phelps, had previously been opposed. The consensus was that with drought, crop failure, low grain prices, and the pool experiencing financial difficulty, the problem was too deep and too complex to be solved without political action. At the 1931 convention, considerable discussion was also focused on western fiscal autonomy and the aforementioned proposed charter of liberty. Phelps reiterated his call to action: "We have met here in conventions year after year and we resolve and resolve. Unless we have some action, we might as well have a bonfire and burn them up."[42]

The delegates voted to enter the political field as an organization and to "seek the backing of all citizens in electing candidates on a policy aimed at ultimate social ownership and non-profit production." The convention resolved that the initiative should come from the local lodges, advising that if 15 per cent of the lodges in a constituency agreed to such a plan, the central office would be requested to hold a convention to nominate a candidate.[43]

THE BIRTH OF THE CCF

By 1931, the UFC passed a motion "condemning the capitalist system and calling for social ownership and co-operative production," and favouring "nationalization of farmlands and a use-lease system of land tenure."[44] Elsewhere across Canada, progressive farm groups, academics, and members of the Independent Labour Party (ILP) had started talking about the formation of a new political party. Many in the province's labour movement, including the ILP (formed in 1929 and led by Regina school principal and city alderman, M. J. Coldwell), were advocating social and economic changes. In the fall of 1931, the ILP outlined a program similar to the UFC, calling for nationalization of banking, a planned economy, and a national health scheme. By 1931, the ILP sought to develop a clear working relationship with the UFC.[45]

The UFC, impatient with the provincial government's lack of action in providing real assistance to hard-pressed farmers and urban dwellers, decided to hold a series of conferences in June 1931. Significantly, labour was invited to participate. In District 12, the UFC executive called an emergency convention in Unity on June 16, 1931. It resolved that a central convention be held in Regina on June 26 and 27, 1931, at which a committee of each of the sixteen districts and members of organized labour would coordinate their demands and present them to the provincial government. Phelps was one of four members elected to this committee, representing Wilkie.[46] On June 26, about eighty farmer delegates and about twenty labour delegates met in Regina. This convention, the first at which agriculture and labour co-operated, selected a committee of seven to act as spokespeople. M. J. Coldwell was one of two representing labour, and J. L. Phelps one of the five representing farmers.[47] The convention drew up a set of twenty-one demands that were presented to the provincial government on June 27. The most important demand was that the legislature hold a special session to deal with the dire economic conditions. A. J. Macauley, representing the UFC, introduced the delegation to the Cabinet and presented the demands; M. J. Coldwell, representing labour, was the first speaker. Coldwell noted that labour was backing agriculture in its demands since it realized that conditions in urban areas would not improve until those in rural Saskatchewan did.[48] Phelps spoke commendably, according to UFC Leader George Bickerton:

> Mr. Bickerton said Mr. Phelps at that time had debated one of the most controversial issues in a manner which deserved recognition and that a reporter present had stated that he had never heard a proposal presented in such a comprehensive way. He had shown the government how finances could be raised to bring about sought for legislation—not in a half-baked manner, but with intelligent proposals.[49]

Premier Anderson stated that his government was already addressing the other demands the delegates had presented and refused to call a special session, disappointing both labour and the UFC and prompting them to action. The town of Wynyard formed the first political unit of the UFC in July 1931. Wilkie soon followed under the leadership of Phelps and Bickerton. On July 31, Phelps co-chaired a UFC District 12 organizational meeting at Unity, where they resolved "to organize a United Farmers' Political Association for the provincial constituency of Wilkie." Phelps was selected to serve on the constituency committee representing Narrow Lake, Starview, and Thackeray.[50]

After deciding to take political action, the UFC established a Political Directive Board to formulate and review policy. This board consisted of the executive of the UFC, along with three members appointed by the UFC convention and three by the ILP. Arrangements were made for constituency committees to send representatives to the UFC annual convention to participate in sessions at which political matters were being discussed. The ILP was also allowed to send representatives from any constituency in which it had a branch.[51]

There were other signs of closer political co-operation. M. J. Coldwell's speech at the Labour Temple in Saskatoon on January 17, 1932, was arranged to coincide with the UFC–ILP economic conference held the previous day.[52] At the sixth annual UFC convention held in Saskatoon in February 1932, agriculture and labour continued to co-operate:

representatives of both the UFC constituency committees and the ILP were granted delegate standing at the convention. Its main business was to organize the farmer and labour groups to engage in political action and to prepare them to field candidates in the next provincial election. The delegates appointed Williams and Phelps convention chairmen. Macauley was re-elected as president, and J. F. Herman as vice-president. Phelps, Williams, and Bickerton declined to accept a nomination for the latter office.[53]

In March 1932, the UFC central office wired its full support to J. S. Woodsworth, as he raised the question of establishing a co-operative commonwealth before the House of Commons.[54] The UFC and the ILP also demanded that the Saskatchewan government reduce farm debt and provide security of tenure against foreclosure. When Premier J. T. M. Anderson refused to meet these demands, the two groups decided to found a new party. On May 26, 1932, members of the "Ginger Group" met with Woodsworth in Ottawa and made the decision to establish a new "Commonwealth Party."[55]

At the first annual joint political convention held in Saskatoon, membership of the Political Directive Board was changed to include the executives of the ILP and the UFC, and on July 27, 1932, they officially formed the Farmer-Labour Party. At this session, the name "Farmer-Labour Group" was selected, and M. J. Coldwell was elected leader. Though George Williams, a popular radical farm leader and the UFC's president since 1929, intended to stand for this position, he withdrew when others advised him that his impromptu visit to the Soviet Union after the world wheat conference in 1930 "had lowered his political stock." Agrarian radicalism had obvious limits.[56] Instead, Coldwell, the more moderate leader of the ILP, was elected president and leader of the fledgling Farmer-Labour Party. As a member of the Political Directive Board, Phelps was at the meeting and was one of the first to join the new party.[57] Discussion at the convention centred on the proposed platform:

> Mr. Phelps stated that he considered that Unemployment Insurance mentioned in the clause should not be necessary if they were going to bring in this new socialist system.... [Since under this new system] there would be no unemployment, he

> thought it showed a lack of faith in the economic program that they proposed to bring in. He thought that health insurance was good and so far as there was no health plank in their platform he thought that this should be added to their policy as it was one of the most important in the platform of any political association.[58]

The philosophy of the Farmer-Labour Group held strong appeal for Phelps. While coming out clearly against the capitalist system and favouring the socialization of state and economic planning, it rejected violence as the road to reform and favoured proceeding within the parliamentary system. It also rejected any dealings with the Communist Party.

Delegates from this new alliance planned to attend the annual labour conference meeting in Calgary in 1932. Along with the Saskatchewan Farmer-Labour Group, others attending the convention included the United Farmers of Canada from the three Prairie provinces, the ILP, trade unionists, and socialists and social reformers of various kinds. This was the meeting that officially gave birth to the Co-operative Commonwealth Federation.[59] J. S. Woodsworth was named leader.

CANDIDATE PHELPS

On Valentine's Day, 1931, Joe Phelps had married Lena Ackerman.[60] Lena, from a pioneer home twelve kilometres west of Saskatoon, was a teacher in the Star View School just north of Wilkie, and was clever and capable. With Lena's support, Joe had taken up the cause and began organizing for the Farmer-Labour Party in earnest.

After July 1932, Phelps was active in the new party within his constituency, becoming a member of the local committee when it was created in October. At a meeting at Wilkie on May 26, 1933, at which Williams outlined the policies of the new party, Phelps introduced him and chaired the meeting.[61] He even decided to enter provincial politics, accepting the nomination as the Farmer-Labour candidate in the Melfort constituency.[62]

Phelps remained on the Political Directive Board and executive of the Saskatchewan Farmer-Labour Group and chaired the second annual convention in July 1933, where his resolution that the name be changed to the Saskatchewan Section of the Co-operative Commonwealth Federation (to correspond with the federal organization) was defeated. It would retain the name Farmer-Labour Group until 1934.[63] Phelps was once again elected to the seven-member Political Directive Board and was also introduced as the Farmer-Labour candidate in the Melfort constituency in the upcoming 1934 election. An archival copy of Phelps's election brochure issued by the "Melfort Farmer-Labor Group (CCF)" lists "Twelve sound reasons why you should vote for J. L. Phelps," which include a call for a socialized banking system, socialized health services, state planning and ownership, and "Human rights above property rights." The brochure also alerts voters that the constituency of Melfort held an agreement with a signed undated resignation should the candidate fail to carry out his pre-election promises.[64]

This was not to be. Phelps had been encouraged to go to Melfort to oppose someone many wished to prevent from running, but the returning officer there refused to take his nomination papers. According to Phelps, this was because he was from Wilkie, but the official reason given by the returning officer was that Phelps had included his signature only once instead of twice as was required, and nominations had closed before Phelps was able to correct the omission.[65] Phelps and his supporters tried unsuccessfully to reverse this decision. He later indicated that if he had had enough money to challenge it, he was certain he could have won, but he did not do so. He added, "I was fed up anyway and at that time I wasn't too anxious about going into it. After a whole bunch of meetings and what not I was played out and I went back to the farm and put my bib overalls on. It was a good experience though."[66]

Although Phelps seemed intent on going "back to the farm," his resolve soon weakened. On October 18, 1934, at North Battleford, Phelps was nominated as the CCF candidate in the federal riding of the Battlefords, but he declined.[67] He continued to lend some support to the Narrow Lake Lodge of the UFC but did not participate much beyond that level.

THE REGINA MANIFESTO

The CCF, officially created at the Calgary meeting in 1932, had commissioned the drawing up of a platform for the new democratic socialist party, to be amended and approved at the follow-up conference in Regina

Election brochure for J. L. Phelps, "Farmer-Labor (CCF)" candidate for the Melfort constituency. Printed by the *Nipawin Herald*, 1934. Permission granted by the Phelps family estate.

in 1933. The CCF's first national convention took place on July 1, 1933, in Regina. The meeting was a much larger gathering than the Calgary conference: 130 delegates, representing seven of the nine provinces, adopted a wide-ranging platform for the new party. The Regina Manifesto called for collective ownership of all resources and the machinery of wealth production in order to co-operatively produce and distribute goods for use and service, rather than for private gain. This was to be achieved through the establishment of a planned national economy; socialization of the country's financial system; development, operation, and control of utilities and natural resources; and socialization of health services. The first paragraph of the Regina Manifesto reads:

> We aim to replace the present capitalist system, with its inherent injustice and inhumanity, by a social order from which the domination and exploitation of one class by another will be eliminated, in which economic planning will supersede unregulated private enterprise and competition, and in which genuine democratic self-government, based upon economic equality, will be possible. The present order is marked by glaring inequalities of wealth and opportunity, by chaotic waste and instability; and in an age of plenty, it condemns the great mass of the people to poverty and insecurity. Power has become more and more concentrated into the hands of a small irresponsible minority of financiers and industrialists and to their predatory interests the majority are habitually sacrificed. When private profit is the main stimulus to economic effort, our society oscillates between periods of feverish prosperity in which the main benefits go to speculators and profiteers, and of catastrophic depression, in which the common man's normal state of insecurity and hardship is accentuated. We believe that these evils can be removed only in a planned and socialized economy in which our natural resources and the principal means of production and distribution are owned, controlled and operated by the people.[68]

In *Dream No Little Dreams*, a biography of the Douglas Government, A. W. Johnson succinctly illustrates the CCF philosophy that underlies its policies and programs: "It consisted of a passionate belief in the common man: in his ability and his right to govern himself; his right to the dignity and self-assurance to which all men are born; and his right to the kind of economic and social security which the CCF believed to be essential to self-realization."[69] The CCF saw democratic socialism as perfectly consistent with individualism, freedom, democracy, and equality of economic and social opportunity, which were equally part of its value system. True freedom required a minimum of economic well-being, along with "a sufficient measure of social security, security of tenure on the farm and in the home, and the opportunity for an adequate education."[70] And it was no pipe dream. Reflecting on the vision put forth in the Regina Manifesto in a 1978 interview, Douglas stated, "As I leave politics, I see about eighty per cent of our Regina Manifesto on the statute books; a publicly-owned Bank of Canada, a Wheat Board, unemployment insurance, family allowance, universal old-age pensions, hospital insurance, Medicare, the Canada Pension Plan, and a national petroleum corporation."[71]

THE WOMEN'S VOTE

Phelps was also strongly in favour of women's rights and cognizant of women's contribution to the farm—and to the new party's chances of electoral success:

> There is considerable difference between principles and platform. I often think a platform is what they get in on but do not ride on. There is a vast difference. There are many political parties, one at least, which is bidding for power, and they will steal anything from your platform. I think if you stick to principles it will be pretty hard for them to steal that. However, there is something else. There has been all the talk about men. I think we all ought to include the women. I am going to tell you that an election can be won or lost on the women's vote. I hope that, in going out to the country, we can make that point clear.[72]

Phelps's comments would prove to be very insightful. In years to come the Liberals did indeed "steal some of the platform" of the fledgling

Farmer-Labour Party, but it would be several more years before parties focused on obtaining the women's vote. In more recent times, too, the issue of political integrity has come to the forefront, with increasing public apathy and disillusionment as political leaders renege on election promises once elected.

In the weeks, months, and years to come, Phelps became increasingly politically active, committed to promoting the Farmer-Labour message. He travelled throughout the province, organizing for the party in the months leading up to the 1934 election, when the first five CCF members, affectionately known at party headquarters as "the quintuplets," were elected. His involvement in the political process and deep agrarian roots combined to shape his expanding social and political consciousness. By 1938, Phelps would be among the ten CCF members who would form the official opposition in the Saskatchewan legislature.

CHAPTER 3

COMMON GROUND

By 1938, the situation on the farm had become very grim: about two-thirds of the province's farm population was on relief.[1] Eight consecutive years of drought and crop failure had left the province near bankruptcy. Provincial income, almost entirely dependent on wheat, tumbled by nearly 90 per cent. Rural and urban communities alike were thrown into the downward economic spiral. The price of a bushel of wheat dropped to forty cents, down from about $2.63 in 1919 and approximately $1.60 in 1929.[2] Even subsistence activities such as growing a garden or keeping a milk cow alive became virtually impossible in many drought-stricken areas. The Palliser triangle, an area covering much of southern Saskatchewan that John Palliser had advised was not suitable for agricultural settlement after his 1857 expedition, was hit particularly hard.[3] Mortgage companies began to take over some farms, and many young men left in search of work. The hardships of the Depression created a great deal of social and political common ground among Saskatchewan people, and contributed to growing support for the CCF's plan.

SPREADING THE WORD

Organizing work often took Phelps away from his young family to travel around the province spreading the party's message, frequently in treacherous conditions. To compensate for his absence from home, he would write newsy letters. In a November 1933 letter written from Choiceland, he described the challenges of political organizing on the prairies:

> We couldn't get quite all the way up north of the Torch River on Friday, so had to leave the car and walk the rest of the way. We got a team of horses to pull the car back to the main road on Saturday.... Stayed at Mr. and Mrs. Taggart's place, the same place Dad and I stopped when we were up here last summer. Don't know when I will get a chance to post this letter, as the mail goes out once a week from many of these places up here.

Fifty centimeres of snow had fallen over a two- or three-day period. Closing his letter, Joe stated, "I'm living on deer and moose meat. There is all kinds of game up here, but I have no time to shoot."[4]

Educating the masses about this new political alternative was consuming a great deal of his time. On a cold evening in January 1933, he was involved in another political meeting in Star City and wrote, "Last night here in this town a lawyer, a merchant and banker asked quite a few questions about our socialist movement, but so far they haven't got me strung up to a tree." On February 27, 1934, on the road again, this time at Brooksby, he wrote, "We have had very good meetings and interest in our movement is sure spreading fast."[5]

By February 1934, momentum was building. He wrote home:

> A real good meeting was held in the Melfort hall last night, with over two hundred attending. A lawyer from Melfort represented the Liberal party. The collection was $13.75, but the rent for the hall was $15.00, so we lacked $1.25. The local committee in charge said they expected we would be shorter than that. Collections at other meetings have been good. I have almost enough money already to pay my expenses back to Wilkie, so I should make out all right. Will get my club bag and mail on Saturday at Gronlid of course.[6]

In jest, he added, "I have only room for one shirt as yet. Think I will pawn the rest to get funds for the campaign, as I really don't need them." Phelps's letters home also contained numerous tidbits of advice on managing the farm.

Phelps became more deeply involved in Farmer-Labour issues and the 1934 provincial election campaign. Frank Eliason, a major player and secretary of the newly minted party, provided inspiration and encouragement for his involvement in politics: "Frank had a great influence on my decision to enter politics, quite a substantial influence. He was like a second dad to me."[7] Eliason, later frequently cited to have been "the glue that held the union together" during the Depression,[8] had become provincial secretary of the UFC in 1929. With the formation of the Farmer-Labour Party in 1933, Eliason had served a dual role as secretary of both the new party and the UFC. Eliason's draft document was accepted as the basis for the program the party adopted, and at the first CCF convention in 1933, Eliason moved that the Regina Manifesto be adopted as a whole.[9]

Wilf Churchman, who later became Phelps's assistant deputy minister, first met Phelps in the mid-thirties while teaching at Fairyland School, near Wilkie. Wilf spent many hours with Joe and Lena and their children. He remembered the little orchestra they had, called the Night Owls, and recalled, "Lena played piano, Joe occasionally took a turn on the drums, and I played saxophone and clarinet. In their home I was introduced to the CCF doctrine, for we had many discussions on the pros and cons of socialism."[10]

THE QUINTUPLETS

In the 1934 provincial election the Liberals, led by Jimmy Gardiner, elected fifty members; the first five Farmer-Labour members elected formed the official opposition. George Williams, former president of the United Farmers of Canada, became the leader of the Opposition. The results were not what the party had hoped for. The press had labelled the Farmer-Labour candidates as communists and Bolsheviks, and had alleged that they intended to nationalize everything. The Catholic Church had openly attacked them. M. J. Coldwell was defeated, as was Tommy Douglas. Coldwell and Douglas would, however, be successful in their bid for federal seats in 1935, the only two CCF members to be elected in Saskatchewan.[11]

During the early thirties, the party was plagued by an internal conflict between George Williams and M. J. Coldwell.[12] Williams had devoted many years to leading various farmers' movements and undoubtedly had been reluctant to withdraw his nomination for the leadership of the Farmer-Labour Party when it was formed in 1932. Perhaps somewhat jealous, Williams was soon convinced that Coldwell was not a capable leader.[13] The conflict escalated with Coldwell's ignominious defeat in the 1934 provincial election: he finished fifth out of seven candidates in the Regina City riding. Williams, on the other hand, had garnered the largest majority of any of the five successful Farmer-Labour candidates. A brief meeting between Williams and Coldwell in Saskatoon on June 23 ended "in a huff." Strife continued when Williams and Coldwell called separate meetings with the elected and defeated candidates, respectively. The Political Directive Board partially resolved this standoff on July 27, when it made Coldwell the official leader and Williams the house leader of the Farmer-Labour Party.[14] When Coldwell relinquished the party leadership on December 13, 1935, after being elected to Parliament, Williams, already the CCF house leader, was immediately named party leader.

Joe had definite opinions about the two men. He respected and admired Williams. Later, he said, "I liked George. George and I got along fine. I didn't agree with him all the time, but on basic things I agreed with him. There was no question about that." Phelps did not hold the same admiration for Coldwell, identifying more closely with Williams's radical socialism than with Coldwell's more moderate views. He later recalled, "I never was close enough to Mr. Coldwell that he confided in me. And I liked Mr. Coldwell fine, but I felt he was just two or three steps up some way.... He wasn't a farmer and if it wasn't for the views he had, I would say he was a high mucky muck. That's all there is to it."[15]

CHANGING PRIORITIES

Joe's interest in the UFC diminished after its 1934 decision to withdraw from politics. In an interview with Jean Larmour in 1982, he said, "I put in my term with the Farmers' Union [*sic*] and they wanted me to stay on, but I said that I thought I had done my share and that I wasn't just leaving them entirely, but that I was going to devote more of my time to the political end."[16] He continued to work with the local lodges of the UFC, presenting some "interesting data from the *Canada Year Book*" at the January 10 meeting of the Narrow Lake Lodge in 1934. At the February 7 meeting, he agreed to become a director, and he and Lena hosted the March 24 meeting. On October 19, 1934, he gave an instructive address to the Lilydale Local Lodge,[17] and he attended the annual

UFC conventions in Saskatoon in 1933, 1934, and 1935, sharing the position of chairman with C. C. Stoliker, G. H. Williams, and J. T. Herman, respectively.[18] However, he no longer displayed his earlier enthusiasm for the organization and declined the nomination as UFC president in 1935.[19]

While he also refrained from entering federal politics in 1935, that year he became a member of the provincial council of the CCF. He was re-elected to this position at the annual convention in July 1936. The next year, he was elected to the CCF provincial executive, a post he held until he was elected to the legislative assembly in 1938.[20] As a member of the provincial council and executive, Phelps worked with such influential members as G. H. Williams, C. M. Fines, M. J. Coldwell, Louise Lucas, A. J. Macauley, Gladys Strum, T. Johnston, and T. C. Douglas.[21]

The Depression years were difficult, and Phelps juggled many responsibilities, including his work as a telephone lineman in the Wilkie district, managing the family farm, his political work, and his young growing family. Stress likely contributed to the stomach problems he struggled with from the early 1930s. Phelps travelled to the Mayo Clinic in Rochester, Minnesota, for surgery on a stomach ulcer, done by Charles Mayo himself. After having a portion of his stomach removed, Phelps remained on a diet made up largely of green tea, fruit, vegetables, oats, alfalfa, and brown bread all of his life. Correspondence in 1937 from Phelps's family doctor, Dr. Hugh MacLean, advised Lena on Joe's diet and the care of his gastric ulcer, and also stated, "Joe is one of the key men in the CCF and if and when we obtain power of the province I am hoping he will be in cabinet."[22] Dr. MacLean, a surgeon who practised in Saskatchewan for thirty years, had tended injured trekkers when the On-to-Ottawa Trek was violently crushed by police in Regina in 1935, and during the 1930s he became an ardent supporter of socialized medicine. He documented many examples of the financial burden of illness and how the Depression was resulting in inadequate medical care, and repeatedly made pleas for reform. His recommendations later became part of the Sigerist report, commissioned by Tommy Douglas to study health care services soon after the CCF formed the government in 1944. The recommendations contained in the Sigerist report provided the basis for the first medicare legislation.[23]

SAW-OFFS

While the CCF had successfully entered the political scene by the mid-thirties, its members were somewhat disappointed with the results. To attract more voters, they needed to make changes. After the 1934 election, the Farmer-Labour Party made the decision to abandon its unpopular land policy, particularly its "use-hold" or "use-lease" policies.[24] It also turned its attention to co-operating with the other political parties, with the shared purpose of defeating the Liberals.

In 1936, the CCF provincial convention approved a resolution to invite "all progressive organizations, political, cultural, and economic to meet in convention to seek to discover a common goal on which we may unite for action and a common goal to which we may unitedly move."[25] The resolution to "unite" was popular. After years of drought and declining prices, there was great momentum among the Saskatchewan delegates to co-operate with all other "progressives," including Popular Front candidates (the communists, under the Unity banner), and even the Conservatives and Social Credit, which had made great gains in Alberta and were opposed to eastern financial control and favoured immediate action to save farms from foreclosure.[26] The national CCF thought otherwise. Woodsworth, the CCF's national leader, opposed any alliances with communists and spoke out strongly against the resolution. He also spoke out strongly against a shift in the policy direction of the party: "Social Credit stands for capitalism, I am a socialist and I'm not going to enter into political alliances with those who uphold capitalism."[27] Williams stood against the leader, stating, "Whether we like it or not the people of this province are demanding unity. How can we ignore the demand of our members?"[28] Saskatchewan delegates, anxious to defeat the Liberals, strongly supported the resolution, with only eight of 312 delegates opposed.[29] The outcome of the resolution speaks to the malleability of the CCF at the time: "The farm leaders wanted immediate economic action and political power, and did not care whether or not the goal was socialism."[30]

The Conservatives, desperate after their humiliating 1934 defeat, were certainly eager to co-operate with the CCF.[31] G. H. Williams favoured "saw-offs," whereby the two parties would agree among themselves where each would nominate candidates, depending on which had the better chance of defeating the Liberals. After the CCF and the Conservatives reached a general agreement, individual CCF constituencies held talks with their Conservative counterparts and "saw-offs" were arranged for the 1938 election.

Williams was much more eager to achieve co-operation with Social Credit after its stunning victory in Alberta. Calgary teacher and radio evangelist William Aberhart (also known as "Bible Bill" for his outspoken Baptist views) had led the Social Credit Party to victory in 1935, preaching economic populism and social conservatism, winning fifty-six of the sixty-three seats in the legislature and over 50 per cent of the popular vote. Aberhart had vowed to field a candidate in every Saskatchewan riding, which posed a definite threat to the CCF in Saskatchewan. Williams and Macaulay visited Aberhart in the fall of 1936, but no definite commitments were made on either side.[32] Joe Phelps strongly supported a general policy of co-operation and urged that a committee be appointed to approach Aberhart directly, rather than working with other Social Credit leaders, stating to Williams, "I feel that for the sake of the future of the CCF and the ideals for which we stand, something can and must be done."[33] Throughout 1937, CCF leaders continued to strive for co-operation with Social Credit. At a provincial executive meeting in September, Williams obtained an agreement to have the CCF approach the Saskatchewan Social Credit League at its October convention and broach the issue of co-operation between the two parties in the next provincial election.[34] When Phelps appeared at the Social Credit convention on October 6, 1937, the delegates passed a motion by a vote of twenty-seven to nineteen to listen to an offer of co-operation. However, when some of the nineteen threatened to leave the convention, Ernest Manning, Aberhart's right-hand man and an Alberta Social Credit MLA, advised that such a motion required unanimous consent. The party executive meekly ruled accordingly on the motion.

The CCF provincial executive continued to make overtures to Social Credit with no success. On October 4, 1937, just two days before the Social Credit convention fiasco, Williams had sent confidential letters to all provincial officials, informing them that while each constituency had the right to determine if it would nominate a candidate or not, "a fusion party or a joint candidate inevitably means a candidate who is controlled by no-one other than himself or herself."[35] In other words, co-operation did not mean union or amalgamation.

Whether Phelps's next actions resulted from his misinterpreting Williams's statement or from his own impulsiveness is difficult to determine. Nonetheless, by January 1938, Phelps was actively promoting the selection of a Unity candidate in Wilkie, one the CCF and Social Credit would jointly nominate.

At this point Williams, Douglas, and Coldwell were in favour of co-operation if it resulted in saw-offs, but rejected the nomination of Unity candidates. As for the situation in Wilkie, Douglas expressed concern "that too hasty action in repudiating this move may allow certain people to jockey us into the position of looking like the ones who are rejecting offers of co-operation." Coldwell rejected the concept of Unity candidates and opposed an alliance with Social Credit. He stated, "Wherever possible, three-cornered contests should be avoided and I would be prepared to consider ways and means of accomplishing that there [in the Wilkie constituency]."[36]

Although Aberhart opposed any notion of co-operating with the CCF, most Social Credit delegates at their 1937 convention had indicated that they were interested in pursuing the possibility. Early in 1938, Joseph Needham, president of the Saskatchewan Social Credit League and MP for the Battlefords, was instrumental in bringing together the Social Credit and CCF constituency organizations in Wilkie at a "Unity" convention, which even devised a common platform for the two groups. While Needham favoured co-operation between the two parties, M. J. Haver, the provincial Social Credit organizer, did not. On January 17, 1938, following the decision of the party executive, Haver publicly repudiated the actions of the Wilkie constituency. Nonetheless, Needham attended a meeting at Wilkie on April 19, 1938, at which Phelps (now a member of the CCF provincial executive) and representatives of the Wilkie Conservative executive drafted an agreement to nominate a United Progressive (UP) candidate in the riding. Apparently, Needham must have then changed his mind. Although Douglas thereafter tried to discuss co-operation with Needham on numerous occasions, he could not succeed "in getting anything of any definite nature arranged."[37] At a meeting in Wilkie on May 21, nominating a Unity candidate was no longer an option. George Hindley, an independent candidate, received the nomination.[38]

In the meantime, the CCF provincial executive decided to approach Aberhart again. On March 18, 1938, Williams wrote a conciliatory letter to Aberhart, once again suggesting co-operation. On April 1, he sent Macauley to Edmonton to broach the subject with Aberhart, but the Alberta premier rebuffed both offers.[39] The Saskatchewan Social Credit League was equally unobliging.

THE MAN FROM SALTCOATS

Co-operation with the Conservatives, which the CCF had sought rather indifferently, was partially achieved, whereas co-operation with the Socreds, which it had pursued doggedly, simply did not materialize. When nominations closed on June 1, 1938, Social Credit had nominated forty-one candidates in fifty-two ridings to the CCF's thirty-one. One of those CCF candidates was J. L. Phelps.

Surprisingly, Phelps became a CCF candidate in Saltcoats rather than in Wilkie. Perhaps he felt discouraged when the Social Credit provincial organization thwarted the attempts he and Needham had made to select a Unity candidate in the Wilkie constituency. Phelps subsequently recalled,

> They wanted me to run in Wilkie. I didn't want to run anywhere. I was busy farming at that time. I farmed quite a farm, and I had just got married and we were starting a family. I didn't want to. I don't say it to blow about it, but I had plenty of opportunities to go into politics in different constituencies. I had different people come to me and say, "Well, now look, we would like to make you our candidate," when I would be out on farm union work. I would say, "Go ahead, get somebody else."[40]

The CCF was gaining momentum. Edgar Kaeding, who was later elected in Saltcoats in 1971 and served as Minister of Agriculture and Minister of Rural Affairs in the Allan Blakeney Government for eleven years, recalled,

> My first recollection of Joe dates back to the day he was nominated to carry the banner for the CCF in the constituency of Saltcoats in the election of 1938. I was an impressionable boy

> of 18, whose family had become caught up in the farm struggles of the 1930s.... Like so many others, we were searching for a better way of life for our rural people.[41]

Edgar Kaeding's father, Emil, who had provided leadership in the local movement to create the Wheat Pool, credit union, union hospital, and the co-op, was the CCF Saltcoats constituency president when the provincial election of 1938 was called. Despite a widespread search, the constituency had been unable to find a suitable candidate by the day of the nominating convention, so Emil reluctantly let his name stand. According to Edgar Kaeding, "It came as a great surprise to dad when he arrived at the convention to discover a brash young man from out of nowhere, being promoted as a likely candidate." The brash young man was Joe Phelps. Edgar continued, "Apparently the CCF central office was looking for a constituency which Joe could contest, and with the approval of some of the executive of the Saltcoats constituency, he was authorized to attend the convention."[42] Joe Phelps was nominated, and both he and Emil Kaeding ended up on the ballot.

When the Saltcoats CCF local organization contacted Phelps by telephone in the spring of 1938, he had reconsidered. He left his seeding, went by train on a Sunday to Spy Hill to meet them that afternoon and evening, and made plans with them "on what [they] were going to do and when [they] were going to do it." He returned home that night, the bona fide CCF candidate for Saltcoats. He added, "I figured if you were going to do something you had better get busy and do it." He also told them "it would not be just a squabble for me and that everybody had to roll up their sleeves and get in there and help or else it was no use," because Asmunder Loptson, the Liberal candidate, was "buying votes right and left and promising roads and every other doggone thing."[43] Phelps's impulsive nature and his dedication to the CCF were becoming readily apparent.

His nomination in Saltcoats created some problems, though. The *Regina Leader-Post* reported that within that riding "dissatisfaction exists among the CCF supporters at the candidature of J. L. Phelps, who came from Wilkie, clear across the province, to defeat two Saltcoats men for the nomination." Since fear existed that this dissatisfaction might cause CCF supporters to vote for a Social Crediter, some suggested that Phelps should withdraw and allow "the nomination of a Saltcoats man as a Unity nominee." This "might consolidate the CCF vote behind one man and spike a Social Credit entrance into the field."[44] This, of course, never occurred.

Phelps was establishing a reputation as a dynamic speaker, and easily won the nomination. Emil, feeling that some of his long-time supporters had deserted him in favour of an unknown commodity, considered resigning from the constituency executive. However, according to Edgar Kaeding, "after several hours of serious discussion between the two men, he agreed to become Joe's campaign manager, realizing that Joe would make an excellent candidate and the important thing was to post a win."[45]

Joe and Lena spent many evenings in the Kaeding home during that 1938 election campaign. Edgar Kaeding recalled,

> I used to enjoy sitting and listening in the living room to the discussions on campaign strategy. On other occasions the whole constituency executive would meet in our home, and often other contemporaries of Joe and Dad would appear, such as George Williams and M. J. Coldwell. Although I was only 18 at the time, I can still remember the crackle in Joe's voice when he got wound up in one of his pet theories. Those were pretty heady days as the CCF movement was starting to catch on around Saskatchewan.[46]

Coverage of the 1938 campaign was limited. The *Yorkton Enterprise* contained the following three short items:

> Stornoway: On Monday evening, May 23 Mr. Joseph Wawryke MP [*sic*][47] addressed a meeting in the hall here in the interests of CCF candidate, Mr. J. L. Phelps.... There was a good attendance and interest shown by the hearers.

> Wroxton: Mr. J. L. Phelps, the CCF candidate for our constituency, will hold a meeting here on June 6th.

> Meadowvale: Those who attended the CCF meeting at Grahame on Tuesday, May 24, were favorably impressed by

> the address of the candidate, Mr. Phelps. The state medicine plank made a particularly strong appeal.[48]

About three hundred people attended a meeting held at Esterhazy on May 26. Phelps claimed

> that if elected...the CCF would give security to farmers on their farms and to urban dwellers in their homes. They would see that debts were reduced to where they could be paid. They would enact legislation to bring about State Medicine...the CCF would pay interest on bonds "if and when funds are available." They would institute a work with wages program; give equal educational opportunities to all and join with others in bringing about control of currency and credit.[49]

An advertisement on June 2, 1938, in the *Esterhazy Observer and Pheasant Hills Advertiser* requested voters to "Elect J. L. Phelps," Saltcoats's CCF candidate, on the following platform: "Honest Government, Complete Religious Freedom, Hospital and Medical Services, Equal Educational Opportunity, Increased Social Services, Single Transferable Ballot, [and] Security of Tenure."[50]

On June 8, 1938, Phelps won the seat handily and Saltcoats was represented by the first non-Liberal in the history of the constituency. The *Wilkie Press* commented, "Feeling locally was generally pleased that Joe Phelps had won handsomely for the CCF in the Saltcoats riding, especially when it was known he was compelled to do all his own campaigning. The Saltcoats seat was considered so doubtful that CCF speakers could not be spared to help the campaign there."[51] Phelps's reputation as a combative politician and a formidable opponent was already well established. The day following the election, the *Leader-Post* published the following statement: "Into the picture comes a slashing farmer, 'Joe' Phelps of the Wilkie district. Mr. Phelps has been elected CCF member for Saltcoats. He is an aggressive personality."

Provincially, the Liberals, led by William Patterson, elected thirty-six members; the CCF ten; and Social Credit two. Two Unity candidates were also successful.[52] In his analysis of the election, G. H. Williams indicated that the CCF was well pleased with the results. He noted that the

CCF not only polled the second-largest vote but also took 35 per cent of the vote against the 44 per cent obtained by the Liberals in the thirty-one seats it contested. He added that of the fourteen members elected as members of the Opposition, ten won on a straight CCF ticket and two others had been endorsed by the CCF. He further added that of the two Social Credit members elected, one was placed in the field by the CCF, in co-operation with other groups, and was actually a CCF member.[53] As in 1934, the CCF again became the official opposition, but for the first time it had the ability to provide a strong opposition in the provincial legislature. This time Joe Phelps was one of its members.

CHAPTER 4

STORMY WEATHER

Joe Phelps settled into his role as a member of the Opposition for the next six years. It was an intensive training ground where he honed his skills in research, debate, and political strategy. His knowledge of parliamentary procedure and Liberal policies gained during these years proved useful in years to come. Twenty-seven of the fifty-two members of Saskatchewan's ninth legislative assembly, which convened on January 19, 1939, were rookies, including Joe Phelps.[1] Phelps's conscientiousness caught the attention of many he worked with. His impulsiveness and aggressiveness also began to emerge as defining personality traits. He admired and emulated his mentor, G. H. Williams, the leader of the Opposition. He also learned much from such seasoned adversaries as J. M. Uhrich, W. F. Kerr, and H. Staines. But it was T. C. Davis, the attorney general and Liberal member for Prince Albert since 1921, who taught Phelps the most about the need to be prepared in parliamentary debate. When Jean Larmour later asked Phelps if he had fought with Davis, he replied,

> Oh God, yes. Damn near upset the desks, kicking them over. But you know, we never hated each other. He was a good sportsman, I'll give him credit for that.... I detested the ground he walked on politically but I have to admit he is clever.... He was sold on one side of the deal and I was sold on the other. That was all the difference. He would go at me like nobody was fooling.[2]

When asked if he tried to work out strategies to trick Davis, Phelps said, "Oh yes. And by God you had to do your homework if you were going to do it with him. And he respected me for it, I think, because I did my homework, too. That's something where I knew what I was talking about, or tried to anyway. You just took your life in your hands in there."[3]

Phelps proved to be a formidable opponent, his combativeness often antagonizing the ruling Liberals. The *Leader-Post* columnist noted that on February 2, 1939, Phelps snapped at Davis, "Pay attention to the business of the house," and pointed a finger at Dr. Uhrich and shouted, "No, you sit down." When the Liberals jeered Phelps, he referred to Liberal speeches and quoted Victor Hugo: "Strong and bitter words indicate a weak case." The reporter continued: "The Saltcoats man scorched Liberals, their policies and deeds with fiery words. He hammered Dr. Uhrich on state medicine. He hammered them on interest payments, declaring that 'the first charge of the province was the welfare of the people.'" Phelps also said that agriculture was "pretty baggy at the knees." Phelps had also given an intelligent response to Davis's question about the statute of limitations and had fully explained the Exemption Act, much to Davis's surprise and chagrin. In addition, he had taken the Department of Education to task by citing statistics "like a government pamphlet" and by indicating that some rural schools were "slum schools." Furthermore, he had insulted the Liberals, calling them "professional confusionists." The *Leader-Post* columnist described the encounter:

> Catch Mr. Phelps...by the tail and how Mr. Phelps can bite...
>
> Liberals learned...that the opposition housed as near a wildcat as a legislator can be. Mr. Phelps, while doing his stint of debating, scratched the premier, Mr. Davis, Mr. Estey, and Dr. Uhrich, and though he had to retract at times, he made the ministers uneasy, nettled, or angry. But wonder of wonders! Mr. Phelps can handle the "Terrible Turk," Mr. Davis. In this legislature, that is something.
>
> Mr. Phelps looks as if he wouldn't scratch a paper cup. But he can make a speech. He made one of the best yet. He is a fighter. He has punch. He has a fine fire of indignation. And best, under fire he is as unruffled as a billiard ball.

Liberals will gun for Mr. Phelps. But Mr. Phelps will take care of himself quite handily.[4]

When the 1939 session finally ended at 9:45 p.m. on April 1, the spent legislators participated in their ritualistic closing act, a paper fight. Not surprisingly, J. L. Phelps became a prime target:

> No year has seen such a wild and lengthy paper fight. In a cyclone of whizzing paper bullets, the gentlemen loosed their pent-up play.
>
> Mr. Davis and Mr. Phelps, true to form, fought a personal engagement for a time. A bunch of Liberals ganged up on Mr. Phelps, burying him in flying paper. Mr. Phelps churned back like a windmill.[5]

During the next five sessions, Phelps had many other acrimonious clashes with the Liberals. Though his chief opponent from the 1939 session, T. C. Davis, no longer sat in the assembly, Phelps soon acquired new adversaries: Premier W. J. Patterson, who was also provincial treasurer; W. F. Kerr, Minister of Natural Resources; and J. W. Estey and H. Staines, successive ministers of education. Since Phelps often questioned government fiscal policies, as well as matters concerning natural resources and education, these men soon became his main opponents. Phelps interrogated the Liberals relentlessly. He persistently attempted to obtain information by asking the same question in different ways. On February 19, 1940, the assembly denied Phelps's motion requesting "the names of all companies, corporations, syndicates, associations, and partnerships engaged in mining, fishing, forestry, lumbering, oil production, and the fur industry."[6] He also requested the value of production of each of the said organizations, the amount of wages paid their employees, and a list of all organizations that had not paid any royalty to the government during that period. He wanted all this information for "each of the past six years." On February 22, he moved an almost identical motion that was again rejected.[7]

Undeterred, on March 7, 1941, Phelps moved four separate motions for returns that essentially requested the same information.[8] Several times during the caustic debate that followed, the Speaker called him to order and required him to withdraw statements. Overwhelmed by the gargantuan nature of the request, Kerr noted that the questions were the same ones Phelps had asked a year earlier and that supplying some of the information requested would be impossible. He added that providing the rest "would be a tremendous task which would not only take up the time of his whole department for a long time but would require extra help to get the answers." Phelps still insisted that the minister's reasons were not good enough. When Estey denied charges that information was being withheld and indicated that these questions were not properly worded, Phelps stated, "I gave careful consideration to the words I was using. I thought I could get under the wire with that one."[9] All four motions were defeated, but not before Phelps had clashed with Omar Demers, the Liberal member from Shellbrook, and told him how to keep order. Interrupting Phelps, Speaker Agar stated he would look after order in the House himself. At this point, Estey demanded that Phelps withdraw his suggestion that the Speaker could not keep order, and Phelps complied.[10] Despite the response he received, his requests for detailed information continued.[11]

POLITICIAN WITH A CAPITAL P

Another testy clash occurred after Phelps used an array of statistics to argue that provincial expenditures for education were inadequate and that children, particularly in rural areas, were being short-changed. In his defence on March 30, 1943, Staines called Phelps "a statistical juggler," declaring that Phelps's statements "savored of the practices of a gutter politician." Staines charged that Phelps had resorted to "selective statistical data" in arriving at his conclusions and that he had made a "discreditable" statement. When Agar required Staines to retract "that word," he did so sarcastically, noting: "I do not want to offend the refined sensibilities of the honorable gentleman from Saltcoats."[12]

In an article written on April 2, 1941, a *Leader-Post* commentator humorously described the Liberals' attitude toward Phelps and explained his reaction to Phelps's three-hour speech:

> [T]his Phelps person is very definitely in the bad books of the Liberals. If all they have said about him be true, he is truly a

> terrible sort of bogey man, an ogre of the very worst order, a "politician" with a capital P, a thorn in their flesh they would willingly have extracted permanently. Mr. Estey referred to his [Phelps's] Friday speech as that "tirade for three hours, most of it without meaning." Some CCF members made their criticisms in a "straight forward, manly way," but much of Phelps's criticisms were based on unfounded suspicion.[13]

In another article, the same columnist described Phelps in this manner:

> Mr. Phelps, of course, the most energetic speaker in the house, brings in quantities of books, pamphlets, and paper to quote from, waves his arms, shouts, scowls, and at one time at least during this session pounded Mr. Brockelbank's desk unmercifully to emphasize some particularly telling point. With Mr. Estey, he is the busiest man in the chamber. His desk is always littered with paper, and he is generally industriously at his desk at work making notes, writing letters, or engaged in some actual physical exercise at his desk."[14]

Besides antagonizing the Liberals, Phelps often provoked the Speaker. On February 21, 1939, after expressing an opinion on the propriety of a statement, Phelps "burst out in tones that jerked members to attention," and the Speaker stated, "I resent the member from Saltcoats, every time the speaker is giving an opinion, shaking his head and waving his arms around. If he continues to do so [I intend] to have him named on the floor of the house."[15]

Phelps again provoked Speaker Agar on April 7, 1943, when he voted against his own motion. For this action, Agar administered "a severe reprimand" and "censured" him for having taken up the time of the House in debating the motion, for causing an expense in printing it, and then for voting against it. Noting that he had never seen anything like it in all his thirty-three years as a member of the legislature, the Speaker added, "Such dishonorable practice should be condemned."[16] Probably, the most colourful instance in which Phelps infuriated the Speaker occurred on April 8, 1942. Deputy Speaker W. G. Ross threatened to have Phelps ejected if he refused to obey an order to sit down. When Phelps refused to do so, Ross had the sergeant-at-arms escort Phelps from the chamber.[17] The Speaker of the House called several of the opposition members to order, told them to sit down, and threatened to have them ordered from the chamber. According to Phelps, numerous requests made to the government to provide the necessary information to vote on matters involving millions of dollars of taxpayers' money had gone unanswered. Phelps described the scene in the legislature:

> I then got to my feet and started to ask some questions, and was called to order, and ordered to sit down by the Speaker. I then asked the speaker if he could tell us [the Opposition] how we could vote intelligently for these expenditures of this money, before knowing what had been done with the money we had voted for this same purpose last year. The speaker then ordered me out of the House, and the Sergeant-At-Arms at once escorted me out.[18]

J. H. Brockelbank, the opposition leader,[19] promptly objected, claiming that Ross had exceeded his authority, and raised a point of order that any elected member was within his rights asking for information before the vote was taken, and further established that the chairman had erred in having Phelps removed from the chamber, arguing that the Speaker could only take such action after a majority vote and at the direction of the legislature as a whole. By the time Ross withdrew his ruling and stated that he would allow Phelps to resume his seat, however, Phelps had already left the building and did not resume his seat that day. Nor was Phelps in the legislature on April 9, 10, or 11. By the time the session ended on April 11, Phelps had returned to his Wilkie farm to do his spring work. Highly indignant, Phelps later contended that he should have received an official notice to return, a notice the government declined to issue. In a letter to his constituents, he wrote:

> I have not gone back, nor at the moment do I intend to go back. My campaign manager has endorsed this action on my part in the Saltcoats constituency and by the Provincial Executive of the CCF. I am doing so as a protest to this sort of thing. I feel, and many others like me, that we are fighting

> as never before, in fields near and far, for the preservation of the democratic rights of the people, and the preservation of our so-called democracy. But if this sort of thing is allowed to continue, it makes an absolute sham of the ideals and freedoms for which we are striving.
>
> Someone simply coming to me without an order of the Assembly and telling me they are prepared to overlook the incident is not enough. If the House, as a whole, or their spokesman, has erred, which they admit, then I feel I am entitled to be escorted back to the Assembly the same way I was ordered out; and receive a formal apology from the assembly, together with a vote of the Assembly to order me seated in my right and proper place as the peoples [*sic*] democratically elected representative in an honourable way.[20]

Although Phelps often exasperated government members and the Speaker, he proved to be an articulate spokesman for the interests of his constituents. Representing a rural riding and himself, a farmer, it is not surprising that from the outset Joe Phelps took a keen interest in agricultural issues. During the 1939 session, he had opposed the Threshers' Lien Act but supported the licensing and bonding of livestock shippers and drovers. He requested that the provincial government urge its federal counterpart to adopt a system of crop insurance for farmers. In fact, four of the six resolutions that he moved or seconded dealt with agriculture, as did three of the thirteen returns he requested.[21] Interested in greater utilization of the Port of Churchill for the shipment of prairie grain since his days on the UFC board in 1931, he continued to question the Saskatchewan government on the issue in the early 1940s.[22]

TEACHERS AND CHILDREN "SHORT-CHANGED"

Another of Phelps's interests was education, especially in rural Saskatchewan. On February 2, 1939, he charged that the government "had evaded its responsibility and that the condition of many rural schools was a disgrace to any country." Concerned that "children and teachers were being 'short-changed' by the government's policy," he claimed that the Liberals always found the money to pay the bondholders but had none for education. He also noted that the average teacher in 1937 earned $488 and claimed that while a student's education in Saskatoon cost $80, the average rural student's education cost $10.[23]

Six weeks later, Phelps objected to a $25,000 increase in the grant for the University of Saskatchewan for the fiscal year ending April 30, 1940, knowing that the government planned to decrease rural schools' grants. He declared, "The rural parts of this province feel that insufficient attention is being paid to rural areas under present conditions. . . . Having in mind difficulties of rural schools and teachers, I think the increase to the university is totally uncalled for. It is not a square deal." He inquired, "What provision is the minister making to make it possible for the rural child to get to the university?"[24] On March 25, 1943, Phelps again "condemned the government for having spent 'too little money' on education in Saskatchewan." Indicating that the Patterson Government "did not even spend all the money we voted the [education] department for that year [1941–1942]," he pointed out that while the legislature had voted for $4,092,000 for education, the actual expenditure had been $4,005,000. He continued: "It is true we have criticized the government on occasion for over-expenditures, but this sort of saving is short-changing the children of the province." He noted that while provincial revenues had increased 35.74 per cent between the fiscal years 1938–1939 and 1941–1942, only 1.09 per cent more had been spent during this same period. This, he maintained, "proves that education is not getting a square deal in this province."[25]

"I DON'T BACK UP ONE INCH."

Early in the first session, Phelps exhibited a keen passion for the development of the province's natural resources. On January 25, 1939, W. F. Kerr introduced legislation to establish an Industrial Development Board. When the bill appeared for second reading on February 6, 1939, G. H. Williams moved and J. L. Phelps seconded "that the said Bill be so amended as to include the principle of direct governmental development of Natural Resources, and operation and/or control of industries either by the Board itself or by other boards or commissions set up by or under the provision of the Industrial Board Act, 1939."[26] Although the amendment giving the government control over the development of Saskatchewan's natural resources was defeated and the bill to establish the Industrial Development Board was later passed, Phelps's action in seconding this amendment indicated that he already held strong views on the subject. On February 2, 1939, Phelps had commended the government for planning to establish the Industrial Development Board, but said he "was not in accord with the idea of development for the advance of the Hudson Bay Mining and Smelting company or the Consolidated Mining and Smelting company that exploited the resources and then when they played out, left Saskatchewan and sometimes the country with profits, leaving behind only 'open holes.'"[27]

During the 1940 and 1941 sessions, Phelps again requested extensive information on the province's natural resources. In 1941, the *Leader-Post* reporter wrote:

> Mr. Phelps wanted to know practically everything there is to know about the natural resources department. He had six questions, of five clauses each dealing with mining, timber, petroleum products, gas, sodium sulphate, clay, coal, gold, other minerals, not to forget the "etceteras," which bulked up the debate. The Saltcoats man admitted he wanted much of this information so he could use it in the budget debate, hoping, no doubt, to make things as embarrassing as possible for the government.[28]

Phelps's concern for natural resources was evident in at least two other debates in which he participated. On March 24, 1942, he reiterated his theme that undeveloped natural resources belonged to the people. He stated, "The government has given away oil leases, but it is not impossible to change that." Noting that companies engaged in mining did not own the coal or ore, he added, "The CCF would reimburse those companies at the replacement value of their equipment." He considered confiscation unnecessary but added, "If it is necessary, I don't back up one inch."[29]

BURNING THE MIDNIGHT OIL

In 1942, Tommy Douglas had assumed leadership of the party after George Williams left to serve overseas. As leader, he set up a planning committee with a number of subcommittees to prepare the CCF to assume power. Phelps's interest in natural resources may have caused Douglas to select his vocal maverick to head the natural resources subcommittee; alternatively, Phelps's place on this subcommittee may have sparked his interest in natural resources.[30] Nevertheless, as the head of this subcommittee between 1942 and 1944, Phelps worked conscientiously to learn as much as possible about natural resources and to critique the Liberal government's resource policies. Whenever he could, Phelps attempted to discredit the government. In fact, when asked later in an interview with Jean Larmour what he had done to try to create a policy for development, Phelps replied, "Oh, just expose what was going on out there. There was lots going on and you just had to dig it out and pick out the parts you wanted."[31]

J. H. Brockelbank also served on the subcommittee, but did not share Phelps's passion for quick and bold action. Phelps recalled in the 1982 interview noted above that he never worked closely with Brockelbank, describing him as "kind of over my head or something—to work with him didn't go well in some way or another." Brockelbank later replaced Phelps as the minister responsible for northern Saskatchewan in 1949, taking a markedly different approach to northern development than Phelps.

Phelps spent hours documenting the committee's findings, discussing strategy, planning how it would present the information, and making sure it was prepared:

> No, I did my homework, if I do say so myself. I was pretty conscientious about it. We burned the midnight oil, Myron [Feeley] and I. He would come down to our house and I would go up to his and we would work hours together on how we were going to approach it and how we were going to do it and then who was going to do what.[32]

Burning the midnight oil likely affected Phelps's ongoing stomach problems. In a letter from the Drake Hotel in Regina to the family, he wrote, "Had some ten or twelve x-rays taken in Saskatoon. It took three days to complete them all. They say my stomach is holding out pretty well, but I must be careful what I eat."[33]

Charles David Cummings, who represented Souris–Estevan for the CCF, also served on the natural resources subcommittee. Cummings recalled,

> Joe was a very positive thinking person, but was a good listener of the opinions of others. He would discuss with each committee member that member's opinion. In fact he would urge each one for an opinion. I enjoyed working with him. He was criticized for being too aggressive. However, we were breaking new ground, and some errors could be expected to occur. A great amount of the Saskatchewan social democratic program was of his making.[34]

The natural resources subcommittee also studied industrial development, considering the feasibility of a wide range of industries. It considered the idea of compulsory government marketing organizations, processing facilities, and secondary industries designed to use the province's natural resources, as well as the development of public utilities. On February 23, 1944, Phelps charged that Saskatchewan was approaching "a monopoly condition" in the lumber, coal, and mineral industries. To remedy this, he suggested "exploratory work to determine the value of undeveloped natural resources, redrafting of timber regulations, improved processing of coal, the introduction of a severance tax, the establishment of a provincial marketing board, [and] a provincial fur exchange and cold storage facilities." He also claimed that the people of Saskatchewan were not getting their fair share of the revenue from natural resources. He stated that in 1935–1936, when the total value of production of natural resources in Saskatchewan had been $7,133,185, the royalties paid to the province had been $700,596; in 1942–1943, when production had jumped to $31,079,497, royalties had only increased to $1,420,811. He concluded, "There was a 485 percent gain in production but only a 100 percent increase in revenue to the province. There should have been an increase of $2,511,936. The people want to know why this money had not gone into the public treasury?"[35]

Phelps was also politically active outside the legislature. At the provincial level, Phelps participated in various constituency conventions outside his own riding. Between June 16, 1941, and June 18, 1942, he addressed meetings in the constituencies of Qu'Appelle–Wolseley, Kelvington, Cannington, Souris–Estevan, and Moosomin on one or more occasions. He also spoke to the CCF youth at their provincial Co-operative Commonwealth Youth Movement (CCYM) convention in

Moose Jaw in 1943. He participated in the CCF Winter Schools in Regina and Saskatoon (open to "all CCF people, candidates, campaign managers, organizers, constituency officers, poll committee members, and other workers") in 1944, sharing the platform with a number of distinguished politicians, and probably in 1942 and 1943 as well.[36] He was also a delegate to the national CCF convention in Regina on December 29, 1944.[37]

He also devoted considerable time to his own constituency of Saltcoats. In January 1940, the *Saskatchewan Commonwealth* noted,

> True to his promise at election time that he would hold public meetings between sessions for the purpose of reporting on happenings in the legislature and to receive suggestions from his constituents regarding matters they wish dealt with at future sessions, J. L. Phelps...has just held a series of very successful meetings. Points covered by Phelps include Two Creeks, North and South Wroxton, Calder, Beresina, Bavelaw, Welby, Glyndwr, Zeneta, Stockholm, Freedholm, Luton, and Hazelcliffe, finishing with a joint meeting at Langenburg with Mrs. Louise Lucas, CCF candidate for Melville federal constituency.[38]

In December 1940, the CCF newspaper again reported that Phelps had just completed a speaking tour in the Saltcoats constituency and that meetings had been held in thirteen polls. He had also attended two zone conventions and a council meeting in another riding and had given several lectures on citizenship at various schools.[39] In addition to this seemingly endless round of speeches and meetings, Phelps also sent weekly letters to his constituents when the legislature was sitting.[40]

PREPARING FOR POWER

Phelps was among a group of prominent members of the national and provincial CCF, including Tommy Douglas, Woodrow Lloyd, Clarence Fines, J. H. Brockelbank, and Oak Valleau, who carefully scrutinized and finalized the party's policy in preparation for the 1944 election. A special three-day conference was held in the Christmas season of 1943 to examine the policy papers and ideas developed by the provincial executive and subcommittees. Frank Scott and David Lewis attended from the national CCF office, as did CCF leaders from British Columbia.[41]

Slowly and steadily, the CCF was gaining popularity throughout Saskatchewan. By the time Liberal Premier William Patterson called the provincial election in 1944, the CCF, now under the leadership of Tommy Douglas, had consolidated its position in the province. In preparation for the election, the CCF opposition proposed an amendment to the Elections Act to lower the voting age to nineteen, which Phelps introduced. In a letter to Lena, he wrote, "The amendment will lower the voting age to nineteen, the same as they have done in Alberta. This will make the Liberals squirm, as we will win if they vote for it, and they sure will lose the support of the young people if they vote against it."[42]

On the national scene, the CCF was on the rise. It had emerged as a serious political threat to the federal Liberals during the war years, after forming the official opposition in British Columbia, Ontario, and Saskatchewan. The popularity of its policies put pressure on the federal Liberal government to begin implementing progressive social legislation. Startled by polls that showed the CCF gaining in voter support, Prime Minister Mackenzie King responded by adopting some of the popular elements of the CCF program. Early on in the war, King implemented a system of unemployment insurance (UI), a labour demand going back to the 1930s. The UI legislation was passed in 1940 and the program went into operation in 1941. In January of 1944, King announced a system of "baby bonuses," and in February his government approved Order in Council P.C. 1003, which formally gave unions access to government-backed certification procedures. King was successful in stealing a lot of the CCF's thunder and thwarting it as an electoral threat at the federal level. Despite the changing face of national politics and federal Liberal efforts to usurp the role of providing a social safety net, however, CCF party faithful remained confident that the social gospel message of Tommy Douglas and the well-oiled party machine would bring victory to the CCF in Saskatchewan.

When the assembly prorogued on April 1, 1944, Phelps had served his apprenticeship as an opposition member. He had learned to tangle with seasoned and astute government members, he had found a niche in the CCF caucus, and he had discovered his own key interests. He also knew the mood of the province and particularly that of the Saltcoats constituency. When Premier W. J. Patterson called an election for June 15, he and the CCF were eager to begin the official campaign.

At dissolution, the legislature consisted of thirty-three Liberals, eleven CCF, and three National Reform (previously Unity and Social Credit) members. Five seats were vacant and seven MLAS were on active service in the armed forces.[43] The five-year term of the ninth legislature ought to have ended in 1943, but, during the session that year, A. C. Stewart (Yorkton, Unity) had introduced an amendment extending the life of the legislature until June 10, 1944. The 1944 legislature also amended the Legislative Assembly Act to give Saskatchewan residents serving in the armed forces three representatives in the next legislature.

Several issues dominated the 1944 election, but the ideological debate overshadowed the campaign. Andrew Milnor writes: "The socialism issue, dormant since the election of 1934, arose to dominate the [1944] election."[44] The Liberals attacked the CCF's alleged anti-democratic nature. Premier W. J. Patterson stated that "the issues facing the electors at the next Saskatchewan election were clear cut, namely the regimentation of the CCF or the individual liberty of the Liberal party."[45] Hon. J. G. Taggart, the agriculture minister, also indicated that "the voter would sit in judgment on these two principles, privileged or socialized possession, and he would decide which principle to support, to which end the issue should be presented clearly, stripped of every detail—Socialism or democracy."[46] T. C. Douglas expressed the opposite view. In one speech he made this appeal to the voters: "You are either voting to go back to the old dog-eat-dog system or go forward to build a new society based on human need."[47]

Besides disagreeing about the merits of socialism versus free enterprise, the two major parties also held widely divergent views on agriculture, education, health, and labour. With respect to the first, the Liberals stressed the steps they had taken to ensure farm security and to reduce farmers' indebtedness. They also insisted they had aided farmers by working with the federal government.[48] However, the CCF soundly criticized Patterson for placing farmers at the mercy of the mortgage companies. Douglas noted that "from 1935 to 1941 the Liberal government had permitted 12,292 foreclosures and evictions in Saskatchewan" and that "today 25 percent of the Saskatchewan farmers are renters, whereas 40 years ago only four percent of the farmers were renters."[49]

The CCF promised that if elected it would guarantee that every honest and industrious farmer would be able to keep title to his land and pass it on to his children. To that end, it adopted a four-point land policy that promised that a CCF government would:

1. protect the farmer from unjust foreclosure and eviction;
2. protect from seizure that part of a farmer's crop that is needed to provide for his family;
3. use, if necessary, the power of moratorium to compel reduction of debts to a figure at which they can reasonably be paid with prevailing prices of farm products; and
4. prevent the growth of debt by placing a crop failure clause in all mortgages and agreements of sale.[50]

The Liberals and the CCF also held differing views about education. The Liberals called for the expansion of existing programs but offered no new ones. The CCF, on the other hand, criticized the government for condoning low salaries for teachers, the poor condition of many schools, and the lack of opportunities for Saskatchewan young people to obtain a higher education. Its sixteen-page pamphlet entitled "The CCF Program for Saskatchewan" advocated establishing larger units of school administration, placing teachers on an improved salary schedule, providing free school texts and supplies to students, making financial arrangements to permit qualified students to attend university, and revising the school curriculum.[51]

The Liberals were also proud of their health services, which included the provision of free treatment for tuberculosis, cancer, and infantile paralysis (polio). In the 1944 session, the government also indicated that it would undertake programs in co-operation with the federal government, such as "a physical fitness program and enabling legislation for a national health program."[52] However, the CCF criticized the Liberal health program as totally inadequate. It advocated moving in stages toward a complete system of socialized health services, with special emphasis on preventative medicine, so that everyone in the province would receive "adequate medical, surgical, dental, nursing, and hospital care without charge."[53]

Concerning labour, the Liberals promised to "support all useful and progressive legislation which [would] tend to improve conditions and employer-employee relations generally."[54] They believed their labour policy was adequate. The CCF disagreed. Endorsing the principle of collective bargaining, it insisted that workers should have the democratic right to organize unions and be guaranteed freedom from discrimination and intimidation. It also promised to increase the minimum wage and to establish a Department of Labour.[55]

This was the platform that Phelps endorsed as he addressed his constituents during the 1944 campaign. Phelps campaigned diligently and often had others speak on his behalf.[56] Since he was a large-scale farmer who lived across the province from his riding, campaigning at this time must have required great effort on his part.[57]

The CCF won the June 15 election by a landslide. Five Liberals and three active service MLAS formed the Opposition.[58] Results showed Joseph Lee Phelps, CCF, farmer, with 3,461 votes, defeating Donald Alexander McKenzie, Liberal, barrister, with 2,874 votes, and Rae Melville Salkeld, Conservative, farmer, with 454 votes. In the new legislature, only three of the Liberal Party's five members—W. J. Patterson, the former premier; A. T. Procter, the former highways minister; and G. H. Danielson—would make any significant impact in the Opposition. The Liberals were in great disarray. Chris Higginbotham, a freelance reporter, noted that the CCF, in contrast, were "more prepared for victory than the Liberals were for defeat."[59] The election of a socialist government in Saskatchewan caused elation and exaltation for some, but it created apprehension, anxiety, and fear for others.

When the CCF under Premier T. C. Douglas assumed power on July 12, 1944, Joseph Lee Phelps was a member of that government. This was not surprising. Phelps was a veteran politician who had shown his mettle in the legislature. Having displayed a keen interest in placing the development of natural resources under public control, he would soon begin to play a dominant role in the new administration.

PART II

IN GOVERNMENT

1944–1948

CHAPTER 5

MAVERICK DREAMER

A well-orchestrated campaign of public speaking engagements and radio broadcasts by the CCF's very popular and sincere Baptist leader, preaching a combination of social gospel and a new economic order, brought victory to Tommy Douglas and his party, and the formation of the first social democratic government in Canada.

The magnitude of the task facing them was immense. The party advocated radical reforms that touched nearly every facet of economic and social life in the province, promising farm security legislation, a new deal for labour, development and support for the co-operative movement, a restructured public school system, socialized health care, and a prosperous mixed economy. The harnessing of the province's natural resources was critical to diversifying the economy and improving the province's financial position, and essential to fund the new social programs. Faced with this revolutionary political and social mandate, Douglas assigned the key natural resources portfolio to Joe Phelps.

In his first few months as Minister of Natural Resources, Phelps initiated literally hundreds of new programs. He began to assemble a power grid that would eventually electrify rural Saskatchewan. He began acquiring aircraft for transportation in the North, leading to the creation of a government-owned airways corporation. He designed and set up a series of conservation programs and created new mechanisms to develop and market the fur, fish, and timber resources that were abundant in the North, and explored opportunities in mining and mineral resources. He began to establish Crown corporations and create a number of innovative business ventures, representing the government's first forays into public ownership. By 1948, the Department of Natural Resources (DNR) consisted of nine separate branches: Forestry; Fur and Game; Fisheries; Water Rights; Crown Lands; Industrial Development; Provincial Parks; Mines; and Legal Surveys on Crown Lands. Innovative new programs were developed in each of the branches, many of which continued for decades to come.

VICTORY

Edgar Kaeding, Joe Phelps's long-time friend and associate, remembers it well:

> I was in Regina on election night, June 15, 1944, one of the thousands of people who sat outside the *Leader-Post* building...watching the returns being posted on the wall of the building. Every time another victory for the CCF was posted, a wild cheer would ring out. As the evening progressed, and it was evident that the CCF had won a major victory, all kinds of celebrations began. Old wood was piled in the crowded street, with the odd rubber car tire thrown in. The street cars which ran on 11th Avenue and Albert Street were almost completely immobilized as revellers would pull the cables off the overhead line.[1]

In July, the new Cabinet was sworn in. Tommy Douglas was premier and would also serve as Minister of Public Health. Just ten days after taking office, he arranged for a commission to survey health services. Chaired by Henry E. Sigerist of Johns Hopkins University, the commission completed the survey within three months, and its 1944 report, though brief, would form the basis for future health care legislation on both provincial and national levels.[2] Medicare began humbly on January 1, 1947, when the Saskatchewan Hospitalization Plan was inaugurated, providing hospitalization to Saskatchewan residents at a cost of $5 per individual, to a maximum of $30 a family.[3]

Clarence Fines, later described as an "enigmatic character whose legacy was to act as the fiscal balance wheel in the Douglas government," would direct the provincial Treasury and Treasury Board.[4] Jack Corman, a solicitor and mayor of Moose Jaw, was attorney general. G. H. Williams was named Minister of Agriculture, and J. H. Brockelbank, a farmer and leader of the Opposition in Williams's absence, was Minister of Municipal Affairs. Oak Valleau, a farmer who, like Phelps, had been active in the policy-planning committees, was appointed provincial secretary and Minister of Social Welfare. J. T. Douglas, farmer and provincial organizer for the CCF, was put in charge of highways and of public works. Woodrow Lloyd, a former president of the Saskatchewan Teachers' Federation, took the education portfolio. He would go on to become "the philosopher of the cabinet whose principled yet practical approach would be felt in all the key government decisions,"[5] and would later lead the party when Douglas left to lead the national party.

Government of the province of Saskatchewan, 1944. Hon. J. L. Phelps, Minister of Natural Resources and Industrial Development, Government of Saskatchewan, 1944. Provincial Archives of Saskatchewan R-B3640-1.

Jack Sturdy, a school principal, was made Minister of Reconstruction and Rehabilitation, while Charlie Williams, popular mayor of Regina, was appointed Minister of Telephones and Telegraphs and Minister of Labour. Lauchlan McIntosh of the Saskatchewan Wheat Pool became Minister of Co-operatives and Co-operative Development, and Joseph Lee Phelps would serve as Minister of Natural Resources.[6]

GETTING THINGS DONE

Tommy Douglas assembled a team of people capable of carrying out his social democratic vision, allowing them enough autonomy to follow through. The professionalism and collaboration that was evident among Douglas's Cabinet set a high standard. In a 1981 documentary, Douglas is described as a circus ringmaster in charge of a tempestuous collection of strong-willed, independent people. He described himself as a conductor:

> I had the baton and I never pretended that I could play all the instruments. I use to say to our caucus, I don't expect to know as much about finances as the provincial treasury or about education as Woodrow Lloyd or as much about resources as Joe Phelps. But my job is to see that you all play in the same key and on the same tune and at the same tempo and if somebody doesn't play that way, then as far as I am concerned he or she is out, no matter how brilliant they are.[7]

When asked if Joe Phelps was a good member of the orchestra, Douglas replied, "He was a good member of the orchestra. Like every other member of the orchestra, once in a while you had to say, just a moment, there are some other instruments. You know this is not a solo effort. And you have to let other people play their part too."[8] Tommy Douglas placed the administration of the DNR squarely in the hands of Joe Phelps, whom he described as an activist and a very pragmatic person. They were breaking new ground, and bold and rapid action was required. Joe Phelps's energy and dedication would be put to the test over the next four years, and he would rise to the challenge.

As Phelps settled into his new job, he soon began to display his energetic enthusiasm, his idealism (perhaps even his naïveté), and particularly his impulsiveness. He was determined to implement the socialist plan set out by the CCF and to do so at lightning speed. As A. W. Johnson notes in "Biography of a Government," "The province was in desperate need of economic development, the party had charted a course which involved social ownership, and it was his responsibility to 'get things done.'"[9] So he did.

Big business retaliated early in the wake of the CCF victory. Imperial Oil stopped exploration in the province. Prudential Life withdrew financial support. Mortgage companies began threatening mass foreclosures. The election of a socialist government in Saskatchewan caused consternation all across North America. The press portrayed the government as everything from anti-business to harbouring a Russian communist connection. Tommy Douglas would, in fact, be called a communist, an atheist, a dictator, and a Nazi during his time in office.[10] In later years, however, praise for Douglas would be unprecedented and his integrity would not be forgotten. In fact, Douglas was deemed the "Greatest Canadian" in a national poll conducted by the CBC in 2004.[11]

Although the press fanned fears of the socialist government's policies, optimism was high. Money the government had said was not available

Joe Phelps, Minister of Industrial Development, Government of Saskatchewan. Provincial Archives of Saskatchewan R-A2892-2.

during the Depression had magically appeared in wartime, when government spending had rejuvenated the economy. The scarcity and deprivation of the Depression was seen, at least in part, as being artificial, something government spending and control of the economy could have mitigated. British political economist John Maynard Keynes had shown that capitalist economies could be made more stable through government control of interest rates and taxation, and by mobilizing capital for investment and spending. The shared misery of the Depression had imbued the public with a sense of communion of spirit and effort.

In this new political and social climate, the new government set about putting its programs in place. Diversifying the economy was seen as the most important step in generating revenues for the province. The Department of Natural Resources was to be the primary instrument of development, and the clearing house for service delivery in Saskatchewan.

THE POOREST GOVERNMENT IN CANADA

George Cadbury, a prominent British economist with private and public administrative experience who joined the government as its chief industrial and coordinating officer in 1946, subsequently stated that when the CCF came to power, Saskatchewan was not only the poorest government in Canada but it also had the highest per capita debt in the country.[12]

With the province nearly bankrupt, the CCF would find it difficult to deliver on its election promises. Although Saskatchewan had gained control of its natural resources in 1930, successive provincial governments had invested little in their development during the Depression. Despite this, by 1940 the value of minerals produced in the province—including ore, sodium sulphate, clay, sand and gravel, natural gas, and coal—had grown from $2.3 million to over $9 million, not to mention the fur, fish, and timber resources of the northern part of the province.[13]

The war increased demand but also created problems, such as the imposition of wage and price controls and labour shortages, which hindered development. Consequently, in 1944, Saskatchewan's economy was still basically dependent on one commodity: wheat.

Both the Liberals and the CCF were concerned about the vulnerability of the province's wheat-based economy. Even before the war, in April 1939, the Patterson Government had passed an act to establish an Industrial Development Board, which was eventually set up in 1942. As the war approached its end, the Liberal government established the Saskatchewan Reconstruction Council to develop policies and plans to deal with problems that might arise after the war.[14] The council presented its wide-ranging report on August 2, 1944. It examined the potential for the development of agriculture, natural resources, power, and other industries in Saskatchewan, and included a separate report by L. E. Kirk, a professor of field husbandry and dean of the College of Agriculture at the University of Saskatchewan, which looked at developing manufacturing or processing industries using farm products as raw materials,[15] in order to "in a very large measure stabilize the province's economy and mitigate the violent fluctuations in wheat prices and production levels."[16] With respect to natural resources, it stressed the need to conserve the province's forests, expand the fish and fur industries, and establish marketing services, as well as suggesting setting up filleting plants. It also recommended that the province undertake geographical surveys and prepare maps to assist in finding and developing mineral resources.[17] Soon after the 1944 election, the Saskatchewan Industrial Board reported to the new CCF government that it had already begun investigating opportunities in the leather, footwear, and woollen industries, as well as the development of sodium sulphates, clay, natural gas, and power.[18] Thus, by August 1944, the new government had received two reports its Liberal predecessor had commissioned to provide advice about how Saskatchewan's economy might be expanded and diversified. This allowed it to hit the ground running, although the CCF had itself invested a great deal of energy in developing economic policies to the same end. In developing its own election platform, it had commissioned a plan for public ownership in the development of natural resources late in 1943, and Douglas had set up several committees to develop policy papers for specific areas.[19]

"ALMOST FLABBERGASTED"

The province was clearly ready for bold and rapid action, and that is what it got with Joe Phelps. Phelps had worked tirelessly on the natural resource policy subcommittee formed in 1943, and had established a reputation as not only a hard worker but also a strong advocate of public ownership. During the previous term, he had been very vocal in his criticism of the Liberal Minister of Natural Resources. The authors of *Tommy Douglas: The Road to Jerusalem* describe him as the "cabinet's maverick" and a "dreamer who generated great enthusiasm among those around him." They also note that "the roadside was strewn with the bodies of those who could not keep up" and that he "paid no attention when others counseled caution."[20]

In *Dream No Little Dreams*, A. W. Johnson examines how the CCF government effectively translated its goals into policies. Much depended on the minister in charge. Rather than relying on the advice and assistance of newly appointed officials in newly established agencies or operating departments as some ministers did, Phelps favoured developing policy using only ad hoc advice as he sought and required it, an approach that "enjoyed the distinction of producing the largest number of changes in public policy in the new government."[21] In part, this was because a great deal of ambiguity surrounded the area of social ownership. While there was general consensus that public ownership of utilities was appropriate, the question of whether industrial enterprises, in particular manufacturing, should be developed publicly was still unclear. The government's capacity for policy analysis and decision making in this area was not resolved, according to Johnson, until the second half of its first term in office.

Phelps took immediate action, announcing on July 22, 1944, in the *Leader-Post* that a complete reorganization of the DNR was underway. L. C. Paterson, who had been employed by the federal government before control of natural resources was transferred to the province, would act as superintendent of the department. The purpose of the overhaul, Phelps announced, was "to obtain a more efficient operation, and to lay the base for the introduction of the policies of the new CCF government with regard to the resources of Saskatchewan."[22]

A number of Royal Commissions and special committees would be set up to oversee the work of the new department. In fact, from October 1944 until early 1945, 196 new acts were passed and four new departments were established.[23]

Phelps soon discovered that he would begin the task of reorganization from scratch. There was no geophysical or geographic mapping in place; northern Saskatchewan was virtually untouched; and despite their planning, previous regimes had taken very few steps to diversify the economy through either resource development or publicly owned enterprises. Later, when asked how he felt about being in charge of this department, he responded,

> Well, naturally, I was almost flabbergasted. I realized immediately the gigantic, tremendous proportions of the job and the fact that very little had been done in some of these fields, and it was virgin territory in some respects.... In regard to the resources they had been running wild almost—I mean with very little control or supervision, and it was certainly a tremendous job.[24]

When Douglas added industrial development to Phelps's portfolio on November 10, 1944, Phelps's work became even more taxing.

In a 1982 interview with Jean Larmour, Joe remembered, "God the things you had to do. It was out of this world. You had to have it on a sheet—which one to take first!" When asked about his work schedule, he recalled, "I would work all day in Regina, and then take the night train out to Prince Albert and wake up in the morning, have breakfast on the train and get off the train to work. I would then work all day and half the night, and then go back down to Regina."[25] Phelps's ministerial papers reveal that indeed his schedule was incredibly rigorous.

HANDLING A CABINET JOB HERSELF

The Phelps family now made the decision to rent out the farm and move to Regina, purchasing a home at 2229 Halifax Street. Although she was content to work in the background, Lena's ever-present support and quick and clever mind were a tremendous help to Joe. Lena would look after domestic duties, accompany her husband to some of the political meetings, entertain guests, and, at times, assist Joe with his speeches.

A 1946 *Leader-Post* article titled "Natural Resources Throne Has a Woman Behind It" attested to Lena Phelps's influence in the department:

> There are people that will tell you that Mrs. Phelps is indeed the power to be reckoned with behind the natural resources throne, that Joe Phelps listens when his Lena talks and that

> she is always on hand when important departmental matters are under discussion at which time her judgement is deferred to before decisions are made . . . Certainly Mrs. Phelps looks and sounds very capable of handling a cabinet job all by herself.[26]

At the time of the 1946 interview, in addition to assisting her husband, Lena was also busy raising three children: Lee, fifteen; Ella, thirteen; and Bruce, eleven.[27] She maintained that her domestic duties were her top priority, stating, "I can make a better contribution as Joe Phelps' wife than by going into politics on my own." The article outlined Lena's many endeavours, including "stumping her husband's constituency to keep his CCF flock from straying," writing books about cookery, "pinch hitting" at various functions, ghost writing and looking after correspondence, as well as lecturing to school children and their parents on industrial development.[28]

Lena would also play a significant role in the drafting of controversial mineral rights taxation legislation that later went before the Supreme Court during Phelps's term as minister, doing extensive research on the legality of the Hudson's Bay Company's ancient rights and claims in relation to mineral rights taxation. On the strength of her explorations, Phelps would later propose that mineral rights revert to the Crown.

Blanche Green was hired as a stenographer in the DNR soon after Joe was appointed to Cabinet. Phelps put great trust in her and even included her in family functions. She became great friends with Lena, and when out-of-town meetings came up, she often stayed with the children. According to Green,

> Joe adored Lena. She was his unsung hero. Lena was proud to be his wife. She was a very kind, happy, outgoing, competent person that really complemented Joe's hard driven work personality. Lena would attend public functions in his absence, and was a good speaker...mind you this may have eventually cost Joe re-election, because his constituents did not see him often enough.... He was busy working on his many projects. Often Lena would come to the office and assist him with duties he felt he didn't have time for, and she welcomed these opportunities.[29]

PERPETUAL MOTION

The office for the Department of Natural Resources located in the Saskatchewan Wheat Pool building on Albert Street in Regina was relocated to the Co-op Creamery building on Albert Street and 11th Avenue in August 1945. The second office was not a particularly fancy one, and Blanche Green recalled:

> When the wind came from a certain direction, we could smell the manure from the stables. The creamery still used horses to deliver milk. That did not bother Joe. He was a farmer, and a little manure wouldn't bother him. He probably had some manure on his own boots. His boots…yes…he always wore those high boots, the kind that lace up at the top.[30]

Doris French Shackleton, author of *Tommy Douglas*, also remarked on his boots, though she thought he stood out as much for his high energy and commitment to the socialist doctrine of the party. She described him as a "standout from the generally harmonious group. . . . He was an impetuous man, who stomped into town in his high boots from his expeditions in the north, needled Fines for new program money, and flared into temper over alleged breaches of the socialist faith."[31]

Green, who was his secretary from 1944 to 1948, was already employed in the department when Phelps was appointed minister. She recalled that before hiring her as his personal stenographer, Phelps asked her to take dictation: "In the memo Joe stated three reasons for his point of view. I noticed that he had only made mention of two reasons. Pointing this out really impressed Joe. Monday morning he offered me the position. I accepted and never regretted my decision."[32]

Green reflected on her first impressions of Phelps:

> I thought he was different, not in a negative sense though. He was so action oriented. We had never seen such a bee hive of activity in the office before, under the old regime. He was a task master, restless and driven. He was always thinking. Joe was a man years before his time. He was a perfectionist. I doubt if he ever quit working. He was the nearest thing to,

> perpetual motion I've seen. Social chitchat was not his thing at all. He was all business, yet he was polite and kind. I don't believe he ever had any fun the way others would consider things fun. He often worked nights. It was important for him that the new CCF government was not open to criticism, so we never went out for coffee breaks. But Joe willingly encouraged us to have coffee brought in. He would be proud of his Department's dedication to duty when someone from the public would tell him they noticed the lights on in the office late at night.[33]

She also recalled, "I never saw him smoke or drink. Joe said he only drank once and lost complete control. He never drank again."[34] Olaf Turnbull, who later served on the executive of the Saskatchewan Farmers Union in the 1950s, and as Minister of Co-operatives and Co-operative Development after being elected to represent Elrose for the CCF in 1960, remembered, "He was quite shocked when he heard that some politicians attending a conference with him planned to attend a cocktail party. Joe didn't need booze—he got high from his audiences."[35]

LOAFERS AND INNOVATORS

After the CCF victory, staffing changes within the civil service became a heated issue. Although some changes were made, many Cabinet ministers kept their staffs almost intact, retaining many deputy ministers, including several that the CCF had denounced in the days of the Liberal regime. Some of the CCF party faithful felt that the Douglas Government did not go far enough in removing employees who had worked in the previous Liberal government from politically sensitive positions.

Phelps was the only minister to make significant changes to his staff, firing fifteen people, many of them at senior levels.[36] Phelps did not hide the disdain he felt toward bureaucrats and bureaucracy. In fact, Shackleton noted that he was impatient with the civil servants he had inherited and "at one cabinet meeting when he was forbidden to chuck all of them out he threatened to rent a room downtown, crowd them all in with one blank piece of paper a day and run his own show elsewhere."[37] According to Phelps, "Some were simply loafers and were riding the bandwagon, simply not pulling their weight and didn't intend to—or some of them maybe didn't have the ability to. I wanted to clean it out but the boys wouldn't let me go."[38]

Douglas came out strongly against political patronage, despite pressure from many partisans, and took steps to ensure that more of the hiring would be done based on merit rather than political affiliation. In 1947, Douglas introduced the Public Service Act, which made the Public Service Commission responsible for hiring, certification, and promotion within the public service. After passage of the act, with the exception of deputy ministers and a limited number of senior positions, ministers were no longer able to select their own personnel.

Phelps preferred to hire people he knew would be loyal. He selected staff based on gut instinct; some were friends and acquaintances, some were hired for their skills or expertise, and others for their enthusiasm and energy. According to Johnson, "He admired innovators and felt that the civil service did not contain enough of the dynamism that is an essential attribute of innovation. So he personally would search out people with ideas, people with a taste for change and people with the energy to bring change about."[39] Phelps worked best with highly motivated, flexible, and competent people with a similar work ethic. Although office staff members were aware that he could be quite "fussy"—insisting, for example, that he have immediate access to files or correspondence—he was never cranky. When left with instructions to pass on to another party, his staff was often advised, "Make sure they don't drag their feet." Working for Phelps was never boring, and many of his staff would later reflect that they appreciated the variety and the many challenges that working for him presented. Some field staff found him demanding, and some could not keep up. Phelps made sure that those that did not share his enthusiasm or work ethic were "uncomfortable in their incompetence," and they generally resigned by choice.[40]

All were aware of his relentless drive and work ethic. Blanche Green recalled, "He said there would be some long days and some short days. But I never saw any short ones!" She recalled Joe being sick for only one two-day period during the four years he was a Cabinet minister, and on that occasion she delivered the office mail to his house.[41] Wilf Churchman, hired as assistant deputy minister in 1946, recalled Phelps's work habits:

> After the Second World War, which I spent in the RCAF, I renewed my acquaintance with the Phelps family in Regina where Joe was Minister of Natural Resources. I soon learned I was working for a workaholic, who expected everyone to work as hard as he did. One night when I was working late at the office, he phoned me and said he had a complaint about one of our field officers in the Hudson Bay region, and would I go and investigate. It was about nine o'clock in the evening, and I said I would go first thing in the morning. "In the morning?" he said, "If you left now you could be in Yorkton for an early start tomorrow." He was right, I was.[42]

LOOSE CANNON?

Tommy Douglas had similar work habits. His daughter, Shirley Douglas, recalled that he was only home for dinner and a short nap each day, and returned to his office virtually every night. Like Douglas, Phelps often only returned home for dinner and after a ten-minute nap would be up and off to work again. Douglas and Phelps also both suffered from stomach problems. Legislative staff recalled that on Cabinet days, at 10:30 a.m., half-pints of milk were served.[43]

Blanche Green reflected, "I couldn't make any personal plans because Joe might call. Many a time I was home at night and was called back to the office to type up a memo or attend to some urgent office matter. Work was his life. I believe he even worked on Christmas." She even had to convince Phelps to give the office staff a Christmas holiday. Green recalled that Phelps was very aware that voters expected the CCF to deliver on their promises and that his favourite expression was, "Nothing ventured, nothing gained—we've only got four years." She also recalled his social conscience and generosity:

> He survived tough times...the Thirties, and he saw a need, a need to help others. Money was never his aim. Constituents would visit his Regina office. They were very hard up for money. Joe would often reach into his pocket and give them money and I never recall him being repaid. I don't believe he ever expected to be repaid.... I believe his vision started way

> back on the farm in the Thirties, when Joe and Lena would spend the winter nights talking about all the changes they would make if they ever got into office. He was ready to go to work and follow through with those plans.[44]

Although at times Phelps could be abrupt and forceful, he was rarely angry, and Green witnessed only one such incident in her four years working for him:

> I was in Joe's office as he was speaking on the telephone with Jack Sturdy, the Minister of Social Services. Joe became very annoyed. I was shocked and surprised when Joe said, "Listen here Jack Sturdy, you're not going to piss up my leg and tell me I'm sweating." Without missing a beat, Joe turned to me and said, "Excuse me Miss Green," then carried on with the phone conversation. That was the only time I ever witnessed him openly annoyed at anyone.[45]

Jessy Paynter, employed as a relief secretary in the DNR in the 1940s, remembers,

> This was one of my first jobs so I was nervous. Joe was always pleasant. He expected a lot from his staff. Joe tore through the building. He was full of energy, yet considerate.... I'll never forget the day when Joe asked me to get him chocolate milk. The creamery was located on the bottom floor. I got the chocolate milk for him, but tipped the carton, spilling the contents on some of Joe's papers. He never said a word! During the time I worked for him, I never saw him lose his cool.[46]

Eleanor McKinnon, secretary to Tommy Douglas for forty-two years, saw Joe Phelps as "a colourful character, a workaholic, devoted to the socialist movement and in particular to the development of Saskatchewan and the programs of the CCF for the betterment of all its citizens." She recalled,

> Each year the Cabinet and planning board held a week-long conference. All the participants were very busy men, and

> were frequently called out for phone calls or some business matter demanding their attention. This disruption to the meetings reached a point where Tommy Douglas asked me not to call any of them out unless it was a matter of life and death. This particular morning Joe Phelps swung in, tossed his hat on the hat rack, and said he was expecting a phone call, and to let him know the moment it came through. When the call came through, I notified Joe and Tommy Douglas motioned to me to tell me something. "I told you not to call anyone out." I bent down and in a whisper I said, "I know you did, but Mr. Phelps told me to call him out immediately the phone call came through, and I'm much more afraid of him than I am of you."[47]

Work in the revitalized department continued at a frantic pace. Some felt the new minister was moving too fast and criticized his disregard for procedures and protocol. Phelps believed bureaucratic procedures and red tape simply slowed him down. Often he would inform his Cabinet colleagues about projects after they had already been initiated. According to some, Phelps was running the department out of his back pocket, often acting as his own deputy minister. Saskatchewan author Murray Dobbin writes:

> Phelps would even write personal cheques for projects and then have the Department of Natural Resources put the money in his account to cover them. His unorthodox approach to administration won him the enmity of civil servants and fellow cabinet ministers, and the respect and loyalty of the small group of socialists he had been able to attract to senior positions in the northern administration.[48]

George LeBeau, a friend who would later collaborate with him on the Western Development Museum project, observed, "As Minister of Natural Resources, he sometimes had difficulty with government people who couldn't see his way of doing things, when an opportunity presented itself. He antagonized many CCF people and members of the Provincial Cabinet, by just going ahead and doing what he thought was best."[49]

Tremendous energy was required, given the comprehensive mandate of the department. Postwar development and reconstruction was high on the government's agenda, including providing long-term employment for men and women being discharged from the armed services. Industrial development would proceed according to the CCF plan for a mixed economy, a combination of private enterprise, co-operative enterprise, and public ownership. Private enterprise would be encouraged as long as it was competitive, and wherever possible the government would support co-operative enterprise. In cases where natural monopolies existed, the CCF favoured public ownership, but the extent had not been clearly articulated by the party, and there were differences of opinion even among Cabinet members. This uncertainty spilled over into the government's first forays into the development of publicly owned corporations, which had been one of the planks of its election platform.

"A BLANK CHEQUE"

Shortly after the CCF took power in 1944, the Department of Natural Resources was expanded to include an Industrial Development Branch to investigate the use of Saskatchewan's natural resources for industrial development. George Cadbury, a devout English socialist from Cambridge University and member of the Cadbury chocolate clan, helped shape policy as chairman of the Economic Advisory and Planning Board (EAPB). Other key economic and financial advisors were Tommy McLeod, Al Johnson (later president of the CBC), Tom Shoyama, and later administrators such as Donald Tansley and Allan Blakeney, who would become premier from 1971 to 1982.

The processing of primary products, including timber, fish, fur, wool, hides, and clay, would form the basis of the new government-owned enterprises. Profits generated by public ownership would be used to fund social programs and further development. Resource development would diversify the economy and provide employment for Saskatchewan people. The first projects in the government's new industrial initiative included plans for a clay products plant, a woollen mill, and a shoe factory. Preliminary investigations were also started for a briquette plant and a pulp mill.

The government introduced an amendment to the Natural Resources Act during the special legislative session in the fall of 1944. It passed easily, giving the minister power "to acquire land or works by purchase, lease or expropriation," and then to operate, extend, alter, improve, and maintain "any mine, factory, plant, machinery, or equipment." Basically, it empowered him to do virtually anything he deemed "necessary to develop and utilize the resources of the province in lands, water powers or forests which were the property of the crown."[50] A second piece of necessary legislation was the Crown Corporations Act, passed on March 30, 1945. It allowed the government to set up Crown corporations by acquiring land or works though purchase, construction, or expropriation.[51]

Before the government could set up publicly owned industries, it needed capital to finance their establishment and operation. The government raised money by two methods. The Mineral Taxation Act, passed in November 1944, required that owners of mineral rights pay a three-cents-an-acre tax to the DNR effective January 1, 1945, or forfeit their mineral rights to the Crown. This tax was aimed mainly at the three largest holders of mineral rights in the province: the Hudson's Bay Company, the Canadian Pacific Railway, and the Canadian National Railway (CNR).[52] The government also raised money through the sale of industrial bonds—over $1 million worth from January 15 to February 28, 1945.[53]

The Opposition strongly opposed all of this new legislation. W. J. Patterson described the amendment to the Natural Resources Act as "one of the most comprehensive and widest pieces of legislation" ever to be presented in the Saskatchewan legislature. Asserting that it gave the minister too much power, he urged the legislature to retain some control over the types of businesses the DNR might enter. A. T. Procter (Liberal, Moosomin) opposed the Crown Corporations Act because it gave the government authority to buy any kind of undertaking "anywhere, even outside of the province." G. H. Danielson (Liberal, Arm River) termed a section pertaining to the Crown corporations bill "a blank cheque" and accused the government of having a "dictatorship and fascist attitude." Patterson also objected to the Mineral Taxation Act because he believed that municipalities rather than the government should receive the revenue from this tax. Later, Procter called the bill to amend the Mineral Taxation Act "absolutely wrong," "confiscatory," and "thievery." The *Leader-Post* commended Procter for attacking this "piece of definitely confiscatory legislation."[54] Nonetheless, the legislation passed.

FULL SPEED AHEAD

The Crown Corporations Act in March 1945 created the framework for government entry into business enterprise, and Phelps became minister in charge of all established Crown corporations. The act gave him the power to acquire land or works, and to purchase, sell, or utilize any natural resources, and Phelps eagerly plunged ahead. In May and June of 1945, in keeping with the CCF policies of social ownership, Saskatchewan Clay Products, Saskatchewan Leather Products, and Saskatchewan Wool Products were established as corporations.

The Saskatchewan Lake and Forest Products Corporation (SLAFPC) was established in 1946 by an order-in-council dated May 23, 1946. It took over activities previously carried out by the Saskatchewan Timber Board and operated under three distinct divisions: the Saskatchewan Timber Board, the Saskatchewan Box Factory, and the Saskatchewan Fish Board. Corporate directors included Phelps, who was chairman and minister responsible; J. H. Brockelbank, Minister of Municipal Affairs, as vice-chairman; George Cadbury, chairman of the Economic Advisory and Planning Board, as chief industrial executive; James F. Gray, resident director, Prince Albert; and M. Kalmakoff, treasurer, Government Finance Office.

Initially the government took a very aggressive approach to public ownership of provincial natural resources. In January 1944, it proposed a plan "for the eventual and complete socialization under provincial administration of all natural resources now controlled by the province." The Natural Resources Act had empowered the minister to "do all things he deemed necessary to develop the resources of the province which are the property of the Crown, including purchasing, constructing and operating buildings, factories, research laboratories, machinery, equipment, or works."[55] However, the degree to which it should pursue public ownership created considerable controversy within the government, and there was concern that it could not afford to alienate private interests operating in the province. As a result, "given these uncertainties within the government's position on public ownership, it is not surprising that the topic occupied a great deal of time in cabinet. One minister recalled having the impression that one-third of the cabinet agenda was devoted to Joe Phelps' items and two-thirds to the rest of the government."[56]

Later, the CCF found it necessary to soften its approach and allow private enterprise to participate to a larger degree than some within the party originally anticipated would be necessary. In January 1947, Phelps took to the airways to address the people of Saskatchewan and discuss the government's plan for continued development. The CCF government would remain firm to its commitment to develop the province's natural resources on a planned basis, and would continue to favour public ownership, but it would also allow private enterprise to operate. Phelps stated:

> The products themselves in their natural state, belong to the people, hence the benefits should be turned over to Saskatchewan citizens in the form of increased health care and social services. In addition, a percentage of the surplus will be plowed back into the particular industry concerned, for its further improvement, expansion and conservation.... [However,] it is not yet practical for the provincial government to operate in some fields of natural resource development [such as the petroleum industry] in Saskatchewan, and in these instances private capital will be permitted to operate, provided it makes adequate contribution to the provincial economy through payment of royalties or some other form of return.[57]

In addition to the development of natural resources, the government was also taking steps toward creating Crown corporations in the province. The Government Insurance Act of 1944 allowed it to establish the Saskatchewan Government Insurance Office. A new Department of Co-operation and Co-operative Development was also set up, as were the Saskatchewan Transportation Company, Saskatchewan Government Telephones, and the Saskatchewan Power Commission.

Phelps's first eighteen months in office represented a period of frenzied activity. He was extremely busy in his role as Minister of Natural Resources and Industrial Development.[58] By October 19, 1945, he had begun to establish a province-wide grid for electrical power. He was also the minister in charge of six Crown corporations, three marketing boards, and a box factory. Furthermore, by the end of December 1945, he headed a department that operated six airplanes. Perhaps only the impulsive J. L. Phelps, with his drive, boundless energy, naive optimism, and zealous socialism, would have undertaken so many ventures in so short a time. However, some of his newly established projects would soon encounter serious problems and many of his Crown corporations would suffer critical financial losses. Indeed, Phelps soon discovered that establishing new Crown corporations was one thing; administering them was quite another.

CHAPTER 6

THUNDERSTRUCK

When the CCF came to power in 1944, about ten thousand people, a population more or less evenly divided between First Nations,[1] Métis, and whites, were living in the North.[2] The white population was concentrated in the three mining communities of Goldfields, Creighton, and Island Falls. Soon after the CCF was elected, Joe Phelps and Premier Douglas took a five-day aircraft tour across northern Saskatchewan to see the situation firsthand. Phelps was the first Cabinet minister to travel north of Prince Albert.

Phelps and the premier were appalled at what they found. The fishing and fur industries were in a state of stagnation and decline, and unemployment was widespread. Indigenous society was, in fact, in a state of abject poverty and social disintegration.[3] The Indigenous peoples in the North lacked education, medical facilities, decent housing, communication, and social services. Road access was poor or nonexistent in many communities, making much of Saskatchewan's north accessible only by air.

Despite the problems and the lack of development, Phelps saw great potential in the North: "My first impression was the vastness of it, just the literal size of the north half of the province and I was struck with the potential of it.... I was almost thunderstruck with the potential, with the literal geographic dimensions. Well I couldn't get over it for weeks, to just digest what all that meant."[4] The North covered over 160,000 square kilometres stretching from Prince Albert to the Northwest Territories and included more than 100,000 lakes, mixed coniferous and deciduous trees, bush, muskeg, rivers, and a vast section of the Precambrian Shield.

Phelps felt strongly that wealth generated by developing the natural resources in the North would provide much-needed resources for social programs, improving the standard of living for northern Indigenous peoples and indeed all of the people of Saskatchewan. In his view, with careful planning and management, the North offered much promise.

First, a plan for improved conservation measures and careful stewardship would ensure the natural resources were sustainable and would remain for future generations. Phelps had very definite socialist ideas about developing natural resources that he most clearly articulated in two radio addresses he gave in January 1947 and December 1948:

> An intelligent development of Saskatchewan's natural resources must be on a planned basis.... Public ownership could produce maximum results in terms of raw materials and subsequent dividends to the community.... The products themselves, in their natural state, belong to the people; hence the benefits should be turned over to the Saskatchewan citizens in the form of increased health and social services. In addition, a percentage of the surplus will be plowed back into the particular industry concerned, for its further improvement, expansion, and conservation.[5]

> The natural resources of any country are placed here by the Creator in order that all citizens might benefit, not only the present generation but our children and all future generations. They are all recognized by the CCF as having a just claim on our resources. Past administrations regarded our resources as something to be exploited for the sake of a few individuals or the shareholders of a few large companies.[6]

MANY CHALLENGES

Development in the North posed formidable challenges. Differences in language and culture were significant barriers to communication that immediately created distance between Indigenous people and the provincial government. Saskatchewan writer Murray Dobbin noted that "Phelps and his workers had no roots in the [northern] settlements, did not speak Cree, had few allies among the native population, and no Indian or Métis organizations with which they could negotiate.... With no responsibility for the programs being imposed on them the Native people felt little obligation to cooperate."[7] Phelps was not discouraged by this, believing that Indigenous culture was based on the same principles of sharing and equality that the CCF was expounding. He felt they would be receptive to the plan if it was designed in their interest. Development would proceed according to the stated goal of the CCF's Native policy of integration. According to Laurie Barron, author of *Walking in Indian Moccasins: The Native Policies of Tommy Douglas and the CCF*:

> The Douglas government came to believe that traditional Native culture had been founded on socialist principles, and for that reason, Native society would be intrinsically receptive to socialist experimentation. Integration as the ultimate goal of the experimentation, implied that Native people would be participants in mainstream society, fully enjoying all the social services and individual political rights others took for granted, all the while enjoying their own cultural integrity and collective rights as Aboriginals.[8]

Phelps was quite aware that the culture and way of life in the North was unique. In an interview with Murray Dobbin in 1976, he reflected, "I was just an upstart coming in there, never knew anything about the north country and I told them straight off always. I said, 'I'm new to this country. I don't know except what you tell me and what I see. I haven't lived it and so I'm going to be careful about how I'm going to tell you about how you should live.'"[9] If his plan for northern development were to be successful, he needed to consult with northern people and get them involved. Ultimately, he knew they would need to buy into the plan if it was to work.

In addition to cultural differences, there were other major barriers. The northern economy was based almost exclusively on trapping, hunting, and fishing, and it was quickly apparent to Phelps that Indigenous people had been virtually indentured to the HBC. The company's monopoly ensured that it was able to control supply, price, and essentially all aspects of the fur industry. Phelps was fiercely opposed to monopolies and was openly hostile to the HBC. Taking steps to reduce its predatory practices ranked near the top of Phelps's long list of priorities.

Geographical factors also presented sizeable challenges. Indian and Métis trappers were scattered throughout the North in isolated, remote locations in an area covering thousands of square kilometres with very limited road access. Not one to be hindered by this sort of barrier, Phelps was quick to take action, advising the government that to address the problem of travel in the North it was essential that it begin acquiring aircraft. By 1945, the government had acquired its first planes.

Complicating matters further was the issue of federal versus provincial jurisdiction. By the mid-1940s, there were approximately fourteen thousand status Indians in Saskatchewan, most living on the sixty-one provincial Indian reserves. The federal government was responsible for their health care, income support, and education. There were many problems on the reserves. Corruption among federal Indian Affairs officials, low-quality education in the mission schools, low standards in health care, and discrimination against Indigenous war veterans were widespread.

There were also significant problems within the Métis community, who numbered approximately nine thousand in 1941. Many of the Métis people living in the North were trappers and fishers. The Métis, people of mixed Indigenous and white ancestry, did not fall under federal responsibility but rather had full Saskatchewan citizenship. According to Shackleton, "They had the right to whatever 'quality of life' was generally made available under CCF government. Because most Métis were brought up by Indian mothers and lived in fringe areas close to Indian reserves, they were regarded as Indian by most of the white population. This meant they were ignored for most purposes."[10] The intent of the CCF Native policy of integration, according to Barron, "seems to have been honoured where Indians were concerned, but far less so in the case of the Métis, who as it turned out, would be targeted for total assimilation."[11]

Given all of these factors, developing a workable plan to manage natural resources in the North was tremendously challenging. There was essentially no meaningful forest, fur, and fish or game policy at that time. In fact, resource policies largely benefitted the wealthy lumbermen, and the fur and fish dealers. Loggers, trappers, and fishers were receiving very little for their work and there were no meaningful conservation programs in place to ensure sustainability of the resources.

Phelps saw the lack of established programs as an advantage—there would be no bureaucratic processes or procedures to slow him down. In the months to come, he designed and established a full range of new programs, many of which remained in the decades that followed. Eiling Kramer would later comment, "The innovative ideas of this energetic Minister laid the groundwork for Saskatchewan resource planning and policy that became recognized as the best in Canada during the next 25 years."[12]

Aware that he faced significant challenges and was not familiar with many issues in the North, Phelps contacted Malcolm Norris, a Métis man with considerable grassroots experience in northern Saskatchewan. Phelps was impressed with Norris: "He just solidified some of the ideas that were taking shape in my mind in regard to a program for development of the north and a new deal for native people . . . The development of the resources and the fish marketing board and the fur marketing services, he was all for those kinds of things." Norris, hired soon after their first meeting, provided a liaison with the people and got acquainted with key figures, introducing the new programs and gathering suggestions. He was active in talking about and developing policy. Phelps explained:

> He must have done a pretty good job because it wasn't very long before the atmosphere seemed to change. The CCF was suspect in a lot of the north. They didn't trust us.... We were bringing in a completely new philosophy and a lot of them were naturally suspicious of us. They started to respond very definitely. I think it was partly a result of the work of Malcolm.... Norris and I spent countless hours discussing hundreds of issues.... He was a contact person...to keep me posted on how our general ideas were going over and what we should do to improve them, to improve the plan, and to improve the mechanism that we were using to apply the plan.[13]

Phelps relied on Norris in many of his northern policy decisions, and readily delegated considerable authority to his Indigenous staff, valuing their opinions and suggestions. In *Walking in Indian Moccasins*, Barron indicates that

> Phelps was also widely respected in certain circles, particularly by the small group of committed Marxists he attracted to senior positions in the northern administration. Included in that group was Allan Quandt, the northern administrator, as well as Jim Brady and Malcolm Norris. The latter two were Métis who had been instrumental in organizing the Indian Association of Alberta.[14]

An incident that took place in Prince Albert reveals that while Phelps was sometimes outspoken, he was a principled and humble man, willing to acknowledge his mistakes. Dobbin recounts:

> Phelps, a powerful and articulate speaker, had ridiculed a northern Indian who levelled a rather inarticulate criticism at provincial government policy. The partisan white crowd was delighted. Norris jumped to his feet and denounced Phelps and the crowd for their cruelty and pointed out that the native people had complaints that deserved attention. Phelps apologized to the Indian. Later, Norris paced the floor, anticipating Phelps' anger over his outburst; Phelps never mentioned it.[15]

By many accounts, this incident is typical of Phelps's character—he could also become quite emotional and was "easily moved to tears" on issues he felt strongly about.[16]

Phelps saw the growth of responsible self-government at the settlement level as a primary objective of northern development, and recognized that it would be necessary to involve Indigenous people in the process. Phelps, along with Quandt and Norris and other DNR officials, began to encourage informal village councils in an effort to increase political awareness. In reflecting on Phelps's approach, Dobbin states,

> Perhaps Phelps' most important contribution was his appreciation of the need for political education and struggle among the native people. He recognized that Indians and Métis had to demand their own reforms. His task was to encourage a grass roots movement which would oppose reactionary

> elements, and out of self-interest, support the basic thrust of the CCF programs.[17]

Dobbin points out that when Phelps left the North after his defeat in 1948, things became much more conservative and bureaucratic. Phelps was much more inclined to involve local people, take chances, and be innovative than the CCF leaders that would follow. "Under Phelps the innovators in the DNR held sway; under Brockelbank the conservative bureaucrats would regain their traditional power."[18]

INTEGRATIONIST REFORM

The CCF was also attempting to deal with Indigenous policy issues on a provincial level:

> It was under the umbrella of CCF integrationist reform that the precursor to the modern-day Federation of Saskatchewan Indian Nations was born.... Unlike in other jurisdictions, such as Alberta, the CCF created a political climate that actually nurtured the right of Indians to organize politically, and it did so in a way and to an extent that was unprecedented.[19]

Phelps participated in a 1945 conference called by Premier Douglas in Regina, inviting Indigenous leaders to put aside their differences and unite in a common cause. Phelps, acting in his capacity as Minister of Natural Resources, welcomed the participants, and in his address commented that the provincial government would end the exploitation of Indigenous people in the fur business, and in the marketing of furs and fish on which the Indigenous people were dependent. He stated that the Saskatchewan government intended to take the lead in resource development, with the goal of assisting Indigenous people. He also announced that two Indigenous people would be appointed to a provincial game advisory committee, and that Indigenous people would be given priority rights in trapping areas.

Throughout its first term in office, the government held a number of meetings with Indigenous leaders. These meetings provided a forum for discussion of the underlying political, social, and economic issues affecting Saskatchewan's Indigenous population. The creation of a single Indian provincial organization was also part of the CCF plan. To this end, Premier Douglas invited more than fifty Indian delegates to an organizational meeting in Regina on January 4, 1946. At the meeting, Phelps vowed that the CCF government would end the exploitation in fur and fish marketing. He stated, "Indians should be given full citizenship rights, including the right to vote, as a prelude to having representation in the provincial legislature."[20] At a general assembly of chiefs in a Saskatoon meeting in February 1946, which nearly one hundred delegates from every band in the province attended, Phelps spoke about the importance of unity for the Indians. This meeting resulted in the creation of a new Indigenous association. Indian leaders agreed to the formation of the Union of Saskatchewan Indians. John Tootoosis of Cutknife was elected president, and John Gambler of Avonhurst and Ernest Goforth of Balcarres vice-presidents.[21] The organization allowed them to carry grievances to the provincial and federal governments with one united voice, and solidified the government's commitment to integrationist reform. Barron noted, "the seminal contribution of the CCF was its dismantling of the historical barriers to Indian organization through which the Indian leadership was free to fashion and evolve its own political organization."[22]

In March 1946, Fred Dewhurst (CCF, Wadena) "introduced a motion in the legislative assembly calling for a federal commission, with Indian membership, to investigate conditions on Indian reservations, with a particular reference to health, education, social welfare, and civil rights." During the debate that followed, Phelps was one of the main speakers to attack the federal government's administration of Indian Affairs. He demanded that "Indian jurisdiction and funding be transferred to the provinces and insisted that Indians be given full citizenship rights, including the right to vote and to drink alcohol in public places."[23]Earlier, at a Saskatoon conference of Indian leaders in 1946, Phelps had addressed the issue of citizenship directly. He cited the Saskatchewan liquor laws prohibiting Indians from purchasing beer and whisky, and stated that he believed the law should be changed to afford full citizenship to the Indigenous peoples of the country. On February 25, 1946, the *Leader-Post* quoted him as saying, "During the war Indians in the services were allowed in beer parlors and didn't make any bigger fools of themselves than white men."[24]

Phelps also expressed concern for the welfare of Indigenous people in a letter to M. J. Coldwell:

> It was a personal pleasure to see the Indians [at the Saskatoon Conference] taking matters more into their own hands and demanding rights as citizens of this Country.... It is now time we regarded the Indians as citizens of the Province in which they reside and the Dominion Government make a grant on a per capita basis in proportion to their population in each province, which money could be expended in a program of rehabilitation for these Indians.
>
> [We] are doing a considerable amount of rehabilitation in the northern part of the province.... We make no distinction between Indians and white men and most of the work will benefit the Natives.
>
> If an Indian is ill, we will send an ambulance plane for him as we do for a white man. In fact, there is no Department of which I know that acts otherwise.

He added that the federal government should stop treating Indians "as their special wards," noted that the provincial fur conservation program treated "the Indians on the same basis as the white man," and asserted, "the present reservations are wholly inadequate."[25] Saskatchewan historian James Pitsula noted that the CCF government was committed to improving the lot of the Indians, believing that equality or "non-discrimination" was the key to solving the Indian problem, and that equality of individual rights could be achieved "by eliminating special status, dismantling the Indian Affairs department, and transferring to the provinces responsibility for administering services to Indians."[26]

The government was also making efforts to address the concerns of Métis people. In 1946, the first Métis convention was held in Regina. There was a plea for land leases, equipment for farming or small industry, building materials for homes, and vocational training. "The southern Métis were among the most disadvantaged group in the province, but more than that, their poverty was highly visible,"[27] and therefore a Métis advisory committee established at the conference requested road repairs, funding for new projects, long-term housing loans, assistance in acquiring blocks of land, and grants for organizers, and the provincial government made efforts to deal with some of these concerns. By 1948, the Métis were included under the free provincial hospitalization program, and by 1949 a group of one hundred Métis had been moved from a southern area near Lestock to Green Lake. Farming and a sawmill operation were initiated, and land and home-building supplies were granted.

Phelps's concern for the welfare of the province's northern residents, particularly of the Indigenous people, was often evident. Some were grateful to the CCF government and to Phelps. Chief Joseph Dreaver wrote, "I would like to say that the Indians and Metis of Saskatchewan greatly appreciated the deep interest in their affairs shown by the present provincial Government. Particularly your efferts [*sic*] as Minister of Natural Resources and Industrial Affairs to improve their chances of acquiring a decent standard of living."[28] On the other hand, many strongly opposed the CCF's policy concerning Indigenous peoples, as Barron and David Quiring point out. Barron acknowledges that the government sympathized with Indigenous people, but argues that its empathy "was riddled with paternalism."[29] Quiring is extremely critical of the CCF's entire policy for northerners, arguing that the government imposed its own agenda on the people without consulting with them or discovering what they really wanted. Quiring's position is that the CCF government tried to bring northerners into the twentieth century by modernizing, assimilating, and socializing them. To do so, it "utilized destructive, paternalistic, and colonial methods to impose its agenda." Though these people had "accepted and valued the existing northern system which had evolved over several centuries…[the] C.C.F showed no concern about wiping it out" because it felt it knew better what was best for northerners. Quiring insists that by destroying the former northern economic and social system and failing to build a workable new economy and society, the government worsened poverty and social dysfunction within Indigenous communities. He singles out Phelps and strongly condemns him for bringing about "the most aggressive intervention" in the North.[30]

While the paternalism evident in the CCF's approach and its lack of a long-term, coherent, collaborative plan to create a stable economic base have contributed to the current lack of prosperity and stability for many First Nations peoples and northern residents, Phelps often acknowledged that he did not know what was best for northerners and made a concerted effort to consult and collaborate with local people to obtain input into the new government programs he was responsible for. Phelps envisioned that the conservation, development, and stewardship of the natural resources, including fish, fur, and timber, would provide employment and economic stability. His personal vision and approach were more idealistic than paternalistic. The large number of non-English speaking northerners made it difficult to obtain local input, and as Quiring points out, the "consultation process did not extend to the other economic and social engineering policies which quickly and dramatically altered reality for northerners."[31]

Phelps was attempting to implement a unique provincial plan within a federal system. The "social and economic engineering" brought about by the imposition of the federal Indian Act is critical to the analysis of the CCF provincial policies and programs. The Indian Act, which denied full citizenship to First Nations peoples and controlled virtually every aspect of their lives, was not in keeping with the spirit and intent of the numbered treaties with the Crown, and it impacted all of Phelps's efforts in the North. The devastating impact of residential schools, for example, which were part of the assimilationist policies of the federal government, is only now being acknowledged, and the intergenerational effects continue to be felt within First Nations families and communities.

Phelps was able to work successfully with the federal government to create the fur conservation blocks, and also tried hard to achieve co-operation between the two levels of government on projects such as housing, fishing, social welfare, law enforcement, and education, but the results were disappointing. Phelps also undertook an extensive economic and social survey of every settlement in the remote areas of northern Saskatchewan. These reports, averaging about one hundred pages per settlement, provided information about living conditions there and made recommendations for improving them.[32] His co-operation with the provincial highways department to build roads in the North for fighting fires and transporting fish and timber proved successful and, in turn, would encourage summer resort development and the tourist trade.

AN AXE TO GRIND

A number of factors worked in opposition to the Indigenous reform policies of the CCF. Not surprisingly, a vast number of vested interests profited by leaving the situation unchanged, as Barron points out:

> There was the powerful triumvirate that historically had dominated the northern part of the province: the Liberal party, the Hudson's Bay Company and church missions. Prior to the CCF, the three had acted in concert in securing Indian votes, furs, and souls, and, collectively, they represented a dominating and controlling interest diametrically opposed to government intervention in the North.[33]

Phelps was extremely antagonistic toward the HBC and often let his hostility toward it be known, attacking its monopoly market position and openly criticizing its policies. His opinion of the HBC was not entirely an objective critique based solely on its monopoly position in the North. As a southern farmer, Phelps had leased land from the company, only to have the lease peremptorily cancelled on seven days' notice. Although the cancellation was made legally on the basis that the land contained neither buildings nor crop, Phelps felt the action was unfair and for this reason, according to Barron, had "an axe to grind" with the company.

In response to the cancellation of his lease, he wrote a letter to the HBC in his capacity as minister of the Crown. Barron provides the following account of that correspondence:

> "Your company have [*sic*] a few Agreements with our Government, and several of them directly with this Department and I might suggest that some of these same agreements are due to come up for revision very shortly; and the same seven days notice in such cases might be quite sufficient to terminate same." That such a statement represented a conflict of interest on the part of the minister seems not to have troubled Phelps. Nor was the implied threat idle posturing. Personally and ideologically, Phelps hated everything the Hudson's Bay

> Company stood for, and he was quite prepared to take on the company head to head.[34]

Phelps spent the next few weeks gathering anecdotal and other evidence to support his contention that the HBC's vested power and interest should be reduced. On March 19, 1945, he presented his case during the budget debate in the legislative assembly. Phelps contended that the HBC charter granted by King Charles II in 1670 was invalid, and, as a consequence, title to the land the HBC had acquired when it surrendered Rupert's Land to the Dominion in 1869 was also invalid. The charter, he hinted, might be challenged in court.

The Mineral Taxation Act, in draft form since October 1944, cemented Phelps's commitment to reducing the HBC's position as a vested interest in the North. The tax would impose annual fees both on private mineral rights and on lands designated by the government to be "producing areas," greatly impacting both the CPR and the HBC, who not only owned vast amounts of land but also had retained mineral rights on much of the lands they had sold. It was estimated that the HBC's holdings of some 2.2 million acres would generate a substantial $66,000 per year.[35]

The HBC took these threats seriously. In an effort to deflect potential negative fallout from the confrontation, it took measures to co-operate and appear conciliatory in its dealings with the Saskatchewan government. To this end, a meeting was arranged. On March 24, 1945, HBC officials met with Phelps and Premier Douglas in an effort to resolve the situation. They alleged that if the company's charter to obtain Rupert's Land had indeed been invalid in 1670, then title to all the land subsequently carved out of that territory was invalid. According to the HBC account, which is the only existing documentation of the meeting, both Phelps and the premier were thrown off guard by this allegation. However, company officials decided on a conciliatory approach after determining from Phelps's response that the government would not back down on its efforts to reduce the HBC's influence. Government plans included taking over the company's leases at Cumberland House.

The HBC proposed that the matter could be resolved amicably if both sides agreed to a series of proposals: first, that both parties agree that all correspondence dealing with the dispute be destroyed and pledge mutual co-operation; second, that the HBC would offer its knowledge and expertise toward conservation in the North; and, third, that the HBC would relinquish its community lease at Cumberland House to become part of the proposed conservation block, on the condition that Phelps agree to leave the company's private lease alone. By creating the perception that it was co-operating with the government, the HBC reduced the risk of government intervention and regulation. As well, it made the government's interest in reforming its long-standing trade practices in the North seem far less justified. "It was clearly in the company's best interests to normalize relations with Phelps and Douglas, and this is exactly what was promised by the results of the Regina meeting."[36]

Although the government reduced the proposed rate of taxation in the Mineral Taxation Act after the meeting, the HBC pursued the matter further, appealing to the Dominion government to have the tax disallowed. In October 1945, a special federal Cabinet committee heard the case, but the HBC was unsuccessful in its attempts to have the act reversed. The company took steps to comply with the legislation, and, in a subsequent meeting with Phelps, agreed to an interim tax payment. In return, the company was given extra time to complete a survey of its lands to determine which mineral rights would be surrendered.

The CPR, on the other hand, continued to fight the tax, suing both Phelps and the attorney general, but lost its suit first in the Court of King's Bench in 1948 and again in the Saskatchewan Court of Appeal in 1950. The CPR's attempt to overturn the tax was ultimately defeated in the Supreme Court of Canada in 1952.

CHAPTER 7

POWER TO THE PEOPLE

Bringing power to the people of rural Saskatchewan is perhaps Joe Phelps's most memorable and satisfying achievement. In his 1982 interview with Jean Larmour, Phelps recalled the task with fondness and a great sense of accomplishment and pride: "That was the biggest challenge I had, and, if I do say so myself, we did a damn good job of it. We put in a foundation that's still there."[1]

In the days leading up to the election of the CCF, the Saskatchewan Power Commission served approximately 45,000 customers in about 140 towns, and operated 1,560 miles of transmission lines. This number represented more than 50 per cent of the power lines in the province.[2] There were approximately eighty thousand farms that needed electric power, but the commission was not meeting their needs. Some were only receiving power on a partial basis, twelve hours a day. The majority of Saskatchewan farms had no electricity at all, and the previous Liberal government "had no plan whatsoever for hooking them up."[3]

COMPENSATION, NOT CONFISCATION

Rural electrification was a project very close to Phelps's heart. His first-hand experience on the farm had convinced him that province-wide power was essential to improving the quality of life in rural areas and stabilizing the agricultural economy. Building an electric power system would also aid in the government's plans for diversification through industrial development and the development of natural resources in the North. To bring about industrial development, three things were necessary: a cheap, reliable source of power; legislation to allow the government to proceed with the socialization of industries; and money to establish and operate those industries. To obtain cheap, reliable electricity for industrial development, the CCF government planned to purchase the various power utilities, integrate them into one provincially owned electrical grid, and supply power throughout the province. Later, Phelps commented that he was more interested in developing the power system than in any of the other things he was doing. He added, "I was always talking about rural electrification." In fact, "I didn't want the Industrial Development. I wanted to spend time on the Power Commission. I wanted to concentrate on it. Even natural resources, I took it under protest."[4]

In the previous term, while sitting in opposition, Phelps had strongly supported the CCF resolution calling upon the government to acquire the existing power sites and develop new ones. Now he had the mandate to make it happen. He was adamant that the task of providing electricity for all would require full government ownership of the entire power system, but he stated publicly that private companies would be treated fairly and that the government believed in "compensation, not confiscation." When asked if expansion of the power system potentially meant subsidizing private companies, Joe replied, "I only think, speak and act in terms of social enterprise these days." He went on to say, "When the provincial government, through the Saskatchewan Power Commission, embarks upon a program of supplying electrical energy to rural areas, it must be prepared to subsidize that development out of the public treasury."[5]

The electric power situation in Saskatchewan in the mid-1940s left a great deal to be desired. The province did not yet have anything like an integrated electric grid. For the most part, Saskatchewan residents obtained their power from individual isolated generating stations. Some cities, such as Regina, owned their own power plants. Others, such as Moose Jaw and Prince Albert, had sold their municipal plants to private companies (in 1930 and 1931, respectively). Most towns in southern and southeastern Saskatchewan also depended on private companies for electricity. Three of the four largest private power companies were American firms: Dominion Electric, Canadian Utilities, and National Light and Power. The fourth was a Canadian firm, Montreal Engineering.[6] The province also had a foothold in the industry. J. G. Gardiner's Liberal government had created the Saskatchewan Power Commission in 1929. It supplied electric power to Saskatoon, North Battleford, and more than one hundred small towns, principally in the central part of the province.[7] As Clinton White has noted, at the end of the Second World War the government of the day faced two choices: "either to dispose of the [Saskatchewan Power] Commission to the privately owned companies and encourage these firms to operate as a single utility, or to take over the holdings of such concerns and establish a province-wide publicly owned monopoly."[8] Phelps was responsible for negotiating the purchase of these various companies.

Phelps relied on his assistant deputy minister, Vern Hogg, to provide accurate research and develop comprehensive proposals, so he quickly recruited him to serve as an advisor and consultant on his work on the power project.

CLASHES WITH THE POWER COMMISSIONER

In October 1944, Phelps and Hogg had an unsatisfactory preliminary meeting with power commissioner, L. A. Thornton. Differences in their political views were evident in the meeting. Thornton, like some members of the Regina business community, did not support the CCF's plan for diversification of the economy, in particular the move toward government ownership and expansion of the power system. Moreover, Thornton was firmly opposed to rural electrification, citing the cost as prohibitive. After a trip to Iowa, Phelps had discovered that the American rural electrification grid used a single-wire instead of a two-wire system, with the return circuit through the ground, which reduced the cost of wire by half and required much lighter power poles. But Thornton rejected the idea and responded, "Lines have to be built to current specifications." It was evident to Hogg, who recalled Thornton's condescending and bureaucratic attitude, that Phelps was not impressed with the power commissioner.[9] If they were to proceed smoothly, with a well-defined policy and program, Phelps would need to secure the services of someone more co-operative to succeed Thornton.

Shortly after the initial meetings with Thornton, Phelps asked him to send copies of the incoming and outgoing Power Commission mail to his office. When Thornton dismissed the request as ridiculous, Phelps promptly took the matter to Cabinet and by the following afternoon the mail began arriving at Phelps's office. After monitoring the Power Commission's correspondence for a two-week period, it was apparent there was demand for hookups to power lines, but it was also evident that there was insufficient electrical generation capacity to satisfy the demand.

Phelps asked Hogg to prepare a brief outlining the current power situation, and to provide recommendations for potential courses of action. It was Friday afternoon, and the brief was to be submitted by Monday morning. Hogg recalled that this was a typical request: "Mr. Phelps was a workaholic, not unusual with farmers, and he expected his staff to be on call in evenings, and weekends, even during holidays."[10] Hogg located a recent report of a commission headed by a professor from the University of Saskatchewan dealing with agricultural electrical power generation, industrial development, and other matters of economic interest for Saskatchewan. This formed the basis of his brief to Joe Phelps. The Monday deadline was met.

Phelps's ideas came together quickly and he soon developed a six-point plan for the Power Commission. In *Power for a Province: A History of Saskatchewan Power*, White outlines the Phelps plan:

> Firstly, the Commission would take over the holdings of private operators. It would actively encourage production and distribution of electric power. Plans would be drawn up at once for expanding its transmission system to provide complete coverage of all rural and urban areas. All new power lines would conform to certain standards and coordinate in an overall plan for electrification of the province. The capacity of its generating stations would be increased to supply energy for the governments' industrial development program. And its rates and contracts would be rearranged on the principle that urban users of power would absorb some of the costs of providing service to rural areas.[11]

FORTUITOUS MEETING

Soon after Hogg's brief had been submitted, the editor of the CCF Party newspaper published an article suggesting that the provincial government purchase the Moose Jaw power plant. Phelps was not convinced that this was the best course of action, but he arranged a meeting with the president of the Moose Jaw National Light and Power Company to assess the feasibility of the purchase and to potentially open negotiations. In the days to come, he arranged meetings with all of the key players in the industry and explained the government's plan to integrate the provincial power system. Preliminary talks included discussions on how the government acquisitions would proceed and the appropriate machinery for negotiating compensation. It was essential that these talks be handled in a timely, diplomatic manner. Corporate negotiations and acquisitions required the advice of someone knowledgeable and experienced in the industry. In this respect, the meeting scheduled with Moose Jaw National Light and Power was fortuitous: Phelps found exactly the person he was looking for.

A meeting was arranged with Halma F. Berry, president and general manager of Moose Jaw National Light and Power. Hal Berry had worked for Iowa Southern Utilities in the United States, and had been transferred to Moose Jaw when the Iowa company purchased the Moose Jaw electrical utility. Berry had worked his way up in the firm, becoming president and general manager of National Light and Power in the 1930s. Hogg attended that meeting and recalled,

> It was evident that Berry assumed the provincial government would develop publicly owned power, but Berry suggested that instead of taking over the Moose Jaw plant, it would be more logical and practical to take over the Dominion Power plant at Estevan, and expand it on the basis of low cost lignite coal from the adjacent coal fields.[12]

Shortly after the initial meeting, the Power Commission arranged for a formal valuation of the Moose Jaw plant. The report revealed that the generating station had an estimated value of $1 million, and the distribution system, including the transmission lines to Mossbank, were valued at approximately $500,000. Against the total were debts of about $3 million, represented by stocks and bonds. When entering negotiations, government advisors had proposed a price of $1 million or so, thinking that the company's annual profits of $90,000 would make it a worthwhile purchase, despite the fact that its debts would remain. After the evaluation, the commission secretary advised Phelps that the disparity between tangible assets and debts would appear to preclude purchase of the stock.[13] Phelps already felt that purchase of the Moose Jaw firm was not the best decision. His feeling was reinforced by Berry, who argued that purchase of his company would not increase the number of electrical consumers, whereas the same money spent on transmission lines would. Berry also offered to supply energy through his company to the commission on reasonable terms. Phelps was impressed with Berry's knowledge of the power business and his approach to it.

MAN OF ACTION

The views of the two men meshed. Berry, like Phelps, believed that the widest possible distribution of electrical energy in Saskatchewan was a priority in the postwar era for reconstruction. Surprisingly, Berry was supportive of Phelps's idea of public ownership of Saskatchewan's electrical facilities.[14] In January 1945, after Thornton's resignation, Phelps persuaded Berry to leave his position with Moose Jaw National Light and Power and become power commissioner for the Saskatchewan government. Convinced that Berry should replace Thornton as commissioner, Phelps had him appointed to this position on January 2, 1945.[15] Berry agreed to be commissioner on two conditions: "Firstly that the government decide whether or not it would purchase or expropriate his company as soon as funds became available, and secondly, that he could locate a suitable man to assume his own position." Phelps postponed acquisition of Berry's firm, and Berry found a replacement. Phelps later commented, "He was a prince of a guy. A hell of a good guy, and he knew his electricity. I could never have done it without him." However, about L. A. Thornton, he recalled, "I fired the power commissioner because he was an ass, in my opinion, and he couldn't say a civil word about the NDP [*sic*], even though he was working for us. He thought he knew everything. In my opinion he didn't know anything, about power even, very little."[16]

Things moved very rapidly after Berry was hired. His appointment met with favour with officials from the other private power companies, who felt he would be sympathetic to their interests. It was also well received in financial circles. Very soon after his appointment, Berry recommended the purchase of Dominion Electric, stating, "I believe it would be possible to buy the common stock of this Company for a figure somewhere between $400,000 and $450,000. This would represent a cost of approximately 60% of the book value."[17] Berry estimated that the earnings of such stock plus federal income and excess profit taxes, which would be retained by the province, would pay for the stock in three years.[18] He predicted that the property could be acquired without any expenditure except payments advanced from the company's own earnings. When Phelps suggested to Cabinet that the government buy Dominion Electric, "some damn near fainted," "some opposed," others had "questions," and still others had reservations and felt the government was "going too fast."[19] Cabinet disagreed, but he remained firm. He later recalled,

> I won out on power. I was pretty rough on that one. I stood my ground and I said, "To hell—I will throw this job in the goddamn ditch unless we are going to go ahead." I just laid it on the line. I remember one time we had a discussion and finally they left it pretty well to me. That was a big assignment but I had confidence in the power commissioner, once we got him in there and got going, then I felt I knew where I was going.[20]

Phelps encountered resistance to purchasing Dominion Electric not only from the Cabinet but also from the Opposition and the newspapers. W. J. Patterson argued that rural municipalities would lose tax revenue if the government bought the company since private companies paid taxes to the municipalities but government-owned ones did not. He maintained that the amendment to the Power Commission Act would give the government vastly increased powers and remove from the legislature "its right of final control." A. T. Procter (Liberal, Moosomin) labelled the bill "a blank cheque on the resources of the province." The *Leader-Post* also argued that this amendment would give the commission "blanket authority." This would mean that "whereas under the existing Power Commission act control of capital expenditures of the commission rested in the legislature with the commission having authority only with respect to operating expenditures, the amendment would eliminate this legislative check entirely, giving the commission the right to embark on capital expenditures." On the other hand, C. M. Fines, the provincial treasurer, defended the purchase, arguing that it was "a vital step in obtaining control of an essential part in a province-wide power setup." Using an array of statistics, he argued that the deal was a good one and insisted that "based on current income…in twelve years the province could own all the assets."[21] The amendment passed. Cabinet accepted a similar proposal within less than a month, and special retroactive legislation was passed permitting the commission to purchase capital stock in incorporated electrical utility companies. After amending the Power Commission Act, the government acquired Dominion Electric Power on March 12, 1945. Between November 1945 and May 1947, it also bought the other private companies.[22] Dominion Electric operated as a wholly owned subsidiary of the commission until amalgamation took place on January 1, 1947.

Plans were made rapidly for the newly acquired company. Fuel at the Estevan Dominion Electric plant was being purchased at roughly a third of the cost of other provincial locations, and plans were made to interconnect Estevan, Moose Jaw, and the southwest under consolidated management. Estevan would become the base load centre for all of the transmission lines in southern and eastern Saskatchewan. Several expensive diesel-generating stations could then be closed down. Plans for new transmission lines were drawn up and approved. The Estevan–Stoughton connection was also approved, and the first steps toward an integrated power system were made. Vern Hogg recalled,

> Within a month, the Saskatchewan Power Corporation was formed, Hal Berry was hired as general manager, and the Dominion Power Company, a public company on the Toronto Stock Exchange, was taken over by stock purchase one hundred per cent by the Saskatchewan government. Joe Phelps was certainly a man of action.[23]

It would take a number of years until the system covered the entire province, and the other Canadian provinces would follow.

If a province-wide power grid was to be sustainable, the team needed to identify and develop sources of electrical energy. Plans were made to expand the Estevan generating station, and estimates on hydroelectric development were obtained. In May 1945, Phelps announced that the government would undertake a survey to determine the feasibility of hydroelectric power generation at Fort à la Corne, east of Prince Albert. When the first natural-gas-fuelled power station at Unity had increased to a size sufficient to act as a base load station for an area extending to Wilkie, Kindersley, and Macklin, the attention of utility officials turned to natural gas transmission and distribution. In September 1945, Phelps announced, "Results of drilling in the Unity gas field indicated that Saskatchewan now has a major commercial gas field which when developed, will be a definite asset in the economic future of the province."[24]

EXPANSION

Phelps respected the opinion of Edgar Kaeding, his long-time friend from Churchbridge, and stopped at his farm during the summer of 1946 to discuss how to get rural electrification underway. Kaeding recalled Joe's words: "I promise that if we can get a sufficiently concentrated group of farmers to sign up, the government is prepared to run an experimental line south of Churchbridge." Kaeding took up the challenge, and a number of meetings were held. He reported that

> Nineteen farms wanted to power-up along the seventeen miles of line. We were asked to put up $800 each for the main power line, and $20 a pole for yard runs. We were also asked to do some labour, since all the power pole holes had to be dug by hand. This was arranged, and in the summer of 1947, we had one of the first rural power projects in Saskatchewan, and what a blessing it was.[25]

The various power plants that were purchased were integrated into a smoothly operating and efficient system. In October 1947, H. F. Berry, chairman of the Saskatchewan Power Commission, noted that the commission had increased its services. There were 1,626 miles of line in service in 1944; by August 1947, it was 3,276 miles. There were 12,989 customers served in December 1944; in August 1947, it was 42,602. In the year ended March 31, 1947, the commission's total earnings after depreciation were $983,000. In 1949, SaskPower became a Crown corporation.[26]

By 2002, SaskPower reported that it operated three coal-fired power stations, seven hydroelectric stations, four natural gas stations, and nine wind turbines, and maintained more than 152,000 kilometres of power lines. It employed 2,350 people on a permanent full-time basis and had a net income of $127 million, providing a dividend of $82 million.[27]

In the documentary *Folks Call Me Tommy*, Douglas reflected on his achievements while in government, noting that the thing that gave him the greatest satisfaction later in his life was driving through rural Saskatchewan with his wife, Irma, seeing lights on the farms where it used to be dark, and realizing that the CCF had reduced the drudgery of farm women. The importance he attached to this program is a tribute to the faith he had in Phelps to make it a reality. Eiling Kramer also reflected on Phelps's assignment to this important task: "Once again this impatient human dynamo organized people and materials in record time, bringing rural Saskatchewan into the 20th century."[28]

The groundwork had been laid to bring power to the people of rural Saskatchewan. Developing a provincially owned and operated power grid proved to be one of Phelps's most important achievements as a Cabinet minister.

CHAPTER 8

AIRBORNE

Opening the North for economic development required extensive travel. A small airline, Mason & Campbell Airlines (commonly known as M&C Aviation), served northern Saskatchewan, but with increasing government requirements, the service was not adequate. Soon after his appointment, Phelps arranged to purchase two aircraft. A Stinson four-seater fabric plane was purchased for $8,160 from M&C in Prince Albert for the DNR on December 12, 1944. It was stationed in Regina and placed at the disposal of all government departments as needed.[1] A second-hand Wacco CF-AYQ float plane, docked on the North Saskatchewan River in Prince Albert, was used for passenger transportation and light hauling in the North. Phelps travelled on this plane with Floyd Glass as pilot for most of his northern tours. The government also required smaller airplanes for forestry and fishery work. The planes were used to help enforce fish and fur regulations, do survey work in the Hudson Bay Junction area, transport government personnel, and protect against forest fires. The two aircraft that Phelps purchased for the government formed the nucleus of what evolved into a provincial air fleet, part of Saskatchewan Government Airways (SGA), another of the government's Crown corporations.

With so many projects on the go, Phelps was always in a hurry. "He hated time wasted travelling, so he bought a Piper Fox [privately] and hired a pilot to ferry him places," Wilf Churchman recalled.[2] Phelps used the aircraft, which was stored at the Regina airport, to attend various board meetings. Churchman, assistant deputy minister to Phelps beginning in 1946, recalled that on several occasions Joe talked about narrow escapes he had while flying in bad weather, incidents he simply brushed off. According to Churchman, "Joe was very devoted to his program goals and bad weather was no deterrent. Even ducks and geese were grounded in bad weather, but the unflappable Joe Phelps winged his way to the important business at hand."[3] Pilot Floyd Glass recalled one of the first flights he took with Joe Phelps on board:

> We were taking off from the North Saskatchewan River at Prince Albert and Phelps was seated in the plane dictating notes to his secretary. When he glanced up the floatplane was heading for the bridge, coming ominously close. At the last minute we went under it instead of over and Joe tapped on the glass saying, the next time he planned a stunt like that could he be so advised?[4]

When the flying training schools closed after the war, hundreds of Tiger Moth trainers became available through the federal War Assets Corporation. By April 1945, Phelps had purchased two Tiger Moth aircraft from the War Assets Corporation for $1,000 each, and subsequently appointed Floyd Glass as superintendent of all aircraft operations and northern district superintendent.[5] The DNR flight program included Lefty McLeod, Stu Millar, Fred McClellan, and Floyd Glass. Lefty McLeod and Stu Millar had been flight instructors at the Elementary Flying School in Prince Albert during the war.[6] In December 1945, the DNR bought a Norseman, which it equipped as an ambulance for the Department of Public Health.[7] Phelps continued to buy planes for the DNR, and by the end of 1945 it owned six.[8]

The DNR fleet performed a number of vital functions, including carrying burning, net and sawmill permits, surveying timber, servicing conservation officer stations and fire towers, and patrolling for fires, as well as carrying on lake research for the Fisheries Branch. Prospecting and geological mapping was also taking place in over half of the northern third of the province, an area of Precambrian shield approximately 230,000 square kilometres in size. Phelps once mentioned to his grandson, David Goranson, that another reason for flying the north was to monitor HBC activities.[9]

In 1946, the DNR began to design and manufacture radios for their aircraft and ground personnel, built in the government radio shop at the Prince Albert airport, under the supervision of a radio engineer. Although primarily intended for fire suppression work, the radio-communication system became an essential resource for northern administrative work and emergency use. That same year, the government created the DNR's Radio Branch to improve medical services and forest fire suppression, and to provide weather data for aircraft and logistical support for business activities. Later, trappers and others working on the land were rented portable equipment to maintain radio communication links. The DNR also aired a daily radio program on the Prince Albert radio station CKBI. The popular *Northern News* broadcast provided a much-needed means of communication in the days before telephone service was available to northern homes.[10]

Phelps was aware that the expansion of air travel was both necessary and beneficial for the province. He included the need for a reliable air link from Saskatchewan into the United States in a brief to the federal Air Transport Board in Saskatoon, and also stressed the need for Saskatchewan towns and larger villages to build inexpensive landing strips or fields to help promote the expansion of air travel. Phelps made the point that airstrips would also benefit natural resources aircraft travelling in the North and could be used by the provincial air ambulance service.[11]

Within two years, the Air Division of the DNR had ten aircraft in service, more than twice the number operated by M&C. The government was able to purchase airplanes from the War Assets Corporation at bargain rates. (Tiger Moths that had been purchased for about $7,000 were sold for as little as $450, and a Norseman originally priced at $38,000 was sold for just $15,000.[12]) Although the government was not operating under a commercial licence in direct competition with M&C, it was cutting into the company's business quite significantly. M&C argued that there was only room for one licensed carrier in the North, raising the possibility of a potential purchase by the provincial government.

The use of government airplanes increased steadily. They were freighting medical supplies, moving building supplies for schools and fish processing plants into the North, carrying fur and fish, as well as transporting government administrators and personnel, doctors, nurses, and teachers. Federal Indian Affairs also contracted Saskatchewan government aircraft to provide all medical flights for treaty Indians, work previously conducted by M&C.

"NOW IT'S AIRLINES"

This increasing demand for air travel related to northern development prompted Phelps to initiate a plan to set up scheduled air service to La Ronge three times a week, as well as two circular routes that would cover most of the main communities in northern Saskatchewan. (M&C was only flying as far as Stanley Mission and La Loche.) The federal government agreed to provide the necessary licensing if the DNR could negotiate to buy out M&C Aviation. In August 1947, shortly after it began negotiating with M&C, four of the province's airplanes and a hangar were destroyed by fire at Prince Albert. Phelps, now desperately in need of M&C's airplanes, radio equipment, maintenance, and overhaul of the shop and hangar, successfully negotiated the purchase of M&C. Phelps obtained Cabinet approval for the purchase of M&C's assets for $115,000

The CF-SAM was the second of two Norseman aircraft purchased in 1946 for use as an air ambulance, the first nonmilitary government service of its kind in the world. Provincial Archives of Saskatchewan, Government of Saskatchewan Photo Services Reference #1949.

and M&C agreed to relinquish all flying rights in the area.[13] On August 15, SGA was established. Many M&C staff remained employed with DNR.

In a radio interview, Phelps and Floyd Glass, general manager of SGA, discussed the new Crown corporation. Phelps explained,

> It's another step in our program to utilize the province's wealth lying "north of 54"—fishing, furs, timber and mining industries. The new airline will cover every important settlement, and provide, for the first time, a first-rate service for all groups, both private enterprise and government departments, engaged in development work.[14]

SGA also announced that the new company would provide the "world's first non-military air ambulance service," critical for residents in remote northern areas where only limited health services were available in a few of the larger communities.[15]

The province would also become the first in Canada to use planes and parachutes to fight forest fires. Smokejumpers, called by radiotelephone, were parachuted in to control fires prior to the arrival of firefighting equipment. Waterbombing by plane was developed later.[16]

An August 19, 1947, editorial in the *Leader-Post*, titled "Now it's airlines," criticized the Saskatchewan government's decision to enter the field of commercial aviation by replacing "free-enterprise" with its own airline. Phelps replied,

> We in the provincial government, feel that we can profit by the federal government's experience [with TCA—Trans-Canada Air Lines] along these lines, and have formed the new undertaking into a corporation at the outset. It may not be too much to hope that someday in the future, your paper may come to realize that the people of Saskatchewan, and Canadians in other parts of Canada, as well as those people of countries such as Great Britain, Australia, New Zealand and others, believe that our transportation systems should be owned, operated, and controlled by the people, and not solely by the shareholders of a few private companies.... Having entered the field of northern aviation for northern development purposes, it is

> our belief that we were well advised to take the honourable course in negotiating for the purchase in a fair, open and above board manner. We could have just obtained a license and entered into direct competition with M&C Aviation, the company we successfully negotiated for.[17]

When the inaugural flight of SGA left Prince Albert airport on October 11, 1947, with five passengers for the long haul to Lake Athabasca, the minister was there to officially open the new service. The passenger list included an RCMP constable en route to a northern post, two children just released from the Prince Albert sanitarium and returning home to Camsell Portage, northwest of Uranium City, the DNR radio technician, and a tourist from Wolf Point, Montana, on a sightseeing and fishing trip.

Air transportation became an essential component in the government's Northern Conservation Service. It was initially very expensive, with considerable wait time and many empty return flights for pilots. This changed when the government began hiring conservation officers who were also pilots. These conservation officers became an important link between the government and the people of the North, and they were present in northern Saskatchewan for almost two decades until the government changed in 1964. Airplanes stationed at Hudson Bay, Prince Albert, Meadow Lake, and La Ronge were leased from SGA and flown by the conservation officers for their day-to-day operations. This made for much more rigorous and thorough enforcement. Fur, game, and fish poachers were aware that a conservation officer could appear at any time. There were no local municipal governments in the North at the time, and since most northern residents made their living from natural resources, conservation officer pilots had contact with nearly all of them at their traplines, fish camps, and in their communities. They delivered fur cheques and government payments, and hauled furs out. Conservation officers often took time to pick up mail or a few groceries for trappers they were going to visit, or would fly the sick or injured out for medical attention.

RECYCLING ON A GRAND SCALE

Airplanes were not the only thing that Phelps had arranged to salvage from the War Assets Corporation. Although the phrase "reduce, reuse, and recycle" was not in common use in the 1940s, his attitude toward recycling was definitely ahead of his time. He could not stand to see waste in any form, particularly in connection with material that could be reused or had significant historic value.

Shortly before VE day, in a speech to a CCF nominating convention at Regina City Hall, Phelps expressed his revulsion at the waste exhibited by the federal War Assets Corporation, whose one objective, he said, was to get as much stuff out of circulation as soon as possible. "You'd be surprised at the amount that can be saved," Phelps stated. He also demanded that when the new Parliament convened in Ottawa it appoint a Royal Commission to inquire into the destruction of war materials by the War Assets Corporation. "The government of the day," he fumed, "was going to have something to answer for."[18]

At one point in the speech, he dramatically yanked a blanket off, exposing what appeared to be junk lying on the stage beside him. With a loud voice, he exclaimed, "Here's the proof," as he pointed to the pile of material. The pile included a searchlight, wire cable, and a fire extinguisher. Phelps explained,

> The material was the remains of part of an aircraft from the Estevan airfield that had been taken off the scrap heap at the Estevan flying school, and I arranged to have it brought to Regina. Don't blame the air force. The War Assets Corporation is responsible. This material is the stuff being bought and paid for with your money. A lot of it could be salvaged.[19]

His persistence finally paid off when Dominion Munitions Minister C. D. Howe, in a speech in Prince Albert on June 4, 1945, said,

> I am prepared to put his government in a position of making large sums of money, by asking the War Assets Corporation to give Mr. Phelps the sole concession for salvaging usable material from our aircraft disposal dumps, with the proviso that he must sell this material directly to the public, and not make its disposal a junk dealer's business.[20]

Phelps responded to this offer in a speech on June 5, 1945, in Lemberg, when he said, "I'll take Mr. Howe up on that proposition. We will undertake to dispose of it. A lot of that stuff could be used to mighty good advantage in Saskatchewan."[21] It was not long before one of the first projects negotiated with the War Assets Corporation in Ottawa came to fruition. A barracks building was moved from St. Aldwyn's airfield, sixteen kilometres north of Swift Current, into the city and converted into an apartment building to house sixteen to twenty servicemen's families. Phelps's concern with preservation would surface again later when he was instrumental in the establishment of Saskatchewan's Western Development Museum.

CHAPTER 9

THE FUR TRADE

Phelps turned his attention to fur marketing and conservation measures early in his term as a Cabinet minister. Fur supplies were dangerously depleted, and conservation measures were desperately needed to turn the situation around. Phelps was also putting his mind to developing initiatives that would stabilize and improve the marketing of fur in the province. As Barron has noted, the fur trapper had long been victimized "by fluctuating fur prices determined on the world market, by the natural cycles in fur-bearing animals, by the excessive profit margins extracted by the trading companies, and by the ability of the fur companies…to manipulate the terms and conditions under which credit would be given to the trapper." The lack of government regulations had led to such "horrendous over trapping" that species like the beaver were close to extinction in some areas.[1] Phelps was incensed at the HBC policy of encouraging trappers to overharvest furs by extending credit, credit that could only be repaid by increasing the number of furs delivered. A plan was desperately needed to encourage a sustainable supply of raw fur in the province and minimize overtrapping. In Vern Hogg's 1943 *Plan for the Development of Natural Resources of Northern Saskatchewan*, he stated,

> The Hudson's Bay Company holds a virtual monopoly on the purchase of furs and over the natives who trap the largest proportion of the total yearly catch. By skillful dealings the natives are kept in a state of servitude to the company. All business transactions between the company and the natives

> is carried out on a barter basis, in much the same manner as it was at the beginning of the fur trade. The natives must trade their furs to the company in return for all the necessities of life, food, clothing, canoes, nets etc.... If a native has money to make purchases he is charged 50% more than the cost price to white trappers.[2]

Once again, Phelps was quick to act. On July 12, 1944, he wrote to J. S. McDiarmid, Manitoba's Minister of Mines and Resources, requesting information about muskrat leases and the sale of furs through a recently established provincial agency. On July 12, he asked J. H. Janzen, a lawyer, about the legality of establishing a central Fur Marketing Agency, and by August 18 he had interviewed some trappers to determine if they were interested in having such an agency. A questionnaire was then sent to fourteen thousand trappers and fur farmers in the province, asking them the same question. Of the 2,800 who responded, 97 per cent of the trappers, 82 per cent of the fur ranchers, and 83 per cent of the fur dealers favoured the proposal. Then, during a special legislative session in October 1944, Phelps introduced an amendment to the Fur Act that authorized the government to operate a Fur Marketing Agency and to regulate trappers' licences and permits.[3]

SASKATCHEWAN FUR MARKETING SERVICE

On November 1, 1944, the government inaugurated the Saskatchewan Fur Marketing Service, with Phelps as the minister in charge and W. H. Lefurgey as its manager.[4] Its main objective was to provide a safe market for all producers and dealers and to obtain the highest prices for furs. Furs would be graded, sorted into lots, and offered for sale periodically by auction. Shippers who were dissatisfied with the prices they were receiving for their furs could place reservations on them or bid on their own goods. The government charged shippers a nominal commission for operating this service. The first fur auction, held on January 9, 1945, sold $91,000 worth of furs. Three subsequent auctions that year sold over half a million dollars worth of furs, a total that far exceeded expectations.[5]

This new initiative did not cause much debate in the legislature. On March 26, 1945, A. T. Procter (Liberal, Moosomin) asked, "Is the minister aware that there has been considerable complaint about fur grading?" To this, Phelps responded, "No, but I am aware there has been a great deal of satisfaction from both dealers and trappers."[6] Though the Opposition expressed little concern about the Saskatchewan Fur Marketing Service, fur dealers were very critical of it. They feared Phelps would eventually impose compulsory marketing of furs, a fear that was well founded. They also thought that it was "unfair competition" for them, since its fieldmen were DNR employees and were paid out of the public Treasury. Its fieldmen also encouraged trappers to sell their furs to the agency. There were also complaints that dealers had to pay fur taxes and licences but that the government had bought the Fur Marketing Service's building with public funds and paid no taxes. Lastly, they complained, "no experienced fur man was in charge of the agency."[7]

On October 19, 1945, the Cabinet converted this agency, the Saskatchewan Fur Marketing Service, into a Crown corporation with the same name.[8] The corporation's purpose was to operate "on behalf of the Province of Saskatchewan the business of buying, selling, storing, processing, and preparing pelts of fur-bearing animals, marketing pelts of fur-bearing animals for and on behalf of the owners thereof and providing marketing services for such owners."[9] The marketing company handled the purchase and sale of all fur produced in the province, providing a market for fur farmers and trappers of wild game. Trappers received an initial payment at the time of sale and a final payment that reflected the actual price received by the Fur Marketing Service in the marketplace. To ensure the success of the two-price fur marketing plan, the government made it mandatory for trappers to sell beaver and muskrat to the service, although trappers were allowed to sell other furs to anyone.[10]

Although well intentioned, the government's fur marketing initiatives were not well received. Edgar Kaeding recalled,

> Joe went about his new job with enthusiasm, but as expected, not all his ideas were popular. I can remember the debates about the Fur Marketing service, in which he proposed all furs be marketed through the service, and that royalties be paid. Many of our smaller farmers used to supplement their income by trapping muskrats during the spring, and they did not relish anyone telling them how many they could trap or where

> they could sell them. These rules stirred up massive resentment in some people, although Joe Phelps' intent was good.[11]

The marketing service was unpopular for several reasons. Trappers resented the 5 per cent commission it took to finance its operations.[12] Furthermore, because trappers were compelled to sell their beaver and muskrat pelts to the Fur Marketing Service, they lost access to the credit that private companies had long provided, which had often been the means of financing their trapping operations.

Not surprisingly, shortly after the fur marketing regulations were established, the HBC mounted serious opposition to the legislation that compelled trappers to sell their beaver and muskrat pelts to the Fur Marketing Service because it meant that it could no longer buy these furs from trappers.[13] The HBC and other firms would not extend credit to trappers who could no longer trade with them and over whom they no longer had any leverage to collect debts. The method of payment also created problems for the trappers. While the Fur Marketing Service gave trappers an initial payment on delivery of their pelts, it did not give them their final payment until after the auction. Thus, trappers often lacked the means to finance their annual trapping activities.

The provincial government responded by establishing its own string of stores under a Crown corporation, Saskatchewan Government Trading. Phelps suggested that the government stores be operated as co-operatives, but according to Laurie Barron, "little serious consideration was given to the idea at the time." However, in 1959 Saskatchewan Government Trading, along with the fish marketing service, was transformed into a co-operative structure known as the Northern Co-operative Trading Services, and by 1961 there were fourteen co-operative retail outlets in the North.[14]

Shackleton reports, "The CCF government's first contact with the Métis people was the attempt to regularize and stabilize fish and fur marketing through government agencies." It was not an immediately acceptable working arrangement:

> Some Métis trappers suspected they could get more through private sales and sometimes the government cheques were slow in arriving. The government tried to foster cooperative

> stores for general supplies in competition with the ubiquitous Hudson's Bay Company. But a cooperative enterprise is not to be imposed on a nomadic and unsophisticated people and development was slow.[15]

DEPARTMENT SHAKE-UP

In October 1944, C. A. LuVerne (Vern) Hogg was hired as a geologist for the DNR from the Canadian Geological Survey, where he had worked in northern Saskatchewan and in mining and exploration in northern Ontario and Quebec. Phelps appointed him deputy minister in 1946, after Henry Lewis resigned from his position as deputy.

Phelps was the only Cabinet minister in the Douglas Government with the dubious distinction of having had three deputy ministers. The first deputy had resigned shortly after Phelps's appointment, stating that he was aware they did not think alike and it would not work out; he was given a position in the land department. Henry Lewis, who had been appointed in April 1945, resigned for undisclosed reasons.

Hogg's promotion did not go unquestioned. Front-page headlines in the *Leader-Post* read, "Phelps-Lewis clash leads to department shake-up." The newspaper published a series of stories speculating on Lewis's departure and stating it had been rumoured that differences of opinion within the department—in particular within Crown corporation operations—were causing the friction. The story also said, "Other rumours were that Mr. Lewis had too definite leftist leanings and because of this the government was endeavoring to dispense with his service."[16] The same story indicated that in the previous two months, two other government employees who were allegedly too radical had been asked for their resignations. Premier Douglas, when questioned by the newspaper on the matter, commented that the differences between Phelps and Lewis were principally the result of a clash of personalities. Lewis's comment to the press was that he and Mr. Phelps were both Irish and sometimes agreed to disagree.[17]

The controversy surrounding Lewis's departure prompted Phelps to charge the *Leader-Post* with irresponsible handling of news. In a statement published in the *Leader-Post* on November 4, 1946, he blasted it for biased and negative reporting:

> Contrary to the thinly veiled hopes of the *Leader-Post* this change of staff does not herald any grave disintegration in the department or its staff. We are proceeding with our program as rapidly as possible in accordance with the mandate given to us by the people of Saskatchewan. If the *Leader-Post* would display as much ingenuity and persistence in publicizing our northern development program, to take one phase of our work, it would not only have an extremely interesting and constructive story to tell its readers but could also pride itself on helping to put across something which will bring additional wealth into the province and do much to improve conditions among the Indians and others who have been eking out an existence in the northland due to the past neglect of former administrations and the callousness of private enterprise.... Mr. Hogg's appointment was in the interest of wise and efficient administration, which I think most people will agree is imperative if our natural resources are to be properly developed and applied to bettering conditions for the people of Saskatchewan, which is our objective.[18]

Phelps preferred to keep the circumstances surrounding Lewis's departure confidential, and took exception to the newspaper printing stories he felt misrepresented the situation. He appointed Hogg as deputy minister based on his credentials, believing he was an expert in his field, aware that he could provide accurate and reliable technical advice as his deputy.

This was not the only incident during Phelps's political career in which he strongly objected to stories printed by local newspapers. Phelps, outspoken and direct in all of his communication, was perhaps somewhat idealistic and naive in his assumptions about how the media should be reporting on government programs. A critical editorial in the *Prince Albert Daily Herald* prompted Phelps to submit a letter to the paper on January 25, 1947. Phelps felt the *Herald*, which had ostensibly been supportive of his development efforts in the North, had turned on him. In his letter he stated, "Care has previously been taken by your paper to refrain from printing anything which might have a damaging effect on northern development. We hope your policy is not being altered."[19] The *Herald* responded by publishing the following comments:

> We are as unlikely to take steps consciously that will have the effect of retarding development of the North, as we are to advocate self-destruction for this community or this paper, and no stirrings of a suicidal mood have been noted lately. Our ideas of what may have a damaging effect on northern development, of course, may often differ sharply from those entertained by Mr. Phelps, but they'll certainly keep on being as honest, sane and earnest as we can make them.[20]

The controversy surrounding Vern Hogg's appointment dissipated shortly after, and Phelps worked closely with him throughout his remaining time as a Cabinet minister. On many occasions, Hogg attended meetings and conferences on his behalf. Hogg recalled Phelps's contributions fondly, describing him as "an honest, tireless and dedicated worker, and a builder, who made a tremendous contribution to the development of Saskatchewan during his short time as Minister of Natural Resources."[21]

FUR CONSERVATION BLOCKS

Hogg recalled that Phelps frequently showed disdain for officials and politicians in Ottawa, referring to them as "scissorbills"[22]—the scissorbill is a water bird that skims the surface to achieve the greatest rewards for the least effort—but one 1944 meeting Hogg attended in Ottawa was very favourable to the province. The federal government committed to pay up to 50 per cent of the cost of setting up the fur management and conservation programs, forest inventory, freshwater biological fishery surveys, and geological surveys. These federal funds were important in establishing many of the base programs within the department between 1945 and 1948, and Phelps's attitude toward the federal government softened considerably. Federal government funding would provide much-needed assistance in the marketing of Saskatchewan furs.

Phelps's approach to the development of fur resources involved both marketing and conservation. His idea was to divide northern Saskatchewan into a number of conservation areas called fur conservation blocks, which would be trapped exclusively by local residents. Under the umbrella of the Northern Fur Conservation Program, these community conservation blocks would be operated as large wild game farms, adjacent to a number of northern settlements, and would provide a predictable and sustainable supply of wildlife. The program would provide an incentive for trappers to join with the government and take responsibility for stabilizing the supply of furs, in order to increase the potential for greater economic reward in the future.

One of the first projects in the program occurred in the Cumberland House area, northeast of Prince Albert. In the fall of 1945, Phelps arranged for an aerial survey of the area to determine the feasibility of the government plan to flood approximately sixty thousand acres and create a large swamp area. The swamp, part of the fur and waterfowl conservation block, was intended to function as a breeding ground for wild ducks and muskrats. The territory to be included in the block had been surrendered to the Saskatchewan government in 1944 by the HBC. Phelps explained the project in the *Leader-Post* on September 10, 1945: "In establishing the block, it is the government's objective to improve the marshes in such a way that hunters and trappers may carry off a more constant supply of muskrats and ducks."[23] By June 1946, the survey was complete and plans were underway. Ducks Unlimited agreed to contribute $100,000 to be used for construction, while the provincial government provided the machinery and supervised the work.

The Fur Conservation Blocks program was based on a joint agreement signed in July 1946 between the provincial and federal governments. The latter, recognizing its responsibility for Indigenous people in the province, agreed to pay 60 per cent of the program's costs. The program applied to the area north of 53 degrees latitude, which was divided into conservation areas or fur blocks. Individuals who had resided within one of these areas for twelve months received exclusive trapping rights. Trappers within these conservation areas elected a five-man council "to assist the department's field officer in planning and fur development."[24] The five-member local trappers' councils had to include both First Nations and Métis representatives from the area, as well as two elected members to administer the blocks. In co-operation with a field officer from the DNR, councils were responsible for establishing and enforcing the conservation quotas for beaver and muskrat, and making sure that all trappers in the block were treated fairly.[25] Muskrat and beaver were trapped on a share basis, with each trapper receiving a quota according to the estimated number of animals in the block. The DNR took 10 per cent of the revenue from the sale of these furs and used some of the money for conservation—"for building dams, sowing wild rice, transplanting beavers, or for anything which would aid in the conservation of the northern fur supply."[26] Trappers were allotted specific areas in which they could trap other animals in season without restriction. Regulations provided that trappers leave enough animals to ensure propagation.[27]

The fur block program was very successful and offered a number of advantages, including ensuring a more stable income for resident trappers and stabilizing the fur supply. Strategic restocking also became a part of the program. By February 1947, sixty-five conservation blocks had been established.[28]

Under the South Saskatchewan Muskrat Trapping Plan, the DNR constructed dykes and dams to raise the water levels in areas to improve the breeding grounds for muskrats. Trappers bought special permits for exclusive rights to trap in certain areas. They had to leave 40 per cent of the muskrats untrapped until the maximum population the area could support had been reached. DNR staff determined how many animals could be trapped by estimating the number of muskrats in the area and dividing the quota among those entitled to trap in it. All pelts had to be sold through the Fur Marketing Service, which retained a 20 per cent share for the DNR. Some of this money was designated for conservation.[29] Many trappers favoured this plan since they could see that such planning would ensure a future for the industry.

In July 1946, the *Leader-Post* reported that the development of the fur conservation block in the Cumberland House area was commanding the attention of local Indigenous residents. Phelps, visiting the area after establishing the conservation block the year before, pointed out that "the benefits of the fur conservation block were demonstrated in striking fashion to Native trappers this spring, when they took off 32,291 beaver pelts—20,000 more than in the previous year."[30] The *Leader-Post* also reported that residents were taking a keen interest in community affairs, erecting a community hall for social functions and meetings and becoming involved in fundraising for other community work.

During his visit to Cumberland House, Phelps advised the residents that "while fur was the main 'crop' for the district, the provincial government will give every encouragement to the development of other activities, such as poultry and livestock raising, growing of garden produce and general farming." The *Leader-Post* also reported that Phelps had inspected the government sawmill being constructed just a few miles from Cumberland House. The sawmill, brought in by barge early in the spring, would provide lumber to erect the dams for the fur conservation project and to build homes in the area. It was expected to turn out from ten thousand to twelve thousand feet of lumber a day.[31]

BOUNTIES, BEAVERS, AND FUR FARMS

In September 1944, the DNR began to re-evaluate its trapping policy. As part of the conservation plan, efforts were made to curtail the illegal trafficking of furs and to enforce fur regulations more rigorously. As a first step, heavy fines were imposed for various offences. Phelps announced in November 1945 that "a reward of $100 will be offered by the department for information leading to conviction for any one of three major offences: Illegal trafficking in furs, exporting furs without the required permit, and the handling of beaver pelts without proper authority."[32] By 1946, the department's annual report noted that the depletion of game resources through the depredations of the timber wolf was becoming serious, and the DNR increased the bounty on timber wolves from $10 to $20 and paid a $2 bounty on coyotes.[33] Trappers were quick to complain, since the Timber Board paid this additional $10 bonus only on wolf pelts sent to the Fur Marketing Service. W. J. Patterson, the Liberal leader, called the action discriminatory and charged that the government paid "special bonuses or rewards out of public funds to those who sold their products to a government agency."[34]

On one northern trip, Phelps talked to a group of Indigenous people near Clear Lake who had never seen a beaver. During the 1945 trapping season, only fifty beaver were legally trapped. Fearing they were facing extinction, the government closed beaver trapping the next season. The meeting prompted Phelps to initiate a program of relocating nuisance beavers from the south to the North, and strategic restocking became part of the program. Another step he took was to have live beavers moved from areas where they were numerous and the water level was too high to places where the water level was too low.

The first such initiative, announced in February 1946, involved a plan to transport approximately one thousand beavers from near Saskatoon to more northern districts. Nuisance beavers that were causing flooding in southern streams were flown north for liberation. Lefty McLeod, a pilot with Saskatchewan Government Airways, recalled the beaver transportation program:

> They had a plague of beaver in the Prince Albert National Park and they decided they were going to transfer a bunch of them around the province. They were delivering them to me down at the breakwater at Waskesiu thirty-five at a time. You should have seen the cages made of chicken wire and two by fours wrapped in galvanized iron so they couldn't eat their way out. The cages weighed more than their contents. The minute you started the engine they would all work themselves into a heap in the center just like a bunch of kittens, and go to sleep. They wouldn't bother you at all.[35]

Twenty- to twenty-five-year-old trappers in Buffalo Narrows and Île-à-la-Crosse reported seeing beaver for the first time in their lives. The policy of trapping beaver alive and transporting them to new areas suitable to their propagation was continued during the mid-1940s with some success. In 1947, the DNR transplanted 647 live beavers into new areas, "the largest undertaking of its kind in the world."[36] Through careful administration and strict enforcement by conservation officers, fifty-five thousand beavers were harvested in the mid-1950s.

Fur farming was another potential area for development. Phelps encouraged co-operative ventures in beaver and muskrat farming, and even had the DNR appoint a veterinarian to assist fur ranchers.[37] Among veterans returning to Saskatchewan from the Second World War, some were anxious to be involved in fur farming and had applied to the provincial government for assistance. Speaking at a conference of agricultural representatives in Regina, Phelps said, "We intend to help them as much as possible. While the program would not be adaptable to certain areas in the province, it might well establish a measure of post war security for perhaps three to four hundred veterans and their families." Taking a dig at the Dominion government, he remarked, "Much money has been spent on PFRA [Prairie Farm Rehabilitation Act] irrigation projects.... Alternatively the Canadian beaver is very abundant and could do a better job of building dams than many engineers.... The money used on PFRA dams had to be repaid, while the beaver-farming project could be made to pay for itself from the sale of pelts." He added, "every woman in Saskatchewan should have a fur coat."[38]

AERIAL TOUR

In the summer of 1946, Phelps took a six-day air tour of the North to meet with trappers and explain the fur conservation program. The *Leader-Post* reported, "Trappers, both Indian and white, were glad to see the 'man from Regina.'"[39] His presence in the North was also reported as "history-making," as no other provincial minister had visited so many northern points. Phelps covered more than 2,500 kilometres in his aerial tour in the department plane. He first stopped at Île-à-la-Crosse to travel by boat to Buffalo Narrows and inspect the fish filleting plant and the new government school. Then he dropped down on Cree Lake for a short stay and held a mid-lake meeting with two fishers, at his request. At Lake Athabasca, he visited the goldfields at Fond du Lac and Stony Rapids, then went on to Wollaston Lake, Southend, and Island Falls to see the Churchill River Power Company's hydro development. From there he went on to one of the government's fish filleting plants at Beaver Lake. Phelps met with a group of trappers at Southend, many of whom spoke English fluently. Solomon Merasty, who said, "I'm glad I met you," expressed the feelings of the Indigenous people at the meeting. "I know ten times more now than I did before."[40]

Following his tour of northern Saskatchewan by aircraft and boat, Phelps announced that "the provincial government's fur conservation program into far northern areas of Saskatchewan will be pushed forward as rapidly as possible," thanks to the support of the federal Indian Affairs department, which covered 60 per cent of the cost of the program.[42]

Innovative ideas and strategies were always on Phelps's mind. In the spring of 1946, he announced that about fifteen thousand new and improved pelt stretchers for muskrat, perfected in the Summerberry muskrat project in northern Manitoba, would be made available to Saskatchewan trappers before the spring season opened.[42] The stretchers were being produced at the government-operated box factory in Prince Albert, and it was believed they would increase the value of muskrat pelts caught in the province. In the past, many pelts had been damaged when improperly stretched on makeshift frames. Protection of the fur during the pelt-stretching process would become even more important if a fur coat industry was to be established in Saskatchewan. That possibility became public when Phelps announced in the provincial legislature on March 21, 1946, that "there was a firm negotiating with the government for starting such an industry."[43]

Later in his term as minister, there would be controversy over the compulsory marketing of timber, fur, and fish through government agencies. Although the marketing boards did serve to stabilize the industries, some producers argued against them. At a public meeting in Big River in August 1947, trappers complained that fur grades were not uniform and prices were too low in many cases. Always an advocate of personal action, Phelps invited the trappers to send their representatives to fur-grading courses as a means of protecting their interests, and concluded by saying that the marketing boards had been established to safeguard producers in much the same way as farmers were protected by the Wheat Board: "The marketing agencies set up by the provincial government compare favorably with the Canadian Wheat Board, and timber producers in Ontario, Manitoba and British Columbia look with envy on Saskatchewan's planned programs."[44]

Of all the Crown corporations Phelps administered, the Fur Marketing Service was by far the most financially successful. Figures indicate that it was continuously in the black. Though it was only established in October 1945, its profits by March 31, 1946, were $1,642. Its profits for the fiscal year ending March 31, 1947, were $32,425.51.[45]

Reflecting on the CCF approach in his later years, Phelps admitted, "We were...and I personally was more concerned in getting the fur trade reorganized so that Native people had jobs that were familiar to them.... In my opinion the priority was jobs in the fur and fishing industries. They knew about those things."[46] Government activity before the CCF had been minimal. Phelps commented, "The government before left it pretty well to the parish priest and I'm going to say the bootleggers and the fur sharks. That was the three groups that run that north country."[47] The conservation block program was successful, and, despite opposition from the HBC and some of the trappers (this although the compulsory components of the fur program were dropped in 1956), the Fur

Marketing Board did, in fact, stabilize prices, and it remained in place in the years to come. The two programs fulfilled Phelps's aim to ensure the propagation of fur-bearing animals and guarantee economic security to the trapper.[48]

CHAPTER 10

FISH, TREES, AND LAND

The big fish companies were also a target of Phelps's contempt. Feeling strongly that the companies were exploiting fishers, "practically stealing the fish," in his words, he took steps to organize the Saskatchewan Fish Board soon after his first ventures into the North. In fact, the fishing industry was the first natural resource industry Phelps decided to bring under government control. With the establishment of the board, royalties were collected for the first time on whitefish, pickerel, and lake trout exported from the province. Special attention was given to controlling and eradicating parasitic infestations, and the work of inspecting both lakes and fish began in the summer of 1944.

THE FISHING INDUSTRY

While fishing had been one of the Indigenous people's main sources of livelihood for hundreds of years, commercial fishing was relatively new to northern Saskatchewan.[1] Commercial fishing north of Prince Albert began in 1891, and there had been an unsuccessful attempt to establish a fish export business in 1898. The industry grew after the turn of the century, and in 1909 Turtle and Jackfish lakes produced over 300,000 kilograms of whitefish. Other northern lakes, such as Big River, Peter Pond, Île-à-la-Crosse, Dore, and Churchill, also became important for their fish production. During the First World War, the demand for fish caused prices to rise and, as a result, the catch also increased.[2] Thereafter, the poundage of fish caught generally remained constant or even declined in some years. However, the last few years of the Depression and the Second World War saw another increase in the quantity of fish caught, as the wartime demand for food and rocketing fish prices expanded fishing operations.[3] By 1943, Saskatchewan was Canada's leading producer of whitefish and was supplying nearly a third of all the trout. By 1944, about 140 lakes were open to commercial fishing.[4]

Still, by 1944 the fishing industry was in a precarious state. One problem was that the more than one hundred lakes from which fish were taken were scattered and isolated. Since many lakes were inaccessible by road, transporting fish to southern railways was very difficult and costly. Climate and geography created another problem. Because people fished mainly in the winter, they froze the fish for transport, often without cleaning them properly or preparing them attractively for market.[5] Another problem was that the fishing industry was poorly regulated. Fishers often hired twenty or more men to fish for them and thus obtained more fish than their allotted share. Since they could catch their limit in one lake and then move on to other lakes, many became fly-by-night operators.[6] Another problem was that fish dealers provided supplies such as nets and equipment and even advanced money to fishers, who were then obligated to sell their catch to these buyers, who in turn often exploited them by paying very little for the fish.

Phelps and the new CCF government moved quickly to address some of these problems. By November 1944, the legislature had approved an amendment to the Fisheries Act that imposed a half-cent-per-pound royalty on pickerel and whitefish and a cent on trout taken for commercial purposes and exported out of the province. A year later, the Cabinet limited the number of commercial fishing licences and limited the poundage of fish that might be taken under any such licence.[7]

MARKETING BOARD

One of the first meetings Deputy Minister Vern Hogg remembers attending, organized and chaired by Phelps, concerned the rejection of whitefish by United States Customs. It was the industry's most serious problem: the larval and adult stages of the tapeworm *Triaenophorus crassus* had infested whitefish, tullibee, and pike in all three Prairie provinces. In 1943, the federal government had commissioned a study into this problem because American customs officials were rejecting so many fish at the border.[8] Just months before the CCF took office, the federal government passed the Whitefish Inspection Act; it resulted in the closure of many lakes because of the substandard quality of fish there. The Saskatchewan government classified its lakes as "A" or "B" according to the federal regulations: fish from "A" lakes could be exported anywhere in the round—unfilleted—since infestation was low, but fish from "B" lakes had to be candled and filleted before they could be sold. To adhere to the Whitefish Inspection Act, the DNR had to close lakes in order to classify them "A" or "B," which often caused fishers to vent their anger at the department.

The decision was made to process the rejected whitefish through filleting plants to be constructed at strategic locations, and to establish a marketing board. Vern Hogg recalled, "A quick decision was typical of Joe. I found he was not one to dither or cogitate on a situation, he was a very decisive individual and quick to act."[9]

Fish Marketing Board warehouse at Beaver Lake, Saskatchewan, between 1945 and 1954. Provincial Archives of Saskatchewan, Government of Saskatchewan Photo Services Reference #2294.

Phelps lost no time in establishing the first filleting plant. On July 10, 1944, he sought information about fish processing from Len Waite, a commercial fish processor at Big River, and by August 1944 a start was made on the Lac la Ronge filleting plant. It was finished the following August. In January 1945, a second plant opened at Beaver Lake near Flin Flon.[10] By July 1945, the Cabinet had established Saskatchewan Fish Products Corporation for the purpose of "carrying on the business of fishing, buying, and selling fish, and establishing fish canneries, fish curing, fish processing plants, and marketing these products on behalf of the Province of Saskatchewan."[11] J. L. Phelps, A. Olson, and K. Dickson were appointed as directors. The Saskatchewan Fish Marketing Board was established in November 1945, with the support of the fishers and the directors of the Saskatchewan Fish Products Corporation. Its purpose was to market all the fish that Saskatchewan Fish Products handled.[12] By December 1945, both filleting plants were in full operation and the Fish Marketing Board in place.

By 1946, the government controlled three of six filleting plants engaged in processing fish in Saskatchewan. A third filleting plant was added at Meadow Lake, adding a mobile unit with a quick-freeze feature. The remaining plants in the North were operated as private companies.

SOLVING PROBLEMS

Early in 1946, controversy began surfacing within the fishing industry over the government's participation, and Phelps scrambled to defend its initiatives. In the provincial legislature in February, Phelps stated, "The fishing industry in western Canada is in a precarious position at present."[13] He indicated discussions at an upcoming conference for government and industry representatives would centre on the Saskatchewan government's fishing regulations. A number of problems were emerging. The scattered and isolated nature of operations made transportation the single largest cost. Geography and climate continued to create additional problems. Fishers were protesting low prices. In the spring of 1946, fishers near Buffalo Narrows had refused to sell their fish at the prices being offered by the private company in the area, two cents a pound for jackfish and five cents for whitefish, but road conditions were making it impossible for them to haul to other fish dealers.[14] There were also criticisms of the government's fish filleting program. A Moose Jaw resident made statements on a radio broadcast at a Regina station in March of 1946, saying that fishers were being compelled to process all fish through the government plants and that Canadian fish were being rejected at the border. In response to these statements, Phelps attempted to clarify the government's fish filleting program. Calling the remarks "deliberately calculated to mislead the people of Saskatchewan, detrimental to the fishing industry and malicious and untrue," the minister responded,

> Regulations for the classification of fish for processing purposes are established by the Dominion government and apply to all fish regardless of which plant they are processed in.... It is obvious that with three privately owned plants in operation, fishermen are not compelled to deliver all fish for processing to a government-owned plant.[15]

Phelps and the government would rely on a Royal Commission for solutions to these and other issues related to the industry, including conservation and the development of provincial fish resources. Phelps announced its establishment in June 1946,

> to study all phases of marketing fish products, including methods of obtaining a uniform high quality product. Also on the agenda of the study will be export and import regulations, trade agreements with the United States government, and freight, express and air rates. These latter items will be studied with a view to having them adjusted to throw a lighter burden on fishermen.[16]

As part of the study, the Department of Natural Resources proposed the investigation of "co-operative fishing." According to this rather unique scheme, the government proposed that boats built by the department be sold to groups of fishers. All members of the co-operative would share equally in expenses and surpluses. The commission would also examine ways to bring about reconciliation between game and commercial fishing regulations in an effort to resolve the long-standing tensions between commercial and game fishers. Phelps explained:

Joe Phelps at Lac la Ronge filleting plant in the summer of 1946. Permission granted by the Phelps family estate.

> There has been considerable friction on this question in the past. Complaints have been received that men operating under a commercial license have been taking all the game fish out of some of the lakes with their nets. Commercial fishermen have complained that any curtailment of their fishing privileges would constitute a serious threat to their economy.[17]

Public hearings by the Royal Commission were scheduled to begin on July 3, 1946, in Prince Albert, and involved twenty-four northern communities. Twenty-five public hearings were held, and the commission heard presentations from more than 250 people. Its two-hundred-page report, completed on February 22, 1947, made many wide-ranging recommendations.

As recommended by the Royal Commission, to explore ways to increase sales Phelps sent representatives to centres in the United States where Saskatchewan fish were being sold. He also appointed former Royal Commission member Angus H. MacDonald the assistant supervisor of fisheries for Saskatchewan. As well, he divided the province into five areas and invited advisory representatives of fish producers to meet with the directors of the Saskatchewan Fish Marketing Board.[18] To prevent fluctuations in the fish market, he advocated the establishment of a centralized interprovincial marketing body for the three Prairie provinces, but no evidence exists that such an agency was formed.

By November 1946, the government was taking steps to eliminate overfishing in northern lakes.[19] A trained fisheries biologist was hired to scientifically survey northern lakes to ensure they were not being overfished or overstocked. Guidelines for fishing limits were established based on scientific study, and fishing regulations were drafted to assign different opening and closing dates to different lakes to regulate the supply of fish. An attempt was made to make local councils, elected by resident trappers, responsible for controlling areas and catches. The councils worked under co-operatives composed of Indigenous, Métis, and white trappers where possible.[20]

The Saskatchewan Fish Marketing Board's payment system had created another problem. It gave fishers two payments: an initial payment when they delivered their fish, and a final one at the end of the season when administration costs had been paid. Many did not understand this two-payment process. The board's initial payment was the same for all lakes and was fixed for the season. Since private fish buyers set prices on a lake-to-lake and day-to-day basis, they often offered higher prices than the board did. Some, who were seemingly unaware that "A" lake fish could be caught and sold in the round while processing "B" lake fish involved extra expense, also thought that the board was unfair when it paid two different prices for whitefish. The "B" fish had to be inspected, filleted, wrapped, boxed, and placed in cold storage. Often, they were so badly infested that half the fish had to be discarded. Lastly, the process of candling fish was also difficult to do successfully because the cysts were often extremely hard to detect. Even when the fish were processed and filleted, some did not pass federal inspection,[21] and still others were rejected at the United States border.

In an attempt to stabilize the troubled industry, Phelps and the government set up bonded warehouses at the railheads: Flin Flon, Big River, and Prince Albert. All dealers had to send their fish to these warehouses so that exported fish could be graded and inspected. To ensure that government plants, warehouses, and freezing plants were economically viable, the government imposed a seventy-five-mile (120-kilometre) radius around its three filleting plants. All fish caught within this area had to pass through the government warehouses and be marketed through the Saskatchewan Fish Marketing Board. Independent operators objected strenuously to the rule, claiming they suffered unfair competition. Len Waite, the owner of Waite Fisheries Ltd., in Big River, expressed his extreme displeasure in a letter to Phelps. He noted, "the territory taken in by drawing a line 75 miles in radius around Beaver Lake, Lac la Ronge, and Meadow Lake actually cuts off a considerable portion of our operation and I may say a very important portion." He insisted that while the Fish Marketing Board would be unable to develop all the territory within that seventy-five-mile radius, "we...are prevented from entering any development within that specified territory." He also complained, "we are actually at the mercy of any overly zealous Fish Board employee and it is rather difficult for you to control the forays they are apt to make from time to time." Waite then concluded,

> The Fish Board is in the position of a favored competitor in the operation of their fish operation. They enjoy numerous privileges and it follows I, as a private operator, am working

> under a handicap.... To arbitrarily take in a territory which may fall in a 75 mile radius of one of your Plants must take in a lot of territory that you do not want or do not even require. You prevent, however, other operators from engaging.[22]

Phelps also believed that, during the transition period from a wartime to a peacetime economy, fishers should be protected by applying the provisions of the Agricultural Support Act, which the legislature had passed in 1944. However, this did not occur.[23] In the fall of 1947, he took yet another initiative to stabilize the fishing industry. To promote the marketing of fish products, he set up and experimented with small fish canning and smoking plants, but these did not prove to be very successful. The last step he took to improve the industry was to distribute 47,180,000 fish eggs and fry to more than fifty lakes during May and June 1948 through the DNR.[24]

While parasitic infestation was the most serious problem Phelps encountered in the fishery, other problems continued to persist. Since lakes were scattered and isolated and winter weather forbidding, transporting fish to the railheads continued to be difficult. Though some portages and roads were built, making all areas accessible by road was impossible.[25] For the most part, fishing took place in the winter, and "cat swings" (convoys of caterpillar tractors pulling sleds) transported most of the fish. At times, this method proved to be very treacherous. In the spring of 1946, conditions were particularly dangerous because the lakes and muskeg had not frozen sufficiently and heavy cracks developed in the ice. Seven caterpillars broke through the ice and two men were lost.[26] Summer fishing required roads, trucks, and strategically placed refrigeration units, so it was very limited. The Fish Marketing Board also used DNR airplanes to transport fish, but this was very costly.[27]

Phelps also had difficulty selecting and training suitable personnel. This resulted in conflicts within the department and the termination of employees. In his zeal to organize the fishing industry, along with the array of other ventures he was juggling, Phelps sometimes neglected to make others aware of his policies or had difficulty communicating policy effectively. This surfaced at the board, management, staff, and local levels.[28] Don Phelps, who was involved with transporting fish from the lakes to the warehouses, mentioned this lack of communication to his brother on at least two occasions. On February 10, 1946, he wrote, "I am convinced the field staff does not know what we are trying to do...you should draft a circular letter of the principals [*sic*] and objectives of the Board for them to carry as an explination [*sic*] to fishermen, it would protect them and educate them and the fishermen to quite and [*sic*] extent." On February 21, 1946, he again wrote, "I feel you should have a meeting with these fishermen before the season ends in order to give them the opportunity of getting firsthand information, none...understand what we are trying to do."[29]

Complicating matters further was the small catch of fish. Markets for Saskatchewan fish, which had increased greatly during the Second World War,[30] declined dramatically after the war had ended. In addition, fish prices decreased between 1944 and 1948. In fact, Douglas described the drop in fish prices as "catastrophic."[31] Because fish that were frozen when prices were low were being dumped, this reduced prices even more.[32]

The multitude of problems within the industry made it less than financially viable. Although the government had imposed a royalty and a checking fee of half a cent per pound on all exported pickerel and whitefish, and a cent per pound on exported trout, during the November 1944 legislative session, this tax could not begin to cover the expenses the Fish Marketing Board incurred.[33] In an unaudited report T. C. Douglas gave the legislature in February 1948, he noted that for the year ended March 31, 1947, the Fish Marketing Board's loss was $34,000, and for the period from April 1 to December 31, 1947, it was $65,000.[34] Phelps rose to argue that fish filleting plants "cannot be expected to pay cash dividends" and that it would be a mistake to expect them "to return substantial profits." He further maintained that the fishing industry should be considered "an investment" in the provincial economy, but opposition members apparently disagreed with Phelps's logic.[35]

Ultimately, the Saskatchewan Fish Marketing Board was unsuccessful. Finding qualified, trained personnel and developing good management programs proved very difficult. The speed with which Phelps had set up the board created misunderstandings and perhaps caused people to resent the project, Phelps, and the government.[36] Phelps's imposition of the seventy-five-mile radius around the government's three filleting plants, which compelled fishers to sell their fish to the board, infuriated many fishers. M. Bodner reported that some fishers told him they felt they were selling their fish to the board at the point of a gun.[37]

For the year ended March 31, 1947, the Fish Board recorded a loss of $34,505.45 after depreciation. In addition, it had received a grant of nearly $40,000 from the DNR. For that period, the Fish Board's loss was greater than that incurred by any other Crown corporation or agency.[38] In 1959, the government transferred the marketing and processing of fish, provisioning of supplies, and distribution of retail goods to co-operatives that had been established for that purpose.[39]

FORESTRY

Timber resources also required attention. By early 1945, Phelps had made plans to tap provincial timber resources as another component in the government's program of industrial development and bring the forest industry under public control.[40] Phelps was concerned that the big timber companies were, in his words, "fleecing the producers." Timber companies were also denuding the forests, and there was a grave need to put conservation measures in place in order to regulate the rate of depletion.

The forests were being depleted by a combination of forest fires and overcutting. In fact, the area depleted by fire exceeded that depleted by legitimate use, but overcutting was also a major problem. Forestry regulations had been lax. Timber berths were readily available, and with an increased demand for lumber fuelled by the war, over four hundred sawmills were operating in the province by 1944. The annual report of the DNR tabled in the legislature in February 1946 showed that the value of forest products marketed in the fiscal year 1943–1944 was $8,142,891, an increase of $3,194,161 over the previous year. Saw timber production was 169,544,208 feet board measure (fbm), more than double that of the last pre-war year.[41] This increased production, however, further depleted the province's timber reserves at a rate the government found alarming.

Conservation and the development of natural resources were critically important to the CCF plan for Saskatchewan.[42] Once again, the new government wasted little time in taking action. Under the Forest Act, four new regulations would take effect on October 16, 1944. These regulations increased the dues to be paid for timber cut on Crown land to bring them into line with those imposed in adjoining provinces. Timber cutting regulations were standardized for all timber berths. The government also created a sliding scale of royalties, based on the selling price of the lumber cut. Lastly, it sold permits only to established mill operators who conducted their own operations because Saskatchewan had too many sawmills for the amount of timber available.[43] On October 19, Phelps introduced an amendment to the Forest Act to change the diameter of the trees that could be cut by licencees who had purchased timber berths from the federal government prior to the transfer of the natural resources to the province. This amendment increased the diameter of white spruce trees that could be cut from ten inches (25 cm) measured eighteen inches (45 cm) from the ground to twelve inches (30 cm) measured 4.5 feet (137 cm) from the ground. This applied only to trees on Crown land.[44]

Phelps scheduled a meeting with provincial district forestry superintendents in August 1945 to discuss the spruce lumber cut.[45] The large numbers of veterans returning from the Second World War had created a residential housing shortage and this greatly increased the demand for timber products. The supply of mature white spruce had been heavily depleted by a combination of forest fires and heavy cutting over the previous ten years. Although the government had originally proposed a 50 per cent reduction in the annual cut in order to restore forest conditions, a compromise solution of a 25 per cent reduction was agreed upon.[46] This would ameliorate adverse forest conditions to some extent, and enable the industry to meet the demand for building materials for postwar housing projects.

ELIMINATING MIDDLE MEN

Early in Phelps's term as minister, he proposed that the Timber Board purchase timber products directly from producers, who would in turn deliver the products to central points for distribution and sale. In the old system, the government simply sold cutting rights on Crown lands. In its place, Phelps proposed that the government contract producers who would cut the timber, perform the processing operations, and turn the product over to the government for sale and distribution. In September 1944, Phelps had sent all sawmill owners and operators a questionnaire asking them if they favoured the establishment of such a board. On November 6, he announced that 91 per cent approved the plan. He suggested that the proposed board market 20 per cent of all lumber cut during the 1944–1945 season, through co-operative retail outlets or to farmers directly.[47] As was the case with other natural resources in northern Saskatchewan, Phelps's plan for development was complicated by federal regulations. He immediately ran directly into a wall of Dominion government regulations. In February 1945, A. H. Williamson, timber controller for the Department of Munitions and Supply, and C. D. Howe, Minister of Munitions and Supply, voiced the federal government's very strong opposition to this marketing plan. Howe indicated that it would add to the difficulty of obtaining adequate lumber supplies for distribution in Saskatchewan. They urged Saskatchewan to postpone implementing its proposal until after the war, and Phelps reluctantly shelved it, but only temporarily.[48] After several months and a number of discussions, Howe reluctantly agreed that if the Saskatchewan government established a marketing board, the Dominion would not interfere.[49] He advised that the matter be deferred until the price obtainable in export markets was no greater than the market price in Canada and there was no longer a need for control in the interest of the consumer. He acknowledged that while formation of a board was not in violation of timber regulations, it could result in shipments of lumber to Saskatchewan from other provinces being drastically reduced.

In September 1945, Phelps announced the formation of the Saskatchewan Timber Board, another new Crown corporation, to be headquartered in Prince Albert.[50] For the first time, the Saskatchewan government would not be buying lumber from private operators; rather, they would market their own timber directly through the board. Since its purpose was to "carry on the business of manufacturing, purchasing, and marketing of timber products on behalf of the Province of Saskatchewan," Phelps now had his desired marketing board.[51]

Confident in the operation of the new board and that problems with the Dominion government had been resolved, in September 1945 Phelps announced, "All railway ties produced from Saskatchewan forests in the future will be contracted for, sold, and distributed by the Timber Board." Previously, producers purchased cutting rights on Crown lands from the provincial government and sold directly to the railways. "Under the new policy, the people of Saskatchewan will save a large sum in brokerage and Commissions, by eliminating the middle man," confirmed Phelps. "Purchasers should find it more convenient to deal with the Timber Board, than a number of private concerns." Phelps also advised that over 80 per cent of lumbermen in the province were in favour of the establishment of the board. Formation of the board would eliminate middlemen, who, according to many timber producers, had been making all of the profits. "Our attempt is to avoid this. The money will go to the people as a whole."[52]

The need for forest products continued unabated as post-Second World War construction carried on. In November 1945, representatives of the pulpwood industry from across Canada met for discussions. Statements issued after a meeting between Premier J. B. McNair of New Brunswick, J. S. McDiarmid, Manitoba's Minister of Mines and Natural Resources, and Joe Phelps expressed concern about the shortage of people to work in the woods. Their common communiqué appealed to farmers, loggers, and war veterans to take jobs in the forests. Phelps described the situation as urgent, and said, "There will be more jobs available and more opportunities for woods workers this winter than ever before."[53]

FOREST CONSERVATION

Stewardship of the forest was something Phelps took very seriously, releasing figures showing that 24,137 square miles (or 43.88 per cent) of Saskatchewan's 63,000 square miles of forest area had been destroyed by fire between 1913 and 1945.[54] In the fall of 1945, he announced the formation of a Royal Commission to inquire into the condition of the forests in Saskatchewan, and to recommend a policy of management and conservation of forest resources. Phelps explained:

> The forestry depletion in Saskatchewan is of sufficient seriousness to warrant a full-scale inquiry. These resources are the property of the people. The present government does not propose to see them ruthlessly exploited without concern for future generations. We must inaugurate a progressive, planned forest management policy that will build up Saskatchewan forests.[55]

The Royal Commission on Forestry began its work on October 29, 1945, and, quickly realizing "the seriousness and urgency of the fire situation," decided to inform the government of its views before the 1946 forest fire season began.[56] The first interim report advocated that the government train men immediately to make up a permanent firefighting staff and that they be assured of a reasonable period of employment. It stressed that emphasis be placed on the prevention of fires rather than on their detection and suppression. It also proposed obtaining the assistance of the RCMP "to combat lawlessness and enforce the regulations." Lastly, it suggested that the legislation be revised to provide for more severe penalties for breaches of the law related to "the destruction or endangering of the forest by fire."[57]

Heeding the Royal Commission's recommendations, Phelps took a number of fire protection initiatives soon after the first interim report was released. The DNR's plans for forest fire prevention and suppression included "standby crews at strategic points" and forming "local settlers' fire detection and suppression committees wherever possible."[58] Educational and publicity measures to acquaint the public with forest problems were stressed. Since carelessness was the main cause of fires, Phelps tried to secure the public's co-operation by conducting publicity campaigns, using brochures, radio broadcasts, essay contests, and posters. He also secured the RCMP's help in enforcing fire regulations and introduced an amendment to the Prairie and Forest Fires Act to increase the maximum fine for causing forest fires, including fines for a first offence of arson rising from $200 to $1,000, and providing a penalty for a second offence of imprisonment up to one year, in keeping with the Royal Commission's recommendations.[59] The final report of the Royal Commission on Forestry was made public in the spring of 1947. The *Leader-Post*'s May 22, 1947, editorial commended Phelps and the government for "this constructive attitude" in implementing many of the recommendations put forward in the interim reports. The editorial also pointed out there had been massive timber losses due to fire: "It is clear that the greatest menace to the province's timbered areas is not over-cutting, but fire.... 278,172 acres of merchantable timber were burned over in one year, with a fire loss of $460,532. In the same year the cost of suppression was almost as much...$414,969."[60] The final report elaborated on the need for fire suppression, and detecting and suppressing forest fires became one of the government's most urgent priorities.

In July 1947, the *Leader-Post* reported that fifty-five fires in Saskatchewan's forests had burned over fourteen thousand acres. Seven hundred acres of merchantable timber and eight thousand acres of young forest growth had also been destroyed. Other areas also experienced the wrath of fire, as it swept over 5,300 acres of grasslands, swamps, and muskegs, which were not forested but were of value as shelter for game and fur animals, and for water conservation. Phelps outlined the government's position on fire suppression, stating, "Most of the fires had their origin in neglected camp fires, careless smokers and land clearing operations, and while I am prepared to impose stiff penalties for fire law infractions, I prefer to prevent the occurrence of fires by educational programs and other cooperative measures."[61] Forest fire suppression became a focus for further planning in the months ahead. To increase vigilance so that fires could be readily spotted, Phelps set up an interlocking system of lookout towers, developed a radio-telephone network, and established daily airplane patrols. He also constructed roads into certain forest areas to facilitate fire detection and firefighting.

Forest fires continued to be a problem during Phelps's tenure, but their numbers decreased. While the long-term annual average was 235 fires per year, there were only eighty-seven in 1944; ninety-eight in 1945; and ninety-seven in 1946.[62]

FOREST MANAGEMENT

In the months that followed, the findings of the Royal Commission were used to launch a number of innovative forestry programs. Authorized timber production was curtailed, fire protection and suppression activities were emphasized, and greater use was made of airplanes and radio in combating fires and carrying on administrative work. The Royal Commission's second interim report had made various recommendations on forest management, but the main one advocated curtailing the annual timber cut to one-twentieth of the merchantable timber available in any area.[63] Because of the great demand for lumber at this time, Phelps could not curtail timber production that drastically, but he did decrease it: spruce production fell from 169 million fbm during the war to 144 million fbm in 1946, to slightly under 112 million fbm in 1947 (of which white spruce fell to 95,000 from 130 million the preceding year and 160 million fbm during wartime).[64]

In response to the Royal Commission reports, Phelps changed the government's forestry policy in another significant way. Up to this time, the government had sold timber on Crown land "on the stump," that is as standing trees. People bought this standing timber in large timber limits, often hundreds of square kilometres in size. Since the CCF maintained that the people of Saskatchewan owned the forests, it developed a new policy: henceforth, the Timber Board would let contracts by tender to operators to cut the trees and saw them into lumber. They would then turn the lumber over to the board for marketing at the railhead.

To further improve forest management practices, Phelps approached the private operators who had obtained timber berths from the federal government under the old policy. He gave them three choices: conform to the new policy of cutting by contract, curtail cutting to one-twentieth of merchantable timber, or surrender their timber berths to the government.[65] The government brought timber berths back under public control if it purchased them or if the owner relinquished them under the terms of his contract. By 1948, only three private operators held timber berths.[66] Phelps also hired additional trained forestry personnel. He discouraged waste of the poplar, a very common tree in the North, by trying to discover possible uses for it. He encouraged better utilization of trees at the sawmill to eliminate waste, and he sought new uses for forest products. To further increase efficiency and improve administration, he transferred the headquarters of the Forestry Branch from Regina to Prince Albert so it would be closer to the centre of its operations.[67] Lastly, on July 1, 1946, he opened the Saskatchewan Forestry School in Prince Albert to offer training in all matters pertaining to the administration of forest areas,[68] the first school of its kind in the Prairie provinces. Although greatly condensed and modified, the course covered a large number of the subjects listed in a modern university course in forest science. Phelps had even hoped to set up some forest farms in Saskatchewan, but he gave up the idea after making many inquiries and receiving numerous negative responses.

In January 1947, he established the Forestry Management Branch, which drew up a twenty-year plan. The *Regina Commonwealth* described this plan as follows: "The principle upon which the cutting policy is based is that the amount of good timber cut in any year should not exceed the amount which is replaced the same year by natural growth. In this way a sustained yield will be maintained."[69] Before the Timber Board could award contracts, it also had to know what forest resources were available. Hence, by the winter of 1946, Phelps had set up a forest inventory to determine the location, extent, and value of the province's forest resources, another of the Royal Commission's recommendations.[70] Crews used aerial photographs and ground surveys to compile this inventory. In another effort to preserve the forests, men removed deformed, diseased, and broken trees and thinned out areas to ensure the remaining trees could develop "under the best possible conditions." Others, called "cruisers," marked trees; operators could cut and remove only these trees.[71] This process would give immature trees a chance to grow and develop. Many areas had been so depleted that the government planted new trees to ensure the perpetuation of the forests there. The DNR transplanted 400,000 trees from tree nurseries in 1946 and 265,000 in 1947.[72]

In forestry, too, financial returns were a problem. While the forest industry was financially more successful than the fishing industry, it still struggled. To March 31, 1946, the Timber Board's net loss was $3,607, but the fiscal year ending March 31, 1947, showed profits after depreciation of $26,993.[73] Perhaps more importantly than profitability, Phelps had taken critical steps in preserving and managing provincial forestry resources for the future.

STEWARDSHIP OF THE LAND

Allocation of Crown lands was yet another responsibility falling within the Natural Resources department. Approximately ten million acres of provincial land were under its jurisdiction. With large numbers of returning veterans, Phelps turned his attention to land allocation, announcing in December 1945 that Crown lands would only be sold to Second World War veterans, who would then be given the option to purchase the land after ten years of leasing from the government.[74] The announcement was part of the Land Branch Rehabilitation Program designed to help settle returning veterans on suitable farmlands. At the same time, it was decided that Crown lands, whether suitable for grazing or grain production, would be disposed of only by lease. Tenure for all leases was set at thirty-three years, with right of renewal and with privileges granted under the lease to endure to heirs of the lessee.

During 1945, field staff of the branch inspected and appraised approximately five thousand quarter sections of provincial lands, and evaluated these parcels for settlement by Canadian veterans. A schedule of rentals based on the value of land for grazing was determined by the quality and quantity of the grass, and the prices producers were receiving for livestock. The selling price after the initial ten-year lease period was to be determined by the productive performance of the land, correlated with the performance of similar land in the district.

Phelps was ardent about good stewardship of the land. Land policy developed under his direction was designed to ensure lands would be used for the purpose to which they were ecologically and economically best suited. During 1947, field agricultural representatives from the department continued land classification assessments. Renewals and new leases were withheld pending the final reports.[75] Of the ten million acres of provincial lands involved, approximately seven million were found to be only suitable for grazing purposes. The survey also disclosed a need for intensive conservation programs with respect to both the physical and economic use of land resources. Following the reports, an amendment was made to the Provincial Lands Act to transfer administration of Crown lands only suitable for agricultural purposes from the DNR to the Department of Agriculture.

In April 1946, the department investigated the idea of establishing a provincial air photo library to centralize and distribute air photo prints.[76] By 1947, the Surveys Branch of the department had established this library so that all departments could efficiently obtain information on lands and resources. It also purchased air photographic equipment in order to undertake aerial photographic surveys, making Saskatchewan one of the few Canadian provinces equipped to do this work.

Although the environmental movement had not yet taken hold in Saskatchewan, years of working the land had left Phelps with a strong affinity for the environment. On one occasion, after viewing what he believed was an unacceptable clear-cut in northern Saskatchewan, Phelps sent Louisiana Pacific out of the province. The environmental effects of the coal mining industry also disturbed him. In an interview with Berry Richards in the early eighties, he stated, "I was struck with the very physical thing of the coal business—the desecration of the land and how they left it afterwards. That really worried me." Phelps did not take steps to develop the province's coal resources, which at the time were considered somewhat inferior. Later, the addition of by-products would increase their value. The department's research indicated that leaving the country level after mining the coal resources would cost a great deal more, and consequently it did not make economic sense.[77] It would be several years until measures would be put in place to raise the environmental standards in the coal mining industry.

Speaking to the People's Forum at Regina City Hall on January 28, 1947, Phelps's early environmentalism was evident. Phelps said in his introduction that

> Heritage is nothing more or less than the people's share as citizens of Canada, in the natural economy of the country. Canada could only grow as a nation in proportion to the expansion of its fundamental resources. Soil, water, minerals, vegetation and animal life are the basis of life, and the future depends on them.... There should be an immediate stock taking of these resources to see how they are being developed for the people and what is being done to protect the people's interest in them.... One of the tasks facing Canadians is that of adjusting human population to the land. There could be a suicide of civilization, without the atom bomb, if people do not conserve soil and water.[78]

His environmental consciousness surfaced again in the early 1950s, while he was serving on the Royal Commission on Agriculture and Rural Life. Phelps would once again stress the importance of conservation and appropriate land use in his fight to preserve the family farm.

CHAPTER 11

NATURE'S STOREHOUSE

Mineral resource development in northern Saskatchewan was yet another area where Phelps applied his energy, chartering an aircraft early in his term as minister to become acquainted, in his words, "with the various stopping places in the north." The uranium mining camp in the Far North at Beaverlodge was one of the stopping places. Phelps asked his wife Lena, who had accompanied him on the trip, to enter the mine with him, but rules specified that women were not to go underground. Not one to blindly conform to procedures, especially those he thought unreasonable, Phelps insisted Lena be allowed to enter the mine, noting later, "The head man was there and he wiped the regulation aside, saying if she wants to go, she should go…and she went."[1] Phelps described taking his wife down the partially dug mine shaft at the mining camp later in two separate interviews. In 1976, he recalled, "My first wife was the first woman that ever went down the uranium mine. We got a special permit to go down."[2] Phelps's daughter, Ella, who had travelled north with her parents, also recalled the trip.[3]

Saskatchewan's uranium deposits were first discovered and developed on the north shore of Lake Athabasca, where uranium mineralization was first noticed by prospectors searching for gold and copper in the early 1930s. When uranium's significance became apparent in 1944, extensive prospecting in the Beaverlodge area resulted in the establishment of the Uranium City mining camp. In the 1950s, sixteen ore bodies and three separate milling facilities were developed in the Uranium City area.[4]

The splitting of the uranium atom in 1939 and the potential for creating a nuclear bomb had transformed the industry, and so, "at the dawn of the atomic age, politics entered the uranium business."[5] In 1943, the federal government banned all private uranium prospecting in its territories and asked the provinces to do the same. On January 28, 1944, Eldorado Mining and Refining became a federal company. C. D. Howe secured the incorporation under the War Measures Act.[6] Robert Bothwell, author of *Eldorado: Canada's National Uranium Company*, noted, "Socialist Regina had no objections to Eldorado's prospecting parties from 1944 to 1948."[7] He also writes, "the development of Beaverlodge took time. It was not until 1949 that Eldorado felt able to risk a large expenditure of money at the future mine site."[8] Construction of the town of Uranium City followed and, "by the winter of 1952–53, local initiative with a minimum of public assistance had created Uranium City."[9] The mining activity at the camp impressed Phelps. "It seemed to me to be a tremendous undertaking, and I just stood back with my mouth open and looked at it." Later, he commented,

> Strangely enough, it was one of the things I pushed to the back of the book because we had so many things to do, and minerals seemed a little bit apart from the people in my thinking, partly because I was a prairie person, for one thing. The minerals were something I felt....well it was like nature's storehouse and nothing would happen if it was left there a little while longer. The forest, the fish and the game were all in trouble. This impressed me more. I saw the urgency to do something in those areas first, something to correct the problems, and some positive programs. "First things first," was the way I approached it, and the fur, fish and timber were already being harvested and were howling for activity.[10]

Given the financial position of the government, there were considerable fiscal restrictions associated with mineral development. Phelps recalled discussions with Cabinet in which it advised that the government should be cautious. In Phelps words, "The boys thought we should walk pretty easy there." He elaborated in a later interview:

> I started early and warned them and informed them. If we were going to do a job in the development of resources in this province it took money and it took real dollars—and lots of them. We couldn't be the poor country cousin forever. You couldn't do it with nickels and dimes. In those days, it was a different kind of arithmetic and a different kind of thinking. The thinking was in hundreds or in thousands sometimes, not hundreds of thousands, or millions like today.[11]

Looking back, Phelps reflected,

> My thinking was pure and simple, straight forward. A partnership deal at that time—a straight partnership. I didn't want the government to go in and start to develop a mine. That wasn't my thinking because we were beginners, beginners in the industry, beginners all the way around in that particular field. It was so new and of course at that time the public including ourselves didn't as well understand the value of minerals. Looking back, we didn't realize the degree of importance minerals really are to any country.[12]

EXPLORATION AND DISCOVERY

Mineral resources were abundant in Saskatchewan, but there had been minimal documentation of the specific locations or the size of the deposits. With typical enthusiasm, Phelps embarked on an exploration and discovery program, beginning in the summer of 1945. He knew from the existing government records that deposits of copper, nickel, platinum, china clay, zinc, lead, chromium, gold, pitchblende, magnetite, chromite, and glass sands existed. Knowing Saskatchewan was lagging behind in the development of mineral resources, Phelps was aware that geological mapping would be essential. In fact, he pledged, "to obtain detailed information on the mineral deposits next year every known mineral occurrence in northern Saskatchewan, will be examined and sampled by the geologists of my department."[13] Geologists spread out over the province.

With geophysical mapping underway, the focus turned to development of provincial mineral resources. Prospecting was also a weak link, limited primarily by the short season and the lack of transportation. To compensate for these obstacles, Phelps arranged the innovative Prospector's Assistance Plan, in which prospectors, accompanied by a government geologist, were transported north, free of charge, in government aircraft. Each month, food and supplies were brought in and mineral samples taken out for analysis. If discoveries were made, the government would become involved in the extraction of the resources. Phelps recalled that Vern Hogg advised that he proceed carefully: "He didn't want me to get in trouble, and have something go haywire afterwards and backfire. It was [a] tricky thing he said, you have to be careful."[14] Prospecting and development work continued, albeit cautiously, in several areas throughout the years that followed, and mineral production continued to increase.

MINERAL TAXATION

In the days before the Crown began reserving minerals from land grants, a number of Saskatchewan's early settlers had obtained title to the minerals on their land along with the surface rights on their homestead from the Dominion. At the time, land titles were acquired solely for agricultural purposes and the mineral rights were not a consideration. Phelps, along with many in the CCF administration who were determined to obtain a greater return from the exploitation of the province's mineral wealth, decided that those persons who had, through this oversight, received mineral rights, "should now be taxed for the privilege of owning them."[15] The Mineral Taxation Act of November 1944 imposed two kinds of taxes. First, it imposed a 3-per-cent-per-acre tax on the 30 per cent of mineral rights that were privately owned, to be paid annually to the DNR.[16] The act provided that if the taxes and arrears on mineral rights remained unpaid six months after they were due, the owners would forfeit their mineral rights to the Crown after due notice had been given. The second tax, called a holding tax, levied up to ten mills on the dollar of the estimated value of mineral deposits in a "proven area" where minerals were being extracted. Both taxes mainly targeted the three largest holders of mineral rights in Saskatchewan: the HBC, the CPR, and the CNR,[17] which had acquired much of the freehold (privately owned mineral rights) during the early settlement period.

Under the act, the HBC was required to pay a mineral tax to the provincial government in order to retain the mineral rights on the thousands of acres of land it held. In January 1946, Phelps announced that the government would not attempt to collect the taxes. Instead, the mineral rights on several thousands of acres of land in Saskatchewan held by the company would revert to the province through the normal operation of the act. Saskatchewan would thus regain control of a large percentage of its mineral rights, which, he remarked, "should never have been alienated from the Crown in the first place."[18]

Although the confrontation with the HBC over the Mineral Taxation Act was resolved amicably, the CPR was not as conciliatory. In the fall of 1945, the CPR had challenged the Mineral Taxation Act's constitutionality, claiming the tax was *ultra vires*,[19] and petitioned the federal government to disallow it, which it declined to do. The CPR thereupon refused to pay the tax for more than two years and initiated legal action against the Saskatchewan government. When an amendment was proposed in 1947 that would require the CPR to pay standard royalties on gravel, the Mineral Taxation Act became a contentious issue once again. The CPR argued that their twenty-one-year gravel lease, about to expire, should be renewed on the same terms as previously.[20]

The matter was discussed in the provincial legislature in mid-February 1947, when A. T. Procter, Liberal MLA for Moosomin, pressed the minister for an explanation for this change. Phelps indicated that a matter of principle was involved. The government's legal advisors had given assurances that the province was within its jurisdiction to enact such legislation, and that, as matters stood, some companies or individuals were in a preferred position. The government's position was that there should be "no preferred class."[21]

The CPR obtained an interim injunction to restrain Phelps from taking measures leading to forfeiture of mineral rights on its lands, alleging the act was unconstitutional,[22] but in the end, after several lengthy court battles that eventually reached the Supreme Court, the mineral tax was upheld. The Supreme Court eventually ruled against the CPR in 1952.[23]

By December of 1947, Phelps announced that total mineral production for 1947–1948 was expected to total $32 million and that technical staff and a newly appointed director of mineral resources were doing preparatory work for a concerted effort to discover new mineral deposits in northern Saskatchewan. He also stated that mineral resources accounted for approximately 45 per cent of the revenue of the department in 1946–1947, totalling $1,093,946, up from $54,000 in 1931 and $209,121 in 1944–1945.[24]

In the 1950s, as Phelps had intended, the Mineral Taxation Act generated substantial revenues for the government with oil, gas, and potash discoveries. Hogg recalled him saying in 1946 that it would not be long until drill rigs were running all over southern Saskatchewan. "How prophetic!" he noted. "By 1955, on a drive from Weyburn to Estevan and on to the Manitoba border at night, one was never out of site of the twinkling of the drill rig lights."[25]

MINING ROYALTIES

The department's first priority was increasing provincial revenues. With this in mind, Phelps had also turned his attention to the matter of increasing mining royalties. Phelps revealed that in 1943, 81 per cent of the coal mined in Saskatchewan had yielded no royalty to the province, but to the CPR, the HBC, and private landowners.[26] Phelps firmly believed that the private companies developing Saskatchewan's mineral resources should pay royalties to contribute to the provincial economy. On June 5, 1945, the Cabinet amended the quartz mining regulations to establish a new royalty schedule.[27] Phelps noted that this schedule would boost mining royalties by about $600,000 annually. Under this new royalty agreement, Hudson Bay Mining and Smelting Co. paid $180,000 to cover the first three months of 1945, almost as much as the company had paid the entire previous year. Phelps estimated that the company would pay about $750,000 in total for the year.[28]

On May 29, 1945, *Leader-Post* headlines read, "$600,000 boost from royalties" from a change in the quartz mining regulations.[29] The new royalty schedule, put in place, according to Phelps, to obtain compensation for the people of the province for depletion of the natural resources, was part of the government's overall resource policy. Royalty revenues, and similarly revenues from developing the abundance of natural resources in the North, would be used to further development and for much needed social programs. Phelps reported that the new schedule was calculated on a sliding scale to conform to fluctuations in the mining industry, and therefore made allowances for adverse conditions or growth within the industry.

Hudson Bay Mining and Smelting Co. was virtually the only quartz mining company operating in Saskatchewan at the time, actively mining quartz and other minerals in the Flin Flon district on both the Saskatchewan and Manitoba side of the border. Phelps had had several amicable discussions with representatives from the company before adjusting the royalty rates. The company, whose operation had grown considerably from when it started in 1931, acknowledged it had long since passed the development stage of its operation, and hence the increase was likely justified. To encourage new private mining activity, Phelps would leave the old royalty schedule in place for the first three years new mining companies were operating in the province.[30]

In 1944–1945, Hudson Bay Mining and Smelting was involved in the mining of gold, silver, copper, and zinc, plus some cadmium, selenium, and tellurium, with a combined value of $18,225,138. Approximately two thousand people were employed in the company's mines.[31] It continued to expand mining operations, and, by December 1946, placed an order for a twenty-one-thousand-horsepower hydroelectric generating unit to be installed at Island Falls at the Churchill River power plant. Phelps publicly lauded the expansion, suggesting it indicated there was an increasing interest in development in Saskatchewan, and that he believed the increased power capacity would lead to increased operations and, in turn, higher royalties.

Extensive gold exploration was underway in northern Saskatchewan in the spring of 1946, along with diamond drilling and general prospecting and the construction of a mill for the recovery of arsenic and precious metals.[32] By March 1946, there was so much exploration activity in northern Saskatchewan that Phelps appointed a resident geologist to assist prospectors, and laid plans for roads to serve several mining developments in the North. In 1947, a highway was completed between Prince Albert and La Ronge.

Salt beds were also proving lucrative. The Natural Resources minister proudly informed Saskatchewan residents in July 1946 that one of the thickest salt beds in Canada had been discovered by the Vera Oil Field Company west of Unity. This 120-metre-thick salt deposit, encountered at a depth of some one thousand metres, was the first salt discovery at a depth that was conducive to commercial production.[33] Previous discoveries, located two kilometres below the surface, had made economic production impossible.

The establishment of a salt industry was ensured in 1947 with the completion of an agreement with the Prairie Salt Company. An extremely important discovery was made when analysis of a rich stratum of salt, approximately three metres thick, revealed it was 21.5 per cent potassium oxide. Phelps's home constituency of Saltcoats was home to one of the largest potash deposits in the world. The potash discovery represented the only source of this valuable fertilizer material to be found in Canada, and he was aware that, if it could be recovered at low cost, it would be very important to both the province and the country. But Phelps did not pursue development of the potash industry, feeling the concept of mining potash was foreign to almost everyone at the time and noting that "people had to recondition their thinking to get potash on the list."[34] The government decided, after more protracted study, that potash would be developed privately, but it would become an important source of provincial revenues in the future. In the 1970s, the NDP government, under the leadership of Allan Blakeney, would take steps to nationalize the industry.

One of the most successful government enterprises Phelps put in place during the CCF's first term in office involved another type of salt that was ready for development: sodium sulphate. Vern Hogg worked closely with Phelps on this project and related the story:

> A group of investors had a lease on Chaplin Lake, fifty miles west of Moose Jaw, and were in default due to non-performance. Mr. Phelps and I met with the group on two occasions, and the group couldn't come to an agreement to commence work on the lease. As a result, Mr. Phelps advised them the Department would proceed to cancel their lease. When the lease became available a few months later, Saskatchewan Minerals, the Crown Corporation, which also operated the brick plant at Estevan, was issued the lease on the Chaplin Sodium Sulphate deposit. The plant was in production two years later, and had made a significant profit in the first full year of operation.[35]

One of the largest sodium sulphate deposits in the province, located at Ingebright Lake about fifty kilometres north of Maple Creek, held by lease by prominent Alberta lawyer Eric Harvey, also became a profitable part of the Saskatchewan Mineral Corporation. In 1944, three American companies mined most of Saskatchewan's sodium sulphate. When one of these companies, Natural Sodium Products Ltd., applied to lease the Chaplin Lake deposits in 1946, Phelps refused the application and undertook to have the government develop the deposits itself. In the summer of 1946, Phelps met with Eric Harvey and negotiated purchase of the lease. On July 9, 1948, the Chaplin plant, the largest of its kind in the world, officially opened. The publicly owned sodium sulphate plant had the capacity to produce 150,000 tons of sulphate a year. It cost more than $1 million and was expected to add between $1 million and $2 million to the provincial Treasury per year. By the early 1950s, the government had built a profitable processing plant. In 1954 and 1981, Saskatchewan Mineral Corporation acquired the existing sodium sulphate plants at Bishopric and Synbouts, respectively, but closed both plants permanently in 1984. In 1988, Saskatchewan Minerals was privatized and is currently a division of Goldcorp Inc.[36]

OIL AND GAS

The CCF government was also interested in oil and natural gas development. In the early 1940s, the petroleum industry was still in its infancy. Heavy oil and natural gas had been discovered in the Lloydminster area in 1934 and near Kamsack in 1937. During the Second World War, the Liberal Minister of Natural Resources, W. F. Kerr, had signed several exploration agreements with Imperial Oil and its two subsidiaries. Under these agreements, the government issued an exploration permit to the company, setting out conditions including minimum work requirements. If the company discovered oil, it would apply for a production lease, and the government could designate a portion of the acreage it leased to the company as a Crown reserve. Since Imperial Oil had exclusive rights over a large area of Crown lands in southern Saskatchewan, it would have enjoyed an advantage over its competitors had oil been discovered, but it was not. By the end of 1943, Imperial Oil and its subsidiaries had invested over $1 million in its search for oil in southern Saskatchewan and had drilled many wildcat wells, but all were dusters.[37]

The search for gas and oil continued after the CCF came to power, but the rate of oil discovery was disappointing. New discoveries in the Unity Valley field increased the province's gas reserve.[38] Nine additional producers operating in the Lloydminster field, giving the province a crude oil production of 37,188 barrels in 1945, augmented Saskatchewan's first commercial oil well, discovered in 1944.[39] According to Vern Hogg, when Phelps was appointed minister, there was little interest in oil and gas exploration in Saskatchewan. Imperial Oil was carrying out seismic surveys and drilling test wells under an agreement made with the previous Liberal government. It was exploring on a large area of about fifty thousand square kilometres of Crown mineral lands extending from the Saskatchewan–United States border north along an irregular line to Davidson and up to the South Saskatchewan River. Hogg recalled,

> The Imperial Oil reservation agreement terminated at the end of 1945 and they did not take any leases. They applied for a new area to the north to Saskatoon/Kindersley and east to Kamsack. Mr. Phelps wanted minor changes in the agreement but the company would not agree and they announced they would withdraw from Saskatchewan.[40]

After the CCF came to power, Phelps made a number of regulatory changes that became effective for the most part after 1945.[41] Phelps also negotiated a new agreement with Imperial Oil. It was similar to the one Kerr had reached with the company earlier, except that it contained a new section concerning production leases. If oil was discovered, "a three-man board would be established to select the lands to be unitized for production," and Imperial Oil could then lease all these lands. While the agreement did not specify annual rentals per acre, it required expenditures of $100,000 per year. The agreement's final clause allowed "the government to terminate the arrangement any time within thirty days of the calendar year end and provide for compensation to the Company for monetary losses."[42]

During the next two years (1945–1946), Imperial Oil and one of its subsidiaries, Norcanols Oil, continued their exploration program. They drilled wells at Swift Current, Morse, Pennant, White Fox, Davidson, and other areas and found small amounts of natural gas at Pennant and Swift Current. Then, in 1947, Imperial Oil announced it intended to leave the province and concentrate all of its exploration efforts in Alberta.

Was this decision the result of the election of a CCF government hostile to business and, more specifically, to the oil industry? Brian Banks argues that it was not. He points out that Imperial Oil's "boycott" of Saskatchewan "did not begin until after it had drilled fifteen wells, acquired geological data on footage of 95,376 feet and obtained considerable geophysical information." He insists "the company's lack of success was an important factor in the decision to concentrate its efforts in Alberta after 1946."[43] Banks asserts,

> Following the lead of Imperial Oil which moved its drilling rigs to Alberta in 1946, multinational oil companies did not invest to any degree in Saskatchewan. Although much has been made of Imperial's boycott of Saskatchewan, considerably [*sic*] exploratory work was completed after the advent of the CCF, Imperial Oil's lack of success in discovering commercial quantities of oil or natural gas, after an investment of more than $3 million, became an important determining factor in convincing oil companies that Saskatchewan was a high risk environment. The Leduc discovery in 1947 also made Alberta very attractive to oil companies. However, in the two success areas, Lloydminister and Unity, moderate expansion occurred. Saskatchewan had 152 oil and natural gas wells in 1948 compared to only twenty natural gas wells in 1944.[44]

Imperial Oil's explanation that it "was quitting" the province because "conditions are not conducive to oil development in Saskatchewan" is questionable.[45] Were conditions "not conducive" because of the government's policy, or were the chances of success just too uncertain?

The government did not itself undertake exploration or development in the petroleum industry at this time, but its long-term intentions remained unclear. In November 1946, the government's *Statement of Policy on Oil, Gas, and Mineral Development* declared, "The policy of this Government is to develop the resources of this province on a planned basis and a basis of public ownership where possible."[46] However, the policy also stated,

> At the same time, we must recognize that the province is not equipped to enter all possible fields of development immediately and when it, therefore, becomes obvious that new private capital can develop any particular project within the best framework of the best plans for either the Province, the Prairies, or the Nation as a whole, then such capital should be given an opportunity to operate in the province, provided it makes an adequate contribution to the Provincial economy by way of royalties or otherwise.[47]

While Phelps had to face the reality that the government would have to permit private companies to explore for and develop Saskatchewan's mineral resources, he did not accept this fact readily. In 1944, he had hinted at "the possibility of the government taking over the Imperial Oil refinery at Regina," and later, in the foreword to a 1945 pamphlet on natural resources, he stated, "Eventually, it is hoped to establish complete social ownership and management of key industries in the development of our resources."[48] He made this observation again in 1946; at the annual provincial CCF convention, he stated that the government was permitting private enterprise to develop oil reserves because it was not ready to take that step itself, but that it "will move at the appropriate time."[49] In 1948, he stated, "If a gas pipeline is built to carry natural gas from an Alberta field to Saskatchewan points, it should be a public utility or at least a public carrier." He further indicated that the government was interested in oil development and had "some intention of going into the oil development field." He added, "All exploration should not be left to private companies and the government should 'give a hand and lend impetus' to research [*sic*] for oil."[50] While it is likely that these statements might create uncertainty for the private oil companies, it seems more probable that they left for greener pastures.

In the summer of 1946, exploration permits that reduced the red tape of special reservation agreements were put into law by order-in-council. In addition to the normal royalty on production, the permits included an "additional benefit" that would accrue to the government.

This additional benefit amounted to millions of dollars, according to Hogg. The first "Crown Reserves" were put into place in 1946 for companies applying for oil exploration permits. A rubber stamp in the shape of a British crown was used to designate the sections and quarter sections that would be held back as Crown reserve parcels on permit maps issued to the oil companies. Approximately 15–25 per cent of the Crown sections were randomly designated Crown reserve parcels. If a discovery were made, the value would be increased when the land was put up for competitive bidding on a Crown land sale. In 1953, a separate small division was set up to administer the Crown reserve parcels.[51]

After the discovery of oil near Cabri in 1946, it was determined that oil development was best left to private enterprise and a lease plan was prepared that reserved a share of the resources (15 per cent of the mineral rights) over and above the standard oil royalty.[52] The decision was made to permit private enterprise to develop oil reserves, gleaning revenue through taxation rather than entering the oil business. Heated debate over the development of oil reserves ensued. Phelps favoured the government entering the field of oil exploration and the possibility of government-owned oil refineries. However, the case for public enterprise was tenuous at best, as the cost of exploration and exploitation was high and the government risked costs exceeding profits. Douglas had argued earlier that both oil royalties and land rental regulations could be established to "capture a fair share of the resources for the people," and that the province could not afford an extensive exploration program. The planning board and natural resources officials argued against public development, advocating a combination of lease and royalty policies, or possibly co-operative development, but many CCF members continued to favour public enterprise.

At the CCF annual provincial convention held in Moose Jaw in the summer of 1946, Phelps became embroiled in an argument about oil reserve development with P. G. Makaroff, CCF provincial council member. Makaroff criticized the government's strategy of permitting private enterprise to develop oil resources in the province and sell stock. He also questioned a statement issued by the government's Bureau of Publications, stating it would now be easier for private concerns and individuals to develop provincial gas and oil industries. Makaroff stated, "This is not in accord with basic socialist principles, and would probably dampen the enthusiasm of many members."[53] Phelps responded that the government was not yet ready to take on oil reserve development but said it would move at the appropriate time. J. T. Douglas, Minister of Highways, supported Phelps's stand at the convention, telling the delegates that at present there was no market for oil being drilled in Saskatchewan fields, and, in fact, the oil was being dumped. He went on to say that a government geologist and engineer were exploring a process that would make the oil commercially profitable. The planning committee later concluded that the co-operatives had limited resources, and in the end the government's decision was to leave the petroleum industry to private enterprise.[54] The first major oil strike occured in January 1952, and after extensive consultation with the oil industry, the government would develop new oil and gas legislation, and Saskatchewan would become an important centre for oil production.[55]

CHAPTER 12

THE PROBLEM CHILDREN

Not all of the government's business ventures were successful. Some of Phelps's "problem children"—the brick plant and the shoe, blanket, and box factories established early in the government's first term—did not prove lucrative, and despite the initial enthusiasm and optimism that accompanied their start-up, they later became political liabilities.

THE BRICK PLANT

The purchase of International Clay Products, the first such government manufacturing venture, was announced in February 1945. In an interview with A. W. Johnson, Tommy Douglas recalled the Cabinet meeting when the purchase was discussed: "The meeting went on and on and my colleagues were deeply divided. Finally I did something I didn't believe in doing. I called for a vote. When it became apparent that the weight of the vote was clearly opposed to the purchase, Joe expostulated: 'But my gosh fellows. I've already bought it!'"[1] Phelps had acted rather impulsively despite a less than hopeful appraisal by his deputy minister and a second cautious appraisal by an engineer from the University of Saskatchewan, in the belief it would provide work for returning veterans and "make available a supply of Saskatchewan building brick and hollow brick tile which will be in great demand during the post war building boom."[2]

Brick making had existed in Saskatchewan for many years. Saskatchewan's first documented case of brick construction dates back to 1877 when Battleford's Land Registry Office was built.[3] When settlers came west, construction increased and brick plants sprang up. By 1913, approximately forty brick-making plants existed in the province. With the recession that year and the war that followed, construction activity declined and plants began to close. The Depression also took its toll. By the end of the 1930s, only three plants remained: International Clay Products in Estevan; Dominion Fire Brick and Clay Products in Claybank; and Bruno Clayworks Ltd.[4] In 1944, Phelps turned his attention to the Estevan plant, which lay near the province's largest lignite coal fields and had been idle since 1932.[5] This time, the private sector took the initiative. On August 22, 1944, I. H. Bowman, vice-president and majority shareholder of International Clay Products, wrote to Phelps and expressed his desire to sell the plant. He indicated that his health would not allow him to continue operating the business. He said that although

An exhibition display demonstrating the multiple industries the government was involved in, including a leather tannery, a woollen mill, a shoe factory, a transportation company, a brick plant, a box factory, a timber board, and a fur marketing service. Photo taken between 1945 and 1954. Provincial Archives of Saskatchewan, Government of Saskatchewan Photo Services Reference #2977, S 73-5-3.

the plant was worth $200,000, he was willing to sell it for less than half that. He claimed the plant had been successful; its profits between 1927 and 1930 had been $75,000.[6]

Phelps sent C. A. L. (Vern) Hogg, the geologist who had joined the DNR in September 1944 and was appointed to work with Phelps and H. W. Monahan on the Industrial Development Board, to Estevan to examine the clay plant and to determine the cost of putting it back into operation.[7] Hogg reported that the buildings lacked "adequate lighting," were "in a very bad state of repair," and "would possibly be condemned by a factory inspector." The brick-making machinery was "to a large extent without adequate foundations," was "15 to 20 years old," and had a "general run down appearance." He also pointed out that several problems existed. First, labour would be difficult to secure, likely because the working conditions for the men were bad. Second, the clay near the plant was unsuitable for the production of face brick and would have to be mixed with better grades of clay imported from the United States. Third, 30–50 per cent of the bricks were spoiled because lignite coal was used for firing them. Hogg thought the plant could produce a million common bricks per month, but added that estimating accurate costs was impossible since the company did not have detailed records. According to Hogg, a profit of $38,000 might be made in a season's production. However, he expressed concern that if production expanded at the rate the DNR anticipated, coal and clay supplies "in the present workings" would be exhausted before the end of the next production season, though these could be obtained from areas near the plant. He estimated the value of the plant and equipment at $66,730 and the cost of additional equipment and repairs at $25,153. He included a company balance sheet dated November 30, 1943, with his report that put the value of the plant's fixed assets at $174,549 and the coal deposits at $85,075.[8]

W. G. Worcester, professor of ceramics engineering at the University of Saskatchewan, undertook another appraisal at Phelps's request. The professor felt the plant was in "a dilapidated and deplorable condition" and seemed to urge caution about taking it over. His November appraisal substantiated Hogg's opinion that the buildings were near the point of being condemned and its machines and kilns required considerable repair. He assessed the value of the machinery, dryers, kilns, buildings, yard, and pit at $107,802.92; the clay and land at $20,001.95; and the coal deposits at $90,023.80, for a total of $217,828.67. Neither Hogg nor Worcester recommended that the government buy the plant.[9]

Nonetheless, Phelps announced on February 1, 1945, that the government had purchased the brick manufacturing plant and other properties of the International Clay Products Company Ltd. of Estevan for $150,000.[10] He indicated that the DNR had received three appraisals and added that the government would modernize and recondition the plant for about $50,000.[11] He expected that the work would be finished and that the plant would be in operation by July. Optimistically, Phelps pointed out that "in view of the extreme housing shortage, the prospects of greatly increased population in Saskatchewan, and the need for many large buildings after the war there was little doubt there would be an early and continuous demand for many millions of building bricks."[12]

Having purchased the Estevan brick plant, the government then proceeded to establish the Saskatchewan Clay Products Corporation on May 15, 1945. It became the government's first "problem child." It faced several challenges. One involved difficulties in repairing machinery and delays in replacing old equipment. While Phelps had stated that the machinery was "in first class shape" since it had been used very little in the past few years, he soon discovered that much of it needed to be repaired. Other equipment had to be replaced, but wartime priorities delayed the shipment of essential equipment ordered from the United States. Phelps indicated that the plant had operated at about one-third capacity for some time because temporary machinery had to be used.[13]

A second problem was the quality of brick that was being produced. Because the existing equipment was unable to grind the clay finely enough, the plant was making a poor grade of brick. In his appraisal, Vern Hogg had pointed out that the clay being used at the plant was unsuitable for the production of face brick. To manufacture face brick, the plant would have to import better grade clay from the United States and mix it with the local clay.[14]

The third problem was that the bricks proved to be difficult to sell. Optimistically, Phelps announced in June 1945 that the plant had enough orders to take the entire season's output. By January 1946, he had to admit that the government did not yet have many orders. By April, the plant had sold only $1,918 worth of bricks to the United States. Later, George Cadbury (who would head up an Economic Planning Board for the government) gave two reasons why these bricks were difficult to sell: political prejudice existed about buying from the government, and the bricks were not cheap because the government was the employer and had to pay good wages. He recalled:

> We never had a good market. They mostly went to Winnipeg and it was a fairly long haul and it made it that much more expensive.... We were very much in the position of wanting to say that we were the best wage payers in the country [thus increasing the price of the bricks] and I think we fell between our ideals and some of the practical possibilities.[15]

However, the main problem was that early studies had underestimated expenses and overestimated profits. Hogg had included a balance sheet to November 1943 in his feasibility study, which valued the fixed assets of the brick plant at Estevan at $174,549.60. He estimated that repairs would cost an additional $25,153, but by February 19, 1946, the government had spent $223,501.59. Hogg had also estimated that the plant could make five thousand bricks per hour, a million common bricks per month, and seven and a half million bricks in a season. In 1945, the plant only produced half a million bricks between its trial runs in September and its forced closure due to a frozen water line in November. Because the Estevan kiln was very expensive to operate, production costs were very high as well. J. G. Nordal, manager of the brick plant, suggested installing a new car tunnel kiln at a cost of approximately $50,000.[16] While Hogg had estimated a net profit of $38,000 for a year, the plant, in fact, suffered a net loss of $769 up to March 31, 1946. On February 19, 1946, W. J. Patterson wryly commented in the legislature, "The brick plant...was purchased at a great cost yet the production to date has been practically nil."[17] The cost of the additional equipment that would be required to make the plant operational was considered prohibitive. Due to the many difficulties encountered, the plant was forced to close in November 1945.[18] By 1946, Saskatchewan Clay Products became the Clay Products Division of Saskatchewan Minerals. In May 1966, Saskatchewan Clay Products Corporation was renamed Estevan Brick Ltd., and in 1969 it was sold.[19]

SASKATCHEWAN BLANKETS

Phelps's second venture into social entrepreneurship was the woollen mill which he established in Moose Jaw. Phelps entered the wool business after consulting with H. W. Monahan, his superintendent of industrial development, and J. V. Clement, a consultant from the United States who had served as general manager for several woollen mills. Both had favoured the initiative. On Phelps's request, Clement had conducted a feasibility study in October 1944, in which he concluded that a provincial woollen mill could be successful in Saskatchewan. Sheep production had increased greatly during the war years—almost doubling in the province between 1939 and 1944 thanks to increased demand and higher prices—and the government also had a strong desire to process more of the province's agricultural products. Phelps acted on Clement's recommendation quickly, but earlier reports on the feasibility of the industry had not been as optimistic.

In 1943, L. E. Kirk had investigated the feasibility of a woollen industry in the province for the Saskatchewan Reconstruction Council, including the availability of raw materials, plant location in relation to freight rates, environmental factors, employment opportunities, benefits to wool growers, and markets. The wool business was already established in eastern Canada: there were 144 mills in Canada, but only eight of these were located west of the Great Lakes.[20] Kirk believed that since eastern woollen industries consistently found range wool from western Canada unsuitable and imported better and cheaper wool from Australia and New Zealand, it was "reasonable to assume that [western Canadian range wool] would not be used by woollen mills if they were established in this province." He maintained that the savings on freight rates would be minimal since shipping wool to Ontario mills would cost about two cents per pound while shipping it to a plant in the West would cost about one cent. Woollen mills would require high humidity and a good supply of water with a low mineral content. Since Saskatchewan's climate was dry, mills would also have to be artificially humidified. A plentiful supply of water was available, but it would require chemical treatment, which would add to the cost. He noted that while the textile industry would require a large amount of hand labour and could employ many, it would still require the services of "a good manager, engineer and personnel officer, as well as certain key employees who know the techniques and fundamentals of the business."[21] He doubted that establishing a local woollen mill would substantially benefit Saskatchewan wool producers. Since their wool was not uniform or in good physical condition, they could not expect to receive high prices until grading regulations were introduced that would make it more profitable for them to "skirt" the fleeces and market the wool in better condition.[22]

Kirk also noted that assessing the market for woollen goods would be difficult. Mills producing cloth faced "a fastidious and highly competitive market," whereas those producing "goods that can enter directly into the retail trade and which satisfy local requirements" were on "a safer basis." He thought that rural communities might use items such as blankets, knitting yarns, coarse tweeds, mackinaw cloth, overcoating, and rugs. However, he warned that here again competition was keen because the retail trade had well-established connections with wholesale houses. Furthermore, many people now wore ready-made clothing. He suggested that the type of woollen mill that had been most successful in western Canada had been based on custom work.[23] Kirk concluded that Saskatchewan should not try to produce woollen textiles since eastern Canada and Great Britain already supplied that market. Nevertheless, he saw no reason why a private or co-operative enterprise might not enter the business of manufacturing woollen goods in Saskatchewan. Success would depend largely "on managerial ability, an intimate knowledge of the business, and...a keen personal interest in its welfare on the part of its operators." He recommended establishing a custom mill and concentrating on a single product such as blankets.[24]

Despite Kirk's rather apprehensive report, Phelps strongly favoured the establishment of a woollen mill. Saskatchewan had a large number of sheep, and the government was interested in creating jobs and raising revenue by using farm products. With his inherent impulsiveness and his fervent desire to socialize industry, he sent H. W. Monahan to eastern Canada and the United States to gather information about their woollen industries.[25] On October 18, 1944, J. V. Clement, a textile consultant, wrote to Phelps. Clement mentioned that he had met Monahan in Boston, stated his qualifications, indicated his desire to survey the wool situation in Saskatchewan, and expressed an interest in obtaining a job.[26] Phelps asked Clement to undertake a survey to determine the feasibility of establishing a woollen mill in Saskatchewan. After Clement had spent twelve days in the province undertaking the study, he submitted his report to the minister on November 22, 1944. Clement estimated that the final cost for capital equipment would be $63,000 and that an additional $5,000 would be needed for miscellaneous mill supplies. He concluded:

> We see no reason why the project should not be a success and may be the means of bringing "outside" capital into the province. If after giving this report due consideration, you decide to go ahead with the project, the writer can arrange to give same his personal attention, which will include purchase and installing of machinery, selection of overseers or foremen, construction of fabrics, installing a practical "foolproof" costs system, and selecting a competent Superintendent or Manager.[27]

H. W. Monahan's preliminary study also asserted that a mill should be able to operate successfully if qualified individuals were secured and if its products were limited to blankets, knitting yarns, and "homespun" cloth. His report concluded:

> Any development that might be decided upon will have to be well designed, well equipped, well managed, and have machinery that is equal to or better than average, found in the mills throughout North America.
>
> With a layout such as this, there is no question as to its ultimate success and the benefits that would naturally accrue to the Province as a result of same. Frankly, we believe that the Province has every justification for going ahead with this development as quickly as conditions will permit.[28]

Ten days later, Monahan submitted a second report to Phelps in which he outlined these additional costs: $2,000 for a heating plant, and $1,000 for a well to supply eighty thousand gallons of water per day. He estimated that purchasing the plant, the machinery, and auxiliary services, and erecting the machinery would cost $113,500. This estimate did not include transportation charges, duty, or sales tax. Nonetheless, he still thought "it would be advisable to try to secure some immediate action on this proposal."[29]

On December 6, this announcement appeared in the *Leader-Post*:

> Plans for the operation of a woollen mill, government-owned and operated, at Moose Jaw were announced Wednesday by Natural Resources Minister J. L. Phelps.... Complete cost of the plant will be $125,000.... Organization of the mill was another step in the industrialization program of the Douglas government, Mr. Phelps said. Its earnings will be used to provide money for social services.
>
> Consumers will get more and better woollens at fair prices and returns to wool producers will be increased, Mr. Phelps said. The opportunity for a woollen mill has been ready in Saskatchewan for 40 years but private enterprise has not seized it.
>
> The mill project was undertaken after thorough investigation.... Preliminary work was done by H. Monahan of the Saskatchewan Industrial Development Board. Detailed study was made by Mr. Clement, who checked all data, including that of the Saskatchewan Reconstruction Council report.[30]

Matters moved quickly after that. On December 11, Phelps informed Clement that the government had decided to proceed with the woollen mill proposal and asked him to start locating and inspecting machinery for the mill. On January 15, 1945, Cabinet authorized $30,000 for the purchase of the Macdonald's Consolidated building in Moose Jaw, and on June 5, 1945, established the Saskatchewan Wool Products Corporation. Clement was named manager of the mill.[31]

Saskatchewan Wool Products Corporation soon became the second "problem child." The first problem encountered was difficulty in obtaining machinery, which delayed the mill's opening. In December 1944, Phelps had announced that he expected the mill to begin operations the following spring. However, when four machines promised for May delivery were unavailable until September, the opening of the plant had to be delayed. Phelps had stated that it would make blankets, mackinaw cloth, ladies' coatings, men's shirtings, hand-knitting, material for quilts and comforters, yarn for handicrafts, and rug yarn.[32] When the Opposition questioned him on March 1, 1946, about what it had produced, he replied that only woollen blankets had been made. Later in the session he had to admit that none had yet been sold.[33]

Three other problems plagued the woollen mill's operations. The first was finding a cheaper supply of good water. The second was disposing of waste from the plant after Moose Jaw City Council passed a bylaw prohibiting the discharge of deleterious or obnoxious substances into its sewer system.[34] The third was obtaining a sufficient amount of soap for processing the wool. In October 1945, the Wartime Prices and Trade Board informed Clement that it could not give him the quota of soap he needed since the oils and fats required to manufacture soap were still in short supply.[35]

Another difficulty resulted from an apparent conflict between Clement and some of the workers. On November 26, 1945, Phelps informed Clement that an employee named Fisher had phoned "to say that conditions had become so unbearable at the Mill that he was tendering his resignation for the third and last time."[36] In a letter to Clement, Phelps expressed his displeasure:

> We have a very large investment in that plant; in fact much larger than was first anticipated or indicated in your first figures to us. Now that this investment has been made it simply must pay dividends and nothing can be allowed to stand in the way. I also wish to state that from time to time key men have left the mill.... I did not take the time to discuss with you every complaint in connection with the Woollen Mill, both verbal and in writing, which was brought to my attention the past nine months [*sic*] it would have absorbed too much of my time. As you will no doubt recall some of the above complaints were referred to you for attention.[37]

On November 29, 1945, Clement resigned, and three weeks later John Moors from Golden Fleece Woollen Mills (in McGrath, Alberta) became the plant's new manager. Finances remained the woollen mill's most serious problem. The original cost estimates proved to be far too low. In December 1944, Phelps had stated that he expected the total cost of the mill to be $125,000. However, by March 1945, Monahan had to admit that "the investment in the project was somewhat above the original estimate." Still, he insisted that the plant would "pay itself out in three years."[38]

In November 1945, J. S. Bevan, chief accountant for the DNR, gave a number of reasons why the original cost estimates had increased. Many expenses had not been included in the original estimate: the excise tax, which amounted to $20,663.01; U.S. premiums on purchases made there, which cost $20,000; duties or tariffs; the costs of remodelling the building; purchasing insurance for the machinery and the building; paying employees until the plant opened; and being forced to purchase new rather than second-hand machinery, exceeding estimates by $40,000.[39] In addition, the DNR had to give the Treasury department a cheque to cover "the [education] tax of tangible personal property brought into Saskatchewan" for the period up to December 31, 1944. J. S. Bevan estimated that the amount of machinery and equipment purchased for the plant for which no education tax had been paid was about $126,325.[40] By February 28, 1946, the provincial treasurer had advanced Saskatchewan Wool Products Corporation $274,417.19 for capital expenditures and $150,000 for working capital, totalling $424, 417.19.[41] Needless to say, none of this had yet been repaid. On April 5, 1946, the *Leader-Post* printed the "Wool Mill cost so far" as $393,309.[42]

By 1946, blankets manufactured at the government mill were being marketed throughout Saskatchewan. The blankets were distributed through regular wholesale, retail, and co-operative trade outlets, and most of the larger department stores. Raw wool, produced in Saskatchewan and purchased from the Canadian Co-operative Wool Growers Association, was being used in production, and the factory employed a number of workers, working several shifts on the looms and working the carders and spinning mules.[43] However, capital expenditures and operating costs including raw materials and supplies were all much higher than was originally estimated.

In 1947, the mill also began manufacturing lighter cloth such as suits and shirts, car robes, and knitting yarn. Improvements were being made to the equipment and the facility, and the future looked promising. By early in 1948, however, things began to change. A Saskatchewan Industries annual report in 1947–1948 stated that a number of Canadian and United States woollen mills had been forced to shut down operations.

The Saskatchewan mill was facing increased production costs and reduced demand for its products. There were also marketing difficulties due to the severity of the winters and general uncertainty in the economy related to crop failures. Production was reduced in 1948, and by December 1948 the mill was showing a loss.[44]

According to Pat Rediger's *The Crowns: A History of Public Enterprise in Saskatchewan*, Clement's original report on wool markets had been oversimplified and based on faulty assumptions. He had, for example, underestimated the cost and availability of the equipment that was needed. Training unskilled labour had also proven expensive. In addition, "the low quality of local wool and the breakage of threads aggravated by the dry prairie climate" contributed to the woollen mill's failure. The woollen mill was shut down in 1954 (six years after Phelps left office) after it had lost $830,000.[45]

Phelps was disappointed in the factory's failure and later stated that many of his other responsibilities took him far away, so he was not close enough to see what went wrong: "I was on policy, you can't get policy and administration, day-to-day operations mixed up."[46] Phelps, more interested and involved in initiating these new ventures, had perhaps relied too heavily on newly appointed officials to administer the newly established agencies. Critics of the government's entry into business pointed to the financial liability, proposing that these ventures were better left to the private sector. Still others cite Phelps's impulsive and less than cautious approach to social ownership.

THE BOX FACTORY

Phelps added the Prince Albert Box Factory to his portfolio of government business enterprises in November 1945 through rather unusual circumstances. The Trade Union Act, enacted by the CCF in October 1944, had greatly expanded workers' rights to organize into unions of their own choosing and to bargain collectively. A newly created Labour Relations Board, put in place to examine complaints of unfair labour practices, administered the act. In the fall of 1945, the board was requested to intervene on behalf of workers employed at the Prince Albert Box Factory. They were attempting to negotiate their first contract and had complained that their employer was refusing to bargain in good faith.

After reviewing the situation, the board ordered the company to enter into a collective bargaining agreement with its employees and issued an order stating that a government controller would take over management of the plant. Thumbing their nose at the board's decision and in a last ditch attempt to avoid bargaining in good faith with the union, the company had responded by selling out its assets to its president and firing all of its employees.[47]

Premier Douglas, quoted in the *Leader-Post* on November 5, 1945, condemned the company for its deliberate and flagrant attempt to avoid the collective bargaining regulations laid out in the Trade Union Act, and stated that they "would be made accountable." Acting on advice from Cabinet and his legal advisor, Morris Shumiatcher, Douglas decided to go a step beyond the act's provision for putting a controller in place at the plant. The ten-day dispute between the Cabinet and management of the box factory culminated when the government expropriated the company and its assets, and the factory became a Crown corporation under the administration of the DNR. The Prince Albert Box Factory then came directly under Phelps's jurisdiction, and Monahan became the factory's controller.

After the expropriation, the *Leader-Post* accused the government of being authoritarian, charging it with a "deliberate and flagrant violation" of its own laws and of being "tyrannical," and insisting that the government ought to have brought the matter before the courts rather than taking this "most high-handed and arbitrary step."[48] The premier later asserted that by changing the factory's ownership and firing all the employees, J. E. Mitchell, the owner of the company, "was defying the government, the court, and the Labour Relations Board" and that "this was the only way to enforce the Trade Union Act. If this man had been allowed to defy the Labour Relations Board, scores of employers might have followed his example, torn up their collective bargaining agreements and in fact thrown their employees on the streets."[49]

The box factory created many new problems for Phelps and the government. Douglas later admitted that they did not really want "a broken-down factory," but since its owner had disobeyed the Labour Relations Board order and defied the government, expropriation was the "only way to enforce the Trade Union Act."[50] Having obtained the factory, the government did not know quite what to do with it. Since no overall plan existed, running it efficiently was almost impossible. W. D. Smith, one of its managers, complained, "There does appear to us a tendency to consider the Box Factory Division as an illegitimate orphan, starting with the Cabinet and following through to the local CCF Study Groups." J. F. Gray, director of Saskatchewan Lake and Forest Products Corporation, also expressed this uncertainty when he wrote, "At the present time I am not at all clear as to what the Box Factory can do.... Apparently, I have the wrong impression as to what it was set up for. There must be some clarification with regard to the possibilities of this factory."[51]

Other problems plagued its operations. The facilities were crowded and inadequate. As one report in 1947 put it, "The plant is far too crowded, both inside and outside. It is difficult to move among the machines, the employees get in each other's way and operations are slowed up. The layout of the plant is too small for its present operation."[52] The box factory also had outdated, inefficient machinery. In describing the machinery, another report spoke of the "very poor condition of the key machines and their obsolesant [*sic*] design"; it described them as "very largely old, outmoded and worn out," and noted the "most serious breakdowns are due to worn out parts in machines which have already been through atleast [*sic*] one fire." W. J. Bague, accountant for the Timber Board, agreed: "This is recommended as an absolute *must*, not only to bring in new machines, but to replace the worn-out, outmoded slow production units."[53]

Under these conditions, Phelps had difficulty finding someone to manage the factory successfully. Between November 1945 and June 1948, four men tried to do so but failed. H. W. Monahan, who had become controller at the time of expropriation, retained the position for only two months. On February 15, 1946, Phelps appointed S. A. Weinstein as manager, but he quit in January 1947. W. D. Smith then became the manager, but in March 1948 J. J. Harrop replaced him. Obviously, having four managers within two and a half years did not promote managerial continuity. Some of these men did not want the job, others were unsuited, still others were untrained. However, none was successful. James Gray of the SLAFPC wrote, "This whole operation has been very unfortunate right from the start, as I am firmly of the opinion that we have never had any manager in the Box Factory who understood how such a factory should be operated.... None of them have had the abilities to be manager of a factory."[54]

While working conditions in the factory improved after the government took over, new sources of conflict surfaced, and once again labour relations became strained. There was conflict between workers; Gray noticed "a peculiar situation within this Union where we have some sort of personal squabble between two groups of individuals." While he could not determine whether nationality, religion, or something else caused this problem, he added that as long as this fight continued, "there is not anyone who can get harmony in this factory."[55]

There was also conflict between management and labour. Smith wrote, "Our hard core problem…is…who is the manager, myself or the Union Committee. When it is clearly established in the minds of all that an employee who fails to meet the required standards of his job must be removed, and further if not suitable elsewhere in the plant then dismissed, then we will be well advanced toward profitable operation in any line we touch."[56] After Smith dismissed two employees, the union demanded their reinstatement. When management refused, some men promptly quit. Phelps dismissed all the employees who had quit their jobs and closed the plant for nine days. He threatened to close the plant permanently and said, "I don't want anyone to get the idea that the government can't close it. It is not a vital industry."[57] The matter eventually went to arbitration, which found for the union. The two men were reinstated, but tension and conflict persisted.

Phelps, as director of the company and also the minister responsible, found himself in the middle of the dispute. In a front-page story, the *Prince Albert Daily Herald* ran the headline, "Phelps's threat seen as labour act violation." C. S. Davis, the lawyer for J. E. Mitchell, the previous owner of the box factory, pointed out that the stand taken by Phelps was "not only the handwriting on the wall for labour, but a clear and unmistakable manifestation of Bolshevism."[58] Phelps had spoken to the employees as they returned to work after the week-long absence and indicated that he would recommend shutting the factory down if they failed to implement a three-point program to increase production, reduce waste, and reduce the unit cost in the next three months, thereby bringing the factory out of the red. The union responded by telling Phelps that it was management's responsibility to make the plant profitable.[59] With intervention by Clarence Fines, acting as premier, the dispute at the box factory was settled quickly and did not produce a rift between the government and the labour movement. Nonetheless, it was an early indication that conflicts could and would erupt to challenge the relationship between unions and their avowedly labour-friendly government.

Financial problems also emerged shortly after expropriation, in part the result of the government's decisions and actions. On November 7, 1945, Morris Shumiatcher negotiated an agreement with the union that gave employees very generous benefits and increased their salaries by approximately ten cents per hour.[60] Furthermore, because the government was eager to avoid litigation, it paid J. E. Mitchell $71,500 for the factory, even though it considered that price exorbitant. These two factors and the many others already discussed resulted in the box factory operating at a loss. Total operating losses to October 31, 1947, amounted to $30,496.12. By April 30, 1948, this had decreased to $17,871.64.[61] The box factory had come under the Saskatchewan Timber Board's jurisdiction after November 5, 1945, and under the SLAFPC's after its formation in May 1946. Saskatchewan Forest Products continued to operate the Saskatchewan Timber Board, the Saskatchewan Box Factory, and the Big River Mill throughout the 1950s. In 1952, a new facility was constructed to meet increased demand, but by the mid-fifties the new plant was experiencing financial difficulties. Paper products began to replace wood as packaging material, and the deficits reappeared. In 1957, the decision was made to cease operations and transfer its assets to the Saskatchewan Timber Board.[62] The box factory closed in 1957 with an accumulated loss of $495,000.[63]

THE SHOE FACTORY

A third Crown corporation, Saskatchewan Leather Products Corporation, was the next business venture Phelps turned his attention to. The *Report of the Saskatchewan Reconstruction Council* provided some background information for the government. L. E. Kirk had pointed out that 98 per cent of the leather industry was situated in Ontario and Quebec. Plants required some highly skilled employees and considerable capital investment. The eighty plants in operation in 1942 were capitalized at $28.2 million, for an average investment of $350,000 per plant. Concerning the feasibility of establishing a tanning industry in Saskatchewan, Kirk added that "starting a new enterprise in Saskatchewan is not at all promising"—a tannery would need to process twenty-five thousand hides per year to be profitable, but the province could not support that large a manufacturing enterprise. Shipping leather as opposed to shipping raw hides to eastern Canada would only provide minimal savings on freight charges, regardless of what many claimed. A producer of leather should have a ready market of at least 50 per cent of his output before he began, but "such a market does not exist in Saskatchewan at the present time." Kirk concluded, "The tanning of leather appears to be one of the least promising enterprises from the standpoint of a new industry for this province."[64]

Despite Kirk's decidedly negative report, Phelps was determined to establish a leather industry. When J. M. Cantor, manager of Western Footwear Ltd., wholesale distributors, contacted him on December 6, 1944, and expressed a desire to establish a shoe factory and tannery in Regina, Phelps was quick to show his interest. Cantor, having tried unsuccessfully to convince eastern firms to open a shoe factory in Regina, promptly submitted a written proposal to Phelps, who apparently turned it over to Hogg.

Once again, Phelps relied on the advice of both government staff and outside consultants. The staff in the Industrial Development Branch reviewed Cantor's report. The report seemed promising, and Cantor and Phelps entered negotiations in 1945. Cantor proposed a partnership in which Western Footwear would invest 25 per cent and the government the remainder. This was rejected, and Saskatchewan Leather Products was established as a Crown corporation, with Western Footwear, an established company, named as the sole distributor. Distribution and sales would be assured, Phelps believed, through the arrangement with Western Footwear.[65]

On January 2, 1945, Hogg submitted a preliminary report regarding the establishment of such a factory that discussed shoe factories in western Canada and the types of shoes that would be suitable for Saskatchewan needs. As for manufacturing costs, it indicated that a pair of men's shoes without counter or toe cap would retail at $4.50.[66] Cantor had suggested that a factory capable of producing eight hundred pairs per day or 240,000 per year would be feasible. Production would be divided as follows: men's work shoes, 50 per cent; women's and young girls' shoes, 25 per cent; children's shoes, 25 per cent. Since Western Footwear would take two-thirds of the production, or 160,000 pairs, government institutions 15,000, and the co-operative stores likely 25,000, a market for 200,000 pairs seemed assured. Hogg suggested buying the machinery and leather from the Mid-West Shoe Company in Winnipeg, which was interested in selling its plant. Cantor estimated that the total cost of establishing this plant would be $125,000.[67] On April 16, Phelps confirmed their "verbal agreement to purchase from Western Footwear Co. the building of the McColl-Frontenac Co. which you [Cantor] have recently purchased on behalf of the Saskatchewan Government for the sum of $20,330." This building, on 7th Avenue and Hamilton Street, would become the shoe factory. As well, Phelps authorized Cantor to buy machinery and equipment for the factory, and confirmed that the government would invest up to $100,000.[68] On May 29, Phelps announced the establishment of a shoe factory, and two weeks later the Cabinet established Saskatchewan Leather Products as a Crown corporation.[69] This Crown corporation would have two divisions: a shoe factory, established on June 12; and a tannery, established on July 12.

The shoe factory, under Phelps's umbrella of new government enterprises, was soon to become a political liability. The rationale behind the business was that it would enable the government to add value to the animal hides already readily available, and also provide employment for Saskatchewan people, producing good-quality shoes and work boots throughout the province. Once up and running, however, the business soon began to show embarrassing losses. Many problems emerged, including a shortage of hides, inexperienced operating and management personnel, difficulties obtaining machinery and equipment, fluctuating markets, and increased prices of chemicals and other products needed in the manufacturing process. Apparently, sufficient research had not gone into the production, marketing, and distribution of the products produced, and the factory ran into financial difficulty.

A very serious problem, once again, was money. Expectations had been extremely high when the government announced that the factory was capable of making one thousand pairs of shoes per day or about 100,000 per year. It planned to employ about one hundred people, giving preference to returned veterans. Western Footwear would take delivery of the factory's entire output, pay the government for the quantity produced, and receive a 20 per cent commission for distributing it. When production did not reach expectations, profits proved to be much lower than anticipated. In his financial statement for Saskatchewan Leather Products for the period August 6, 1945 to March 31, 1946, C. H. Smith, auditor of utilities, noted that from September 30, 1945, to March 31, 1946, the factory had produced 18,594 pairs of shoes. The average cost of manufacturing shoes to date was $3.13¼ per pair, but the selling price was only $2.30½.[70] The net loss for the period from August 6, 1945, to March 31, 1946, was $14,757.21. In addition, capital and operating advances totalling $175,000 had been made to the shoe factory and the tannery. Smith's statement did not include a detailed analysis of the tannery's finances since it had not begun to operate until May 1, 1946; however, its losses from May 1 to October 12, 1946, amounted to $7,612.[71]

Other problems concerned the corporation's management and subsequent labour problems. For instance, "Mr. Aldrich," dismissed in September, was reinstated in October "after discussion of the labour situation at the Factory." In December 1945, employees formed the National Union of Shoe and Leather Workers, which was affiliated with the Canadian Congress of Labour. Workers held an unauthorized work stoppage on the afternoon of December 18 when Managing Director Cantor announced they would not be paid for four days over Christmas when the factory was closed.[72] In a report to the Saskatchewan Leather Products board of directors on March 16, 1946, Cantor stated, "While the results are far from satisfactory as I feel a plant of this kind should show a fairly substantial profit, there are factors that . . . make this impossible and as long as we are handicapped by these the best we can hope for is to break even or show a small margin of profit." These factors—which had reduced the shoe factory's profit by $958 per month—included giving workers at least a 2 per cent higher wage scale, a twenty-minute daily rest period, a forty-four- rather than a forty-six-hour work week, and one day of sick leave per month.[73]

The tannery, which opened on May 1, 1946, also struggled. Very select leather was required to make good shoes, and the tannery did not produce such a high-quality product. Furthermore, the shoe factory was the tannery's only outlet, and that plant was less than a successful venture.[74]

An analysis of competitive pricing, supply, and potential distribution problems might have made the factory more successful. The shoe factory "suffered from too small a market to permit exploitation of scale economies." Merchants complained that salesmen told them it was "company policy" to refuse to sell their products to merchants that were handling Saskatchewan Leather Products footwear. In some cases, "dealers in specialized machinery and patented items [were also] unwilling to sell to 'socialist' crown corporations."[75] Tanilen, a chemical essential in the tanning of hides and only available from South America, suddenly became unavailable. Phelps recalled that some delighted in seeing the government enterprises in trouble: "The powers that be. You can't put your finger on who the hell did it but they were all helping each other. They were going to get at the government by cornering the market on tanilen—they cut off the supply."[76] The shoe factory and the tannery were closed in 1946 with a cumulative combined deficit of $156,000.[77]

Phelps was often criticized for his approach to running some of the government enterprises. In *Tommy Douglas: The Road to Jerusalem*, McLeod and McLeod write, "Phelps rarely notified the rest of his cabinet colleagues of his actions in advance, but if they asked him to slow the pace, he would reply, 'never say whoa in the middle of a puddle!'"[78] In fact, by the end of December 1945, each of the three "problem children" was experiencing serious difficulties. While part of the fault for this rested with Phelps himself, he was not solely to blame. In his enthusiasm to launch these enterprises as quickly as possible, he frequently acted without sufficient planning or preparation. Those who undertook feasibility studies, likely buoyed by Phelps's enthusiasm, also tended to be overly optimistic in their predictions. It is important to note that Phelps, having been given a "blank cheque" and a socialist mandate, was acting in good conscience; but while he could establish these endeavours, neither he nor the government had a plan or "a mechanism for meshing them together."[79] Indeed, given the massive changes that were being implemented, the government did not have the administrative machinery in place for detailed and integrated economic and budgetary planning. In the spring of 1946, Phelps announced the establishment of a Crown company Accounting Division within the DNR:

> We realize the great difference between governmental accounting and industrial and commercial accounting, and have made this reorganization to separate these functions. Saskatchewan people who are the owners of the new industries operated by

> the government, can feel confident the Department of Natural Resources is sparing no effort in developing the necessary organization to do the job with maximum efficiency.[80]

In November 1946, the government established a Budget Bureau to coordinate the budgeting practices of the departments. With limited resources and massive plans in health services and education, as well as natural resource development, budget analysis and control became key elements in policy formation, and conflict was arising over Cabinet control over departmental activities. Department budgets were submitted to the Treasury Board (a ministerial committee made up of the premier, the attorney general, the deputy provincial treasurer as secretary, and chaired by Clarence Fines) for critical review: "This new machinery enabled the premier and the provincial treasurer to ensure that the cabinet view prevailed over the departmental views whenever the two diverged."[81] As a result, Phelps would not experience the same level of autonomy he had during the first half of his term as Cabinet minister.

SITTING ON JOE'S TAIL

To assist Phelps and the Cabinet, the government had established an economic advisory committee, comprised of University of Saskatchewan academics G. Britnell, F. Cronkite, and V. C. Fowke, as early as September 1944.[82] Douglas had announced that the work of this committee would be "purely advisory" but "the heart of the government's plans for its socialist and co-operative activities." He added, "It will serve as a kind of coordinating agency for several departments which will be intimately concerned with the government's plans for economic development." It was to advise the DNR on the development of natural resources and power and to undertake studies that might be useful in formulating plans for future economic development. John Richards noted that the economic advisory committee prepared some academic and "relatively superficial reports on additional sources of revenue, equity of the provincial tax structure, amending the distribution of federal and provincial jurisdictions under the British North America Act, and on industrial development." On the last subject, it advised, "the government should enter any particular industrial field only after searching investigation and on competent technical advice." Richards noted that since Phelps by this time had committed the government to several Crown corporations, "such advice can be interpreted as an implicit critique of Phelps's impetuosity, or as a plea for the government to procure the requisite economic expertise, or both." The committee soon disbanded.[83]

Douglas realized that if the government were to be successful in its numerous public ventures, it would require a planning expert to help sort out the problems that had been encountered and set up a system of controls. By mid-1945, he found the expert he sought in George Cadbury and tried to persuade him to come to Saskatchewan.[84] In his work for the British Air Commission in Washington, Cadbury visited Regina for a few days in June 1945. He attended a Cabinet meeting and spent some time with Tommy McLeod.[85] McLeod had been Tommy Douglas's urban organizer before and during the successful political campaign of 1944 and was working as an economic advisor to the premier after the election.[86] He would later become the first director of the government's Budget Bureau and then deputy treasurer for Saskatchewan before leaving the government in 1952.[87] Cadbury must have been impressed, for on January 1, 1946, he became chairman of a new government agency, the Economic Advisory and Planning Board, and chief industrial executive. There, "One part of his persona would be dedicated to planning, the other to bringing order to the crown corporations."[88] The EAPB consisted of Chairman G. W. Cadbury, acting on behalf of the premier, and four Cabinet ministers: C. M. Fines, J. H. Sturdy, L. F. McIntosh, and J. L. Phelps. McLeod was designated as secretary, and Dr. Morris Shumiatcher served as legal counsel. This committee's staff soon began to provide expert advice on economic and commercial matters, and helped formulate long-term plans for existing business ventures.

Cadbury lost no time in bringing order to the Crown corporations. When he assumed his position, he did not plan to make any recommendations for three or four months. Nonetheless, in three weeks, on January 24, 1946, he informed Douglas that he believed "one or two questions of major importance...must be settled immediately." He recommended a method for maintaining much stricter control over the formation of Crown corporations, appointing an official secretary for each of them, and providing strict control of their accounts.[89] If another of Cadbury's roles was to "sit on Joe Phelps' tail," he lost no time in doing that either.[90]

On January 25, 1946, he confirmed an earlier conversation he had had with Phelps, in which Phelps stated that his department's various enterprises could be divided into three categories. Some were industrial projects: Saskatchewan Wool Products, Saskatchewan Leather Products, and Saskatchewan Clay Products. Others were marketing boards: the Saskatchewan Fish Marketing Board, Saskatchewan Fur Marketing Service (or Saskatchewan Fur Marketing Agency), and Saskatchewan Timber Board. Lastly, there was also the Saskatchewan Power Commission. Cadbury noted that he and Phelps had agreed that Cadbury would become a director of the Crown corporations categorized as industrial projects and also would become a member of the Power Commission. He assumed these directorships in short order.[91] Cadbury did not single out Phelps's ventures, though, since he soon became a director of each of the government's new Crown corporations.

The EAPB also brought about major changes within the Crown corporations themselves. In May 1946, SLAFPC was formed; it comprised the former Timber Board, Fish Products Corporation, Fish Marketing Board, and Saskatchewan Box Factory. In July 1946, Saskatchewan Industries was incorporated; it absorbed Saskatchewan Wool Products and Saskatchewan Leather Products. In 1946, Saskatchewan Minerals took over Saskatchewan Clay Products and added a Sodium Sulphate Division. Of the many Crown corporations and agencies Phelps had initiated, only the Fur Marketing Service remained untouched by administrative reorganization by July 1946.

Some personnel shifts occurred at this time as well. H. W. Monahan, whom Douglas had appointed superintendent of the Industrial Development Branch on September 15, 1944, resigned on April 29, 1946. L. C. Paterson, acting deputy minister for the DNR until April 1945, quit on August 17, 1946.[92] Henry Lewis, appointed deputy minister on April 2, 1945, clashed with Phelps and resigned in July 1946. Lastly, Hogg, who joined the department as a geologist in September 1944 and became assistant deputy minister in February 1946, was appointed deputy minister on October 30, 1946.

The department's many structural and personnel changes, together with the immense amount of work Phelps undertook, the hectic pace he set for himself, and the many frustrations he experienced, all took their toll. Even Phelps realized he could no longer keep up with everything.

On August 23, 1946, he wrote the following letter to A. Campbell, superintendent of the Leather Products Division:

> It is with real regret that owing to extreme pressure of business in other lines, I found it necessary to ask the Cabinet to relieve me of responsibility both as Minister in Charge and as a Director of Saskatchewan Industries. The work of this Department is assuming such proportions that my activities in certain fields must be curtailed.
>
> In compliance with my request, the Cabinet have now decided to place my colleague, the Hon. J. H. Brockelbank, as Minister in Charge, and Chairman of the Board of Directors of Saskatchewan Industries. Mr. Brockelbank is a capable man and will be a real asset....
>
> Although I have been Minister in Charge since the organization of the Shoe Factory, I have only served a very short time as a director of Saskatchewan Leather Products—in fact I attended only one meeting as such. We have experienced numerous difficulties in the operation of the shoe factory.[93]

On August 26, he wrote three similar letters to the managers of the tannery, Saskatchewan Clay Products, and Saskatchewan Wool Products. Phelps's association with the Industrial Development Branch of the DNR had officially ended.[94]

On August 13, 1946, the Cabinet deleted Phelps's name as an appointed member of the board of directors of Saskatchewan Industries. When the board heard the news at its meeting on August 26, Cadbury moved that the secretary write Phelps, indicating the directors' appreciation for the initiative and leadership he and his wife had given during and after the organizational period of the various divisions of the corporations, and the unanimous desire of the present directors that they continue to take an interest in the activities of the corporation and be associated with its activities in any way that could be arranged.[95]

Political opponents later cited the failures of the "problem children" as examples of why government should not be involved in business, but other government-owned businesses were doing very well indeed. While the box factory eventually went out of business, along with the government's leather and shoe factories and the wool products company, Saskatchewan Government Insurance Office (SGIO) was a tremendous success. Saskatchewan people were eager to have their insurance premium dollars for farm, home, and auto insurance stay in the province:

> The "problem children" as the senior advisors dubbed [the government-owned entrepreneurial ventures] never really threatened the financial health of the government, although they took up a disproportionate amount of its time and attention. These junior members in the family of Saskatchewan Crown corporations accounted for only about five per cent of total government investment in industry. The power, telephone and insurance companies would generate profits that far exceeded the losses sustained on the woollen mill, the brick plant and the shoe factory.[96]

Did Phelps accept blame for the failures? During a video documentary, eighty-one-year-old Joe Phelps was asked if he was embarrassed by things people look back at now and call political fiascos, like the shoe factory. He responded cheerfully, "No, not embarrassed at all. That is all part of progress. I accept that as part of progress." Referring directly to Joe Phelps, Tommy Douglas commented, "If any minister has two good ideas out of five, I raise him very high. I never worry about the bad ideas. Treasury Board and the Cabinet will root out the bad ideas and eliminate them. The people I worry about are the people who have no ideas at all."[97]

CHAPTER 13

TURNING POINTS

In November 1947, the *Leader-Post* reported on a Moose Jaw evening radio broadcast, quoting Attorney General J. W. Corman: "Hon. J. L. Phelps will go down in history as the first minister of natural resources who in the interests of the entire province ever took northern Saskatchewan seriously. Mr. Phelps has applied vision and imagination to the solution of northern problems."[1] The attorney general also stated Phelps was "the first to have ever attacked the feudal empire existing there under the overlordship of the Hudson's Bay Company and smaller entrenched middlemen who were holding the people in bondage." While Phelps had not made "an unqualified success of the vast work of northern reorganization left on his doorstep by the 'do-nothing' Liberals," he stated that Phelps "had to start from scratch and was bound to fall short of perfection."[2] Corman, speaking on behalf of the government, and indeed many of the people of Saskatchewan, felt that Phelps's work to encourage and promote development in the North had been largely successful. Many voters would not share this sentiment.

CLAPTRAP, HALF-TRUTHS, AND PURE TRIPE?

In the spring of 1948, Phelps's attention turned to the impending election. The Douglas Government was seeking a fresh mandate from the voters based on its accomplishments during its first term in office. When the premier dissolved the legislature on May 19, 1948, and announced June 24 as the election date (and July 22 as the date for the deferred contests in the two northern seats), the campaign was underway. Douglas declared that the two main issues were "whether the people wanted to maintain and extend the program of social security begun during the CCF's tenure in office and whether the province was going to have a program of industrial development 'which will be for the people, by the people.'" The CCF slogan was "Backward to Do-Nothing Liberalism" or "Forward to CCF Accomplishment."[3] The Liberals, on the other hand, argued that the real issues "arose out of the fundamental differences both in philosophy and policy between the two parties." As advocates of free enterprise, they declared that the main issue was "socialism and where it leads in the end and its ultimate effect on the lives of people."[4]

Phelps ran in the Saltcoats constituency again and campaigned hard.[5] His campaign emphasized development of the province's natural resources, including plans to build additional plants to process forest products, the utilization of lignite coal, extension of the power system, and further innovative initiatives for northern development. As usual, he had many irons in the fire. He had reported to the provincial legislature in mid-February that the Saskatchewan Fur Marketing Service had made a net profit of $61,601 for the period ending September 30, 1947. Ten scheduled sales had been held by the fur marketing service in Regina, with gross sales amounting to nearly $2 million.[6] Approximately 10,200 shippers had shipped their furs to the marketing system.

Phelps's support for the marketing boards was unwavering despite some criticism and controversy, and he was adamant when, as part of a two-hour marathon address in the provincial legislature, he stated that

> Provincial marketing boards for primary products such as fish, fur and timber will play one of the greatest roles in the future economy of Saskatchewan, because the principle of orderly marketing has been accepted by the people.... If I had to discontinue some government departments, the marketing boards would be the last. Just as the orderly marketing of wheat is now an accepted principle, so is the principle of the orderly marketing of furs, fish and timber, and it is here to stay.[7]

Opposition critics opposed the government's marketing board policy for placing undue restrictions on northern fishers, trappers, and timber producers. On one occasion, a heated exchange took place between Phelps and opposition leader, W. J. Patterson, in which Phelps's character and ability came under attack. Phelps labelled Patterson's comments as a lot of "clap-trap, half-truths, and mostly pure tripe,"[8] and pointed out that prices paid to producers by the province's three marketing boards—fur, fish, and timber—were as high as those paid by private dealers. He also noted that, in fact, the Fur Marketing Service had paid higher average prices than private fur buyers.

Throughout the election campaign, Phelps spoke passionately about the government's policies, and in particular economic policy, placing his emphasis on fiscal planning for the future: "The purpose of government is to give leadership, and the one thing that will give stability to the province, the Dominion, and all nations, is continued confidence and expansion."[9] Phelps, like many who had lived through the thirties, had been deeply affected by the Depression and repeatedly cautioned against governments being in debt: "The CCF government is one of the first to start paying off the provincial debt. Former Liberal administrations have added to it, with few exceptions, year after year." He continued, "If the government continues its present rate of debt reduction, in twenty to twenty-five years, the province might be on a cash basis; thus saving the present interest charges, which are draining the government treasury."[10] Even Phelps may not have realized how accurate and insightful this comment really was. The CCF government would, in fact, successfully turn the provincial economy completely around, from a near bankrupt state to having an A credit rating seventeen years later.

Ideology became a key issue during the election campaign, with opposition parties strongly critical of the socialist policies of the government. Conflict between the new social order and free enterprise triggered heated debate. Phelps came out strongly in favour of social ownership, stating, "It did not matter how they sugared the pill, free enterprise is still capitalism. Capitalism is on trial. Look at the number of unemployed in Canada at present."[11] He also rejected any communist connections: "The CCF will have no truck nor trade with the communists. The only way to eradicate communism is to remove the cause of communism."[12]

Labour issues also sparked controversy. Early in its first term, the CCF brought in the most progressive labour legislation in North America, strongly supporting workers' rights to unionize and the collective bargaining process. However, when public sector workers and workers in the newly created government enterprises, such as the shoe and box factories, began to unionize, tensions had emerged. If the government's experiment in social ownership was to succeed, the new Crown corporations would have to make a profit, and, as minister responsible for industrial development, Phelps frequently found himself in the middle of this conflict.

Phelps continued to suggest that the government would enter into oil exploration and development, and that exploration should not be left solely to private companies. The search for oil meant a large financial risk, but his position was clear: "Large volume production is necessary, and it is not something in which you can dabble your toes. It is possible the province will get a drilling rig, which can be secured at a reasonable cost, and drill holes of its own." The oil-producing area in Saskatchewan was estimated at 170,000 square miles. In early 1948, there had been talk about a possible pipeline from Alberta to Saskatchewan. Phelps had already contacted the other Prairie provinces on this matter and clarified his position on the issue at a People's Forum in February at Regina City Hall. "If a pipeline is built to carry natural gas from an Alberta field to Saskatchewan points, it should be a public utility, or at least a public carrier," Phelps told the crowd. When asked by opposition leader Patterson if this was a government statement, Phelps responded that he was exercising his right to speak as a citizen of the province.[13]

Not all election debate focused on social and economic issues. On June 14, 1948, the *Leader-Post* reported on a controversy in the Pelly election campaign. Phelps was speaking in support of D. Z. Daniels, CCF candidate for the constituency, at a meeting at Ministik Beach, outlining the provincial government's position on natural resources development. John G. Banks, the Liberal candidate in the constituency, claimed Mr. Feusi, the ranger at Madge Lake, was a nephew of Joe Phelps, and implied that Mr. Feusi was incompetent. In response, Mr. Feusi took the platform in his own defence. According to the *Leader-Post*, Feusi, at considerable length, spelled out the improvements he had made in the park and accused the Kamsack and District Board of Trade of using the approaching election as a political tool.[14]

Phelps initially appeared to be winning the Saltcoats seat based upon early polls from the larger towns, but when the more remote rural polls came in, Phelps had lost to the Liberal candidate, A. A. Loptson, by a slim margin of 325 votes. Final poll results showed Loptson at 3,945 votes, Phelps with 3,620, and George Dulmage, a Social Credit auctioneer, with 807. Cabinet minister Oak Valleau was also defeated. The voters gave the Douglas Government a second term, but with a reduced majority: the CCF won thirty-one seats while the Liberals captured eighteen. Fourteen sitting CCF members, including Joe Phelps, were defeated.[15]

MOVE TO CENTRE

During its first term in office, the CCF had become increasingly aware that it would be difficult to create the socialist utopia it had envisioned without dramatically increasing provincial revenues. In *Saskatchewan: A History*, John Archer suggests that "so noticeable was the muting of socialistic policies, as the run-up to the 1948 election occurred, that Attorney General J. W. Corman was reported to have stated that the election, when it came, would be fought on a free enterprise capitalist model, versus a free enterprise CCF model." Archer noted, "the CCF had sought to achieve a redistribution of the available income in as equitable a manner as possible. But lacking power to control income tax, interest rates, wheat prices, freight rate and international trade, this was no easy task."[16] To increase revenues, the CCF would continue to focus on effective utilization of the province's natural resources in the years to come. They would remain in power until 1964 and continue to emphasize the practical aspects of "humanity first," but after 1948 there was a decidedly more measured approach to economic and social reforms.

The election results emphasized what Douglas and his Cabinet colleagues already sensed, namely that "change and turbulence which was the product of change, had to give way to some measure of stability if the CCF Government was to remain in power."[17] They had to consolidate the many innovations they had begun rather than introduce new ones. They also knew that the government had to become more moderate in its approach; it had to shift further to the centre. Likely, they realized that persuading Phelps to moderate his philosophy would be difficult. Although Douglas had mentioned in his campaign that his government would "pledge itself to a policy of planned freedom which will lead to security for all and progress for our province," he added,

"It will not be social security or social service that will be *foremost* in Saskatchewan affairs in the next four or five years [emphasis added]." Indeed, foremost "will be the agricultural and industrial development of the province on which living standards must depend.... The task in the second term will be to increase the wealth production of the province in order to make more money available to provide a higher standard of living for those who are unable to work."[18] Joe Phelps, with his zeal for developing industries, no longer fit into the plan. Certainly, the government also realized that Phelps's policies in the North and the losses in some of the newly created Crown corporations had cost the CCF votes. Significantly, Douglas replaced Joe Phelps as Minister of Natural Resources with John H. Brockelbank, who was much more moderate and cautious.[19]

DEFEAT

The 1948 defeat marked the end of Joe Phelps's political career.[20] His departure from the legislature caused some to rejoice but others to grieve. Douglas would later comment that Phelps was "one of the most volitile [*sic*] and virile speakers in the Saskatchewan political history. He was a real loss to us."[21]

Many blamed Phelps's defeat on his busy schedule, suggesting he had neglected his constituency. According to Roy Romanow, Phelps's strong leadership skills were in demand all over the province, which often took him away from his constituents. Romanow, who would lose his own Saskatoon seat by nineteen votes in 1982 but later become premier, also noted that Saltcoats was "not known as a hotbed for new social change."[22] Eiling Kramer made these comments:

> He lost the Saltcoats constituency largely because he had been too busy to take care of the politics at home. This is a sorry comment on voter appreciation for a man so busy doing his job as a Minister, that he did not leave time for touring his constituency, kissing babies, shaking hands and visiting at fairs, picnics and fowl suppers. He paid the political price by losing his seat, but Saskatchewan gained much from his foresight and dedication. It is hard to believe that four short

> years as a Minister, could have had such lasting impact on Saskatchewan life.[23]

Many constituents were apparently concerned that he had not spent enough time in his own riding and that he seemed out of touch with them. As an opposition member, he had maintained close personal contact with those who had elected him. He had regularly attended meetings and conventions, sent newsletters, and personally knew many of his constituents. After becoming Minister of Natural Resources, however, he could not devote as much time to these tasks. This was often evident. As early as August 1944, he wrote,

> Naturally, we are very busy here. In fact the job of taking over the Department is considerably more extensive than I had at first anticipated.... I will not be able to get down to the Constituency until this fall.... I am suggesting that my wife take over some of the work of the Constituency from now on. I will not have as much time to devote to the people of Saltcoats Constituency. This is simply the price they will have to pay for having a Cabinet Minister represent them.[24]

Responding to criticism that he had not attended the 1945 annual meeting of the Fish and Game League, Phelps expressed a similar concern: "I realize it is impossible for one outside the Department to appreciate the tremendous amount of work there is to do in this office.... In fact, I very seldom get time any more to visit my own Constituency as the administrative duties of the Department have priority."[25]

Phelps was aware of his dilemma in trying to fulfill his dual roles as the MLA for Saltcoats and as the Minister of Natural Resources. Responding to several requests that he attend local conventions within his own constituency, he replied,

> Now you ask for a week in Saltcoats. The general public feel that I have a responsibility to them and should try to stay on the job for which I have been selected. Naturally, I am now beginning to wonder how my time can be divided and who has the greatest demands on it.... It is realized that my own

> Constituency can justly claim some time. On the other hand, it is hoped that you and members of the Executive will see there is a limit to what can be done.[26]

Phelps's role as Minister of Natural Resources gave him little opportunity to deal with his southern, rural constituents since most of his work dealt with northern Saskatchewan. When his constituents felt neglected, many no longer supported him.[27] When Berry Richards later asked Phelps if his role as Minister of Natural Resources had been instrumental in his defeat in the 1948 election, Phelps replied, "Yeah, I don't think there is any doubt about that." He thought that being unable to get to his constituency "for weeks on end" might have caused people to think he had deserted them. He also sensed that there was "very little liaison between what we were doing in the Department and the people of Saltcoats," where 90 per cent of the people were engaged in agriculture. He added, "People at that time wouldn't have understood" the significance of the discovery of potash and its implications:

> Burns, the fellow that told me that it was there…the core samples and what not. He told me, he said, this could be, you got one of the biggest potash deposits in your constituency, or maybe any place in Canada.... Using potash as a fertilizer, that was almost new at that time. You didn't use fertilizers at that time here. Look after nature…no no it was a new ball game entirely. People had to recondition their thinking in order to get potash on the list.[28]

The intervention of James G. Gardiner, the federal Minister of Agriculture, may also have been a factor in Phelps's defeat. Gardiner addressed Saskatchewan audiences at least six times during the election campaign. He pointed out to rural voters how the federal Liberal government was helping farmers: selling Canadian wheat to Britain, making additional equalization payments for coarse grain sales, and paying farmers a high price for their wheat. Gardiner also used scare tactics, warning that if the CCF remained in power, it would "take over the grain elevators." He also claimed that the CCF would "take delivery of the farmers' grain, take it to the wheat board, and then give the farmer what they thought he should get. The balance of the money would be used for provincial requirements."[29] It is also noteworthy that Saltcoats had voted Liberal in every provincial election from 1905 to 1929 and would be solidly Liberal again from 1948 to 1971. While Phelps and the CCF were able to win the seat in 1938 and 1944, it returned to the Liberal fold in 1948.[30]

Reflecting on the 1948 election in 2012, farm leader Chris Hansen reminisced, "We were not all that surprised when Joe lost in Saltcoats. All the 'big guns' from the opposition were focussed on that constituency and there was always a bit of local concern about someone from the west side of the province running in that constituency."[31]

Throughout the election campaign, the Liberals made much of any personal indiscretions they were able to uncover about Phelps during his four years in office. In the fall of 1944, he had "stored" two nearly new one-and-a half-ton DNR trucks at his farm and had used them to haul two loads of grain for a neighbour to a siding thirty miles away. While he had collected $94 for the rent of the trucks and insisted that the government planned to dispose of them, the incident hurt his reputation.[32] A. T. Procter (Liberal, Moosomin) stated, "I do not think that is sound business for any government. That is one of those sordid things that leads to unrest and suspicion in the public mind. It tends to lead to a want of confidence in the ministers. I sincerely hope that those kinds of things will not be permitted in the future."[33]

The Liberals also denounced Phelps for hiring his brother Don to help at the Beaver Lake Fish Plant. Don had been on a "temporary assignment" for at least a year, and while he had not received a salary, he had obtained $550 for expenses.[34] Phelps was also strongly criticized for taking his wife and two grown children along with him on a trip to the North in a government plane in 1946. In a letter to the *Prince Albert Daily Herald* on May 27, 1947, Phelps had argued that he saw no reason why his family could not join him. Besides, he insisted that he had paid $90 for the trip. In a letter to the editor of the *Daily Herald*, E. F. Fournier maintained that Phelps's trip had actually cost $995 because a larger plane had been required to carry four passengers. He also insisted that carrying passengers on a government plane was "illegal." To a question in the legislature about who had accompanied him on his "six day tour of the north," Phelps had responded, "Department records do not reveal complete information pertaining to all plane flights."[35] This was later shown to be incorrect when Floyd Glass, the northern superintendent and Aircraft Division head of the department, testified at an unrelated trial in Prince Albert and stated that records of all flights were kept, which included both the names and numbers of passengers. In a letter, Phelps accused the lawyer of making "petty jibes."[36] Fournier further noted that Phelps had not revealed that he had taken his family on the trip or paid the $90. He accused him of being "evasive in the Legislature to the point of practically concealing facts and figures."[37]

It is likely that Phelps's indiscretions resulted more from idealism and naïveté than from duplicity. Phelps probably saw no harm in storing DNR trucks and helping his neighbour, hiring his brother to work at the fish plant, or taking his family along on a trip. However, the indiscretions noted above are likely what Quiring had in mind when he stated, "patronage and suspected corruption also likely added to Phelps' defeat." While "suspected corruption" is an overstatement, Phelps's actions may have embarrassed his fellow MLAs and gave the Liberals an endless opportunity to badger and harass him and the government.[38] Reflecting on the intensity of the election campaign in a later interview with Berry Richards, Phelps recollected,

> In fact I had one fellow come to me after, three years after the election was over, when I was in the Farmers Union and he made an appointment to see me from Flin Flon country, and he came down here and he said, I come to settle up with you. And I said you got no settling with me. And he said, well I was the fellow, the fisherman from the north that was hired by the Liberal Party. I spent many many weeks in Saltcoats constituency, and that was my job—to spread the idea of what you have been doing to the north country and how the things you have done has ruined it. He said, I wasn't sure myself at the time I was doing it, that it was as bad as they told me to make it, but he said, now after three years seeing what's gone on, he said, my conscience now is bothering me much about what I did, I gotta come and settle with you. And I said, the fact that you came is enough to support me. We all make mistakes. Well, he said, I sure made one. I said I don't hold it against

> you. And he could hardly understand that. I said maybe you did me a favour.... I wasn't married to that job.[39]

ITS MOST RADICAL MEMBER?

After his defeat, Phelps blamed what he termed "concessions to labour" for the party's election losses.[40] At the CCF convention, he stated, "The CCF had gone plenty far in its labour legislation and it was time the party took stock of the situation."[41] In his opinion, the CCF had antagonized farmers by reaching out for labour support. He argued, "on too many occasions the CCF had taken the stand that labour was always right...perhaps it was not always right and that the employer was not always 'the big bad wolf.'"[42] Warning the CCF to take stock of the situation, he said, "We appreciate help we received from labour, but we must impress upon labour that there are two sides to every question.... We have sought to drive employers and employees apart. It should be our effort to bring labour and management closer together." He added, "The CCF may have lost support in rural areas because it moved too fast in its labour legislation to the detriment of those living there."[43] Phelps may also have been alarmed by the corruption within the American organized labour movement that had come to public attention in Canada at the time, and felt strongly the party should reconsider its future relationship with labour.[44]

In *Agrarian Socialism*, Seymour Lipset observed that Phelps, although often characterized as the most radical member of the Douglas Cabinet, was conservative in his views on labour, noting it is ironic that Phelps, "who has been quoted as a critic of labour, entered the CCF government as its most radical member."[45] Phelps, perhaps like many Saskatchewan farmers, felt the interests and concerns of farmers were somewhat at odds with organized labour. Although the formation of the CCF ostensibly represented a melding of the farm and labour movements, conflict remained, creating a degree of internal tension within the party. Labour historian Glen Makahonuk describes the relationship between unions and the CCF as paradoxical: "While the unions were urging the CCF to go further with its programs of labour law reform, the business lobby and agrarian petit bourgeois not only outside the CCF, but also inside it were continually pressuring the Douglas government not to do so."[46] In more recent decades, opponents of the left in Saskatchewan have at times capitalized on vestiges of this rural-urban split.

It is somewhat puzzling that despite his many years working for wages as a lineman, Phelps was so quick to blame labour for the party's election losses. It seems likely that his experience as a manager of socially owned businesses was an alienating experience, and it was at times difficult for him to reconcile with his own petit bourgeois roots or his experience as a worker. His response is indicative of the overarching paradox within the CCF noted above: it was a party made up largely of farmers, with a platform derived from the socialist labour movement. Phelps was also disappointed in his own defeat and anxious for an explanation. Perhaps, as a consequence, he did not take time to consider and analyze the situation but rather echoed and expressed the anti-labour sentiment he was hearing from other farmers whom he regarded as the base of the party.

In a 1981 interview, Tommy Douglas reflected on Phelps's political style, noting that he did not, in fact, consider Phelps a radical. Although he was very progressive on issues such as public ownership, in Douglas's opinion he was more of a "small-c" conservative on some issues. Tommy Douglas commented, "He was an activist. People make a great mistake in always assuming that an activist is necessarily a radical. Joe was an activist, a very pragmatic person. He saw something that had to be done, what's the shortest distance between two points. Where we are to where we want to go. He drove for it."[47] This is an accurate description that encapsulates the somewhat contradictory and paradoxical nature of Phelps's political orientation. Phelps's approach of tackling issues head on, "letting the chips fall where they may" (a favourite expression of his), may have become a political liability. Historian Murray Dobbin suggests that

> his unorthodox methods, his disdain for the bureaucracy, and his political independence, had created considerable tension in the cabinet. He had been highly effective in the CCF's struggle for power, but once there, he had become something of a liability. Some members of the cabinet and the party quietly welcomed his defeat, and they had no inclination to return him to a position of sensitive political responsibility.[48]

Others such as Edgar Kaeding felt that more than any other single factor, the fallout from the creation of the Fur Marketing Board was to blame for Phelps's defeat in the 1948 provincial election. However, despite the unpopularity of some northern development initiatives, Phelps's efforts in the North did not go unacknowledged. Many DNR supervisors and managers were extremely distressed that he would not be returning to the North. Dobbin observed,

> If the problems in northern Saskatchewan were more political than administrative, the authority and political protection of a cabinet minister was required. Phelps could no longer play that role, but perhaps hoping to retain the strength of his personal prestige, seven Department of Natural Resources program supervisors and managers sent a long submission to Premier T. C. Douglas, asking that Phelps be appointed to some position within DNR. Outlining the deficiencies of the northern development program, they hailed Phelps as "one who stood alone in his unwavering faith in the possibilities of northern development." They received no response.[49]

There would be no attempts to find a new seat for Joe Phelps. A suggestion was made that "the Wadena seat—the safest CCF seat in the province—might be opened for 'Fighting Joe,'" but the CCF executive took no such action. The Douglas Government was even cool to providing Phelps with a position in the civil service.[50] After the 1948 election, Douglas and the new government became much more cautious in the enterprises they undertook and much more conservative in the manner in which they governed. Brown, Roberts, and Warnock note that the government-owned manufacturing concerns became economic and political liabilities, and that by the 1950s they had abandoned this strategy: "There was a left-right debate about whether these [oil, gas, coal, potash, and other minerals] should be developed by the public sector. The right-wing strategists won out and most resources were developed by private corporations, usually with capital from outside the province and often outside the country."[51]

THE NORTHERN RIDINGS

When Phelps's defeat was announced, L. M. Marion (Athabasca, Liberal) and Robert E. Lee, president of the Independent Voters' Association of Cumberland, challenged Phelps to contest either constituency in the deferred elections that were to be held on July 22, 1948. Lee's telegram to T. C. Douglas read:

> Mr. Premier, a great many people of the north last night received the news of the defeat of the late minister of natural resources with much gratification. Our only desire now is that you will send this socialist dictator up here to contest the seat of Cumberland constituency so that the people who have suffered most under the dictatorship of Joe Phelps may have the opportunity of venting their feelings towards this arch suppressor of the rights of free people.[52]

Needless to say, the CCF executive did not ask either candidate to withdraw to make way for Phelps. Determined to defend the policies he had instituted in the North by supporting the two CCF candidates, Axel Olson and Joseph Johnson in the Athabasca and Cumberland ridings, respectively, Phelps set up a temporary office in a government building in Prince Albert to campaign on their behalf. Reports out of Prince Albert were that "the government is ready to leave no stone unturned in trying to retain Cumberland, and gain Athabasca from the Liberals." The *Leader-Post* put it this way:

> Resources Minister J. L. Phelps, who is looked upon as the "king of the north" by the many trappers, fishermen and lumber operators who inhabit the northern part of Saskatchewan, has gone back to the area of the province that has become a familiar haunt for him in the past four years. But it is in a somewhat different capacity this time.[53]

During the campaign, Phelps soon found critics both inside and outside the CCF. Carlyle King, a member of the CCF Election Strategy Committee, wrote the following letter to Premier T. C. Douglas:

> The Committee…expressed itself emphatically that Joe Phelps is not running the show up north.…Joe is to work under Mrs. Wheaton's direction in so far as he takes part in those campaigns.
>
> …I had a long distance call from Joe Phelps.… He gave me a long tirade of abuse. He said that everything I had done was wrong, that I was personally responsible for the loss of seats in the provincial election, that I had exceeded my responsibility in putting Mrs. Wheaton in charge, and that I was not telling the truth. I listened patiently to the long recital of my failures and shortcomings as provincial president, but when he proceeded to curse me in profane and dirty language, I hung up the phone. Next day from Prince Albert he phoned again, and wanted to be polite. I informed him that I was holding no further conversation with him until he apologized for the abusive attack and profane language of the day before. He said: "Let's forget it and start over." I said no emphatically and hung up.
>
> …I do not think I deserve to be blamed by a Cabinet Minister for the losses in the election and to be abused in profane and dirty language. I believe that I am entitled to a written apology. I am aware that you cannot make a Minister do anything he does not wish to do, but I am asking you to tell Mr. Phelps…that he ought to write me an apology. If one is not forthcoming, I propose to take the matter to the Provincial Council and tell the Council that I do not intend to continue in a position of responsibility in the organization if that kind of attack by a Cabinet Minister goes unrebuked.[54]

While Phelps was often outspoken and did not hesitate to speak his mind, the "long tirade of abuse" and use of "profane and dirty language" that King refers to are not consistent with any other descriptions of Phelps's character or behaviour. Clearly, Phelps had antagonized some of the leadership within the party. The *StarPhoenix* observed,

> Political observers in Saskatoon, including CCF supporters, admit these results can be evaluated in only one manner—

> unpopularity of policies touching northern trappers, fishermen, and lumbermen. Coupled with the personal defeat of Mr. Phelps, they say the elections in the far northern seats, and their election affiliation, have been thrown squarely into Mr. Phelps' lap. He can win and continue to boss the north, no doubt with changed programs, or else tread the path followed by innumerable other unsuccessful politicians.... Hence, in tackling the two northern seats, Mr. Phelps faces a tough assignment, but no one can accuse Joe of not fighting. He has never shied away when "the going was tough," and with his political future at stake he can be relied upon to stage a real battle. He is certain to make a desperate effort to salvage Cumberland from the collapse of his board-administered domain, for on that constituency hinges his political future.[55]

The *Leader-Post* of July 8, 1948, also speculated on Phelps's presence in the northern political campaign, noting, "Sources close to the government have suggested that the northern people have had enough of Mr. Phelps and his restrictive policies, and his appearance there, in his present capacity, may do more harm than good."[56] His participation in the northern election campaign also triggered the continuing debate in the *Daily Herald*, which surfaced in an editorial on July 12, 1948. His political campaign in northern Saskatchewan was referred to as a "lame duck session."[57] The *Herald* elaborated: "The resemblance presented by the activities of Mr. Phelps, of course, is obvious. For the past four years he has both personified, and almost literally been 'the government' in the Far North. He was defeated in the election of June 24, yet he continues to exercise all of the powers of the government in the Far North."[58] The newspaper criticized Phelps for having an immeasurable campaign advantage through his use of the transportation service and the communication systems in the northern ridings, which the newspaper stated were "largely his own creations and his to command."[59]

Many northern residents complained about the measures Phelps had imposed on the fishing, timber, and fur industries. Some called him autocratic and dictatorial. In fact, G. H. Danielson (Liberal, Arm River) called him "the Grand Mufti of Northern Saskatchewan," "the King of the North," and "the Colossus of the North." L. M. Marion (Liberal, Athabasca) also stated that people in the North referred to Phelps as "Uncle Joe" (a reference to Joseph Stalin) and "Dictator of the North." He added, "Now virtually everything connected with trying to earn a living comes under the control of the Minister of Natural Resources."[60] The word "tyranny," which had appeared in Liberal advertisements, may well have been directed mainly at Phelps. Still others observed that some of the Crown corporations that he had set up had suffered severe financial losses.

Despite Phelps's valiant efforts and the CCF's northern policy initiatives, the Liberals took both Athabasca and Cumberland on July 22, 1948. Athabasca elected Louis Marion, a Liberal, defeating the CCF's Axel Olson of Prince Albert. Cumberland elected Lorne Blanchard, also a Liberal, defeating CCF candidate Joe Johnson of Cumberland House. The Liberal victories in the North were not entirely unexpected. Dobbin noted that despite the fact that no other political party had ever taken initiatives on Indigenous issues, there was an emerging Indigenous hostility to the CCF government. He explains:

> The provincial government also encountered opposition from the Catholic church and private business in the north. The Church, with its considerable influence over native people, denounced the CCF as "godless" and "communist" and the Hudson's Bay Company, private traders and fish companies, attempted to sabotage the government's fur and fish programs. Living among the native people gave white entrepreneurs and clergymen an advantage over the handful of CCF employees in the field. Any native complaint about the government was richly exploited, and used as ammunition against the CCF and their reforms.[61]

The province's newspapers described the defeat of the CCF candidates in Athabasca and Cumberland as "a stinging slap in the face to the Douglas government." Clearly, the people of those ridings had "voiced their dissatisfaction with the socialist experiments which the administration imposed on the fishermen, lumbermen and trappers." "Under the dictatorial drive of Mr. Phelps," they had experienced the reorganization of their industries, the implementation of marketing boards, and the "rigidly controlled timber, fur, and fish production and regulated prices and methods of sale." Through their vote, they had repudiated the government's coercive northern policies and Joe Phelps, who had initiated and administered most of them.[62]

FAILURE IN THE NORTH

The resource policy envisioned and implemented by Phelps was part of an overall CCF plan intended to improve the standard of living in the North. There were, however, a number of problems inherent in the CCF's plan for development. With six different provincial departments delivering services to the North, in addition to the federal Department of Indian Affairs, CCF policy in the North was fraught with problems. For example, Department of Education policy required that mothers and children leave the traplines and fish camps to attend schools in the settlements (mothers' allowances were contingent upon school attendance) so that the children could be prepared for the kinds of jobs that might be available in the south. The old economy based on fur and fish (with prices dependent on external markets) was inadequate to provide a solid economic base for the rapidly increasing northern population, but, cut off from the field education of the bush economy, children were now schooled in preparation for jobs that simply failed to materialize in the North.[63]

Dobbin makes the point that ultimately the CCF failed to implement meaningful social policy because its policy did nothing to account for the lack of a viable economic base. Instead, it created economic dependence. He suggests that "the CCF's plan for northern Saskatchewan in education, health, and social development, meant the people would have to adapt to the system; the system would not adapt itself to the people."[64] Both Dobbin and Barron contend the CCF approach to Indigenous policy was paternalistic, concluding it did not collaborate fully and equally with the First Nations and Métis people but rather imposed its plan for the North. Barron maintains that the government's reforms were rooted in notions of intervention and control. He insists that while the government was well-intentioned, its policies were ethnocentric and paternalistic. Barron points out that, administratively, most of the North was under the jurisdiction of the Northern Affairs Branch of the DNR. Since Phelps held this portfolio, he played the key role in dealing with the North's political, economic, and social challenges.[65] Barron argues that the policies Phelps introduced in the North created serious economic problems there.[66] He further argues that "the DNR was mandated not only as a manager of the northern economy but was also as a manager of the people" who lived there.[67] Many of the solutions proposed to resolve the problems in northern Saskatchewan were, in Barron's words, "little more than reflections of the values and agenda of southern society, and control was carefully maintained in Regina."[68]

Similarly, David Quiring offers a harsh assessment of the CCF government and of Joe Phelps's approach to northern development. Quiring asserts that the CCF government tried to bring northerners into the twentieth century by modernizing, assimilating, and socializing them, and in so doing "utilized destructive, paternalistic, and colonial methods to impose its agenda." He maintains that the government destroyed the northern economic system and worsened poverty and social dysfunction within Indigenous communities. He singles out Phelps and strongly condemns him for bringing about "the most aggressive intervention" in the North. While Quiring acknowledges that the CCF did ensure that parish priests, bootleggers, and "fur sharks" no longer dominated the North, he asserts that it failed to establish a workable alternative. He also identifies the DNR as the "strong colonial arm" of the government that began "greatly expanding its presence and power in the North."[69]

Alternatively, one can argue that the strongest "colonial arm" was in fact the Indian Act and the assimilationist policies, including the residential school system, of the federal government. In contrast to Quiring, northern resident Karla Radloff argued in her thesis, "Cooperative and State Ownership in Northern Saskatchewan under the CCF Government," that the overriding purpose of CCF policy was to improve the social and economic position of northerners. She concluded that by using social ownership as its main policy instrument, the CCF government did, in fact, achieve many of its "policy-specific" goals in the North: "It eliminated the monopolies held by northern traders; it stabilized the northern fish and fur industries through orderly marketing; it increased prices to fishers and trappers through cooperative marketing; it decreased the cost of goods in the north; and it generally decreased the influence of private industry in northern Saskatchewan." She also argued that

> the CCF government's policies of social ownership led to the development of co-operatives in Northern Saskatchewan, which were the first of their kind in Canada, as there were no other Aboriginal or Northern co-operatives previously incorporated. Even though the CCF government's program of co-operative development among Northern Aboriginals was a top-down initiative of limited success, it is significant because it was a pioneering effort that produced an early model for others to draw upon and learn from in subsequent years.[70]

Dobbin acknowledged Phelps's personal efforts to involve northerners in the CCF plan, and noted that when Phelps was defeated and did not return to the North, there was a definite decline in progressive initiatives. The Department of Northern Services became much more conservative, and emphasis shifted toward more bureaucratic administrative procedures. Dobbin states:

> Phelps was more than willing to take on the reactionaries in northern Saskatchewan. He tried to wrest control of a special fur lease from the Hudson's Bay Company at Cumberland House, and attempted to buy out the HBC's trading posts. His cabinet colleagues, however, feared the political consequences of confrontation.[71]

Phelps likely also struggled with resistance from the existing staff and senior administrators he relied upon to implement the government's new programs. Quiring noted that Phelps had an uneasy relationship with senior employees, which undermined morale and at times created defiance: "Not all district superintendents or other high-ranking employees complied readily with Phelps's order that they submit details of their daily activities. Those who defied Phelps or did not promptly carry out his orders received reprimands. He also closely monitored expenses."[72]

Geographical, economic, and cultural factors, as well as the division of responsibility between federal and provincial jurisdictions, combined to reduce the long-term success of some of the early CCF programs in the North. Although there was some progress with issues of concern to First Nations and Métis people, in 1953 Premier Douglas admitted that the government was only scratching the surface. Later, in the 1950s, Douglas concluded that First Nations and Métis problems must be dealt with simultaneously, and that there was a need for federal and provincial governments to collaborate. According to Shackleton, what Douglas did for the Indigenous peoples of Saskatchewan was to "give them the vote and the right to drink liquor like white people. The first benefit was offered repeatedly and accepted reluctantly; the second was eagerly sought and was granted with misgivings."[73] Even Quiring acknowledges that "other governments across Canada, including those that did not adopt socialist policies or other aggressive programs of directed change, experienced similar failures in their northern regions" and that "although greatly weakened, the old forces [the pre-existing Euro-Canadian capitalist and church institutions] continued to affect events during the CCF era."[74]

In the years to come, things would not improve for many of the province's Indigenous people. McLeod and McLeod note:

> Over the next thirty years the Indians moved to Saskatchewan's cities in large numbers, along with their Métis cousins. Instead of municipal welcome, they met with racism, unemployment and poverty. No government federal or provincial, Liberal, NDP or Tory, ever put together a political consensus among the white majority to address the problem.[75]

Notwithstanding future problems, initial efforts by the CCF government were positive. Barron concludes:

> The CCF did express a sympathy and empathy for Native people that was unprecedented in provincial history. The government was genuinely troubled by the plight of an oppressed and disfranchised minority in its midst, and its response was a concerted effort to integrate Métis and Indians into provincial society on a basis of individual equality and fairness.[76]

Schools, hospitals, and nursing stations were built. Conservation measures were put in place to ensure that fur, fish, and timber resources produced sustainable yields for future generations. Marketing boards were set up to safeguard the fur, fish, and timber industries, and the

Fur Marketing Service and the Timber Board both showed profits. Producers received prices that were comparable to or higher than those previously received from private dealers, and orderly marketing stabilized returns for the future. A radio-telephone communication system was established. Saskatchewan Government Airways was operating as a Crown corporation, an air ambulance service had been established, and a road had been built from Prince Albert to La Ronge. The formation of the Union of Saskatchewan Indians (the precursor of the Federation of Saskatchewan Indian Nations) was an important step forward that allowed First Nations peoples to begin to carry their grievances to the provincial and federal governments with one united voice. Within his short mandate, Phelps had accomplished a great deal.

CHANGING GEARS

After ten productive years in the Saskatchewan provincial legislature, six years in opposition and four in government, Phelps changed gears and

Newly installed electric meters signalled electricity had been installed on the farm, July 1955. Provincial Archives of Saskatchewan, Government of Saskatchewan Photo Services Reference #55-167-01.

moved on to a new challenge. Husky Oil had offered him a position in Lloydminster, but after being flown out for two or three days and taking a "sashay around," he decided being an oil tycoon was not for him.[77] He accepted a position with the Power Commission to continue his work on rural electrification. His appointment was announced in the *Leader-Post* on November 26, 1948,[78] along with H. F. Berry, who was appointed chairman, and G. W. Cadbury, chief industrial executive. The committee would undertake a study to expand rural electrification in the province.

After accepting the new post and finding himself working within the bureaucracy, which he disliked intensely and viewed with hostility, Phelps quickly became dissatisfied and frustrated. He believed that rural electrification was proceeding too slowly, and that Clarence Fines and George Cadbury were reluctant in their support of the program. "They were doing some window dressing and I wanted to do the job," Phelps stated in a later interview.[79] Staying only long enough to assist in drafting the policy embodied in the Rural Electrification Act of 1949 and the program aptly titled "Lighting Up Saskatchewan," Phelps resigned his position with the Saskatchewan Power Commission in the spring of 1949 after four months.

Phelps's groundwork, however, ensured that rural electrification did, in fact, proceed. The Douglas Government took steps to ensure that the benefits of postwar economic success and growing material prosperity extended into the rural areas that had been so devastated during the thirties. Between 1949 and 1955, thousands of farms were connected to the provincial power grid, bringing lights and electricity to the farms and significantly lightening the load for rural people in the years to come.

PART III

ACTION AND ACTIVISM

1948–1983

CHAPTER 14

"IT'S TIME TO PUT THE SPURS AND KNUCKLE DUSTERS ON"

By midlife—his work in government drawn to a premature conclusion—Joe Phelps was ready for a new challenge. The abrupt end to his political career had taken him by surprise, and he was stunned by the results, though in his own words he was not "married to that job."[1] After a brief time with the provincial power corporation, Joe, Lena, and the children moved to Saskatoon in 1949. His decision to return to the farm and the farm movement was natural and not surprising given the opinion he expressed after his defeat about the "very evident drift of the CCF away from its agrarian origin towards the role of merely being the political arm of organized left wing labour in Canada."[2]

Joe Phelps returned to his roots, seeking inspiration and a chance to integrate his experience as a farmer, a politician, and a social activist. The agricultural policy of the early Farmer-Labour Party and the CCF had been fraught with well-intentioned but less than popular policies. The original land-use lease policy conceived during the formation of the party amidst the devastating drought and the Depression was abandoned early on, and other ideas such as the controversial co-operative farming initiative had ultimately "failed after a promising start" by the end of the CCF's first term in office.[3] The 1944 CCF program for agriculture was far-reaching and perhaps overly optimistic. In addition to its comprehensive farm security program,[4] it had advocated for the closing of the Winnipeg Grain Exchange; setting parity prices for farmers (prices that would bring farmers their fair share of the total national income); establishing marketing boards with producer representation; regulating the livestock industry; establishing an agricultural bank and a farm implement board to manufacture and distribute farm implements; and setting up government grain storage facilities, import and export boards, and a vast soil and water conservation program.[5] The realities of the province's financial situation had mitigated against the implementation of much of this program during its first term in government, and Phelps perhaps felt that he could have more influence on agrarian policy from outside the CCF. Leading farmers in their protracted quest for fair and equitable treatment through the rejuvenated Saskatchewan Farmers Union movement provided just such a challenge.

During the same period, Phelps's interest in preserving the history of Saskatchewan fast became a passion and led to the establishment of the Western Development Museum, which, through his persistent efforts to collect and display the artifacts of the era, remains a permanent tribute legacy to Saskatchewan's pioneers. Five years of service were devoted to the Royal Commission on Agriculture and Rural Life, as he sought to preserve the traditional family farm and its associated way of life.

He persisted in his relentless work ethic and his pursuit of new challenges and adventures. His thoughts, often expressed while pulling on his suspenders and letting them snap back against his stomach, or with his eyes flashing, accompanied by a lusty thump on his desk, continued to resonate in his characteristic expression: "By jingles, you've got to raise your sights if you want to get the job done!"

A NEW CHALLENGE

After ten years as a politician, Phelps returned to the movement that originally led him to politics, a cause he had first championed as a young man. His next challenge was to breathe new life into the moribund organized farm movement.[6] Although by his own recollection, Phelps had only a "total of 72 schooling days after leaving grade 6,"[7] he recalled writing essays about how farmers needed to work together while he was attending the small rural school near Wilkie as a child.[8] By the age of eighteen, he was heavily involved in farm politics, serving as district director for the Saskatchewan Grain Growers Association and organizing a tour of northwestern Saskatchewan for J. S. Woodsworth, whose social gospel message included the need for a strong and vibrant farm organization. But at the time a storm was brewing in the ranks of the SGGA over the marketing of wheat and how to best serve farmers in maximizing price returns.

By the 1920s, Phelps had "jumped ship" from the SGGA to the Farmers' Union of Canada, the break-away group under the leadership of L. P. McNamee of Kelvington, favouring 100 per cent compulsory contract pooling, joining in its crusade to sign up farmers to 100 per cent wheat marketing contracts. The SGGA favoured a slow, conservative approach, and members were signing up farmers to five-year voluntary pool marketing contracts, reflecting a sharp difference in approach. These were dynamic and exciting times, and historical accounts attest to the bad blood between the leaders of the two organizations over the marketing issue.[9] By 1924, sufficient contracts had been signed by producers to enable a Wheat Pool provisional board to co-operatively market wheat on the international market for the first time. Aaron Sapiro, a California lawyer specializing in co-operatives, had provided the focus and inspiration on marketing strategies required by farmers to attain their goals. During a sponsored visit to Saskatchewan, he stressed the need for the two organizations to amalgamate, which occurred on July 15, 1926, in Saskatoon, and thus the United Farmers of Canada, Saskatchewan Section was created.[10]

Phelps was well grounded in the politics and policies of the voluntary farm movement when he attended what might have been the final convention of the UFC in November 1949. The UFC's membership had declined to only a few hundred paid-up members in thirty-seven locals, and debt was accumulating.[11] Already well connected with many farm families by virtue of his high-profile Cabinet positions and his close association with the ambitious rural electrification program, Phelps had become popular throughout rural Saskatchewan at a time when the CCF held strong rural appeal. His reputation for championing causes inside and outside of government was well established. The challenge extended to Phelps by members at that convention was to attempt the revitalization of the movement.

A NEW IDENTITY

Phelps accepted the challenge on two conditions. First, that the name of the organization be changed—the UFC was too closely associated with the CCF. Phelps had been a member of the UFC delegation that had joined with the Independent Labour Party of Saskatchewan to form the Farmer-Labour Group in 1932, the forerunner of the CCF. Changing the name would enable them to build a new grassroots movement without political history or affiliation, based on the solidarity and collective action inherent in the earlier Farmers' Union of Canada, the group that had spearheaded the formation of the Wheat Pool in the early twenties. The approximately one hundred farm delegates present at the convention voted unanimously to change the name. The United Farmers of Canada (Saskatchewan Section) became the Saskatchewan Farmers Union.[12]

Second, Phelps insisted that membership fees be raised to a meaningful amount. Speaking to the membership at the nominating convention, he argued, "We hear these people say if we raise the fees we'll lose all of our members. We have done a pretty good job of losing them as it is. The world will not take a farm organization very seriously on only a $2 membership. If you're going to pay 'two-bits' to keep it going, then all you can expect is a 'two-bit' organization."[13] Phelps went on to say that they should consider a fee schedule that resembled the closed union shop, whereby no one could farm in Saskatchewan unless they were licensed with the SFU. He continued to advocate a check-off dues system throughout his term in office.

Phelps emphasized the need for a more active approach, noting that the UFC had been functioning primarily as an educational organization and needed to shift its priority to becoming more of a protective body. The Saskatchewan Wheat Pool was increasingly usurping its role as the voice of the farmer. The problems of agriculture were urgent, and in a society where other groups were forming powerful organizations to lobby on their behalf and achieve public awareness, a more active approach had become essential. In his words, "I say it's time to put the spurs and knuckle dusters on."[14]

With reformed policy, a new identity, and an agreement to increase membership fees, Phelps was elected as the first president of the SFU. To liquidate the $12,000 debt of the UFC, the membership fee was increased to $5 per farm unit from $2, and the official publication of the UFC (renamed the *Union Farmer*) was restructured; James F. C. Wright, a noted author, was hired as editor.

Phelps accepted this new challenge with energy and passion. He would ignite a "virtual prairie fire of reorganization."[15] He attributed the state of decline in which he found the organization in 1949 to a number of factors. First, when the wheat pools were formed in the twenties, many directors, delegates, chairman, and local committeemen had been recruited from the UFC and other existing farm organizations. The growth of the co-operative movement, including the grain, poultry, and livestock pools, had also drawn a significant number of people away from the UFC, leaving fewer suitable candidates for continued leadership in the farm organization. Farmers assumed that the commercial co-operatives would take care of their interests. Participation in the political arena had also contributed to the decline in membership. When the FUC and SGGA merged to form the UFC and members of the UFC, in turn, participated in the formation of the CCF in the thirties, the UFC lost a number of experienced people and had since failed to recruit sufficient numbers of replacements. Once again, this fuelled the growing sentiment that there was no need for a general farm organization, with many believing farmers' concerns would be looked after through their affiliation with the CCF. After ten years working within government, Phelps had rethought his position on this matter and had this comment at the nominating convention: "Some say that with the CCF government in Regina, all the farmer's problems are solved and so we don't need the UFC. Mr. Chairman, as time goes on you may find yourself disillusioned on that point."[16] Now, more than ever, Phelps felt strongly that farmers should not rely on government representatives to solve agricultural problems:

> My experience has indicated to me that governments no matter what party they represent only move as and when they are pushed by the pressures of organized groups. There is a strong need for pressure. Organized farmers must consistently and forcefully present the farmers' viewpoint and press for action. Farmers unions are the logical vehicle to carry out this function because by embracing members from all political parties, and because they do not have any commercial

> ties, they are able to speak for all sections of the agricultural community. No single commercial enterprise co-operative or otherwise can speak for all farm interests, nor is there any joint co-operative yet evolved which is qualified to do so.[17]

Through his experience in government, Phelps had become well aware of the influence government boards had on agriculture. He was also painfully aware that there was very limited producer representation on many boards whose activities directly affected farmers' interests. In fact, many government policies were being made without any significant input from boards or producer groups. Rather than expecting commercial trading organizations or government representatives to operate on their behalf, farmers needed to insist that their voices be heard through direct representation. They needed representation on the Wheat Board, and they needed to be in a position to speak directly to provincial and federal governments and insist, for example, on getting a better price for agricultural products.

Postwar problems on the farm were numerous. Chris Hansen, who was elected SFU vice-president in 1954 and became president in 1955, describes the conditions on the prairies when Joe Phelps became president of the SFU:

> The late 1940s were turbulent times on the prairie agricultural scene. When the war ended, thousands of veterans returned either to their home farms, or to seek homesteads in new areas. The key to the farm economy at this time was the price of wheat, and farmers were locked into wheat agreements that were signed during the war to support the war effort. Many farmers believed the agreements were set up to keep wheat prices from going too high, rather than to benefit farmers.[18]

This was no doubt the case. But while the price of wheat had been controlled under wartime agreements, the price of farm inputs began to escalate rapidly after the war. With the rapid change from horsepower to large-scale mechanization, agriculture became less of a self-contained industry. Farmers required a large cash investment in machinery and equipment to carry on farming operations, and many accumulated high interest charges on their debt. Along with large combustion engines came rapidly increasing fuel and other input costs. Phelps would later comment, "If you take a look at the way farm costs have crept up on farm prices, you can see a lot of farmers are just living on depreciation." Attempting to address this growing cost-price squeeze would continue to be the primary focus of the SFU's work. Phelps spoke with inspiration and conviction about the need for "parity prices" to offset the price injustices farmers were suffering in the marketplace, as well as the problems created by rising costs of production.

STRENGTH IN UNION

Under these conditions, there was strength in joining together in common cause in much the same way workers joined together to form trade unions. The *Union Farmer* stated the group's purpose in a special supplement that included a brief historical synopsis of the organization: "The SFU is a non-political organization of which all bona-fide farmers may become members regardless of race, religion or political views. The purpose of the union is to strive to accomplish through organization what the farmer is unable to do for himself."[19]

That purpose was reminiscent of the early Farmers' Union of Canada, which believed that farmers joined together with one united voice could face off against the powerful interests. A number of forces would later combine to reduce this sentiment. Solidarity among farmers could be eroded by crop failures, low prices, the high cost of inputs, as well as drought and pests, all factors to which farmers have been vulnerable since the early settlement days. Some would later conclude that farmers as a group do not really believe strongly enough in the motto "in union there is strength."[20]

Phelps had a very practical rather than an ideological perspective about the purpose of the union. In his words, "the union's only reason for being is to provide service to members." He felt that potential members would be drawn to the SFU if they saw that the program supported their interests and that they could have real input and influence policy. For this reason, Phelps advocated policy development at the grassroots level. The primary objective of the union, Phelps stated on a number of occasions, was to raise the standard of living for farm families, and in particular to protect the interests of smaller farmers who were the most numerous and the most likely to be neglected without a general farm organization in which they could have a direct voice.[21] His sympathies were with the small farmer. Joe's son Bruce later recalled, "The Depression and the possibility of losing the family farm was a big influence on dad. His brothers said, 'walk away' and dad said 'no!'"[22]

Phelps thought that prairie farmers united in a democratic grassroots organization could fight the big interests. Like the earlier farmers' movement, his was a populist approach, in that a basic antagonism between the people and the "powerful interests" was inherent in his philosophy.[23] The union would rely on strength of numbers to wrestle with the big companies that were threatening their way of life. Like a trade union, the farmers' ultimate weapon was a strike, and Phelps supported their right to strike, stating,

> The right of any farmer to market his products, or withhold it from the market as he chooses, must be as undisputed as that of labour to strike, or of any other business man to open or close his business. This point accepted, the right of farmers to strike is clear. I believe that a strike, while justifiable in extreme circumstances is a weapon of last resort. Nevertheless the farmers union does not disclaim a belief in direct action if this should ultimately become necessary.[24]

Although Phelps defended the right to strike in principle, he advocated open and vigorous debate as the preferred route toward solutions, believing that humans were basically reasonable. Even the "bad apples" could be rehabilitated in his view. He rarely gave up completely on anyone. The 1946 delivery strike called by the UFC had likely impacted his views. The strike was an effort to achieve some kind of parity pricing for farm products, and it had generated a great deal of conflict within the movement:

> The Wheat Pool overruled some of their own local committees who decided to participate in the withholding strike and close down the local elevator. The Pool leaders would have nothing to do with the strike and insisted that the elevators be kept open. Moreover, they regarded the strike as ill-advised and impetuous—a blatant disregard on the part

> of the UFC for the channels of agitation which the Pool had built up during the thirties—namely the Saskatchewan Federation of Agriculture. There is little doubt that the UFC had no faith in the effectiveness of these channels.[25]

The 1946 strike affected even families: Chris Hansen, who grew up in Theodore, a small community west of Yorkton, and whose father was active in the UFC local lodge and also on the local Wheat Pool committee, was asked to join the picket line. In 2012 he recalled, "I was 17. Frankly, it was an embarrassing experience."[26] The conflict may have contributed to the low state of affairs that Phelps found the organization in when he agreed to become leader, and it fuelled the desire for rejuvenation of a grassroots organization free from political and commercial ties.

GRASSROOTS INPUT

Phelps turned his attention to building a strong grassroots organization. Organizational meetings were held throughout the province. Frank Eliason, the secretary of the UFC, stayed on initially. Other elected officials, such as Vice-President Joseph Hoffman, Women's President Elsie Hart, and executive members including Alfred Gleave and George Mirka, also attended numerous meetings throughout the province. Paid organizers were hired to promote the organization and locate local leaders. The task was monumental and took them far and wide across the province. Herb Schulz, an indefatigable and renowned farm organizer, self-described proselytizer for the Manitoba Farmers Union, and son of Jake Schulz, Phelps's counterpart in Manitoba, recollects what it was like organizing farmers in the 1950s: "My pay was five dollars a day and out of pocket expenses...and it was not easy. Sometimes I drove a hundred miles to a scheduled meeting to find a lone attendee—the hall caretaker who came to collect his fee."[27] Other times, local farmers were less than receptive. Nevertheless, by April 1950 Phelps was able to report that SFU membership had grown to over seven thousand.[28] The organizing blitz continued as Phelps reminded members of the importance of unity:

> The need of an active farm union was never more apparent than it is at the present time. With every other section of

> society, business, professional, and labour becoming stronger and stronger, farmers have no other alternative but to build an organization equally as strong. Farmers should always keep in mind the fact that we as a group outnumber any other economic group in Canada, and there is no reason why we could not be the strongest, both numerically and financially, if we have the good judgment to band ourselves together in a strong, active farm union.[29]

Grassroots input formed the foundation of SFU policy. Phelps knew the key to strong organization was through member participation in the democratic process. This brought forth a broad range of policy resolutions from locals on social and economic issues that were debated in conventions and helped form the basis of the SFU policy program. Such debates were at times lengthy and sometimes heated, but seldom fractious. Local lodges, requiring a minimum of eight senior members, provided a venue for farmers to get together and discuss their common problems. Locals were also encouraged to sponsor projects in their communities and set an example of co-operative spirit. Resolutions passed at the local lodge moved to the sub-district, then the district, and finally the provincial level, where, if passed by a majority at the annual provincial convention, they became policy. A two-thirds majority was required for constitutional change. Seventeen annual district conventions and numerous public meetings were held annually throughout the province, each district electing a district director, a women's director, and a junior director. The president and women's president made three annual tours of the seventeen districts, amounting to travel of approximately seventeen thousand kilometres.

SFU membership was limited to farmers, farm labourers, and retired farmers. Rural teachers or others closely associated with agriculture could become associate members by a two-thirds vote of the local lodge but could not act as delegates to conventions. There were no restrictions on political persuasion. Phelps did not hesitate to state his opinion on membership: "Radicals and even Communists may gain entrance. In any really democratic society they are few in number and cannot ultimately prevail against the reason and desire for fair play which has always been characteristic of our farmers."[30] The majority of SFU membership was more likely to be in the moderate centre of the political spectrum, as those who adhered to more extreme right- or left-wing ideologies had left the movement to join other organizations in the thirties.

Women played a significant role in the leadership of the SFU. Farm women were given an equal voice and assumed full membership and leadership rights. Women's directors were elected at the sub-district and district levels. At the provincial level, a women's president, as well as two additional women's directors at large, were part of the seven-member provincial board. Phelps was supportive of women's involvement, saying, "They have proven they can make a valuable contribution not only in organizing but in helping shape policy and carry it through effectively."[31] Throughout his life, Phelps was always comfortable with and respectful of women. This was not typical of the times but was perhaps more common in the prairie West, where many women worked alongside men on the farms, than elsewhere.

Phelps's first year as president was a busy one, and as he had in government, he juggled a large number of tasks and responsibilities. In the spring of 1950, at the annual conference, Phelps directed the provincial executive to go "full steam ahead." In a *Country Guide* article published shortly after Phelps became president, the writer H. S. Fry noted,

> During the period when I interviewed Mr. Phelps he was a very busy man. He was attempting to keep in touch with the active organization of the union; he was arranging an interview with members of the federal cabinet on matters on which the Farmers' Union of Alberta, Saskatchewan, and Manitoba were officially protesting; and in between he was attempting to help harvest a frozen crop of wheat.... He was operating a self-propelled combine and hurrying to get away elsewhere on Farmers' Union business.... He was dusty, hungry and depressed and irritated by the low grading of the crop and the wide spread between grades.[32]

CONFLICT WITH THE POOL

Phelps had an uneasy relationship with the Saskatchewan Wheat Pool, which did not welcome the resurrection of the voluntary farm movement.

The essence of Phelps's running battle with the SWP was cartooned in the April 1951 issue of the *Union Farmer*, which depicted Phelps as a bull in the SWP china shop with the headline, "Who's Going to Shut the Door?"

Maintaining a diplomatic public decorum was a delicate problem. After all, the majority of SFU members were also shareholders in the SWP, which was an important lynchpin in the co-operative movement. It should have been one big happy family, but the undercurrent was there and can perhaps only be understood through a brief recall of SWP history.

After the successful launching of the Wheat Pool in 1924, it was generally accepted that the UFC would serve as the educational and policy arm of the farm movement, while the pool would serve as its commercial marketing arm.[33] UFC membership dues were collected from farmers' grain deliveries through Wheat Pool elevators. This arrangement worked successfully until the SWP overpayment on initial grain prices in the fall of 1929, which virtually ended the Wheat Pool's direct marketing function. It turned its attention increasingly to questions of policy and education, placing it at odds with the UFC. While the UFC took strong exception to the Wheat Pool announcing itself as the education arm of various co-operative organizations in 1937, there was little the UFC could do about it, having been drained of leadership by its participation in the formation of the CCF in 1932. The loss of its dues check-off left it financially weak and vulnerable. The pool increasingly filled the education and policy vacuum in rural communities through its field service staff, while the UFC, though still active, struggled to compete.

Phelps was well aware of this sequence of history and had, to no avail, attempted early in 1950 to have the voluntary organization recognized by the pool as the education and policy arm of the farm movement. Shortly after the SFU reorganization, Phelps and Alf Gleave, an SFU executive member, arranged a meeting with Wheat Pool board members to discuss a request for financial assistance in rebuilding the SFU. In his book, *United We Stand*, Gleave recalled,

> We did not have a full day, just a few hours, but it was sufficient to the need and we received our answer quite simply: the SWP would not give any assistance to the SFU in rebuilding. It was also rather plain to me that for some of their directors the direct membership organization was a lost cause or at least

> an unnecessary part of the farm scene. I had grown up supporting the co-operatives and the SWP and I fully expected their answer would be in the affirmative.[34]

In 1951, with the support of a large delegation of SFU members, Phelps arranged a meeting with the SWP board of directors to discuss "spheres of activity." Stuart Thiesson, then assistant secretary of the SFU, attended the meeting and recalled that after Phelps's formal statement outlining its historical role, J. H. Wesson, SWP chairman, coolly dismissed the SFU proposal by stating that the pool considered itself "a farm policy organization as well as a commercial organization."[35] This did little to endear the SWP directorate to Phelps or attending SFU members.

By contrast, the United Grain Growers (UGG) organization had willingly extended the SFU a grant of $2,000. Gleave reports, "In subsequent years I met J. E. Brownlee, then president of the UGG, and found him sympathetic and favourable to the SFU, since he regarded it as an integral part of prairie farm organization."[36]

"HE WAS WITH THE CROWD AND THE CROWD WAS WITH HIM."

Under Phelps, the SFU maintained a strong educational function. Phelps's reputation as a dynamic and powerful speaker, honed through his political career, drew many to listen as he spoke to labour organizations, university students, farm unions from other provinces, co-operatives, political rallies, school trustees, and others, to both educate and garner support for the SFU. In those days, before the ten-second sound bite, public speaking was an art, and Phelps was a master.[37] His speeches were long and dramatic, and he rarely used notes. Notes would distract him, because, according to Olaf Turnbull, a SFU vice-president during this time, "He had his mind on the crowd. He was with the crowd and the crowd was with him. He reacted by instinct, gauging situations by what he felt."[38] Others have noted that at an almost primitive, instinctual level, Phelps quickly became aware of any corruption or dishonesty that was present in a room full of people.

To bring home a point, Phelps would often use stories and anecdotes.[39] Phelps's folksy and genuine style appealed to farmers. Indeed, leaders including Grant Devine, Saskatchewan's Conservative premier during the 1980s, would borrow expressions such as "Never say whoa in the middle of a mud puddle" that Phelps had coined during his time in Cabinet.[40]

Phelps had a number of themes he emphasized and reinforced during his speaking engagements, in his monthly reports to the membership that appeared in the *Union Farmer*, and in his comments to the media. One theme he was passionate about was that farmers needed to take responsibility for finding solutions to their problems. Speaking to a gathering of SFU members in August 1950, he said, "'Help yourself' might well be a slogan of the SFU, Organization of the farmers, by the farmers, for the farmers, can only come about when each and every one of us begin to help ourselves. It is not good enough to leave it to 'George' to do it for us. Nobody has been able to find out for sure just who 'George' is."[41] The solution, in his opinion, was collective "self-help" within a strong and influential farm organization.

During the same address, Phelps went on to talk at length about the rising cost of machinery and how input costs were reducing farm income. He stressed the importance of running the farm like a business: "I think the very nature of our business is one of the reasons why we developed so much self-determination and initiative and fought so many of our battles, because in order to make a success of farming today, you've got to be a business man of the first order. Farming is becoming bigger and bigger business." He suggested that should they meet a farmer who did not have time for union activity, "You just have a little talk with him, and you say, listen, anytime you get so busy that you haven't got time to look after the business end of your business, you may soon be out of business."[42]

A FIGHTING ORGANIZATION

By 1951, the SFU had grown to over seven hundred lodges and nearly fifty thousand members. It had also accumulated a number of assets, including half-interest in a building and enough office equipment, furniture, and fixtures to equip two offices, a head office space in Saskatoon and a small branch office in Regina. As well, the *Union Farmer* had grown to a circulation of some twenty-three thousand. There was no debt and nearly $20,000 in the bank. "Concrete proof," according to Phelps, that they were making progress. Keeping the organization in the public eye was a key part of Phelps's plan. He proved masterful with the media and drew upon experiences and knowledge from his past. He remained faithful to historical policy principles of the UFC in his attempts to reclaim the legitimate educational and policy role for the voluntary movement that he felt had been hijacked by the Saskatchewan Wheat Pool in the 1930s. It was undoubtedly for historic reasons that Phelps invited Aaron Sapiro, the 1920s grand master and catalyst of co-operative marketing and farmer unity, to address the SFU's December 1951 convention. Sapiro electrified the audience of over a thousand people at Saskatoon's Third Avenue United Church.[43] Having this legendary lawyer in attendance not only increased Phelps's stature but represented an important historic and educational experience for all who attended. In 1951, Phelps himself affirmed SFU's commitment to continuing to fight for farmers' rights: "You and I must re-dedicate ourselves to the basic ideals of our organization. More than ever before, we must live up to our reputation as a fighting organization which will never pull its punches in the battle for security for the prairie farmer."[44]

Western farmers' grievances were numerous, and Phelps was never hesitant to bring them to public or political attention. Among these were requests for an immediate increase in the domestic price for wheat, which would be based on a parity price formula.[45] Producer representation at the policy level of the Canadian Wheat Board, a more equitable grain delivery quota system, and a long-range livestock marketing and production policy were also high on the list of policy demands. Retention of the statutory Crow Rate was an important issue even at that time. The Crow's Nest Pass freight rate was based on a 1897 agreement between the CPR and the Laurier Government, put in place to help finance the rail line through the Crow's Nest Pass and facilitate access to mineral deposits in southwestern British Columbia: "In exchange for a federal cash subsidy, the CPR agreed, *in perpetuity*, to lower rates on flour and grain moving east to the Lakehead and on certain settlers' items moving west." The new rates provided a significant transportation subsidy to prairie farmers, resulting in a cost of only "half a cent to move a ton of grain a mile." The rates were eventually altered in the 1980s and, by 1995, eliminated altogether,[46] but some thirty-five years before the demise of the Crow Rate, farmers could read the writing on the wall. Phelps never lost an opportunity to reiterate these demands to the media.[47]

A NATIONAL VOICE

The need for a strong and unified national voice became increasingly evident, and Phelps turned his attention to this end. Negative encounters with the Saskatchewan Wheat Pool board had resurfaced through the Farmers Union's inherited membership in the Saskatchewan Federation of Agriculture (SFA). Throughout the forties, the UFC leadership had received little support in its drive for parity prices from the SFA, which in matters of policy was dominated by pool perspectives as a number of SFA member organizations had no direct policy interest. There was no question from the outset that Phelps would be less patient with the SFA, and, in turn, the Canadian Federation of Agriculture, in his demands for farm legislative changes and parity prices than the UFC had been.[48]

At the 1951 SFU convention, delegates voted after lengthy debate to withdraw membership from the SFA. With this vote, members who were loyal co-operators in the commercial sense had opted to recognize the SFU as their organization of choice in farm policy. It represented a definite victory for Phelps's leadership but opened up another challenge: to broaden the organization's national presence in farm policy.

The Interprovincial Farm Union Council (IFUC) had been organized as a policy liaison body between the UFC and Alberta Farmers Union in 1945, in preparation for the launching of the previously mentioned farm nondelivery strike. With the reorganization of the movement, Phelps seized the opportunity to broaden the base of the IFUC beyond the SFU and the now renamed Farmers' Union of Alberta under the leadership of C. J. Stimpfle. Contacts had been made with farmers in Manitoba in 1950, where organizational interest was high. The Manitoba Farmers Union emerged under the dynamic leadership of Jake Schulz. The MFU quickly became a member of the IFUC, broadening its base to full Prairie province representation. Within a year, the movement included a new farm union in Ontario under the leadership of George Sutherland. A British Columbia Farmers Union was established in the Peace River area of northern BC and northwestern Alberta under the leadership of Tom Aylesbury, and was known as the BC Bloc.[49]

There is no doubt the expansion of the IFUC was directly attributable to Phelps's organizational skills. He served as IFUC chairman throughout his SFU presidency. Bringing provincial farm unions under a national umbrella was an important and necessary strategy in order to present a unified approach to federal policy issues. At that time, the issue of compensation owing to farmers under the British Wheat Agreement remained a major irritant, and wheat prices, controlled by federal agreements, remained the key to the farm economy. The IFUC requested a twenty-five-cent-per-bushel payment; at the time, farmers received 8.3 cents. The sudden growth of the farm union movement caught the attention of federal politicians. Cabinet ministers such as Agriculture Minister James Gardiner and Trade and Commerce Minister C. D. Howe accepted invitations to address farm union conventions.

LABOUR AND AGRICULTURE

Achieving a better understanding between organized labour and organized agriculture also became a focus of Phelps's energies. His position on organized labour had softened somewhat after he left government, and his comments reflected a growing awareness of the interrelationship between the two groups. The health of the provincial economy and therefore the economic prospects for workers, he believed, were dependent on agriculture, the primary industry in Saskatchewan. Low farm income meant farmers did not have enough money to buy industrial goods, and reduced sales of industrial goods meant fewer jobs for workers. Workers' and farmers' needs were inextricably connected in the capitalist economy, and democracy itself depended upon both groups maintaining a high standard of living. In Phelps's words,

> To make our democratic system function efficiently, there must be greater understanding among organized farmers, organized labour, and other groups in the national economy. This cannot be done unless the people who produce the nation's food, and the people who produce other goods and services, are able to maintain decent living standards. If we permit democracy to fail in Canada, I fear that we will never get a second chance to make it work.[50]

The progressive labour legislation brought in by Tommy Douglas's CCF government had spawned a flurry of organizing activity by the trade union movement, and the Canadian Congress of Labour (CCL), formed in 1940 to act as the voice of industrial unionism in Canada, was growing rapidly. Despite opposition from some of the SFU provincial board, Phelps convinced the membership they should make contact with the CCL. Meetings were organized with its president, Aaron Mosher. Both Phelps and Mosher had been active in the founding of the Farmer-Labour Group in 1932, the forerunner of the Saskatchewan CCF. The viewpoints of the two leaders dovetailed and led to the formation of the Canadian Farmer-Labour Economic Council (CFLEC).[51] Meetings between leaders of the IFUC and the CCL were held periodically to discuss broad-ranging economic and social issues affecting the two groups.[52]

Phelps recalled meeting with Harold Banks, the head of the Seafarers International Union, in an interview that was rebroadcast on the CBC radio program *As It Happens* in 1988:

> Now the Seaman's Union...farmers say we didn't have anything in common. But they were the ones that manned the boats that took our wheat and if they went on strike we were up the creek. I felt that we should contact them and get them to see what our problems were, and we should see what some of their problems were. Now we didn't always agree with them, but we did get a fairly good working relationship. I remember the first time I met Mr. Banks; I was almost shocked to see that he carried a revolver all the time, in his holster, right under his arm. That scared me...but I think we made some progress.[53]

Phelps served as chairman of the CFLEC (which was later renamed the Canadian Farmer Coordinating Council) throughout his tenure as IFUC chairman. The networking that resulted after the formation of the council enabled the farm union on several occasions to contact labour leaders in such sectors as grain handling and meat processing to communicate about concerns where industrial disputes might affect farmers' interests. Although connecting with labour reflected a shift in the policy and strategy of the revitalized movement, it became increasingly evident that the SFU was not directly affiliated with the CCF or any other political party.

Phelps travelled to Ontario frequently, "maintaining his usual breakneck speaking schedule even in unknown territory."[54] Membership in Ontario made the IFUC a plausibly national organization, providing long-sought legitimacy in Ottawa. Joe Phelps and MFU President Jake Schulz, known as the "Terrible Twins," enjoyed working together immensely, and their combined effort was effective at the national level.[55] Bruce Dodds, who is familiar with the extensive Ontario Farmers' Union (OFU) collection of documents, recalls the importance of interpersonal relationships:

> Joe and Jake got on famously with Ontario president Albert Cormack, a committed Tory, and enjoyed plotting with him how to influence the government through Cormack's party contacts and activities.... Phelps' good relations with Cormack even extended to antique farm machinery—letters

At a joint meeting of the Interprovincial Farm Union Council and the Canadian Congress of Labour, held on October 23, 1953, at the King George Hotel in Saskatoon, the Farmer-Labour Economic Council was formed. Executive from left to right: G. H. McIntosh (MFU), W. G. Davies (Saskatchewan Federation of Labour), Joe Phelps (SFU), A. R. Mosher, President (CCL), Dr. E. A. Forsey (Research CCL), A. B. Wood (Farmers' Union of Alberta). Photo by Len Hillyar, Commercial Photography, Saskatoon, Saskatchewan, in the *Union Farmer*, December 1953, 13. Permission granted by the Phelps family estate.

> occasionally end in discussion of choice items Albert had located and that Phelps was arranging to transport back to Saskatchewan. Much of the correspondence with Ontario is on Western Development Museum stationary; he indicates in his letters that he spent almost as much time there as he did at the SFU office.[56]

The organization was building momentum and attracting new blood from a number of different fields. In June 1951, Stuart Thiesson joined the staff of the SFU, first as an associate secretary and later as executive secretary of the National Farmers Union in 1969.[57] Thiesson recalled, "I saw Joe the first day on the job. I was young, green and ignorant. Frankly, I was a bit scared! Here obviously was a very experienced and dynamic person. He seemed to size me up and then finally said, 'If you have the authority, you have the responsibility.' Enough said! I never forgot it!"[58] Thiesson worked closely with Phelps during the remaining three years of his term as president, and found that his strong sense of responsibility and work ethic began to permeate the organization: "Joe provided leadership. He was a strong leader. Work came first. We worked long days, many nights and lots of overtime. Joe worked you hard, but he never asked you to work harder than he did himself."[59]

Continued efforts were put into building up membership numbers. A *Union Farmer* special supplement distributed across the province outlined the organization's program in an attempt to solicit more members. The rapidly growing SFU, now boasting eight hundred locals, sought to establish producer marketing boards and parity pricing for wheat and other farm products; increase floor and ceiling prices in a new International Wheat Agreement (IWA); and broaden the Agricultural Prices Support Act to include cereal grains. Further, it sought to increase producer involvement in policy-making, with producer representation on the Advisory Committee negotiating the IWA and on the Canadian Wheat Board.[60]

Several noteworthy gains had already been made. The SFU had sent a number of delegations to Ottawa, and submitted briefs to the federal government and to various government-appointed boards concerned with marketing farm products, as well as making submissions to the provincial government. The SFU could now have union dues deducted from income tax, and had secured a provincial inquiry into the farm machinery industry and some amendments to the Farm Implement Act. As well, its lobbying had resulted in an increase of six cents a bushel on wheat sold on the domestic market and through the IWA. Finally, a SFU representative had been appointed to the Grain Standards Board, and it had been instrumental in the establishment of a provincial Royal Commission on Agriculture and Rural Life.

TRAGEDY

By 1952, Phelps was successfully turning the organization around when he was called upon to take on another challenge. In the early fall of 1952, Premier Douglas asked Phelps to join the Royal Commission on Agriculture and Rural Life, set up to investigate social and economic conditions in rural Saskatchewan. Sadly, just before he was asked to join the commission and mid-stride of all the success he was having in rebuilding the farm movement, tragedy fell upon the Phelps home. His wife Lena had taken ill in August 1952, less than a year after the birth of her fourth child, and was hospitalized at Saskatoon City Hospital.

An exploratory operation revealed a brain tumour. She was told to consult with Dr. Penfield in Montreal, one of Canada's leading neurosurgeons. Joe and his daughter Ella accompanied Lena to Montreal by train, but the doctor found the tumour was inoperable. Returning home on a CNR train on September 13, 1952, Lena died as the train approached Longlac, Ontario.[61]

Phelps and the family were devastated. Along with her role as mother to four children, Lena had been a tremendous help and support throughout Phelps's political career, always finding time to accompany Joe to meetings and assist in his political work and in the farm movement. She had refused to accept office in the SFU, but she had been a farm activist in her own right, organizing conventions, writing a regular column in the *Union Farmer*, and attending Farm Women's Weeks at the University of Saskatchewan, from which policy resolutions were forwarded to the UFC and later the SFU.[62]

The *StarPhoenix* paid tribute to Lena Phelps in its editorial of September 16, 1952:

> The death of Mrs. J. L. Phelps, will come as a shock to many of the farm people of Saskatchewan. Mrs. Phelps was well known

> throughout the farm community and in many other circles. She was known not only as the wife of the President of the Saskatchewan Farmers Union, but also for her own activities in the [farm] movement. Mrs. Phelps possessed an abundant energy and a great drive to which she gave expression in many ways on behalf of the Saskatchewan farmwomen. Mrs. Phelps will be greatly missed in the Saskatchewan Farmers Union and other organizations.[63]

Premier Tommy Douglas attended the service in the role of both minister and friend, and offered words of support. Speaking at the service, Douglas, who had just recently returned from meetings at the League of Nations in Geneva, recalled that he first met Lena Phelps when asked to attend a community meeting at the Narrow Lake schoolhouse. The meeting, chaired by Mrs. Phelps, was being held to discuss world peace. The premier stated that while attending the meeting, he realized, "if we are to have peace and understanding in the world, it will be because everyday people expressing their desire for good fellowship with others are coming together to study the problems of others in relation to their own."[64]

Afterwards, Phelps questioned his future involvement in the Farmers Union. This was a fragile time in his life:

> This has been an extremely difficult year for me, not only from the standpoint of the union itself, but also for the loss of my dear wife, who has for the past almost twenty-three years, been such a source of inspiration to me. At times it just seemed impossible to carry on, and I feel sure if it had not been for friends and family's counsel and enthusiasm, on many occasions I would have ceased to try.[65]

Many in the organization, including Bernice Norman (who had been elected women's president in December 1951) and her husband Ronald, provided moral support to Phelps at this critical time.

Eighteen-year-old Ella was devastated by her mother's death. She remained at home and looked after the household in the months that followed, and then left to marry. Ella's brothers also left home, twenty-one-year-old Lee to marry and Bruce to travel. It seemed best to everyone in the family that Lena's brother Bruce Ackerman and his wife Marion, who lived just outside of Saskatoon and did not have any children of their own, would raise Gordon, just a baby at the time.

Reluctantly, Phelps continued as president of the SFU and accepted the appointment to the Royal Commission. He continued to devote himself tirelessly to the issues of transportation, prices, and orderly marketing, which remained the focus of SFU policy. Retention of the Crow's Nest Pass agreement and opposing further freight rate increases were the top priorities. The SFU continued to strive for further advancement of marketing initiatives, including participation in the signing of the first International Wheat Agreement, and defence of the Canadian Wheat Board system of marketing and protein grading of wheat. It also continued to fight for parity prices for farm products and to seek farmer control of marketing agencies for farm commodities, including beef and pork marketing boards, and to explore ways and means of solving the problem of farm isolation.

"I HAVE THE FLOOR NOW AND WHAT THE HELL ARE YOU GOING TO DO ABOUT IT?"

There was no doubt Phelps was in charge of writing policy briefs to the federal and provincial governments or the Canadian Wheat Board and Canadian Grain Commission (CGC). His submissions were never short and always covered a broad range of policy issues. Occasionally, he would request research material from staff. The request was always prefaced by urgency and impatience and correspondence signed with the closing, "in haste."[66]

Herb Schulz describes a meeting in February 1952, when the IFUC met with the board of grain commissioners:

> Below were several dozen Farmers Union people, led by jut-jawed, trigger-tempered Joe Phelps. Phelps presented the union brief. It contained a veiled suggestion that the board was overly sympathetic to the grain elevator companies. The board chairman stopped him: "Mr. Phelps. That is not correct."
>
> "I say it is and I say we have plenty of evidence." Phelps was challenging the integrity of the board. Visibly annoyed,

> the chairman interjected, but Phelps was adamant: "Mr. McKenzie, I have the floor."
>
> "Mr. Phelps, the chairman of a meeting always has the floor."
>
> Phelps stood and leaned forward like a leashed Doberman: "Mr. McKenzie, I have the floor now and what the hell are you going to do about it?"[67]

There were certain issues that were particularly bothersome to Phelps but none more so than that of the accumulation of grain overages resulting from producer grain deliveries to country elevators. The Canada Grain Act allowed for dockage deductions from grain for weed seeds and other foreign materials, and also a shrinkage allowance to accommodate for weight loss through evaporation. It was evident to Phelps that elevators accumulated overages because these allowances were too high. They also occurred if the proper weight had not been accorded the grain upon delivery. Adding insult to injury, in his view, was the Canadian Wheat Board's practice of paying elevator companies the initial grain price for overages before they passed through the system. The Canadian Grain Commission was responsible for policing the degree of fairness in the setting of these allowances. Phelps was not impressed with the assurance of the chairman of the commission that the CGC was the "watchdog for the farmers over the grain trade."

Former SFU President Chris Hansen recalled,

> They [the Grain Commissioners] hated his guts. And the feeling was mutual. Joe believed that one of the main weaknesses in the Canadian grain marketing system was the lack of an effective regulatory function to keep the grain trade honest. He was convinced that farmers "were being taken to the cleaners" on grading, dockage, moisture content and even weight of their grains. Joe considered the Board of Grain Commissioners totally incompetent, and did everything he could to expose their weaknesses.[68]

The highlight of Phelps's battles with the commission was the much-publicized Kreutzweiser Case, in which a farmer from Crystal Springs, Saskatchewan, was refused delivery of his grain at a pool elevator in Brancepath. The crux of the case hinged on the elevator operator's refusal to accept grain on a subject to grade and dockage basis, as was the farmer's right according to Canada Grain Act regulations. The Saskatchewan Farmers Union filed its complaint to the CGC about the Saskatchewan Wheat Pool's agent refusal to accept Herbert Kreutzweiser's grain.[69]

The board of grain commissioners conducted a hearing in the Legion Hall in Saskatoon on December 17, 1952. The SFU was represented by Morris Shumiatcher, who drew a comparison between the biblical "no room in the inn" and there being "no space in the elevator." The one-day public hearing was attended by large numbers of farmers, and the publicity that followed drew public attention to the case. Although the final results were inconclusive, there is no doubt this effort drew public scrutiny to the work of the board, and probably had a direct correlation to eventual changes to the regulatory function and grading system for Canadian grain, with major benefits to farmers.

A two-price system for wheat came to fruition in 1953. "Earlier, Prime Minister Louis St. Laurent and C. D. Howe, Minister of Trade and Commerce, had both rejected the two-price system as unworkable," according to Phelps. In 1953, Phelps announced,

> Now, I am happy to be able to report that the principle of a two-price system has been established. Mr. Howe has announced that the price of durum wheat in Canada has been increased over and above that of the export sale price. This is another indication that the two-price system principle has been accepted, and now we must bring pressure to bear to have it extended into the general field of agricultural prices.[70]

In 1954, when the CGC called a two-day meeting in Winnipeg to discuss its annual report, Phelps attended with brief in hand and his debating fettle at its prime. The *StarPhoenix* quoted Phelps:

> I raised so much hell they didn't get through their agenda in the two days scheduled for their annual meeting in Winnipeg. They were damn nervous. I detested the Grain Exchange and often thought the Saskatchewan Wheat Pool

> was one of their men Fridays. I've always been a loyal Pool member but I've been pretty critical of it because it did not work closely enough with the organized farm movement. Its leaders wanted to be number one in the agricultural scene and they had the dollars to back it up.[71]

CHECK-OFF

Phelps knew that financial stability was necessary to the survival of a voluntary membership organization. This struggle was also taking place within the labour movement. Dues collection had been the bane of union activists in Saskatchewan for decades. Activists spent countless volunteer hours after long working days visiting members' homes to collect dues before they gained the right to have union dues deducted from members' paycheques by the company and transferred to the union's bank account. This ensured stability and provided the financial resources necessary for organizing, bargaining, and fighting contract disputes. The union shop, a closely related issue, assumes that everyone working for an employer benefits from the union's efforts, and therefore all workers should share in the costs and duties associated with maintaining the union. Canada's most widely heralded battle for union security occurred in the fall of 1945 at the Ford plant in Windsor, Ontario. The issues of the dues check-off and the union shop were at the heart of the dispute. When both sides refused to compromise, a bitter strike erupted. The strike ended when both sides agreed to binding arbitration under Ontario's Justice Ivan Rand. The result was the Rand Formula, which ruled that all current members of the bargaining unit would have union dues checked off, but no one would be required to join the union. Those hired subsequent to certification would be obliged to become union members.[72]

To bring financial stability to the SFU, Phelps requested that the provincial government amend the Rural Municipality Act to enable the SFU to assess a half mill against all farmland in Saskatchewan on the grounds that all farmers benefitted from the SFU's efforts. As established in the Rand Formula, all members would contribute, but membership would be paid additionally on a voluntary basis, to achieve voting rights. A brief was presented to the provincial government on February 24, 1953, on this issue. A second meeting with the Cabinet was held on July 4, with a large delegation in attendance. The province turned down the request but did provide enabling legislation for a voluntary requisition, whereby a farmer could authorize a rural municipality to collect SFU dues on his behalf.[73] The SFU would, in turn, provide the rural municipality with a list of names from which dues collections were authorized. It was not totally successful, but where rural municipalities and their municipal secretaries were cooperative, it worked very well and became a major stabilizing element for SFU funding for a number of years. The voluntary requisition was lost in 1970 when, with urging from the Saskatchewan Association of Rural Municipalities, the Ross Thatcher Government refused to amend the Rural Municipality Act to accommodate the name change from the Saskatchewan Farmers Union to the National Farmers Union.[74]

In attempting to achieve financial and membership stability for the SFU, Phelps had always recognized that members required something tangible from their membership that they could recognize as being personally beneficial. The SFU income tax service was inaugurated at a time when many farmers were filing income tax returns for the first time. Members also received free legal advice through the offices of J. M. Goldenberg, QC, and general legal information through his popular monthly legal column in the *Union Farmer.*

With membership increased to more than 100,000 farm men, women, and juniors in 1,067 locals scattered throughout the province, and many assets accumulated, the organization found itself much better off than before Phelps had taken office. It now owned a half-interest in an office building, $10,000 worth of office equipment, and two centrally located lots in Saskatoon for a future office, and had built up a fund of $34,000 for a new SFU office. Phelps's legacy was not only a large increase in membership and physical assets. As he approached his final days as president in 1954, he took time to reflect on his five years with the SFU, stating they had created a very substantial organization with a strong education program and legal and income tax departments that were giving valuable service to members. More importantly, the SFU had missed no opportunity to present agriculture's problems and needs to governments, boards, and other relevant parties.[75]

"HEADING FOR THE GATE WITH HIS COAT TAILS FLYING"

At the 1954 annual meeting with the board of grain commissioners in Winnipeg during his final days as president of the SFU, Phelps had members of the board "squirming uncomfortably in their chairs," as he later recalled, but was unable to stay as he had to return to Regina for his second wedding the next day. He married Eva Nyholt, women's director of the Saskatchewan Farmers Union, on July 22, 1954, less than two years after his first wife's death. Although he was busy, he was also lonely. He was a family man, an emotional man, and he was unhappy alone. Joe's kids were all living on their own by this time, and without Lena to hold the family together, they were leading distant and separate lives. Eva's late husband, Jack Nyholt, had been active in the Farmers' Union of Canada movement, and was often on the road with Phelps in the 1920s promoting the Saskatchewan Wheat Pool. Eva had met Joe for the first time in 1947 when he was Minister of Natural Resources for the provincial government. After her husband's death in 1953, a writing assignment for the *Battlefords News-Optimist* required that Eva interview Joe and they became reacquainted. Eva and Joe shared a commitment to the farm movement and their socialist ideals—she had been a member of the CCF since 1933.

Phelps stepped down as president of the SFU in December 1954 when his five-year term ended. Fred Woloshyn was elected president and Chris Hansen vice-president. Fred served only a few months, resigning when he became embroiled in a conflict with the board, and Chris Hansen became president.[76] As for Phelps's future career,

> Time and circumstances no doubt will, as usual, be the determining factors. For the next few months I have obligations to fill as a member of Saskatchewan's Royal Commission on Agriculture and Rural Life. I plan to have more time to spend with my family, and to devote more attention to the farm, which to some extent has suffered as a result of the demands made by public life, and later by farm union work. And then, as many of you know, there is my special hobby, the Western Development Museum. That is going to occupy a considerable portion of my time and energies.[77]

Phelps's ability to push for change had revitalized the movement, resulting in a strong and unified voice for farmers. In his fight to build the organization and protect the family farm, he refused to compromise his principles. At a time when farmers needed to, in his words, "stand up and be counted," his bulldog approach served him well. He was a controversial figure, but certainly he was the right man at the right time to lead the resurrecting of the farm movement. He was both loved and hated for his politics and his methods, but no one could seriously dispute his loyalty and commitment to farm families and rural communities. Chris Hansen reflected on Phelps's influence and uncompromising attitude:

> I can't think of many people who have had such a profound influence on my life. We often argued and had deep differences of opinion on appropriate approaches, but fundamentally always believed in and fought for the same basic goals. His dynamic personality, vision, drive and commitment to ideals, were a real inspiration to anyone who believed in the same things. He often created his own enemies by his lack of flexibility and diplomacy. Yet it was this very uncompromising attitude that made him such a dynamic force, first in the CCF government, and later as the leader of the SFU.[78]

Roy Atkinson, who became president of the National Farmers Union in 1969, reflected on Joe's contribution: "He certainly was dynamic. Joe was a remarkable man. Anything progressive in this province, Phelps had a hand in it. He was always heading for the gate with his coat tails flying.[79]

CHAPTER 15

THE WESTERN DEVELOPMENT MUSEUM

Many have credited Joe Phelps with being the primary driving force behind the establishment and development of Saskatchewan's Western Development Museum (WDM), which contains one of the largest collections of historical artifacts in North America and provides a valuable historical record of western pioneers. There were many who shared Phelps's vision, both in government and among the public, generously contributing hard work and financial assistance to make the dream of preserving this history a reality, but others did not share his initial enthusiasm for the project. Eiling Kramer remembers, "During the Forties, Joe's efforts were ridiculed by many including some of his cabinet colleagues. The collection was stored around Saskatchewan in old airport hangars and was referred to as Joe Phelps' 'junk piles' or the CCF 'garbage dump.'"[1] Phelps, on the other hand, envisioned—in his words—"a kind of a Smithsonian institution for western Canada."[2]

Phelps began to collect pioneer artifacts at his farm in the late 1920s. The idea for the museum started simply as a desire to preserve Prairie history by collecting some of the machinery and engines from the homestead era, such as hand tools used by the pioneers and both unusual and ordinary agricultural machinery. Horse-drawn equipment, in particular, was quickly becoming obsolete, and so Phelps set about collecting this old farm machinery and other interesting artifacts. A local auctioneer assisted him in these early efforts. Phelps recalled, "Percy would go to a sale, and if there was an item that he thought I would be interested in, especially if there was a good rig or a horse drawn vehicle available, he would bid it in whether I was there or not, call me about it the next time he saw me, and let me know where I was to go to pick it up."[3] A lot of the items in the original collection were obtained this way. The idea for the museum was kindled when Lou Hantleman, the MLA for Elrose, visited Phelps's farm at Wilkie in the mid-1930s and was mightily impressed with the size and quality of Phelps's rapidly growing collection.

Phelps also recalled discussions that took place in the early forties with his friend W. C. "Billy" Wells, pioneer farmer and a principal owner of Wells Construction. Wells was interested in preserving artifacts from the construction industry, in particular some of the unique equipment his company had used for road building in the early years, which he collected on his farm near Baldwinton. Both Phelps and Wells were keenly aware that without a concerted and coordinated effort this history might be lost, and so they came up with the idea to obtain an air force hangar to get the equipment under cover and preserve it. The war effort was also creating a sense of urgency. Many pieces of older farm equipment were being melted down, and junk dealers often obtained the few pieces that remained. In fact, by 1942, it had become illegal for anyone to keep scrap metal that could be used in the construction of tanks, ships, and other war-related equipment.[4]

True to his populist ideals, Phelps's idea was to form a grassroots museum. The organization would be controlled by the pioneers and donors of the exhibits and would exist for the purpose of preserving Prairie history. To this end, Wells and Phelps, together with Evan Hardy, dean of agriculture and engineering at the University of Saskatchewan, formed the first three-member committee in 1943, with Phelps acting as chairman.[5] Within a few weeks, they had obtained their first hangar and had started gathering and transporting machinery.

The original Western Development Museum was located at the site of the North-West Mounted Police Memorial and Indian Museum in the Battlefords.[6] Restoration of this museum had been Phelps's first foray into historical preservation, falling under the ministerial direction of the DNR. Historian Campbell Innes had collected many articles and papers over the years and had tried unsuccessfully to persuade former governments that the history and artifacts should be housed and preserved. According to Eiling Kramer, Innes spent years trying to get funding, until he got the ear of the new Minister of Natural Resources and Industrial Development, Joe Phelps.

In 1945, a committee was formed to administer restoration of the North-West Mounted Police fort. Restoration began under Phelps's personal direction, and in 1946 Frank Swon and Campbell Innes, both members of the Canadian North West Historical Society, approached Phelps to pursue the idea of setting up a separate museum of pioneer machinery and implements. Part of the fort was already being used to store the agricultural tools and machinery that the fledgling museum committee had been accumulating. Phelps was able to obtain a government grant of $10,000, which kicked off the project.[7] All of the original participants continued to donate their services and, after the financing was obtained, expenses paid out were limited to the transportation and refurbishing of the equipment when an item was donated.

Gathering artifacts for the museum was an ongoing concern for the committee. As minister, Phelps was involved in extensive travel around the province, often travelling by aircraft, and some of his best finds were made while flying low over farmland. Phelps saw a lot of discarded farm machinery during his travels, including trucks, engines, and other junk he considered valuable historical artifacts. He would carefully pinpoint the location of the equipment on a map and alert the other committee members to its whereabouts. Later, they would call on the farmer to see if he would donate it. Often, if Phelps spotted something interesting while travelling by air, he would ask the pilot to make a landing so he could take a closer look.[8]

On April 21, 1949, the first official meeting of the Western Development Museum board took place in Saskatoon at the University of Saskatchewan, with Phelps as chairman and director, and Roy Potter as secretary. Other members included Evan Hardy, University of Manitoba Dean of Agriculture Grant MacEwan, and Frank Swon.[9] Most of the new exhibits gathered were donations, some were contributed on loan, and the three-member committee purchased others. The DNR contributed a number of steam engines, gas engines, and boilers that had been procured as part of a plan for northern development. The federal Department of

Agriculture contributed the first government grant to help finance the stockpiling of the various items that were scattered throughout the country, and the museum continued to be eligible for federal capital grants each year thereafter. The museum received its first provincial government grant in April 1950.

Phelps was particularly interested in salvaging and preserving the old steam tractors, many of which were being bought up for scrap. He loved these machines and was interested not only in collecting them but also in restoring them to operating condition to ensure that the knowledge of the art of steam was not lost. Edgar Kaeding recalled Phelps's work with the Western Development Museum:

> He showed up one day to see if I had any old-time machines to contribute. We had an old steamer that the trees had grown into on a farm my Dad had bought. It was strictly a belt machine; it had no transmission to move itself and had to be pulled into position for belt work by a team. Many pieces were missing, but Joe thought it could be resurrected. Some weeks later when I returned to that quarter, I found a pathway cut into the thicket and the steamer was gone![10]

Steam restoration became a valuable part of the project, and George LeBeau, Phelps's long-time friend and fellow collector, recalled that volunteers came from as far away as the United States to offer their services, in part so the art of steam would not be lost:

> The steam car project was a good example of how Joe worked.... The boiler of the steam car had to be rebuilt. Part of the restoration involved replacing about three and a half miles of steel wire [lagging] needed to wrap around the boiler for heat insulation and extra strength, to withstand the steam pressures that would be generated. Joe found a cable company in England who would supply the steel wire and who would donate it all with no cost to the Western Development Museum.[11]

Phelps and LeBeau spent many hours together ferreting out old equipment. George fondly recalled one of their best finds: "The deal took many years, but we got a 1929 Chevrolet car donated with only seven miles on it and the speedometer reading was accurate."[12] By 1946, a collection of artifacts and machinery had also been gathered on a plot of land on 33rd Street in Saskatoon.

Writing to farmers all over the Prairies inquiring about farm machinery and, when possible, acquiring it, Phelps's boundless energy for the project continued. Newspaper ads in 1947 called for donations of machinery. In April 1947, the *Battlefords News-Optimist* quoted Phelps saying, "An entire chapter of early history is in danger of being completely lost, unless we take immediate steps to gather up and preserve the remaining pieces of equipment and machinery used by the first white settlers who broke our prairie sod for agricultural purposes."[13]

Phelps formally announced the establishment of the original Western Development agricultural museum on August 25, 1947.[14] A hangar at the North Battleford airport had been acquired from the War Assets Corporation to store and exhibit farm machinery, and the plan called for a museum that would be open to the public in the future. People in the Battlefords area accelerated their efforts to collect antique farm equipment for preservation and display after the announcement. The founding committee arranged for a number of storage buildings during this period of rapid growth, including the old Cushing Mill building in Saskatoon, farm barns, and a number of storage sheds and yards. Cleaning, restoration, and painting of the various exhibits, as well as arranging to transport new displays, was a massive undertaking, requiring a great deal of energy and effort.[15]

The museum, which had been placed under the direction of the Department of Public Works, received further attention in the Saskatchewan legislature on April 2, 1949, when the Western Development Museum Act was passed. The act provided that a board would run the museum, and on April 21, 1949, the first board of directors meeting was held, with directors E. Roy Potter, Grant MacEwan, Evan Hardy, Frank Swon, and Joe Phelps as chair. Phelps remarked, "It can now be said that the Western Development Museum is an established institution, the value of which will increase with the years, in preserving in visual form the story of the pioneers of the west."[16]

The North Battleford museum opened to the public in the summer of 1949, and the Saskatoon location, situated at the Saskatoon airport, opened to the public year-round. By this time, the museum had accumulated a combined collection of over three hundred exhibits, including those that had been donated and those awaiting transportation. The first WDM annual report boasted that there were ninety-two exhibits on display at North Battleford, with an additional seventy-three awaiting reconditioning, and in Saskatoon seventy-one exhibits displayed and fifty-five awaiting reconditioning. The original display was largely made up of equipment from the Phelps farm. By 1950, exhibits had grown to 461. Already the museum was attracting some sixteen thousand visitors from around the world to Saskatoon and seven thousand to North Battleford. A fee of twenty-five cents was being charged to view the exhibits. Phelps stated,

> The museum has been able to collect and preserve machinery and equipment which in many instances, cannot be duplicated anywhere in the world. Gradually but surely the museum is acquiring a collection which is even now regarded as one of the outstanding exhibits of Western Canada and which, as the years go by, will be of increasing value and interest as a permanent and colourful record of Western pioneer days.[17]

The Western Development Museum had also acquired a hangar at Moose Jaw to store a collection of artifacts. Soon, a vacant hangar was also acquired at Yorkton. Early in 1950, however, the Department of National Defence requested the return of its hangar in Moose Jaw, and the museum had to move all of its machinery from Moose Jaw to the hangar in Yorkton. A short time later, the defence department also requested the museum move out of the Saskatoon hangar. Saskatoon exhibits were placed on vacant lots and in empty barns on the Exhibition grounds. By 1952, however, the City of Saskatoon had donated a large tract of land on 11th Street West to the museum. Grants from the city and the provincial government aided in relocating the displays, and by 1953 the Saskatoon WDM had reopened at the new site on 11th Street West in a hangar moved from Swift Current.[18]

The WDM continued to gain artifacts and recognition under Phelps's leadership. By 1952, he was able to report that "the Western Development Museum project was unanimously approved and recognized by the

Historic Sites and Monument Board of Canada, as a project of national importance and value, and the Canadian Broadcasting Corporation sent special men and equipment to take pictures for television and newsreel purposes."[19]

In 1954, as chairman and managing director of the museum, Phelps was approached to organize an attraction for the provincial Golden Jubilee celebrations to be held in 1955. The first Thresherman's Reunion had been held in 1952 as part of Saskatoon's seventieth anniversary celebration. In October 1954, a week-long Old-Time Thresherman's Reunion was held, cementing the tradition of shows and demonstrations associated with the Western Development Museum. Steamers were steamed up, gas engines cranked, wagons greased, horses found, oat sheaves brought in, and men assembled to revive the sights, smells, and sounds of the early pioneer days on the prairie.

Phelps named George LeBeau show director, and the first show, dubbed "Pion-Era," was launched in July 1955. Local citizens, service clubs, as well as the provincial government, city councils, and women's groups, all joined in. By the winter of 1955, a women's group headed up by Mrs. Eva Phelps was involved in a number of domestic exhibits for the show, including kitchen, parlour, and dining room displays that featured baking, rug-hooking, washing, weaving, and spinning demonstrations. In 1957, the women's group officially formed the Women's Auxiliary to the museum and launched the restoration of the Colony House, one of the first houses built in Saskatoon in 1883.[20] Both the Pioneer Thresherman's Club and the Women's Auxiliary continued to be instrumental in putting on the Pion-Era show, keenly interested in restoration and in accurately depicting for the public how things were done in the earlier days.

Pion-Era gave a human face to static displays, bringing the exhibits to life and allowing visitors to relive the past. A July 1991 article in *Canadian Geographic* by Monique Roy-Sole described what it was like: "The air was filled with the acrid smell of smoke and dust. Gargantuan steam engines, tractors and threshers, choke and spew hot oil and cinders as they rock back to life with a deafening roar."[21] By 1959, plans to include a pioneer village, additional museum display buildings, showgrounds, and an old-fashioned farmstead had been approved by the City of Saskatoon and the provincial government. By 1961, the first phase was complete and the pioneer village officially opened.

Phelps's fascination with collecting and preserving Saskatchewan's historical artifacts from the settlement period continued through the 1950s. He served as chairman of the WDM board from 1949 to 1961. On April 24, 1963, he was elected honorary chairman of the board of directors by a unanimous vote, acknowledging his tremendous contribution as the motivator, guide, and driving force behind the project.[22] While the board acknowledged that the contributions of many others had been significant in the development of the museum, it stated very clearly that Phelps was largely responsible for making the vision a reality. At the official opening of the new Western Development Museum in North Battleford, a plaque was unveiled honouring Phelps's contribution. It reads: "This museum is dedicated to the pioneers of Saskatchewan and to Mr. J. L. Phelps, who through his devotion to preserving the pioneer life of Saskatchewan has earned for himself an outstanding place in the history of our province…Board of Directors, W.D.M., North Battleford, 25 May 1963."[23] The plaque is prominently displayed beside the front door as you enter the museum in North Battleford.

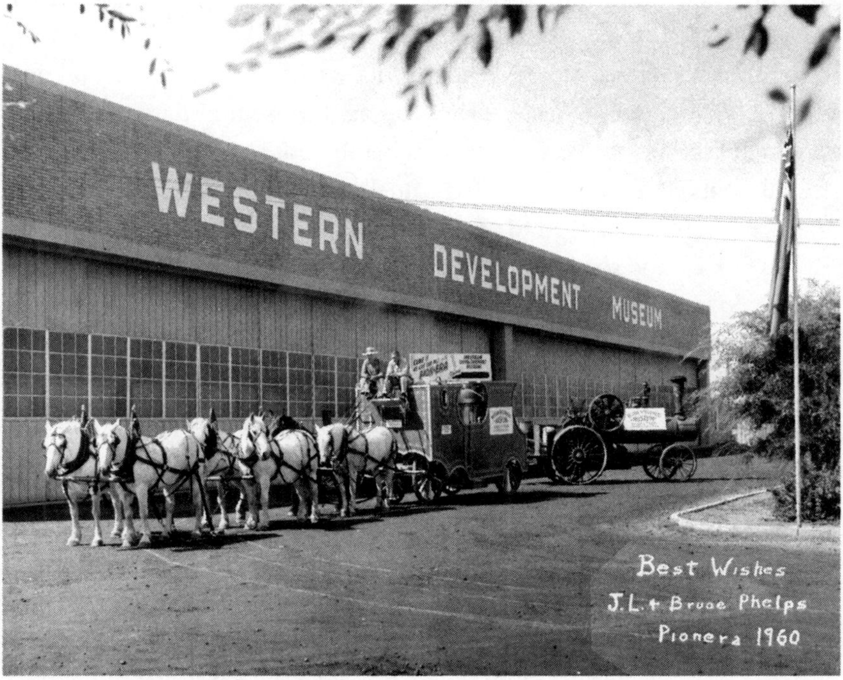

Joe Phelps and Bruce Phelps at the Western Development Museum's Pion-Era, 1960. L. J. Smith Photography. Permission granted by the Phelps family estate.

Ironically, in 1966, Phelps became embroiled in a dispute with the museum over ownership of some of the artifacts, filing a lawsuit against the museum and claiming ownership of a number of exhibits. The disagreement with the WDM board resulted in a long, protracted legal battle in civil court. According to an article in the *StarPhoenix* on April 3, 1999, the WDM alleged that Joe Phelps had twenty-two of its exhibits, while Phelps contended that the WDM had ninety items belonging to him.[24] Over a decade later, and after a trial in civil court that included 120 witnesses and approximately $150,000 in legal fees, Phelps and the museum reached an out-of-court agreement.[25] The museum kept most of the exhibits, although the museum and Phelps paid one another for certain exhibits and exchanged others.

Phelps cited the terms and conditions laid out during the grass-roots formation of the organization prior to the Western Development Museum Act, which passed in 1949. The original committee had stipulated that articles that were on loan or had been donated did not become the property of the museum unless they had been purchased outright, but rather fell under the discretion of the board. The courts, however, did not see it this way. Section 28 of the second Western Development Museum Act, passed in 1963, reads as follows: "All property real and personal belonging to the Western Development Museum Board on the date on which this Act comes into force, is hereby transferred to the museum and all debts and liabilities of the said Western Development Museum Board are hereby declared to be the debts and liabilities of the museum."

The family was so profoundly disturbed by the situation that no one was thinking straight. Confronted with the news that he would have to remove his artifacts from the museum's storage in Saskatoon, Phelps called on his family. He told his granddaughter that he needed her to fly out from British Columbia immediately to help him move the artifacts, even though she was working as a teacher and could not ordinarily leave her class, and despite the fact that the work might be better done by a brawny young local man hired for less than the cost of the airplane ticket. Joe Phelps called and the family answered, without question. She tells of a bitterly cold day on the back of a half-ton truck, with the unmistakable feeling that she was doing the right thing.[26]

Apparently, the dispute had less to do with ownership of the artifacts and more to do with how Phelps felt about the state of the organization.

The museum, which began as a small, grassroots movement, had in his opinion become static and self-serving. Although this was, perhaps, a natural progression for an organization that was becoming a much larger, more professional, and impersonal institution, as the founder, Phelps found this difficult to accept and had become increasingly disillusioned.

Despite the dispute, Phelps remained involved with Pion-Era, later renamed Saskachimo. In a 1971 article, he wrote,

> As a director of Saskachimo I am positively ashamed at the inconsiderate way we have treated our friends and neighbours the native people. The ground we have allocated for their use with their teepees this last two years has looked more like a mud hole than a sensible persons camping ground. They have reason to feel slighted. By comparison at the original Pion-Era grounds they had their own special area where there was natural grass and well-drained [*sic*] and they knew for sure that they were welcomed in a genuine western way at any or all seasons of the year. Chief Wm. Eagle is entirely justified in his recent criticism, so now let us move them on to their own original site and let us smoke the real Pipe of Peace and thus restore our long held record of being a hospitable people.[27]

In his later years, Phelps remained passionate about the Western Development Museum. Son-in-law Bob Little recalled,

> I remember one time in Saskatoon a strong wind blew the canopy off one of the museum's steam tractors. Joe immediately phoned [Roy] Romanow at his home to ensure that the canopy was restored as soon as possible. Mrs. Romanow answered the phone, indicating that [her husband] was sleeping. Joe's immediate response was, 'Well, get him up!' Joe was very direct about what he wanted to do, and he got his point across clearly. 'Can't' was not a word in his vocabulary and he used to say there was no such word. Joe had no fear. If something interested him he would follow through.[28]

In March 2000, the Western Development Museum celebrated its fiftieth anniversary, with celebrations drawing a total of 200,000 visitors to the museums. The current number of exhibits is estimated at 3,700, with a valuation of approximately $3 million. A compilation of attendance figures published in the museum's anniversary celebration booklet reveals it has attracted over seven million visitors from 1949 to 2000.[29] Eiling Kramer fittingly describes Phelps's contribution:

> Saskatchewan is indebted to Joe Phelps and the hundreds of people who supported him in making the dream come true. The right person in the right place at the right time to provide leadership and government finance, culminated in the success of Saskatchewan's great Pioneer Museum complex. The Western Development Museum is a lasting monument to this fiery farm leader who not only dared to dream but also backed it up with action.[30]

CHAPTER 16

THE PEOPLE'S COMMISSION

Beginning in 1949 and continuing through the 1950s, Joe Phelps juggled a number of demanding responsibilities, serving concurrently as president of the SFU and chairman of the Western Development Museum. In addition, he was appointed to the Royal Commission on Agriculture and Rural Life, established by order-in-council on October 31, 1952, to investigate the rapidly changing social and economic conditions in rural Saskatchewan. Phelps played a key role in the five-year study, coined the "People's Commission"—a massive project led by a team of leaders chosen for their practical first-hand experience with rural issues.

The study combined extensive public consultation and discussion through a series of community forums involving thousands of Saskatchewan people with input from the academic and scientific communities. Conducted under rigorous academic standards, the study stands as a rare example of participatory democracy that successfully involved rural people in discussions of the social and economic issues that were affecting them. After four and a half years of work, the final report and recommendations of the Royal Commission were released in 1958 in fourteen published volumes containing 275 recommendations and totalling over three thousand pages.

Phelps was in agreement on all but one of the final reports. In volume eight, the final report on farm prices, he felt he differed significantly enough from the majority of the members to record his dissension in his own minority report outlining his areas of concern and his alternative recommendations. He cited his lifetime of experience in practical farming and his long and close association with the policies advocated by farmers themselves through their own membership organizations as the reason he felt compelled to present an alternate point of view. In his opinion, the commission failed to tackle the problems related to farm income with the boldness and vision that were required to protect and defend the traditional family farm and its associated way of life. In his introductory remarks he states, "I regard the three points with which I intend to deal—farm prices, farm population and farm organization—as basic problems for which satisfactory and workable solutions must be found before any of the other numerous recommendations proposed by the Commission can prove effective."[1]

Many of the conclusions drawn by the commission foreshadow what has been expressed in more recent decades regarding efforts to save the family farm. Sadly, rural depopulation continues to accelerate, a trend that might have been reversed if recommendations such as those contained in the final reports of the Royal Commission and in the Phelps minority report had been implemented.

The thirties and forties had been decades of turmoil for Saskatchewan's farm families. Many left the land because of drought and low prices during the Depression, and later, during the Second World War, to serve overseas. In the years that followed, mechanization brought with it increased dependency on credit and rapidly accumulating farm debt, as farmers expanded their operations in an attempt to remain viable. As farms became bigger, rural depopulation accelerated, which in turn led to decreased rural services and job opportunities. Local governments found it difficult to adequately service the declining population, or undertake improvements that would reduce rural isolation or increase educational opportunities for rural people.

Farming is risky business at the best of times—prices, markets, and weather are critical variables over which the farmer has little control—but many farmers recognized that something had to be done to avert what was clearly becoming a crisis in Canadian agriculture. Organizations like the SFU lobbied the government to address the problem. In response, Saskatchewan's CCF government formed the Royal Commission on

Agriculture and Rural Life to find ways to strengthen the rural economy. Rural issues were important to the CCF. The party relied on rural support to get elected. Farmers, represented by the United Farmers of Canada, Saskatchewan Section, had been instrumental in the formation of the party and formed the base of its electoral support. With this in mind, and the 1952 election in the offing, Premier Douglas assembled the group that would lead the study.

The six-member team was chaired by William (Bill) B. Baker, an expert in rural sociology and social psychology and director of the School of Agriculture at the University of Saskatchewan. Joe Phelps's lifelong participation in agriculture, both actively farming and as president of the SFU, combined with his Cabinet experience, made him another obvious choice for appointment. The SFU's efforts to remedy farm problems had received a lot of publicity, and in two of its previous annual submissions to the government the organization had asked the government to establish a Royal Commission. The Saskatchewan Wheat Pool also had a long history of serving farm interests, and Charles Gibbings, the young vice-president of the pool, was therefore a natural choice for the commission. Gibbings would serve as SWP president from 1960 to 1969 and would later become a commissioner of the Canadian Wheat Board. Harry Fowler was chosen to represent the co-operative movement. A women's perspective on social, family, and rural life questions was also considered essential, and Nancy Adams of the Homemakers' Association, a rural women's organization, was chosen. T. H. Bourassa, a businessman from Lafleche with a lifetime of service to the community, was chosen to represent the rural business community.

The makeup of the Royal Commission was criticized for having close ties with the CCF government, and Phelps's appointment contributed to this sentiment. Critics alleged that Phelps's political background and his position as president of the SFU, which was sometimes mistakenly assumed to be affiliated with the CCF, would compromise the independence of the commission and taint its findings. On more than one occasion, however, the commission was critical of government policy. The interim report on Crown land settlement, for example, criticized the CCF's handling of the administration of northern settlement and angered many civil servants.[2]

Phelps initially served on the works committee of the commission, studying marketing, markets, and prices. He was also responsible for studying the issues of rural electrification and land tenure. Before commencing work on the commission, however, Phelps made a number of suggestions to William Harding, who had been seconded from the civil service to act as secretary to the commission. In a letter dated September 6, 1952, Phelps raised concerns about the staffing of the commission, citing the proposed appointment of a public education and classification analyst, and noting that "a top heavy personnel list" might impact the operating budget. His attitude toward bureaucracy was once again evident. He suggested that current public servants who were "restricted in their present employment to the point where they were quite ineffective and possibly more or less rusting away" could take on some of the work of the commission, reducing the commission's costs because they were already in the public employ. "On the other hand," he conceded, "there are a lot of people in the public service that are not much good on their jobs and certainly wouldn't be much good to the Commission."[3]

Phelps also emphasized the importance of personal responsibility. The commission must be careful, he argued, not to endorse programs that would support farmers who were operating inefficiently. He wrote, "The Commission would need to make pointed inquiries to check on present inefficiency with regard to existing farm practices.... Consumers, as such, may be quite within their rights in stating that they are not prepared to subsidize inefficiency in production."[4]

Always a practical man, he wanted the commission to focus on achieving lasting and meaningful results rather than pie-in-the-sky dreams, and to plan for implementation:

> There does not seem to be much use in the Commission drawing up a grandiose blue print unless they [farmers] are in a favourable mood to accept the plan and secondly have the necessary marketing to protect their interests such as an effective farm union or some other type of economic organization to guard their interests in a world that is completely organized around them.[5]

And, finally, he noted there must be "some continuing agency or rural planning Commission to assist in carrying through with any plans that are finally adopted."[6]

Phelps was an early environmentalist. In the letter he also noted, "conservation of water, soil and forests might be emphasized more."[7] This comment would prove to be very insightful, and William Harding would echo this sentiment later, in 1985, when he concluded that the commission had

> failed to look critically at the fundamental nature of prairie dry-land farming. The approach to land use was traditional and technological and did not consider the effects of annual crop monoculture, mechanization and the use of herbicides and other chemicals on the soil. While soil fertility and conservation were not part of the concerns raised by the public involved in the study, there was a body of literature on the subject at the time.[8]

By the early months of 1953, the study was well underway. Ninety-five community forums were held, and local committees prepared reports and presented briefs at the local community hearings that followed. Ninety communities and eighty-six local organizations and individuals submitted briefs at the fifty-seven community hearings held throughout the province during the post-seeding period of 1953. A total of 236 briefs were submitted to the commission at provincial conferences and hearings: seventy-two from provincial organizations, forty-four from government departments and agencies, thirty-six from university colleges and departments, sixty-three from individual civil servants, and twenty-one from other individuals.[9] Intensive surveys, field interviews, and mailed questionnaires to selected groups provided additional information. Many other individuals with specialized knowledge and experience also took part in the study.

The commission was the first to involve the public to such a large extent and to employ such a wide range of information-gathering strategies. Once assembled, the information was organized and analyzed, and the commission's study and interpretation of these findings formed the basis for the recommendations assembled in the final reports.

THE FINDINGS

It took fourteen volumes to contain the final results.[10] Volume one outlined the parameters of the study and the scope and character of the investigation. Volumes two through thirteen summarized what were identified as the key forces involved in economic and social change in rural Saskatchewan at the time: mechanization and farm costs, agricultural credit, rural roads and local government, land tenure, rural education, movement of farm people, agricultural markets and prices, crop insurance, the home and family in rural Saskatchewan, farm electrification, service centres, and farm income. Each volume contained an analysis and detailed history of the issues raised at community forums, and an integrated analysis of the social and economic factors involved. Rural problems were viewed as being inextricably interrelated, rather than as existing in isolation. The final volume outlined the recommended program of improvements, and summarized and integrated the commission's findings.

Even after issuing its final reports, the commission did not want to quit. The commissioners recommended that they go back to the public in order to plan for implementation. This did not happen:

> The government's patience with a Commission which seemed to have no ending was exhausted, as was the money to support another phase of the inquiry. The government also felt that, in a strictly legal sense, the final act of any board of inquiry was the submission of its final report to the government and the Commission should cease to exist at that point.[11]

Of the 275 recommendations, 102 required federal government involvement for implementation. Twenty-six of the 125 recommendations for which the provincial government was responsible were viewed as being "generally feasible for early implementation."[12] Crop insurance, which became a reality in 1960, and cash advances on farm-stored grain are the direct result of the commission's work, and rural electrification became more widespread in the years that followed. The Family Farm Improvement Act, proclaimed in 1960, encouraged the construction of rural sewer and water systems, and rural roads were also improved. The Agricultural Machinery Act, passed in 1958, improved the quality and durability of agricultural implements. Federally, the Prairie Grain Advance Payments Act, passed in 1959, gave farmers cash advances on farm-stored grain.[13]

However, like many other Royal Commissions, many of its other recommendations were never acted upon. Nonetheless, the results are impressive and some fifty years later the reports stand as a valuable and relevant reference source. William Harding, the secretary to the commission, commented in 1985:

> There is still much in these reports of value to society. Nothing much has really changed since the reports were written except that the forces pushing people off the land, widening the gap between rich and poor in agriculture throughout the world, making agriculture more commercial, more export-oriented and less sustainable, making society more centralized and people more isolated, have strengthened.[14]

Farms continue to get larger, and the rural population continues to decline. Costs continue to rise and farm income continues to fluctuate. The Saskatchewan Association of Rural Municipalities is still fighting for the preservation of rural municipalities, and rural residents are still fighting school closures. William Harding had these comments:

> If the Commission's recommendations on land tenure, credit and farm income had been implemented, particularly those directed to the federal government, the trend might have been slowed and more people could have lived more secure and satisfying lives on the farm. A similar conclusion can be made in connection with mechanization and commercial farming.... If the Commission's recommendations had been implemented those changes might have come about in a more rational manner with much less damage to those who have since suffered from bankruptcy, dislocation and soil degradation.[15]

In her master's thesis, "These Changing Times: A Study of the Saskatchewan Royal Commission on Agriculture and Rural Life," Paula Ray Rein concludes:

> In 1952, the Royal Commission on Agriculture and Rural Life was expected to produce a blueprint for rural Saskatchewan's future. Today in 1994, it could be argued that the chief value of its reports is the insight they offer into a rural society in the midst of dramatic change.... The Royal Commission showed that although change was inevitable, it could have positive aspects.[16]

THE MINORITY REPORT

In his minority report, Phelps disagreed with the majority's recommendations on three issues: farm prices, rural depopulation, and the need to create a strong and adequately financed educational and protective farm organization. Both farm prices and rural depopulation were considered by all members to present a major threat to agriculture, but Phelps differed from the majority in both his interpretation of these issues and his related recommendations. The issue of farm organizations was not, strictly speaking, an area of disagreement but had been determined to be beyond the scope of the commission from the outset. Phelps, however, considered them so important to the future of agriculture that he would not take no for an answer. Phelps argued that only a strong protective farm organization could inform and educate the public, and so sway public opinion and hence government policy. Phelps further argued that it was necessary to make the public aware of the real state of the industry, which could only be achieved if agriculture used the same standard accounting practices as other industries; this would reveal that fixed charges, including interest, taxes, and depreciation, exceeded operating surpluses and resulted in a net deficit. Failure to do so "has given the general public a completely false picture of the very grave financial problems confronting agriculture today" and "kept the industry of agriculture teetering even in its more prosperous periods on the brink of bankruptcy."[17]

He also pointed out that "Consumer prices bear little relationship to the return the farmer receives for his wheat, his beef, his honey, his fruit or any other food product he has to sell," and he advocated a widespread educational campaign to inform the public. Phelps was ahead of his time on this issue. In recent decades, farm organizations have tried to inform consumers and gain public support by pointing out the percentage of the consumer price that actually goes to the farmer. Farm prices were recognized by all members of the commission as a key component in the farm economy. However, they differed on the specifics; Phelps, as usual, favoured parity pricing.

Phelps presented three specific recommendations in his discussion of farm prices. First, he reiterated his call for the establishment of prices based on 100 per cent parity for all farm products consumed on the domestic market, a concept he had advocated throughout his involvement in the farm movement. He explained the concept of parity pricing as "The ability of farmers generally to market sufficient of their production at prices that are in balance with the cost of goods and services they must buy in order to produce." This was, he argued, the "foundation stone on which agriculture must stand or fall."[18] This did not necessarily mean higher prices but rather prices in line with the cost of manufactured goods, other raw products, and services. Farm prices, he noted, would be high when other prices were high and drop proportionately when other prices were low, and thus remain in line with the cost of goods and services purchased by the farming community.

Phelps's attachment to the idea of parity pricing was not surprising, for the concept had been part of the agricultural policy of the CCF laid out in the Regina Manifesto in 1933, which called for "an equitable relationship between prices of agricultural products and those of other commodities and services."[19]

During the thirties, Douglas and the CCF had argued for more meaningful farm policy, advocating the orderly marketing of farm products, production subsidies, and cheaper credit. The CCF saw a need to reduce farmers' debt load and make it more difficult to foreclose on farmers, and advocated strategies such as parity pricing, but the concept was fraught with difficulties. Selling prices based on the farmers' costs of fuel, seed, labour, and credit were difficult to establish. The size of the farm, distance to market, soil types, rainfall, weeds and pests, as well as the availability of labour were all contributing factors to cost.

Phelps's second recommendation involved a system of deficiency payments on export products. Cash settlements under this policy would represent the difference between domestic parity price and that received on the world market. Any excess of price over parity in periods of higher-than-normal prices would be turned back to a fund to compensate for payments made from it during periods when world prices were below parity levels. Phelps noted farmers' willingness to forego peak prices during wartime, in return for a promise of stabilized prices over the long haul.

The third recommendation Phelps made with respect to prices was that cash advances on farm-stored grain be made whenever there were grain surpluses.

Phelps also strongly objected to the commission's contention that rural depopulation was inevitable. The commission report concluded that fewer and fewer farmers would produce more and more food in the future, and that 50–60 per cent of rural youth would not be absorbed into agriculture but would rather migrate elsewhere to find employment.

Between 1936 and 1951, more than one-third of the province's rural population (348,966 people) moved out. All of the commission members, including Phelps, attributed the declining population to low and variable farm income, the effects of the Depression, the trend toward larger operating units, and the lack of material comforts, educational opportunities, and social advantages in rural Saskatchewan. Phelps stated,

> Granted that power machinery makes it possible for one large farm to produce more than a dozen farms operated by horse power, granted that depressed prices and living conditions have driven thousands from the land, granted that distance and isolation have tended to herd people into urban areas, I still do not believe that it is desirable, or efficient to have the bulk of our population crowded together in cities, while vast stretches of land are owned and operated by a few large landholders.[20]

Phelps concluded in his minority report that definite steps could be taken to reverse this trend. He noted the province's overdependence on the wheat economy, stating that "perhaps the time has come when the province should endeavour to develop a type of farming not devoted almost entirely to wheat with its dependence on export markets over which we have little or no control."[21] Although many farmers have diversified in more recent years, the focus on wheat production continued to erode the number of family farms in Saskatchewan in the decades following the commission. Phelps suggested that cropping practices should be examined. While some areas were suited to large-scale, dry-land, farming techniques, others were better suited to dairy and beef production, forage crops, vegetable production, and other sideline occupations. Irrigation and intensive production should be encouraged in suitable districts, providing opportunities for farmers to make a decent living on a comparatively small acreage.

Phelps looked to an increasing urban population, a result of increasing industrial development, to provide not only job opportunities in the cities but a market for the products of small farms. He suggested family farmers be assisted in intensifying cultivation and diversifying crops where soil types, moisture conditions, and location made such practices feasible. Recently, some small farmers have been successful in their efforts to intensify their operations and increase revenues generated per acre rather than increasing the number of acres farmed, reminiscent of Phelps's vision in the late fifties.

Phelps also offered the innovative suggestion to create a land bank fund, with joint provincial and federal input, which could be used to enable young people and others who wished to farm to acquire land from people desirous of selling or from elderly farmers who otherwise could not afford to retire. The creation of a land bank did take place later, under the Blakeney Government during the 1970s, but it proved to be unpopular. Advocates of the program argued the concept was sound, but the implementation was flawed.

If massive changes were introduced into the industry such as those outlined in the commission's recommendations, farmers would require a strong provincially funded protective organization to safeguard their interests. Phelps argued that because they were commercial concerns with financial interests of their own, the grain-handling co-operatives had not always been able to speak for farmers. Policies that might be advantageous for individual farmers, such as payments for farm storage, the abandoning of diversion charges, and cash advances on farm-stored grain, would potentially affect their revenues, and so they chose not to implement them. Phelps stated, "Many farmers who are loyal supporters of the pool recognize the weakness of the present setup. Under present day conditions I believe the creation of a sufficiently strong farmer's education and protective organization is only possible if financial stability is achieved."[22]

The next decades saw a number of farm leaders come and go, and many of the problems in agriculture continued to compound.[23] The Saskatchewan Farmers Union continued to fight some of the same battles Phelps had led it through in the early fifties, including its fight for parity pricing and to secure a contributory insurance plan. Transportation also became a perennial issue. Efforts to lobby for reorganization of the elevator system and requests for changes in the rail system were not successful. The SFU continued in its persistent and vigorous support and advocacy for marketing boards, and to seek long-term credit for general farm operations at low interest rates.

Membership in the SFU declined in the late fifties, and attempts were made over the years to meet with the Saskatchewan Federation of Agriculture, Federated Co-operatives, and the Saskatchewan Wheat Pool to achieve one voice for agriculture. The SFU maintained that commercial groups did not provide a voice for the farm movement, and it continued to advocate for a general grassroots farm organization. The chasm continued to widen between the co-ops and the union, which, according to historical information assembled by the SFU in 1969, is "an anomaly in most respects since virtually every SFU member is a Wheat Pool member and a firm supporter of the co-ops."[24]

Herbert Schulz argues that many of the decisions taken in the 1950s resulted in the current crisis in agriculture. His colourful and poignant memoir recounts the bitter and divisive politics and internal strife in Manitoba between the co-operative movement, the various organizations representing farmers, and the Manitoba Farmers Union. Schulz paints a poignant picture of farmers betrayed by the leadership of their own co-operative organizations and left to suffer the consequences of the "free market." Schulz recalled a speech in the mid-fifties by Joe Phelps at a MFU convention that opened with a characteristic slam of his fist on the table:

> When industry receives generous benefits from the taxpayers, it is "job creation" but when farmers ask for a decent price it is a subsidy. And that comes mostly from those who already have price guarantees giving them cost of production plus profit returns. Our government subsidizes just about every industry in the economy. Shipping, railways, banks, coal mining, gold mining, are on the public dole. Imagine! The

> gold mining industry was subsidized $13 million last year and what contribution does it make to human welfare compared with the food producing industry? We have minimum wage laws for those working and unemployment insurance for those who are not. We have fixed railroad, airline, and telephone rates to guarantee their owners a return on investment. Our government subsidizes newspapers, those great apostles of free enterprise, so we unwashed masses can read their propaganda that farmers must not have subsidies. Farmers operate in an international economy over which we have no control. Our governments must recognize this.[25]

While grassroots organized around the principles of voluntary crop insurance, producer-controlled commodity boards, cash advance payments on stored grain, and a parity pricing system, in the end the philosophy of the sanctity of an unobstructed marketplace won out. While some gains were made and some battles won, the issue of parity pricing, so adamantly supported by Phelps and others in the Farmers Union movement, remained unsolved.

According to Schulz, postwar debate about the future of agriculture became polarized between those that saw government intervention as a means to enlarge markets and increase farm income, and those that saw it as an impediment that limited farm income. Those advocating for increased aggregate farm income through government intervention saw social, as well as economic, value in sustaining the family farm and rural communities, as Phelps advocated for in his minority commission report. The "free-market" argument, embraced by the public, national policy-makers, and politicians of the day, dominated. Laws of supply and demand, which dominated other industries at the time, were, however, inadequate to improve the lot of farmers. More efficient production, brought about by combining rapidly improved technology, larger machinery, more fertilizer, larger farm size, and larger investment (from 1950 to 1960, farm indebtedness increased by 88 per cent)[26] inevitably resulted in fewer farmers and lower prices. Producing more simply lowered prices and, in turn, the number of farmers shrank to fit income available: "A fork was taken in the road that led to the current destination and the way back has not yet been found."[27]

Schulz recounts another of Phelps's speeches:

> Joe Phelps—the other terrible twin—raged:
>
> What in hell do they mean by a surplus of wheat? How can we have a surplus of food when most of the world is hungry? The problem is not overproduction, but under-consumption. Peoples are no longer isolated from each other. The extravagant waste during the War and modern communications, have opened the eyes of the underdeveloped world to the wealth of the West. Our surpluses are what most of the world does not have enough of, yet our farmers are being technologically displaced while our government are [*sic*] too stupid to understand what is happening elsewhere or too arrogant to care. The population of the world is exploding. Our bounty is not a curse but a national treasure. Instead of curtailing food production, our government should be concentrating on getting it to those who need it.[28]

Schulz concludes,

> The philosophy of shrinking the number of farmers to fit available income, rather than increasing aggregate farm income to sustain the farmers reached its logical culmination in the late sixties in two major studies—one federal and one provincial—which obsessed with overproduction, recommended a drastic reduction in farm population "faster than the natural rate of attrition" and more sources of credit for those remaining. The recommendations, consciously or otherwise, seemed designed to make the world safe for agribusiness.[29]

After the Royal Commission on Agriculture and Rural Life made its final report, Phelps once again turned his attention to new challenges, but farming remained close to his heart. In August 1982, the fiery farm leader was honoured for his many accomplishments. Nominated by the National Farmers Union, Phelps was inducted into the Saskatchewan Agricultural Hall of Fame, a fitting tribute for his lifetime of service.

CHAPTER 17

ACTION NOW

After an unsuccessful bid for a federal NDP seat in North Battleford in January 1962, Phelps turned his attention to new challenges.[1] Like many seniors, Phelps often travelled west to Vancouver Island, which offered the same pristine natural potential he found in northern Saskatchewan during his years as a Cabinet minister. Over the years, some members of the Phelps family had left Saskatchewan to settle in British Columbia, including Joe's sister Eva, who had moved from Wilkie to Vancouver in the mid-fifties; his daughter Ella and her family; and his brother Fred and nephew Ray, who had been in British Columbia for several years, actively involved in property development. Phelps would maintain his home in Saskatoon, but his sister Eva's old-fashioned, pioneer-style home, in an unorganized municipal district about eight miles northwest of Victoria, provided a home base during Joe's time on the island. Thanks to a foray into property development, Phelps was able to secure additional retirement income, assist his children and grandchildren, and provide a focus for his boundless energy.

In the 1960s, Joe and Fred Phelps each purchased a half-section of land in what would become the community of Langford, British Columbia. In the early 1970s, Joe had the land surveyed for the purpose of rezoning it into small lots. Fred's son Ray Phelps, a contractor in the area, built houses on the property.[2] Joe and Ray Phelps also purchased property at Malahat that was sold to BC Highways, and purchased undeveloped land near Thetus Park in partnership with another interested individual, which was later expropriated by the BC government because of watersheds located on the property.[3]

"SEVEN KINDS OF HELL"

Sometimes Joe's go-for-it attitude got in the way of his concern for the environment, or perhaps he never understood the fragility of British Columbia's coastal environment as he had the prairies. His nephew Steve Phelps recalled Joe urging Ray Phelps to commence development on property in the Phelps Subdivision at Langford. A stream ran through the property, and Ray was reluctant, preferring to wait for the fisheries department to give the final clearance. Phelps, becoming impatient after waiting for several months, went ahead and hired a crew to start clearing the timber. Work came to a sudden halt when the heavy equipment got mired down in an area near the stream. Nonetheless, Phelps enjoyed the development work and was undeterred by barriers or by the physical limitations that came with age. His grandson Rick Goranson recalled, "In Langford Joe had difficulty walking. His legs were giving him trouble. Walking through the property he was developing would have been far too much for him. But that didn't hold him back! He sat on the bucket of my loader and I drove him around the property, which delighted grandpa immensely."[4]

Periodically, Joe would take the notion to fire up a vintage steam tractor and take it for a drive on the gravel road in the subdivision, not regular practice in the neighbourhood, and this contributed to a growing opinion that he had become quite eccentric in his senior years.[5] Rick Goranson also recollected that Phelps "carried quite a bit of money with him in case he had a fender bender. In that event I think he would want to settle the claim right on the spot."[6]

Phelps maintained his interest in farmers' concerns, writing articles in farm magazines on diversification and food production,[7] and he continued to pursue his passion for preserving the past. A 1968 local newspaper article titled "Exhibit Site Sought," in the *Victoria Daily Colonist*, reported that Phelps, a local contractor and "owner of one of the largest vintage farm equipment collections worth approximately $1,000,000," was attempting to organize a vintage machinery exhibition, with operational exhibits from all of British Columbia's major industries, in the greater Victoria area. The article reported that Phelps was concerned that a great deal of valuable mining and forestry history was being lost, as much of this equipment was being sent to the junk pile. "Somebody's sleeping at the switch," Phelps stated.[8] His efforts to lobby the government to fund this venture were not successful. More recently, however, a national historic site that recreates an early sawmill opened near Port Alberni in 2000.

Phelps had made contact with like-minded people on Vancouver Island through the Saanich Historical Artifacts Society, and found a welcome home for some of his antique agricultural tractors, separators, and small engines at the Saanich museum, home to a collection of steam tractors and a variety of agricultural and forest-clearing machinery.[9]

David Hopkins, steam engineer at the Saanich museum, remembers the day Joe Phelps's steam tractor was run from the old Saanichton Fair Grounds to Willard Mitchell's farm: "That journey took place through fields with planks and tires laid to cross the roads. The steam tractor then sat silent in Mitchell's farmyard for several years, as it needed some boiler work. Joe wanted work done on the tractor, but the Saanich museum lease had run out. Joe hired a truck and low bed to move it out to the Luxton Fair grounds.... Joe Phelps could raise seven kinds of hell if he wanted to get his way."[10]

The Luxton fairgrounds, located between Langford and Sooke and owned by the Metchosin Farmers Institute, provided an ideal place for Joe Phelps's machinery collection. All of the machinery was transported and then secured and protected from the elements in a large shed built in 1977 specifically to house the Joe Phelps collection. A large threshing machine brought from Saskatchewan stands in the corner. It fell off the truck in transit, and Joe and his elderly driver reloaded the thresher, determined to deliver it to the Farmers Institute. A 1917 grey Mogul tractor, gas-powered with steel wheels, is also proudly displayed. Phelps made many trips with a long flatbed trailer unit to bring the collection out to British Columbia from Saskatchewan. The museum employs mechanics, blacksmiths, carpenters, and certified steam engineers to maintain and operate the equipment.

Beginning in 1969, he had championed yet another cause: senior citizens' rights, working as an activist within an organization whose name fittingly describes his character, Action Now. Phelps joined Action Now in the late sixties, serving as vice-president, bringing his usual direct and sometimes abrasive approach to the cause. In an interview with Sheila Baptie, Phelps commented,

> Seniors do a lot of bitching and bellyaching, but to get right out and do something for themselves as a group, that's just beginning to take hold. Too many of us go around with our hats in our hand, kind of apologizing for being senior citizens. I think it is time we raised up our chin a little bit, and aimed a little higher, particularly in regard to our basic old age pension, which is less than $200 per month.[11]

Self-help was once again the recurring theme that prompted his involvement in the cause of senior citizens. He noted that while various other groups had voiced support for the rights of the elderly, "Seniors must take up the cudgels for themselves and fight to protect their interests."[12]

In their senior years, Joe and his wife Eva welcomed their grandchildren and even the spouses of their grandchildren into their home while they were attending university. Family was important to them and kept them active and involved. Controversial issues remained at the forefront, however, and Phelps continued writing briefs. Once again, his knowledge of government procedures and his experience both in Cabinet and as president of the SFU were valuable to Action Now, aiding in its preparation and submission of documents to the government, especially since, according to Phelps, "Governments don't act, they react to what people want or should have."[13]

Baptie, who noted that Joe Phelps had developed quite a reputation for radicalism, wondered if the senior citizens also considered him radical. Phelps responded,

> Oh, some of them I think do. Oh yes. I think that would be quite fair. I regard that as a compliment rather than as a criticism though. We have helped to build this country, collectively, why can't we organize ourselves in such a way that senior citizens are treated fairly. We don't want Christmas all the time, but a fair square deal for senior citizens on the same basis as everybody else. Is that asking for something unreasonable? I don't think so.[14]

"WHAT SOCIETY OUGHT TO BE"

After a long, active, and determined life, Joseph Lee Phelps, born August 12, 1899, in Belleville, Ontario, died at home in Saskatoon of a heart attack on Tuesday, March 15, 1983. His funeral service was held on Saturday, March 19, at Mayfair United Church. He was buried at Wilkie. During an evening session on March 21, 1983, members of Saskatchewan's legislative assembly praised Phelps for his public service. Allan Blakeney, leader of the NDP Opposition and MLA for Regina Elphinstone, described him as

> a person of boundless energy and firm commitment, and great organizing ability. Joe Phelps was not satisfied with the status quo, with, I venture to think, any status quo. He believed in the need for change and the possibility of change. He...[had a] restlessness in achieving his objectives, which did not always fit lightly into the system of cabinet solidarity. I am painting a picture of a man who was, at least in his younger years up to 60 or 65, a person who lived life at the full gallop. When he got older, into 75 and 80, it was perhaps at a fast canter. I think none of us who have seen Joe in action can have anything but admiration for his drive, his initiative, his commitment to others. These activities were never for the financial benefit of Joe Phelps or Joe Phelps' family. They were all in the furtherance of his vision of what society ought to be.[15]

Ned Shillington, NDP MLA for Regina, said:

> He had boundless energy, and he had a faith in his society and his fellow men, which led him to believe that virtually anything could be done if one simply took the time to explain the merits of what you were doing.... It was not in his nature to put himself first. He put his society first. He was an individual who wanted really nothing for himself. He wanted only a better society. He worked very energetically for that, and made contributions toward that end which very few of his generation could match. I join, Mr. Speaker, with my colleagues on

> both sides of the House, in paying tribute to one of the giants of Saskatchewan in yester-year.[16]

Perhaps the greatest tribute to Joe Phelps was made by his friend and associate from the Farmers Union movement, Stuart Thiesson:

> Joe was a proud man, who knew what he believed and why, and more importantly, was prepared to do something about it....
>
> Joe did many things in his waking hours...such as hard work; championing causes, often at considerable odds, that were not widely embraced or popular; tackling projects, some of which will remain as monuments to his life in the history of this province and nation, long after those of us present have passed from the scene. He was a doer, one who was often impatient with the status quo. How often he would say with his eyes flashing, accompanied by a lusty thump on his desk, "By jingles, you've got to raise your sights if you want to get the job done!" And he did! A forceful and flamboyant orator, he had the charisma to stir the most passive souls with a sense of indignation, and hope. His adversaries claimed he was only a rabble-rouser, but they were wrong.[17]

At the 1983 convention celebrating the fiftieth anniversary of the Regina Manifesto, Tommy Douglas spoke for the last time, emphasizing that the fight for social justice would continue, the greatest work was yet to be done—the building of a productive, caring, and peaceful world. In Douglas's words,

> In a movement like ours, as socialist movements around the world have shown, we're not just interested in getting votes, we are seeking to get people who are willing to dedicate their lives to building a different kind of society—a society founded on the principles of concern for human well-being and human welfare.[18]

Joe Phelps was willing.

EPILOGUE

"NEVER SAY WHOA IN THE MIDDLE OF A MUD PUDDLE!"

In 1981, Phelps talked about the approach he had taken throughout his life:

> I think when the chips are down, it isn't a matter of how many rolls of money you got in your pocket, or how much credit at the bank, or how much you got on deposit, those are convenient things all right and you can do things that you couldn't do otherwise.... I think to be at peace with your own mind is one of the biggest things, and if you are at peace with yourself, if you feel that you are doing something for society... something to improve the human race as a whole, then you got a purpose in life and a life that's got some meaning to it.... I think that I have made my contribution. I've tried to do it conscientiously. Sure a lot of people haven't agreed with me over the years, but that's how changes are made, isn't it.[1]

Joe Phelps was a planner, a builder, and a visionary—a man with a fiery spirit ahead of his time. He spoke passionately about the environment, conservation, recycling, reforestation, women's rights, and peace at a time when these views were not commonplace, even within the most radical political and social movements of the time. He was also shaped by the times, particularly the uncertainties of agriculture and the social and political movements that sprang out of the economic conditions of the Great Depression. He showed great foresight into the future of agriculture and rural Saskatchewan and the social, political, and global consequences of actions that were being taken at the time.

Phelps could not have achieved all that he did without the support of the women in his life. As the cliché goes, behind every great man is a great woman—or two or three. Their "invisible" work and ongoing support gave him the freedom to pursue his interests and his political aspirations—to travel, to organize, and to work the long hours he did. Joe Phelps admired and relied on the women in his life. He grew up on a small prairie farm, his father ill, but his mother nurturing and capable. Strong, capable, intelligent women remained a major influence throughout his life, and he relied on their support both at home and in his political endeavours, often stating very sincerely that he "had been blessed to know three wonderful women—a mother and two wives."[2] While he relied on the women in his life, he also supported them and was a strong advocate of equal rights for women, speaking publicly about women's issues as early as 1931.

Phelps played a pivotal role in the Douglas Government's innovative socialist experiment in Saskatchewan. Phelps's dirigisme—the belief that by exerting a strong directive influence and regulatory role over the economy, the state could achieve greater gains for all—is a unique part of Saskatchewan's history and remains part of the collective psyche and common understanding of the role of government in the province to this day. The role of collective action, social planning, Crown corporations in the economy, and the grassroots sentiment around these ideas are woven into the fabric of what has become Saskatchewan's unique culture. Joe Phelps was a colourful individual to be sure, but it is his relentless work ethic that stands out clearly as his most dominant personal characteristic. Unquestionably, he was conscientious, diligent, and serious about his work, and this energy was directed toward what he believed was in the best interests of the government and Saskatchewan people.

Despite his lack of formal education, Phelps achieved great success. It is possible that his limited education may have heightened his desire to prove himself and his already extreme work ethic, and it may also account for the interest he took in education after being elected. His folksy demeanour stands in contrast to some of the people in positions of power with whom he came into contact, and this may have contributed to his dislike of bureaucratic people and procedures. However, his charm and the force of his personality often allowed him to bend the rules or go around bureaucrats or others he felt were blocking him. He also had a highly developed gut instinct and was quick to assess situations, make decisions, and take action, and quick to detect any sign of corruption. His actions and methods were bold and unorthodox.

Phelps had a keen ability to pull together the right people and resources to make things happen quickly and efficiently—in his words, "the day before yesterday"—and for this reason he quickly assumed positions of authority and was highly valued both within government and other organizations. He worked best when he was in a position of power, and quickly became uncomfortable and dissatisfied in situations where he was simply a cog in the wheel or lacked the authority or autonomy to make decisions. He was fully committed to whatever he was involved in, and this propensity to forge ahead despite obstacles earned him a reputation as a man of action. It also garnered intense criticism from his opponents and sometimes his colleagues.

Phelps was criticized for moving too quickly, for surrounding himself with those who thought like he did, for ignoring the advice of experts and colleagues, for antagonizing many within the legislature and his department. Some of his colleagues believed that in his enthusiasm to realize his socialistic dream for the province, he acted imprudently, hastily, and recklessly. Phelps's colleagues often learned of developments only after they had occurred; the McLeods have noted that "Phelps ordered the purchase of at least one plant without consulting the cabinet, and he resorted to tears when his colleagues threatened to reverse his decision."[3] In the flurry of activity, he was often unable to consolidate existing projects before beginning new ones. In fact, W. J. Patterson once pointed out that Phelps announced "so many different things at so many different times that the government may have some trouble in consolidating them and the people have difficulty keeping up with them."[4] It is difficult to even contemplate how he managed so many projects simultaneously. He failed to communicate adequately with members of his department and with the public, and at times failed to find qualified trained personnel to run his various programs.

Jim Wright, founder and first editor of the *Union Farmer*, gave this description of Phelps:

In public life, Joe Phelps was the dynamic pragmatist in action—a restless, driving, impatient innovator. His brain wasn't the computer type, it was like the crystal set of the early days of experimental radio—full of surprises—because you had no way of knowing in advance what wave length you were going to be in on next.

When Joe's built-in antenna got an idea, he demanded action faster than immediately. Often enough he couldn't hold it until the office opened and the staff appeared in the morning. In consequence, his subordinates were rarely pleased but never surprised when the phone rang at midnight or six a.m. and Joe was on the other end of the line. As he was what might be termed "on duty" twenty-four hours a day (I do believe he was churning up innovations while he slept), he expected his deputies, lieutenants, or whatever, to be available day and night, seven days a week.

The great stirrer-upper, it really bothered him to see something jell; as a result his immediate subordinates were rarely given time to consolidate an idea before Joe had shot two or three more at them.

One of a series of secretaries of the Saskatchewan Farmers Union when Joe was president got around the problem temporarily by being always readily available when Joe called the chap in to the president's office. Joe would shoot a brain wave at the secretary who would wear an alert look on his face, nod agreement and make as if he were taking a few notes.

Joe: "Yip, yip, yip. That's it. Let's get cracking on it!"

Whereupon the secretary would walk briskly back to his glass-fronted office, sit down behind his desk and look very busy while waiting for Joe to summon him again in what might be ten minutes time.[5]

THE "PROBLEM CHILDREN"

Five of the Crown corporations Joe Phelps initiated failed. The brick plant and the shoe factory/tannery shut down operations before the end of Phelps's term in office, and the woollen mill, box factory, and Fish

Marketing Board were closed in the fifties. He encountered many problems and difficulties in the government's first business ventures, some due to unforeseen circumstances, some through pre-existing problems, and some of his own making. Trying to implement all of the new initiatives at the same time undoubtedly added to the complexity of Phelps's work. There was no road map, no clear policies and procedures, and limited financial resources. Moreover, the province was attempting to implement a socialized economic program within a federal capitalist system. All of these factors contributed to the complexity of initiating and managing these operations.

Many of Phelps's other initiatives, however, including the sodium sulphate plant, Saskatchewan Airways, SaskPower, the Fur Marketing Board, and the fur, forestry, and fish conservation measures put in place in northern Saskatchewan were tremendously successful. While the unsuccessful enterprises create a negative view of Phelps's legacy, and have often been lambasted by political opponents, it is important to note they were not financially significant in the larger scheme of things. In fact, in 1949, Premier Douglas noted that the "Experimental and 'Problem Children'"—the Fish Board, the shoe factory/tannery, and the woollen mill represented only 4.9 per cent of the total government investment in Crown corporations. Douglas noted that as of March 1, 1949, the government's $35,540,504 investment in Crown corporations had realized a profit of $3,152,502.17.[6] Richards and Pratt acknowledge that although the failures of the various initial Crown ventures assumed "mythic proportions" in the province and became "political albatrosses" for the CCF government, the Crown corporations' financial record could not be described as particularly grim.[7]

These early forays into social ownership represent a unique period in Saskatchewan's history, and the issue of responsibility is complex. The success or failure of all of the new initiatives rests on a combination of ministerial responsibility, the decisions of Cabinet and CCF policy, and the civil service put in place to carry them out. It is clear that, at times, the relationship between Phelps and the Cabinet was difficult. Phelps freely admitted that his Cabinet colleagues did not always agree with him, stating that the Cabinet thought "I did too many damn things" and admitting that he "got alot of backfire" from Cabinet "on some things." Although C. M. Fines, the provincial treasurer, tried to restrict Phelps's spending, Phelps "never found him difficult." In fact, he considered Fines "a good fellow to work with." When asked about his relationship with T. C. Douglas, Phelps replied that Douglas never scolded him but that the premier had talked to him "pretty straight two or three times when there was quite a bit of tension."[8] Richards and Pratt state that by 1946 Fines knew that, financially, Saskatchewan's "experiments in social ownership must remain just that—small experiments, not wholesale takeovers as Phelps proposed." Notably, they conclude that, ideologically, "Fines and Phelps personally embodied the tensions within the government between the moderate and the radical."[9] Douglas recalled that with Phelps, "You could always count on him being on your side if you were raising some question that was extremely controversial . . . Phelps wasn't really so radical, you know, he just jumped to the left side of any issue that came up. He liked to make a noise."[10] According to Al Johnson, while it is difficult to judge whether Cabinet supported Phelps's projects enthusiastically or reluctantly, "'Corridor gossip' has it that the Cabinet was divided, and that Mr. Phelps was able to get some of his projects approved only because of a good deal of uncertainty as to the proper role for social ownership."[11]

While some of his Cabinet colleagues may have agreed with Phelps in principle, they may also have been uncomfortable with the pace of change and with Phelps's freewheeling approach and lack of accountability:

> While the cabinet in principle favored such a diversification, certain members were wary of their colleague's entrepreneurial ambitions. Phelps in turn chafed at the constraints upon his ability to act—whether it be the recalcitrance of cautious bureaucrats within his department (of the senior staff he inherited he dismissed the deputy minister plus four of six senior branch heads), budgetary controls exercised by the Treasury (he insisted on a single budget vote for 'conservation and development' in order to minimize the details of accountability), or the necessity of procuring cabinet approval.[12]

Although in the fall of 1944 the government seemed to encounter "difficulties in crystallizing its position on social ownership," Phelps had no such problems.[13] He had already announced that the government was planning to own and operate a pulp mill, to cancel some lumbering and fur trapping agreements when they came due, to consider negotiating "compulsory government marketing of natural products," and to establish "public ownership when it was in the public interest."[14] Phelps said in 1944, "It is the intention of the Government to effect an orderly change to social ownership in the industrial development of our natural resources."[15] It must be noted, however, that before the Douglas Government assumed power, many and perhaps most members of the CCF shared Phelps's view on social ownership and subcribed to the principles laid out in the Regina Manifesto, which embodied the fundamental ideological orientation of the party. The CCF did not replace the Regina Manifesto with the more moderate Winnipeg Declaration until 1956.[16] McLeod and McLeod note that Phelps's enthusiasm for "'the eventual and *complete* socialization' of natural resources under provincial control [emphasis added],"[17] an idea proposed by Phelps's party committee on natural resources while the party was still in opposition, never wavered:

> Above all, he [Phelps] loved the idea of public ownership of industry, and paid no attention when others counselled caution.... He acted without trying to establish whether he could sell the products or even manage the operations. The resulting tangle posed a challenge to George Cadbury and the Government Finance Office.[18]

According to Radloff, Phelps's policies were based on recommendations made to the pre-election CCF committee in Vern Hogg's 1943 *Plan for the Development of Natural Resources of Northern Saskatchewan under Social Ownership and Control* for the creation of a state-owned northern airway service and public ownership of the fur, fish, and timber industries.[19] Phelps seized upon the recommendations outlined in Hogg's report with dogged determination. His unwavering commitment to social ownership and what some in the party deemed his fervid socialism,[20] along with his impetuosity, contributed to tension within the Cabinet. Yet his impetuosity, which so often created problems, was coupled with innovation and initiative. George Cadbury called Phelps's initiative "absolutely invaluable." Douglas noted that, while at times Phelps was "disconcerting," he was "a man of ideas."[21] Al Johnson, who became deputy provincial treasurer under Clarence Fines in 1952, found

Phelps's "impetuosity" completely foreign, "but he stated that Phelps' 'unorthodox' approach produced the most substantial policy changes of any minister during the formative first two years of office."[22]

In many ways, Phelps was given a "blank cheque" and a portfolio far too big for any one person to handle. One might speculate that the Cabinet was fully aware he would "go full steam ahead" but simply allowed him to test the waters. Later, when Phelps's enterprises were registering losses and it anticipated that it would not be well received by the voting public, the position of Cabinet and the policy of the party moved markedly toward the centre. Clearly, the project of social ownership in Saskatchewan was controversial, and reactionary forces were quick to respond. Although many in the party moderated their position on social ownership, Phelps remained committed. The leadership of the party, fearing loss of support at the polls, no longer saw Phelps's social entrepreneurialism as an asset politically. It is interesting to contemplate what might have been had the government made the decision to persevere longer and put in the needed resources to make these businesses successful. Richards and Pratt conclude,

> The first term of office betrayed a failure to grasp an essential aspect of private or public entrepreneurship, namely the willingness to take risk. The only leaders who consistently displayed that willingness were Phelps and to a lesser extent Cadbury. The victors in the administrative reorganization of 1946–48 abandoned the relatively sophisticated analysis of the potential for public investment made by Cadbury and the Planning Board in late 1946. Instead of concentrating their limited capital and entrepreneurial resources into the new resource industries as then recommended, the government balked at any further public ventures or even joint ventures.[23]

Notably, in M. J. Coldwell's book *Left Turn, Canada*, there is only cautious discussion of the Saskatchewan government's aggressive approach to social ownership,[24] perhaps an indication that at the federal level the position of the CCF on social ownership had already moderated significantly by 1944. Phelps's defeat in 1948 marked a watershed for the government; his departure left a void since no one remained to represent the radical agrarian wing of the party, or to actively pursue social ownership with the same zeal as Phelps had displayed.

While the policies of the CCF and the leadership of the party have been the subject of intense critical and historical analysis, scholars have tended to disregard the impact of the civil service and its failure or success in carrying out the will of the party. Phelps struggled with the bureaucratic barriers he faced in the implementation of CCF policy, particularly the challenges of bringing about innovative change within an established and cautious civil service. He had a deep-seated aversion to bureaucracy, which he saw as a tremendous barrier to progress and true advancement. Bureaucratic rules and policies in established organizations put in place to maintain the status quo were abhorrent to him. By extension, he perceived organizations controlled by bureaucrats as stagnant and self-serving, and in some cases reprehensible. He repeatedly questioned privilege, convention, and the status quo. This attitude contributed to the strong opposition he faced at times. Richards and Pratt note that Phelps "despaired of the lack of entrepreneurial initiative among the career civil servants he had inherited in his department."[25] He disliked having "to rely on a powerful body of professionals," for this would only "mean debate and delay." Besides, he believed that the party had debated these issues endlessly for the last decade, and now "it was time to act, to experiment, to take risks."[26] Al Johnson stated, "Mr. Phelps chose his advisors on an *ad hoc*, almost random approach,"[27] the antithesis of the civil service, where working through established channels is the norm. It seems likely that Phelps was often unable to clone his own enthusiasm, and individuals within the civil service that resisted dramatic changes, either actively or passively, contributed to his frustration and impetuosity.[28]

A FARMER FIRST

Being a successful farmer was the one constant, and perhaps the role that was most central to Phelps's identity. Phelps's "radical socialism" was tempered by his petit bourgeois roots and rural way of life.[29] As a farmer, he was used to being self-reliant and working independently. Reluctant to delegate authority, he tended to direct and control projects himself, a formidable task indeed.

Living through the Great Depression had a profound effect on Phelps's values and beliefs. Although the fear of communism tempered some of the socialist fervour spawned during the Depression, Phelps, along with countless others, looked to a planned economy for relief from the difficult conditions. Phelps's sense of social responsibility became imbedded in a desire for a better world, a new economic order in which wealth was distributed more equitably through safety nets and social programs. Social ownership, as proposed in the Regina Manifesto, was thought to be the engine for this social transformation. Phelps has been called the most "radical" member of the Douglas Government;[30] however, his unique brand of agrarian socialism might best be described as a combination of grassroots populist sentiment, petit bourgeois impulse, and more radical socialist ideals.

The struggle to balance his ruggedly individualistic nature, fostered by his roots on the farm, with his role in the socialist movement emerges repeatedly in Phelps's life. In Johnson's words, "The ultimate paradox for Joe Phelps was that he was a supreme individualist bound by a collectivist ideology, and bound under parliamentary government to act as one of a collective."[31] As both a politician and as a farm leader, his emphasis on self-reliance was clearly evident, as was his strong belief in socialist principles. During his work in government (in particular, in northern development), his intent was to invest in people, to provide them with the means to become self-sufficient. Within the farm movement he repeatedly emphasized personal responsibility, but at the same time advocated programs that would cushion people from the harsh realities of the weather and markets—factors over which they had no control. He strived to create an even playing field—a social and economic order in which equal opportunities were available to all. Phelps's challenge was one of balancing personal responsibility, manifested in his relentless work ethic, with social responsibility, evident in his acute social conscience.

Joe Phelps's ideal society was not the socialist ideal of a "dictatorship of the proletariat" but rather a democracy of small holders—petit bourgeois capitalists. He viewed big capital, monopolies, and even labour (if viewed as an institutionalized class entity) as foreign and inimical.[32] Phelps strongly identified with the socialist ideal of "humanity first," but contrary to the conventional leftist view he saw the petit bourgeoisie, not labour, as the revolutionary class. His efforts to create publicly owned utilities, to control monopolies, to create single-desk marketing powers in agriculture, and to achieve political unity and alliance with labour would allow his republic of small holders to prevail. In this, his economic perspective alone marks him as a unique historical figure. That he defined and advanced his work in terms of socialism, distinct from more labour-oriented or less radical Cabinet colleagues, is even more remarkable. He viewed labour less as a distinct economic class than as a kind of entry vehicle for eventual farm or small business ownership. He saw improved farm and small business conditions as a better route to improving the lives of working people than collective bargaining. In this way, employees could rise to the level of proprietorship, creating a steadier demand for labour and assuring the potentially prosperous alternative of self-employment.

Phelps's unwavering support of parity pricing for farmers is closely linked to his petit bourgeois political impulse in that ensuring adequate income for farmers would also ensure adequate income for local processors, suppliers, and retailers, which, in turn, would create a viable local economy and offset the advantages of larger firms that had the potential to prosper because of low farm prices. Phelps's early participation in the farm movement, sparked by dissatisfaction with his own economic circumstances, was a pivotal experience in his life. Difficulties on the farm, juxtaposed with his exposure to the benefits of collective action, contributed to his inclination to political life. During the twenties, many had come to realize that co-operative initiatives were inadequate without key government supports and compulsory participation.[33] Phelps believed that the path to social change was through grassroots organization supported by social and economic reform through the democratic system. In Phelps's words, spoken in 1931 at the UFC annual convention, "Anything that starts from the top down—suggested by officials of organizations is doomed to hit the rocks some time. But, something generated from the bottom is going to be solid."[34]

Although Phelps is often characterized as the most radical member of the Douglas Government, his views on social ownership were no more or less radical than the other founding members of the CCF that supported the Regina Manifesto in the early thirties. In other ways, he was much less "radical" than other members of the government, most particularly in his views on the labour movement. Phelps did not identify strongly with his role as a worker or sympathize with the trade union movement as a young man. Although he spent over twenty years working as a telephone lineman, there were virtually no references to this aspect of his life in any of the sources consulted, including archival material or interview transcripts. It appears that he viewed his role as a wage labourer as simply a means to an end. It provided enough money to run the farm, support the family, and pursue other interests—a temporary solution to a cash flow shortfall. His role as a farmer was much more significant and influential in shaping his beliefs and the way he approached his life's work. It was not until mid-life, during his years working within the Farmers Union movement, that he began to see common ground between the interests of farmers and labour.

MOVEMENT POLITICS

Phelps drew energy from the potential to make a difference. He was drawn to social movements that emphasized real change—purposeful activity channelled toward reforming particular aspects of society—as opposed to partisan politics. Throughout his life, Phelps's contribution was the most meaningful and effective in the earlier stages of a movement's organizational development, during the period of unrest, discontent, and collective excitement.[35] His return to the farm movement in the fifties to rejuvenate the SFU fulfilled his organizing zeal at the grassroots level.

He believed very strongly that the Farmers Union provided an independent function not easily duplicated by more politically accommodating organizations, and remained aggressively committed to the protective function of the union. Indeed, some believe his vision of the Farmers Union as a mass organization unencumbered by ties to farmer-owned commercial organizations is what was lacking in the fight to retain the Canadian Wheat Board (CWB) in recent years. The pro-CWB elected farmer majority on the board was unable to stave off the federal government, "in the absence of a more vigorous grassroots resistance to assert what is repeatedly been shown to be the popular will."[36] In 1987, Allan Levine, in *The Exchange: 100 Years of Trading Grain in Winnipeg*, concluded that farmers had chosen stability and security over gambling on the highest price on the open market, and conceded, "the reality [is] that the [Wheat] Board is here to stay, a fact which pleases the majority of western wheat farmers."[37] Even Levine's book, which attempts to redress the negative image of the Grain Exchange, did not predict that the government would override the will of the majority of the farmers and remove the Wheat Board's monopoly selling position.

Phelps was undoubtedly what some sociologists call a charismatic leader—a leader who attracted people through the force of his personality.[38] Although he enjoyed being in the limelight, he did not seem to be driven as much by ego as by an overwhelming commitment to whatever movement he was involved in at the time. He was forthright and outspoken, and diplomacy was not his preferred political strategy. As a leader, he was fiery and passionate, often a tough taskmaster, but at the same time a soft-hearted and emotional person, easily moved to tears. He was, undoubtedly, flamboyant and compelling.

Like many charismatic leaders, he became disillusioned with organizations in their later stages. His participation in the grassroots movement, which spearheaded the formation of the Saskatchewan Wheat Pool; in the founding of the Farmer-Labour Group; as a Cabinet minister in the first social democratic government in Saskatchewan; as a leader in the rejuvenated Saskatchewan Farmers Union; and, later, in the senior citizens movement are all evidence of his passion for movement politics. Indeed, Phelps was criticized for being a "dreamer." After he had addressed the 1946 United Farmers convention, the *StarPhoenix* noted that Phelps was a visionary who built "pretty dream castles." It then concluded,

> As a member of the Opposition, Phelps had an undisputed nuisance value. He was also valuable in the Opposition because he could dream and could set up distant goals to be ultimately aimed at. But is the dreamer an effective administrator? He [Phelps] commands one of the most important posts in the Cabinet—a post that calls for a hard, shrewd common sense above all else. Mr. Phelps's speeches, including the one to the United Farmers, seldom seem to present him in quite this light.[39]

Phelps believed that vibrant grassroots movements were the primary vehicles for facilitating reform and the route to social change. He was deeply committed to the movements he was involved in, generating tremendous excitement and momentum and great bursts of organizational activity. His charisma and energy were contagious, and resulted in remarkable growth and progress, often within a relatively short period of time. Phelps and his counterparts in the Farmer-Labour movement and later in the Farmers Union movement canvassed and "barnstormed" literally hundreds of rural communities, spreading their message, and Phelps excelled at it. He was a superb grassroots organizer; his energy and enthusiasm were a tremendous political asset during the early stages of a movement. Farm activist Bruce Dodds maintains,

> Joe's evangelical farm leadership helped bring about the second great revival of 20th century farm activism in Canada. Together Joe and Jake [Schulz, leader of the MFU] and the leaders of the Farmers' Union of Alberta (FUA) brought half the farm people in their respective provinces into the Farmers' Union, an achievement not seen since the heady days of the United Farmers and Pool campaigns.[40]

Conversely, this same desire to maintain grassroots participation, excitement, and momentum also made Phelps somewhat of a political liability as the organizations he was involved in became more established. When the initial unrest had been satisfied through collective action and the organizations became more established, he lost interest or became disillusioned.[41] These situations marked the critical turning points in his life.

In *Agrarian Socialism*, Lipset discusses the institutionalization of social movements, which he labels "bureaucratic conservatism." Although Lipset acknowledges that organizations can become ends in themselves, he describes individuals who, like Phelps, continue in their active pursuit of the original goals:

> An answer to the stagnation lies in the bold actions of such men as the "agitators" of Saskatchewan, who are not satisfied with anything but utopia.... As long as there are social organizations that produce men who do not accept the status quo, who see "the inhumanity of man to man" as a crime, there will be hope in the human race.[42]

Farm activist Bruce Dodds aptly asks the question:

> How will history judge Joe's efforts? As a heroic but ultimately futile attempt to stave off the destruction of the agriculturally based community he was so much a part of? Or as a harbinger of the as yet unrealized potential of free men and women to control their communities, economy and work process through a progressive democratic petit-bourgeois approach that combines capitalist and socialist ideals? Which view is correct? I don't know. But I can say this—I don't think the world has travelled far enough down Joe's road yet for anyone to really know.[43]

Joe Phelps took the road less travelled, and even when the cost was high he remained committed to his principles.

NOTES

INTRODUCTION

1 Herbert Schulz, correspondence with the author, January 2007.
2 *Regina Commonwealth*, May 30, 1962, 5.
3 Lorne Brown, Joseph Roberts, and John Warnock, *Saskatchewan Politics from Left to Right, '44 to '99* (Regina: Hinterland Publications, 1999), 1.
4 Gregory Marchildon, foreword to *Dream No Little Dreams: A Biography of the Douglas Government of Saskatchewan, 1944–1961*, by A. W. Johnson (Toronto: University of Toronto Press, 2004), xv.
5 Herbert Schulz, *Betrayal: Agricultural Politics in the Fifties* (Calgary: University of Calgary Press, 2004), 3.
6 Bruce Dodds, correspondence with the author, January 2007. Bruce provided an insightful and comprehensive critique of an earlier version of this manuscript. In it he discusses the notion of greatness in the context of Phelps's work and career.
7 Herbert Schulz, correspondence with the author, January 2007.
8 Carla Goranson, interview by Larry Shaak, March 2001, transcript, private collection. Carla Goranson is Phelps's granddaughter; she also recalled that Joe always wore suspenders and carried a huge, heavy, brown briefcase filled with "all kinds of papers, some of them tattered," wherever he went.

CHAPTER 1

1 George Phelps, sworn statement, July 7, 1909, R. W. Crump, witness, Homestead Records, Provincial Archives of Saskatchewan.
2 May Cousins, "Faith in the Future—A Pioneer Feature," *Battlefords News-Optimist*, undated.
3 The Eighty Year History Society, *A Harvest of Memories: A History of Rural Wilkie* (Battleford, SK: Turner-Warwick Printers, 1984), 765–766.
4 John H. Archer, *Saskatchewan: A History* (Saskatoon: Western Producer Prairie Books, 1980), 56–57.
5 Joe's father and mother had been born in Ontario but were respectively of Irish and Dutch descent.
6 George Phelps, sworn statement, December 10, 1908, R. W. Crump, witness, Homestead Records, Provincial Archives of Saskatchewan.

7 Cousins, "Faith in the Future." The homestead location is "NE ¼ Sec. 26-41-19 W3rd." It still remains in the Phelps family name.
8 Bill Waiser, *Saskatchewan: A New History* (Calgary: Fitzhenry & Whiteside, 2005), 494.
9 Pierre Berton, *The Promised Land: Settling the West, 1896–1914* (Toronto: McClelland & Stewart, 1984), 22.
10 George Phelps, sworn statement, July 7, 1909.
11 Cousins, "Faith in the Future."
12 This according to Joe Phelps's second wife, Eva. Eva Phelps, interview by Larry Shaak, July 2003, transcript, private collection.
13 Bruce Phelps, interview by Larry Shaak, July–August 2001, transcript, private collection.
14 Waiser, *Saskatchewan*, 21.
15 Archer, *Saskatchewan*, 360.
16 Ibid., 122.
17 Ibid., 123.
18 S. M. Lipset, *Agrarian Socialism: The Cooperative Commonwealth Federation in Saskatchewan: A Study in Political Sociology* (Berkeley: University of California Press, 1967), 43.
19 Archer, *Saskatchewan*, 149.
20 Eighty Year History Society, *A Harvest of Memories*, 764.
21 H. S. Fry, "Joe Phelps, President, Saskatchewan Farmers Union," *Country Guide*, November 1, 1950, n.p.
22 This was taken from the typewritten copy of Stuart Thiesson's eulogy for Joseph Phelps, given at Mayfair United Church in Saskatoon, Saskatchewan, on March 19, 1983, private collection.
23 Fry, "Joe Phelps."
24 Ibid. Phelps told Fry in *Country Guide* that he had exactly seventy-two days beyond grade six: "After I had been in Grade VI for a few days I had a bad abscess in my jaw as a result of which I was home for a very long time. I probably would not have gone back at all, except that the teacher who was going with the Imperial Oil agent in Wilkie where my parents had decided to send me for grades VII and VIII, asked him to drive out to our place. She talked to the folks and the result was that I went back to school for the balance of the term and managed to get my entrance to Grade VIII." Shortly afterward, the war broke out and his father was ill, and he had to stay home and look after the farm. When his brother returned from the war, he was too old to go back to school.
25 *Regina Commonwealth*, May 30, 1962, 5; Eighty Year History Society, *A Harvest of Memories*, 211, 220, 223, 765–766.
26 J. L. Phelps, interview by Jean Larmour, June 1, 1982, transcript, Provincial Archives of Saskatchewan, 4–5.
27 Duff Spafford, "The Origin of the Farmers' Union of Canada," *Saskatchewan History* 18, no. 3 (Winter 1965), 89–98.
28 Fry, "Joe Phelps."

29 Eighty Year History Society, *A Harvest of Memories*, 764.
30 J. L. Phelps, interview by Larmour, 6.
31 Eiling Kramer to Ella Little, "A Literal Snapshot of Joe Phelps," undated correspondence, private collection.
32 Muriel Phelps, interview by Larry Shaak, July–August 2001, transcript, private collection.

CHAPTER 2

1 Archer, *Saskatchewan*, 188.
2 Garry Fairbairn, *From Prairie Roots: The Remarkable Story of the Saskatchewan Wheat Pool* (Saskatoon: Western Producer Prairie Books, 1984), 1–16.
3 George Hoffman, "The Entry of the United Farmers of Canada, Saskatchewan Section into Politics: A Reassessment," *Saskatchewan History* 30, no. 3 (1977), 99–109 (note 23).
4 Fairbairn, *From Prairie Roots*, 15.
5 See Stuart A. Thiesson, "Farm Movement (1901–49)," *Encyclopedia of Saskatchewan* (Regina: Canadian Plains Research Center, University of Regina, 2005), 319, and Waiser, *Saskatchewan*, 261.
6 Waiser, *Saskatchewan*, 261.
7 Ibid., 263.
8 Archer, *Saskatchewan*, 195.
9 Waiser, *Saskatchewan*, 262.
10 Archer, *Saskatchewan*, 196.
11 *Wilkie Press*, December 16, 1925, 1.
12 Eighty Year History Society, *A Harvest of Memories*, 764. This source indicates that Phelps participated at the convention that brought about this merger. It is difficult to tell how active his participation was. Apparently, he was not one of the ten members of the amalgamating committee that was formed at the joint convention of the two organizations held on January 29, 1926, as the *Western Producer* did not list him as one of the ten trustees the UFC selected (*Saskatoon Western Producer*, February 11, 1926, 3; July 22, 1926, 1).
13 Archer, *Saskatchewan*, 196.
14 Archer, *Saskatchewan*, 205.
15 A Phelps family photo dated January 1931 shows Joe Phelps beside an automobile. It is uncertain if this was their first car.
16 Waiser, *Saskatchewan*, 274.
17 Ibid., 278.
18 Phelps was elected to this position at the annual meeting held on February 23, 1927. Fry, "Joe Phelps."
19 Lipset, *Agrarian Socialism*, 75.
20 J. L. Phelps, interview by Larmour, 7.
21 *Wilkie Press*, November 20, 1929, 1.

22 *Wilkie Press*, April 16, 1930, 1; July 2, 1930, 5; July 16, 1930, 1; February 4, 1931, 1; *Saskatoon Western Producer*, March 13, 1930, 9.

23 *Wilkie Press*, April 6, 1931, 1.

24 Ibid., December 10, 1930, 1–2.

25 Friedrich Steininger, "George H. Williams: Agrarian Socialist" (master's thesis, University of Regina, 1976), 53.

26 George Hoffman, "The Saskatchewan Farmer-Labour Party, 1932–1934: How Radical Was Its Origin?" in *Pages from the Past: Essays on Saskatchewan History*, ed. D. H. Bocking (Saskatoon: Western Producer Prairie Books, 1979), 210.

27 Hoffman, "Entry of the United Farmers."

28 *Wilkie Press*, January 14, 1931, 1.

29 *Saskatoon Western Producer*, January 15, 1931, 2.

30 Charter of Liberty, UFC Minutes, Annual Convention, 1931, United Farmers of Canada (Saskatchewan Section), Papers, Provincial Archives of Saskatchewan, 467.

31 J. L. Phelps, interview by Larmour, 11.

32 The minutes of the meeting read: "Phelps—Mrs. St. John—That the Resolutions committee draw up a resolution on Public Health to be submitted to the Board tomorrow morning, which if ratified will be recommended to the Annual Convention. Carried." Minutes of the UFC Board of Directors meeting, 1930, United Farmers of Canada (Saskatchewan Section), Papers, Provincial Archives of Saskatchewan.

33 Ibid.

34 Minutes and Reports of the 1930 UFC Convention, United Farmers of Canada (Saskatchewan Section), Papers, Provincial Archives of Saskatchewan, 214–216, 225–227.

35 Jim Warren and Kathleen Carlisle, *On the Side of the People: A History of Labour in Saskatchewan* (Regina: Coteau Books, 2005), 122.

36 J. L. Phelps, interview by Saskatchewan Archives Board staff, December 1970, audiotape, Provincial Archives of Saskatchewan.

37 Ibid.

38 Ibid.

39 Ibid.

40 Ibid.

41 *Saskatoon Western Producer*, December 18, 1930, 9.

42 Charter of Liberty, UFC Minutes, Annual Convention, 1931, United Farmers of Canada (Saskatchewan Section), Papers, Provincial Archives of Saskatchewan, 467.

43 Ibid., March 5, 1931, 1.

44 Hoffman, "Saskatchewan Farmer-Labour Party," 210.

45 Walter D. Young, "M. J. Coldwell, The Making of a Social Democrat," *Journal of Canadian Studies* 9, no. 3 (August 1974): 50–60; J. William Brennan, *Regina: An Illustrated History* (Toronto: James Lorimer & Company, 1989), 131.

46 *Wilkie Press*, June 24, 1931, 1.

47 Ibid., July 1, 1931, 1.

48 *Saskatoon Western Producer*, July 2, 1931, 5. Premier J. T. M. Anderson was in Ottawa at this time and missed this meeting. Hon. W. C. Buckle was the acting premier.

49 *Wilkie Press*, August 5, 1931, 5, 8–9.

50 *Wilkie Press*, August 6, 1931, 1; *Saskatoon Western Producer*, September 10, 1931, 5. Within a few months, most provincial constituencies were holding UFC political conventions with the determination to bring into effect a strong and virile political organization.

51 Minutes of the 6th annual UFC convention, February 1932, United Farmers of Canada (Saskatchewan Section), Papers, Provincial Archives of Saskatchewan, 222–228.

52 *Saskatoon Western Producer*, February 4, 1932, 5.

53 *Saskatoon Western Producer*, March 3, 1932, 5; *Wilkie Press*, March 2, 1932, 1.

54 *Wilkie Press*, March 24, 1932, 5.

55 The "Ginger Group" had been formed in 1924 when a small number of progressives voted with Woodsworth in Parliament rather than with the leader of the progressives, Robert Forke, who supported the Liberal government.

56 Walter D. Young, *The Anatomy of a Party: The National CCF, 1932–61* (Toronto: University of Toronto Press, 1969), 22.

57 *Regina Commonwealth*, May 30, 1962, 5; *Esterhazy Observer and Pheasant Hills Advertiser*, June 8, 1944, 3.

58 Minutes of the first annual Farmer-Labour Group joint convention, 1932, Farmer-Labour Group, Papers, Provincial Archives of Saskatchewan.

59 No evidence exists that Phelps attended either the Calgary conference in 1932 or the Regina meeting in 1933. Nevertheless, Phelps, with his keen interest in farm movements and his desire to become involved in politics, must have been elated by this new party's formation and by the policies it espoused.

60 "Phelps, Joseph Lee," Clippings File Biography, Provincial Archives of Saskatchewan.

61 *Wilkie Press*, October 26, 1932, 1; June 2, 1933, 1.

62 Ibid., August 11, 1933, 1.

63 Minutes of the second annual Farmer-Labour Group joint convention, July 1933, Farmer-Labour Group, Papers, Provincial Archives of Saskatchewan.

64 Brochure for J. L. Phelps, candidate for Melfort constituency election, 1934, private collection.

65 *Saskatoon Western Producer*, June 14, 1934, 1; *Wilkie Press*, June 15, 1934, 1, 4; July 6, 1934, 1, 3; J. L. Phelps, interview by Larmour, 9.

66 J. L. Phelps, interview by Larmour, 9.

67 *Wilkie Press*, October 26, 1934, 1.

68 Co-operative Commonwealth Federation, *Regina Manifesto*, Programme of the Co-operative Commonwealth Federation, adopted at First National Convention held at Regina, Saskatchewan, July 1933 (Regina: Service Printing Co., 1933), 1.

69 A. W. Johnson, *Dream No Little Dreams: A Biography of the Douglas Government of Saskatchewan, 1944–1961* (Toronto: University of Toronto Press, 2004), 34.

70 Ibid., 27.

71 T. C. Douglas, "Reflections of a Hard-Headed Dreamer," *Reader's Digest*, 1979, 94. In recent years, some of these, including the Wheat Board, have been lost.

72 Minutes of the UFC annual convention, 1931, United Farmers of Canada (Saskatchewan Section), Papers, Provincial Archives of Saskatchewan.

CHAPTER 3

1 Johnson, *Dream No Little Dreams*, 2.
2 Archer, *Saskatchewan*, 188.
3 Barry Potyondi, *In Palliser's Triangle: Living in the Grasslands, 1850–1930* (Saskatoon: Purich Publishing, 1995). See the *Encyclopedia of Saskatchewan* for a map and description of the area commonly known as the Palliser Triangle. "The boundary of the Palliser Triangle is not fixed like a political boundary. Rather it fluctuates depending on climatic cycle, or the purpose of the person mentioning the region. Since Palliser's original pronouncement, the area that people generally call the Palliser Triangle has shrunk. Today boundaries of physio-graphic regions such as the brown soil zone or the mixed grassland prairie ecoregion are often used to indicate the Palliser Triangle" (http://esask.uregina.ca/entry/palliser_triangle.html).
4 Joseph Phelps, personal correspondence to the Phelps family, private collection.
5 Ibid.
6 Ibid.
7 J. L. Phelps, interview by Saskatchewan Archives Board staff, 9.
8 Bruce Dodds, correspondence with the author, January 2007.
9 George Hoffman, "Eliason, Frank," *Encyclopedia of Saskatchewan* (Regina: Canadian Plains Research Center, University of Regina, 2005), 292.
10 Wilf Churchman, interview by Larry Shaak, November 2000, transcript, private collection.
11 Johnson, *Dream No Little Dreams*, 23.
12 Steininger, "George H. Williams," 108; Young, "M. J. Coldwell," 50.
13 Steininger, "George H. Williams," 95.
14 Ibid., 131–148.
15 J. L. Phelps, interview by Larmour, 10, 15.
16 Ibid., 8.
17 *Wilkie Press*, January 19, 1934, 1; February 16, 1934, 1; April 5, 1934, 8; *Saskatoon Western Producer*, November 8, 1934, 7.
18 *Saskatoon Western Producer*, July 6, 1933, 2; August 2, 1934, 2; July 25, 1935, 3.
19 Ibid., July 25, 1935, 3; August 29, 1935, 8.
20 *Saskatchewan Commonwealth*, June 2, 1938, 3.
21 *Esterhazy Observer and Pheasant Hills Advertiser*, June 8, 1944, 3; *Wilkie Press*, July 23, 1936, 3; *Saskatoon Western Producer*, July 22, 1937, 1, 30.
22 David Goranson, correspondence with the author, July 2012.
23 Jacalyn Duffin, "The Guru and the Godfather: Henry Sigerist, Hugh MacLean, and the Politics of Health Care Reform in 1940s Canada," CBMH/BCHM 9 (1992): 191–218.

24 George Hoffman, "The Saskatchewan Provincial Election of 1934: Its Political, Economic, and Social Background" (master's thesis, University of Saskatchewan, Regina Campus, 1973), 233–236; Steininger, "George H. Williams," 120–122.
25 Steininger, "George H. Williams," 244.
26 Lipset, *Agrarian Socialism*, 139.
27 Ibid., 142.
28 Ibid., 4.
29 Steininger, "George H. Williams," 244.
30 Lipset, *Agrarian Socialism*, 142.
31 Ibid., 255–258.
32 Ibid., 261.
33 Steininger, "George H. Williams," 262.
34 Ibid., 264.
35 Minutes of the CCF Provincial Council Meeting (October 16–17, 1937), 5, Co-operative Commonwealth Federation, Papers, Provincial Archives of Saskatchewan; Steininger, "George H. Williams," 265.
36 Steininger, "George H. Williams," 266–267.
37 Ibid., 274.
38 *Wilkie Press*, April 22, 1938, 1; May 27, 1938, 1; June 3, 1938, 1. In the Wilkie constituency the three candidates for the June 8 election were John Knowles, Liberal; F. R. Beggs, Social Credit; and George Hindley, Independent.
39 Steininger, "George H. Williams," 274–275; Ken Andrews, "'Progressive' Counterparts of the CCF: Social Credit and the Conservative Party in Saskatchewan, 1935–1938," *Journal of Canadian Studies* 17, no. 3 (Fall 1982): 66, 73; David E. Smith, *Prairie Liberalism: The Liberal Party in Saskatchewan, 1905–1971* (Toronto: University of Toronto Press, 1975), 236.
40 J. L. Phelps, interview by Larmour, 17.
41 Edgar Kaeding, "Reminiscence of a good friend and mentor, Joe L. Phelps," correspondence to Doug Charrett, April 10, 2001, private collection.
42 Ibid.
43 J. L. Phelps, interview by Larmour, 17–18.
44 *Regina Leader-Post*, May 23, 1938, 3.
45 Kaeding, "Reminiscence of a good friend and mentor."
46 Ibid.
47 Joseph Wawrykow was a CCF MLA, representing Gimli, Manitoba.
48 *Yorkton Enterprise*, June 2, 1938, 8.
49 *Esterhazy Observer and Pheasant Hills Advertiser*, June 2, 1938, 1.
50 Ibid., 3.
51 *Wilkie Press*, June 10, 1938, 1. Interestingly, in Wilkie, J. Knowles, the Liberal candidate, was elected; F. R. Beggs, the Social Credit candidate, came in second; and G. Hindley, the Independent candidate, was last.
52 *Saskatchewan Executive and Legislative Directory, 1905–1970* (Regina and Saskatoon: Saskatchewan Archives Board, 1971), 53. When Liberals Hubert Staines from Athabasca and Deakin Hall from Cumberland were elected in

deferred elections on June 28, 1938, the Liberals had thirty-eight members in the legislature. Although the CCF had doubled its number of members elected, its popular vote dropped from 103,582 (24.1 per cent) in 1934 to 82,582 (18.8 per cent) in 1938. It is important to note, though, that while the CCF ran forty-seven candidates in the 1934 election, it fielded only thirty-one in 1938. Six constituencies ran Unity candidates, so CCF voters in such instances likely would have supported those candidates.

53 *Saskatchewan Commonwealth*, June 15, 1938, 1.

CHAPTER 4

1 Fourteen Liberals, nine CCF, two Social Credit, and two Unity members were rookies. Joining Phelps as newly elected CCFers in the legislature were John A. Young (Biggar), Myron H. Feeley (Canora), Peter A. Howe (Kelvington), Jacob Benson (Last Mountain), Oakland W. Valleau (Melfort), Tom Johnston (Touchwood), John H. Brockelbank (Tisdale), and Joseph W. Burton (Humboldt). *Saskatchewan Executive and Legislative Directory*, 53–55.

2 J. L. Phelps, interview by Larmour, 21, 28.

3 Ibid., 23.

4 *Regina Leader-Post*, February 3, 1939, 13.

5 Ibid., April 3, 1939, 11.

6 Saskatchewan, *Journals of the Legislative Assembly* (1940), 45.

7 Saskatchewan, *Journals* (1940), 58. This time, however, he changed the time period in the motion from "the past six years" to "for the year 1939."

8 Saskatchewan, *Journals* (1941), 44–50. In the first return he requested information about mining; in the second, forestry; in the third, all types of petroleum products, natural gas, and tar; and in the fourth, information about sodium sulphate, clay, bentonites, and other minerals.

9 *Regina Leader-Post*, March 8, 1941, 8.

10 Ibid., 11.

11 Ibid., March 9, 1943, 8; March 10, 1943, 13. On March 8, 1943, Phelps again made several motions for returns that required lengthy, detailed information. The first asked for copies of all tenders submitted to the government in the years 1939 to 1942 for supplies for mental hospitals, jails, and other public institutions. He also wanted all correspondence relating to these tenders. A second asked for information about the amounts paid by each government department, board, and commission to each person or company for gasoline, fuel oil, and grease. He also requested details on who ordered each item; the amount charged per unit; the grade ordered and the grade supplied; to whom and by whom each purchase had been paid; whether the bid was by tender, bid, contract, or otherwise; the date of order and payment; the voucher number covering the transaction; the purpose for which the purchase had been made; and the grade of the material. Premier Patterson stated that to provide all the information requested would practically

entail rewriting the public accounts. A. C. Procter added that to obtain part of the information would require the examination of six thousand vouchers in one department alone. Both motions were defeated, but not before Phelps had charged the government with refusing to provide him with information.

12 *Regina Leader-Post*, March 31, 1943, 5.

13 Ibid., April 2, 1941, 11.

14 Ibid., April 7, 1941, 11.

15 Ibid., February 22, 1939, 9. To "name" was a procedure that warned the offending member of improper conduct in the legislature. Agar threatened to have Phelps ejected if he continued that conduct. This was the first time in decades that any member had been so threatened.

16 Ibid., April 8, 1943, 14.

17 This marked the first time in at least twenty-five years that anyone had been ejected from the legislature. Some could not remember it ever having occurred before.

18 Press release prepared by Joseph Phelps and published in a local newspaper as "Letter to constituents," April 1942, private collection.

19 J. H. Brockelbank succeeded G. H. Williams as opposition leader when Williams joined the army and went overseas in 1941.

20 Press release, "Letter to constituents." The letter closes with: "If you disapprove of my action or have any suggestions to offer, I would appreciate hearing from you. Your obedient servant J. L. Phelps, MLA Saltcoats constituency."

21 Saskatchewan, *Journals* (1939), 57, 63–64, 68, 74.

22 Minutes of the UFC Board of Directors meeting, 1931, United Farmers of Canada (Saskatchewan Section), Papers, Provincial Archives of Saskatchewan.

23 *Regina Leader-Post*, February 3, 1939, 17.

24 Ibid., March 18, 1939, 15.

25 Ibid., March 26, 1943, 14.

26 Saskatchewan, *Journals* (1939), 64.

27 *Regina Leader-Post*, February 3, 1939, 17.

28 Ibid., March 8, 1941, 8. Concerning this debate, W. F. Kerr replied that such information was unavailable, that Phelps had previously tried to obtain that information in 1940, and that Phelps now was attempting "to obtain a little cheap political capital by trying to create the impression that the government was trying to suppress information." Phelps then charged the government with withholding information or of being guilty of inefficiency in the Natural Resources department. In a later session, Kerr stated that Phelps had tried to establish that there was "'inefficiency on the part of myself as minister and the department staff' and that the natural resources were being exploited by companies, corporations, and syndicates." He insisted that Phelps's remarks were "thinly-disguised bits of propaganda for Socialism." While Kerr "complimented the Saltcoats member for his thirst for information and his industrious research," he added that Phelps "was unable to correlate his information, 'with the result that he suffers from a type of hopeless indigestion of the material.'" See *Regina Leader-Post*, April 1, 1941, 5.

29 *Regina Leader-Post*, March 25, 1942, 4.

30 Thomas H. McLeod and Ian McLeod, *Tommy Douglas: The Road to Jerusalem* (Edmonton: Hurtig Publishers, 1987), 123–124. John Richards and Larry Pratt state the CCF established this committee in 1943 in *Prairie Capitalism: Power and Influence in the New West* (Toronto: McClelland & Stewart, 1979), 101.

31 J. L. Phelps, interview by Larmour, 27.

32 Ibid., 11.

33 Joseph Phelps, personal correspondence to Phelps family, February 1943, private collection.

34 Charles Cummings, personal correspondence to David Goranson, September 5, 1992. Charles was ninety-three years old at the time he sent the letter. Goranson, Joseph Phelps's grandson, had asked Cummings to comment on his memories of Goranson's grandfather.

35 *Regina Leader-Post*, February 24, 1944, 17. Interestingly, in this debate Phelps suggested two other government undertakings. The first concerned "the development of new power sites and acquisition of existing ones to provide a province-wide network of electric power lines," and the second pertained to "the extension of air routes in the northern part of the province."

36 These distinguished men were Colin Cameron, MLA from British Columbia; William Irvine, CCF leader from Alberta; Dr. Carlyle King, vice-president of the Saskatchewan CCF executive; David Lewis, national secretary of the CCF; and T. C. Douglas, MP and provincial leader of the CCF.

37 *Saskatchewan Commonwealth*, January 5, 1944, 1.

38 Ibid., January 3, 1940, 7.

39 Ibid., December 11, 1940, 7.

40 Ibid., February 12, 1941, 6; June 10, 1942, 7; July 8, 1942, 6; January 13, 1943, 3.

41 Johnson, *Dream No Little Dreams*, 41.

42 Joseph Phelps, personal correspondence to Lena Phelps, private collection.

43 Raymond Merle Sherdahl, "The Saskatchewan General Election of 1944" (master's thesis, University of Saskatchewan, 1966), 20; *Regina Leader-Post*, May 10, 1944, 1, 12. Five vacancies existed: four had been Liberal seats and one a CCF seat. Seven members were on active service, four for the Liberals and three for the CCF.

44 Andrew Jackson Milnor, "Agrarian Protest in Saskatchewan, 1929–1948: A Study in Ethnic Politics" (PhD dissertation, Duke University, Durham, NC, 1962), 154.

45 *Saskatoon StarPhoenix*, May 9, 1944, 12, quoted in Milnor, "Agrarian Protest," 154.

46 Ibid., May 11, 1944, 17, quoted in Milnor, "Agrarian Protest," 154.

47 Ibid., June 12, 1944, 3, quoted in Milnor, "Agrarian Protest," 154.

48 Sherdahl, "Saskatchewan General Election," 73–75.

49 *Regina Leader-Post*, May 20, 1944, 4. In a subsequent issue of the same paper, Hon. J. W. Estey, attorney general, vehemently denied this figure, branding the statement as "absolutely untrue." He indicated that only 6,740 foreclosures and cancellations had taken place in the inclusive seven-year period from 1935 to 1941. *Regina Leader-Post*, May 26, 1944.

50 Peter R. Sinclair, "The Saskatchewan CCF: Ascent to Power and the Decline of Socialism," *Canadian Historical Review* 54, no. 4 (December 1973): 432.

51 Lewis H. Thomas, "The CCF Victory in Saskatchewan, 1944." *Saskatchewan History* 34, no. 1 (Winter 1981): 9.
52 Sherdahl, "Saskatchewan General Election," 68.
53 *Regina Commonwealth*, May 31, 1944, 7; Thomas, "CCF Victory," 9.
54 *Regina Leader-Post*, May 20, 1944, 4.
55 *Regina Leader-Post*, May 20, 1944, 4–5; Sherdahl, "Saskatchewan General Election," 82–87; Thomas, "CCF Victory," 9.
56 *Yorkton Enterprise*, May 11, 1944, 1; June 8, 1944, 13; *Esterhazy Observer and Pheasant Hills Advertiser*, May 11, 1944, 4; May 18, 1944, 1; May 25, 1944, 6; June 1, 1944, 1; June 8, 1944, 3, 5; June 15, 1944, 1; June 22, 1944, 1. During the campaign, Phelps gave two radio broadcasts and spoke five times within his own constituency. In addition, he had Mrs. J. L. Phelps, his wife; Mrs. E. E. Kaeding, president of the Saltcoats constituency; Berry Richards, the MLA from The Pas, Manitoba; and Harold Winch, leader of the Opposition for British Columbia, speak at meetings on his behalf. Between May 27 and June 14, twelve CCF meetings or rallies were held within the Saltcoats constituency.
57 The Saskatchewan road map indicates that the distance between Wilkie and Saltcoats is 513 kilometres or 319 miles.
58 *Saskatchewan Executive and Legislative Directory*, 49–52.
59 C.H. Higginbotham, *Off the Record: The CCF in Saskatchewan* (Toronto: McClelland & Stewart, 1968), 59.

CHAPTER 5

1 Kaeding, "Reminiscence of a good friend and mentor."
2 Duffin, "Guru and the Godfather."
3 Archer, *Saskatchewan*, 276.
4 Marchildon, foreword to *Dream No Little Dreams*, xix.
5 Johnson, *Dream No Little Dreams*, 62.
6 The new Cabinet had eleven members. The Cabinet consisted of C. M. Fines, provincial treasurer; J. W. Corman, attorney-general; O. W. Valleau, provincial secretary; J. H. Brockelbank, Minister of Municipal Affairs; W. S. Lloyd, Minister of Education; J. T. Douglas, Minister of Highways; C. C. Williams, Minister of Labour; J. H. Sturdy, Minister of Reconstruction; and L. F. McIntosh, Minister of Co-operatives. Douglas retained the health portfolio for himself. When G. H. Williams returned from overseas, he became Minister of Agriculture. Archer, *Saskatchewan*, 260–261.
7 Sheila Baptie, *Joe Phelps: An Impatient Man* (Winnipeg: Points West, 1981), video transcript, Provincial Archives of Saskatchewan.
8 Ibid.
9 A. W. Johnson, "Biography of a Government: Policy Formation in Saskatchewan, 1944–1961" (PhD dissertation, Harvard University, Cambridge, MA, 1963), 182.
10 Elise Swerhone, *Tommy Douglas: Keeper of the Flame* (Montreal: National Film Board of Canada, 1986), film, 58 min.

11 See CBC, "And the Greatest Canadian of all time is...," CBC Digital Archives, http://www.cbc.ca/archives/entry/and-the-greatest-canadian-of-all-time-is.

12 George Cadbury, interview by Jean Larmour, June 15, 1981; January 21, 22, 1982, 6, transcript, Provincial Archives of Saskatchewan; Brian Banks, "The Co-operative Commonwealth Federation Government and Economic Planning in Natural Resources and Industrial Development, 1944–1946" (honours essay, Department of History, University of Regina, 1977), 18.

13 Archer, *Saskatchewan*, 263.

14 Ibid., 255.

15 Saskatchewan, *Report of the Saskatchewan Reconstruction Council* (1944), 9. The foreword listed the topics to be discussed in Appendix 5, "Industrial Utilization of Farm Products in Saskatchewan": alcohol; synthetic rubber; starch, syrup, sugars; wool and woollens; vegetable oils; flax fibre; fuel and paper from straw; preservation of fruits and vegetables and processing of meat; leather; imitation fur from sheep pelts; and plastics.

16 L. E. Kirk to J. G. Taggart, August 2, 1944, Joseph Lee Phelps Papers (M15), Box 31, "Mimeographed Reports, Radio Addresses, Circular Letters, Etc. (2)," Provincial Archives of Saskatchewan.

17 *Natural Resources: A Background Paper*, January 13, 1982, 1, Jean Larmour Papers, Provincial Archives of Saskatchewan; Banks, "Co-operative Commonweath Federation," 61.

18 Saskatchewan, *Statutes of Saskatchewan*, 9, George VI (1939), Chapter 9; *Natural Resources*, 1, Larmour Papers.

19 *Natural Resources*, 1–2, Larmour Papers. Vern Hogg had been a member of the staff of the Geological Survey of Canada and had made several recommendations concerning the development of northern Saskatchewan. Douglas had met Hogg in Ottawa in March 1944 and asked him to come work for his government if and when it was elected. Because of a previous commitment, Hogg was unable to come to Saskatchewan until September 1944 (see Johnson, *Dream No Little Dreams*, 130). Phelps had been on the committee to develop policy on natural resources and industrial development.

20 McLeod and McLeod, *Tommy Douglas*, 123.

21 Johnson, *Dream No Little Dreams*, 67, 76.

22 "Reorganization Is Under Way," *Regina Leader-Post*, July 22, 1944.

23 Archer, *Saskatchewan*, 264.

24 J. L. Phelps, interview by Berry Richards, 1976, transcript, Provincial Archives of Saskatchewan, 1.

25 J. L. Phelps, interview by Larmour, 7.

26 *Regina Leader-Post*, September 7, 1946.

27 Lena and Joe Phelps had five children: Lee, Ella, Bruce, Gordon, and Leila. Leila was born on June 15, 1937, but passed away on November 17 that same year.

28 *Regina Leader-Post*, September 7, 1946.

29 Blanche Green, interview by Larry Shaak, 2000, transcript, private collection.

30 Ibid.

31 Doris French Shackleton, *Tommy Douglas* (Toronto: McClelland & Stewart, 1975), 148. Shackleton has worked as a freelance journalist, as an editor for the Department of Labour, as a CBC journalist, and as a public relations assistant for the NDP caucus.

32 Blanche Green, interview by Shaak.

33 Ibid.

34 Ibid.

35 Olaf (Ollie) Turnbull, interview by Larry Shaak, July–August 2001, transcript, private collection. Elected in the Elrose constituency for the CCF in 1960, Turnbull served as the Minister of Co-operatives and Co-operative Development. He was the Minister of Education from 1962 to 1964. He was also an executive member of the Saskatchewan Farmers Union in the 1950s.

36 McLeod and McLeod, *Tommy Douglas*, 129.

37 Shackleton, *Tommy Douglas*, 148.

38 J. L. Phelps, interview by Richards, 13.

39 Johnson, *Dream No Little Dreams*, 72.

40 Blanche Green, interview by Shaak.

41 Ibid.

42 Wilf Churchman, interview by Shaak.

43 McLeod and McLeod, *Tommy Douglas*, 125.

44 Blanche Green, interview by Shaak.

45 Ibid.

46 Jessy Paynter, interview by Larry Shaak, July–August 2001, transcript, private collection.

47 Eleanor McKinnon to David Goranson, July 18, 1992, private collection.

48 Murray Dobbin, *The One-and-a-Half Men: The Story of Jim Brady and Malcolm Norris, Métis Patriots of the 20th Century* (Vancouver: New Star Books, 1981), 169.

49 George LeBeau, interview by Larry Shaak, 2001, transcript, private collection.

50 Saskatchewan, *Statutes of Saskatchewan*, 8 George VI (1944), Chapter 8.

51 *Natural Resources*, 2, Larmour Papers.

52 *Regina Leader-Post*, October 31, 1944, 5; *Saskatchewan Commonwealth*, November 1, 1944, 1.

53 *Saskatchewan Commonwealth*, March 7, 1945, 1.

54 *Regina Leader-Post*, November 1, 1944, 16, 19; March 28, 1945, 20; March 31, 1945, 1, 11; April 2, 1945, 11.

55 Johnson, *Dream No Little Dreams*, 71.

56 Ibid., 69.

57 Ibid., 68.

58 The response Phelps sent to Ross Thatcher, declining an invitation to be guest speaker at a meeting of the CCF on November 10, 1944, at Mossbank concerning the upcoming federal election, is typical of responses he often gave. He wrote, "Owing to the fact that we are so busy reorganizing our departments and preparing legislation for the session which is now in progress, it is impossible for me to make any commitments at the present time. Our department has more

heavy legislation going before this session than possibly any other department and as a result I am going to be doubly busy." J. L. Phelps to Ross Thatcher, October 20, 1944, Joseph Lee Phelps Papers (M15), Box 30, "CCF, 1944–1946 (4)," Provincial Archives of Saskatchewan.

CHAPTER 6

1 The term "Indian" is deferred to in the book in both quoted material and when used in a historical sense, as this was the terminology of the time.
2 F. Laurie Barron, *Walking in Indian Moccasins: The Native Policies of Tommy Douglas and the CCF* (Vancouver: UBC Press, 1997), 138.
3 Ibid., 3.
4 J. L. Phelps, interview by Murray Dobbin, June 1976, Indian History Film Project, transcript, Provincial Archives of Saskatchewan, 3; *Saskatchewan Commonwealth*, August 2, 1944, 1. The two politicians were appalled at the deplorable conditions of the people there. When they returned from their trip on July 31, 1944, they promised a new deal for the North. For a fuller discussion of these conditions, see Barron, *Walking in Indian Moccasins*, 142–143; David M. Quiring, *CCF Colonialism in Northern Saskatchewan: Battling Parish Priests, Bootleggers, and Fur Sharks* (Vancouver: UBC Press, 2004); and Anthony G. Gulig, "In Whose Interest? Government Indian Relations in Northern Saskatchewan and Wisconsin, 1900–1940" (PhD dissertation, University of Saskatchewan, 1997).
5 *Regina Leader-Post*, January 21, 1947, 3. The broadcast occurred that week but no exact date was given.
6 J. L. Phelps, "Natural Resources: Forests, Timber," December 19, 1948, audiotape, Provincial Archives of Saskatchewan.
7 Dobbin, *One-and-a Half Men*, 171.
8 Barron, *Walking in Indian Moccasins*, xix. Integrationist policies foster the retention of First Nations language, values, and cultural identity, and, at the same time, full participation in mainstream society. Assimilationist policies, on the other hand, imply gradual loss of language and cultural identity.
9 J. L. Phelps, interview by Dobbin, 9.
10 Shackleton, *Tommy Douglas*, 200.
11 Barron, *Walking in Indian Moccasins*, xix.
12 Kramer to Little, "A Literal Snapshot."
13 J. L. Phelps, interview by Dobbin, 9–11.
14 Barron, *Walking in Indian Moccasins*, 141.
15 Dobbin, *One-and-a-Half Men*, 170.
16 Chris Hansen to David Goranson, August 30, 1992, private collection.
17 Ibid., 171.
18 Ibid., 176.
19 Barron, *Walking in Indian Moccasins*, 213.
20 Barron, *Walking in Indian Moccasins*, xviii, 70.

21 "Union for Indians," *Regina Leader-Post*, February 25, 1946.

22 Barron, *Walking in Indian Moccasins*, 80.

23 Barron, *Walking in Indian Moccasins*, 85, 86. For a discussion of the CCF provincial policy on Indigenous people, see Barron, *Walking in Indian Moccasins*; James M. Pitsula, "The Saskatchewan CCF Government and Treaty Indians, 1944–64," *Canadian Historical Review* 75, no. 1 (March 1994): 21–52; Quiring, *CCF Colonialism*; and Gulig, "In Whose Interest?".

24 "Full rights for Indians urged by Phelps," *Regina Leader-Post*, February 25, 1946.

25 J. L. Phelps to M. J. Coldwell, March 8, 1946, Joseph Lee Phelps Papers (M15), Box 31, "Correspondence, M. J. Coldwell, 1944–1946," Provincial Archives of Saskatchewan.

26 Pitsula, "The Saskatchewan CCF," 23.

27 Barron, *Walking in Indian Moccasins*, 45.

28 Joseph Dreaver to J. L. Phelps, January 14, 1946, Joseph Lee Phelps Papers (M15), Box 27, "Trapping Leases General, 1944–1946," Provincial Archives of Saskatchewan.

29 Barron, *Walking in Indian Moccasins*, 204.

30 David M. Quiring, "Battling Parish Priests, Bootleggers, and Fur Sharks: CCF Colonialism in Northern Saskatchewan" (PhD dissertation, University of Saskatchewan, 2002), 5.

31 Ibid., 5.

32 *Regina Leader-Post*, November 15, 1947, 3. Approximately eleven thousand people, mostly First Nations and Métis, lived in this region. These reports included such information as the population of the settlement, the income from fishing and trapping, food costs, living conditions, and general aspects of life in the North.

33 Barron, *Walking in Indian Moccasins*, 177.

34 Ibid., 187.

35 Ibid., 189.

36 Ibid., 190.

CHAPTER 7

1 J. L. Phelps, interview by Larmour, 18.

2 "All Power Lines to Be Taken Over," *Regina Leader-Post*, July 15, 1944.

3 Bruce Dodds, correspondence with the author, September 2012.

4 J. L. Phelps, interview by Larmour, 34; J. L. Phelps, interview by Richards. In 1949, the government converted the Power Commission into a Crown corporation. Ironically, Phelps, who was keenly interested in rural electrification, resigned from the corporation because he believed rural electrification was moving too slowly. Cadbury and Fines were reluctant to push such a program. According to Phelps, they thought people should be encouraged to leave the country "to the jackrabbits." Douglas denied that the two opposed rural electrification, but said they "simply wanted the Government to avoid committing itself to programs

it might not be able to finance." See Clinton O. White, *Power for a Province: A History of Saskatchewan Power* (Regina: Canadian Plains Research Center, University of Regina, 1976), 156, 177.

5 White, *Power for a Province*, 134.

6 Ibid., 72–77, 81–83, 103.

7 Ibid., 100–102, 116–117.

8 Ibid., 129.

9 Vern Hogg, "Joe Phelps, A Prairie Populist," correspondence to David Goranson, January 27, 1993, private collection.

10 Ibid.

11 White, *Power for a Province*, 134.

12 Hogg, "Joe Phelps."

13 White, *Power for a Province*, 136.

14 Bruce Dodds, correspondence with the author, September 2012. Dodds notes that Ontario Hydro dates back to 1906. Manitoba had dominant public ownership and investment by the 1920s, though not a fully integrated public system until 1953.

15 White, *Power for a Province*, 133; J. L. Phelps, interview by Larmour, 34–35.

16 J. L. Phelps, interview by Larmour, 34–35.

17 White, *Power for a Province*, 138.

18 White, *Power for a Province*, 140.

19 J. L. Phelps, interview by Clint O. White, January 1975, transcript, Provincial Archives of Saskatchewan, 9.

20 J. L. Phelps, interview by Larmour, 44.

21 *Regina Leader-Post*, February 21, 1945, 1, 10; February 28, 1945, 1, 8; March 1, 1945, 9; March 8, 1945, 14.

22 Ibid., February 28, 1945, 1, 8.

23 Hogg, "Joe Phelps."

24 "Hydro Survey in the North," *Regina Leader-Post*, May 18, 1945.

25 Kaeding, "Reminiscence of a good friend and mentor."

26 Ibid.

27 H. F. Berry to Valleau and Phelps, October 4, 1947, Joseph Lee Phelps Papers (M15), Box 39, "Correspondence Berry, 1947," Provincial Archives of Saskatchewan; *Regina Leader-Post*, February 12, 1948, 5; Saskatchewan, *Crown Corporations, Province of Saskatchewan, Annual Report* (2002), 3, 4.

28 Kramer to Little, "A Literal Snapshot."

CHAPTER 8

1 Saskatchewan, *Journals* (1945), February 21, 1945, 139; *Regina Leader-Post*, January 2, 1945, 3; *Saskatchewan Commonwealth*, January 3, 1945, 1.

2 Wilf Churchman to David Goranson, January 31, 1995, personal correspondence.

3 Wilf Churchman, interview by Shaak.

4 David Goranson, interview by Larry Shaak, March 2001, transcript, private collection.

5 T. C. Slimon to K. F. Saunders, April 19, 1945, Joseph Lee Phelps Papers (M15), Box 1, "Aircraft 1945–1946"; J. L. Phelps to T. C. Slimon, April 20, 1945, Joseph Lee Phelps Papers (M15), Box 1, "Aircraft 1945–1946," Provincial Archives of Saskatchewan.

6 Saskatchewan, *Wings Beyond Road's End: Airplanes Over Saskatchewan's North* (La Ronge, SK: Saskatchewan Education, Northern Division, 1992), 58.

7 J. L. Phelps to C. D. Howe, December 18, 1945, Joseph Lee Phelps Papers (M15), Box 1, "Aircraft 1945–1946," Provincial Archives of Saskatchewan. By December 1945, the DNR had bought a Norseman that it had equipped as an ambulance for the Department of Health, since the DNR did the flying for other departments in the North. In fact, Phelps noted that he had read with a great deal of interest an article in the *Reader's Digest* that referred to him as the "Pied Piper of Aviation." J. L. Phelps to William Thomas Piper, January 9, 1946, Joseph Lee Phelps Papers (M15), Box 1, "Aircraft 1945–1946," Provincial Archives of Saskatchewan.

8 Joseph Lee Phelps Papers (M15), Box 5, "Economic Advisory Committee Recommendation," Department of Natural Resources and Industrial Development: Summary of Activities during 1945 and Plans for 1946, n.d., Provincial Archives of Saskatchewan. In January 1947, Phelps announced that the provincial government's aircraft division at Prince Albert now had ten planes in operation. The DNR owned three Norsemen, four Tiger Moths, a Mark V. Anson, a Waco, and a Fox Moth. It had purchased seven of these planes from War Assets at an average cost of $750 each; see *Regina Commonwealth*, January 29, 1947, 2. On August 15, 1947, the government purchased the M&C Aviation Company of Prince Albert and all its physical assets for more than $100,000. This purchase became Saskatchewan Government Airways, another Crown corporation; see *Regina Commonwealth*, August 20, 1947, 1, 12.

9 David Goranson, conversation with the author, 2006.

10 James Winkel, *Northern Saskatchewan: A Transformation* (Regina: Saskatchewan Northern Affairs, 2002), 14.

11 "South air link delays traffic," *Regina Leader-Post*, October 10, 1946.

12 Saskatchewan, *Wings Beyond Road's End*, 58.

13 Ibid., 61.

14 Ibid., 62.

15 Winkel, *Northern Saskatchewan*, 13.

16 Archer, *Saskatchewan*, 272.

17 "Now it's airlines—following the TCA pattern," *Regina Leader-Post*, August 22, 1947.

18 "Phelps wants probe of war materials," *Regina Leader-Post*, May 5, 1945.

19 Ibid.

20 "Phelps accepts Howe's offer," *Regina Leader-Post*, June 6, 1945.

21 Ibid.

CHAPTER 9

1 Barron, *Walking in Indian Moccasins*, 144.

2 Karla Radloff, "Cooperative and State Ownership in Northern Saskatchewan under the CCF Government" (master's thesis, University of Saskatchewan, 2004), 20–21, note 29; C. A. L. Hogg, *Plan for the Development of Natural Resources of Northern Saskatchewan under Social Ownership and Control*, 1943, 5, R-33.5, 37 (9-4) "Development of Natural Resources," Provincial Archives of Saskatchewan.

3 J. L. Phelps to J. S. McDiarmid, July 12, 1944, Joseph Lee Phelps Papers (M15), Box 16, "Fur Marketing, 1944–1946 (2)"; J. H. Janzen to J. L. Phelps, July 18, 1944, Joseph Lee Phelps Papers (M15), Box 16, "Fur Marketing, 1944–1946 (2)"; Summary of legislation Phelps introduced during special session, October 19, 1944, Joseph Lee Phelps Papers (M15), Box 28, "Legislation, 1946," Provincial Archives of Saskatchewan.

4 It was also called the Saskatchewan Fur Marketing Agency.

5 Article in *Fur of Canada*, August 1944, Jospeh Lee Phelps Papers (M15), Box 15, "Fur Marketing, 1947–1951 (1)"; J. L. Phelps to T. C. Douglas, February 9, 1945, Joseph Lee Phelps Papers (M15), Box 4, "Purchasing Department, 1944–1946"; Summary of DNR Activities, n.d., Joseph Lee Phelps Papers (M15), Box 5, "Economic Advisory Committee Recommendations, 1945–1946," Provincial Archives of Saskatchewan.

6 *Regina Leader-Post*, March 27, 1945, 15.

7 Ibid., January 11, 1945, 3.

8 Ibid., April 2, 1946, 4. Interestingly, by this date Saskatchewan had eleven Crown corporations; Phelps administered six of them.

9 Re Establishing a Fur Marketing Service, October 18, 1945, Joseph Lee Phelps Papers (M15), Box 28, "Orders-In-Council, 1944–1946 (1)," Provincial Archives of Saskatchewan.

10 In an effort to conserve beaver and muskrats, it enforced quotas on the selling of these pelts. The easiest way it could do so was to have the government agency handle all these furs.

11 Kaeding, "Reminiscence of a good friend and mentor."

12 W. H. Lefurgey to D. McEwen, May 25, 1945, Joseph Lee Phelps Papers (M15), Box 16, "Fur Marketing, 1944–1946 (2)," Provincial Archives of Saskatchewan. When the Fur Marketing Service sold furs at auction, it also charged a royalty of two cents per rabbit to twenty-five cents per badger, a lotting fee of twenty-five cents per pelt, as well as the selling fee of 5 per cent.

13 Barron, *Walking in Indian Moccasins*, 145. Barron noted that the compulsory aspect of the agency was so unpopular that the government abandoned it in 1956.

14 Ibid., 172.

15 Shackleton, *Tommy Douglas*, 200.

16 "Phelps-Lewis clash leads to department shake-up," *Regina Leader-Post*, May 15, 1946. The second story appeared in the *Leader-Post* on July 26, 1946, and was

titled, "Lewis rumored through." Vern Hogg declined comment when asked if Lewis had resigned or been dismissed. Phelps said only that changes were being made in the DNR.

17 "Phelps silent," *Regina Leader-Post*, May 17, 1946.

18 "Phelps protests handling of news—Hogg appointment story criticized," *Regina Leader-Post*, November 4, 1946.

19 *Prince Albert Daily Herald*, January 24, 1947.

20 "Labouring the Obvious," *Prince Albert Daily Herald*, January 25, 1947. There are several other letters to the editor written by J. L. Phelps that appear in the *Prince Albert Daily Herald* in 1947. For example, "A Letter from Mr. Phelps," April 14, 1947; "Mr. Phelps Tells Prince Albert," May 9, 1947; "The Readers Write—Letter to the editor, J. L. Phelps," April 26, 1947; "Use of Government Planes," June 7, 1947; "Answering Mr. Davis," August 11, 1947.

21 Hogg, "Joe Phelps."

22 Ibid.

23 "Survey for fur, Conservation Plan," *Regina Leader-Post*, September 10, 1945.

24 *Regina Commonwealth*, February 11, 1948, 2. In a radio broadcast in May 1948, Phelps stated that these councils were elected at the trappers' annual meetings and held office for a year "with Indians, whites, and Metis having equal rights and representation according to their numbers." *Regina Commonwealth*, May 12, 1948, 12.

25 Barron, *Walking in Indian Moccasins*, 146.

26 "Far north flight spreads fur conservation scheme," *Regina Leader-Post*, July 10, 1946.

27 Barron, *Walking in Indian Moccasins*, 146.

28 *Regina Leader-Post*, February 5, 1947, 11.

29 *Regina Commonwealth*, February 11, 1948, 2.

30 "Community effort seen at Cumberland House," *Regina Leader-Post*, July 13, 1946.

31 Ibid.

32 "Clamps down on fur trade," *Regina Leader-Post*, November 7, 1945.

33 *Regina Commonwealth*, June 12, 1946, 12. Actually, municipalities paid the $2 bounty for coyote pelts and the government reimbursed them $1. In March 1947, the DNR raised the bounty on wolves to $25. Saskatchewan, *Debates and Proceedings of the Legislative Assembly of Saskatchewan*, March 25, 1947.

34 *Regina Leader-Post*, February 20, 1946, 1, 8; G. H. Danielson (Liberal, Arm River) also protested, "This is handing out a special reward to get business. It is one of the worst things I have ever heard of." *Regina Leader-Post*, March 22, 1946, 21.

35 Saskatchewan, *Wings Beyond Road's End*, 65.

36 *Regina Commonwealth*, June 5, 1946, 9; Saskatchewan, *Debates and Proceedings*, February 9, 1948, 12–13.

37 Joseph Lee Phelps Papers (M15), Box 26, "Dr. Peter South veterinarian, 1945–1946," Provincial Archives of Saskatchewan. South resigned after a very short period because he felt the department needed a more qualified man.

38 "Interest in beavers," *Regina Leader-Post*, February 18, 1946.

39 "Far north flight spreads fur conservation scheme," *Regina Leader-Post*, July 10, 1946.
40 Ibid.
41 Ibid.
42 "Stretcher for pelts," *Regina Leader-Post*, March 4, 1946.
43 "Fur coat industry seen for province," *Regina Leader-Post*, March 26, 1946.
44 "Resources program outlined," *Regina Leader-Post*, January 21, 1947.
45 *Regina Leader-Post*, March 24, 1947, 6; Government Business Enterprises, Profits and Losses Before and After Depreciation, Before Interest on Advances, Year Ended March 31, 1947, February 9, 1948, Thomas Clement (T. C.) Douglas Papers, IV. 152, (4-14), "Crown Corporations, January 1946–October 1949," Provincial Archives of Saskatchewan.
46 J. L. Phelps, interview by Richards, 4.
47 J. L. Phelps, interview by Dobbin, 19.
48 *Regina Commonwealth*, May 29, 1946, 12.

CHAPTER 10

1 Anthony G. Gulig, "Sizing up the Catch: Native-Newcomer Resource Competition and the Early Years of Saskatchewan's Northern Commercial Fishery," *Saskatchewan History* 47, no. 3 (Fall 1995): 3–11. Gulig notes that when commercial fisheries were expanded in northern Saskatchewan, resource-regulating agencies strongly favoured commercial fishing and frequently disregarded the treaty rights that Indians possessed. For a fuller discussion of this topic, see Gulig, "In Whose Interest?"
2 Saskatchewan, *Report of the Royal Commission on the Fisheries of Saskatchewan* (1947), 21–23, 43–44. In 1916–1917, fishers received 4.5 cents per pound compared to 1.5 cents per pound the previous year.
3 The fish catch likely increased dramatically when the Depression was at its worst and people, unable to find other jobs, turned to fishing to make a living. Besides, during the Depression, fishers might have been able to sell their fish quite easily since fish was a cheap source of food.
4 The destruction of the Great Lakes fishing industry because of lamprey infestation was an incentive to expand fishing operations in Saskatchewan. New lakes were opened and production increased, "pickerel by 33 percent, whitefish by 58 percent, and trout by 73 percent" during the war years. See Barron, *Walking in Indian Moccasins*, 148.
5 Barron noted that the Saskatchewan fishing industry faced obstacles not found in Manitoba or the Great Lakes. In Manitoba, three-quarters of the commercial fishing took place on Lake Winnipeg, which annually produced about fifteen million pounds. Saskatchewan's production was scattered over many lakes in widely separated areas, with Reindeer Lake, the most productive lake, producing about one million pounds. Only eleven lakes topped 150,000 pounds per year, and most produced much less. Because most of Manitoba's fish was caught in

one lake, building one road to transport the fish to a southern railhead would be much cheaper than attempting to transport fish from many inaccessible areas in Saskatchewan. Barron indicates that these "structural obstacles" made the industry in Saskatchewan uncompetitive during peace time and that the war merely masked the reality that under normal circumstances producing fish cost much more in Saskatchewan than it did in Manitoba or the Great Lakes. See Barron, *Walking in Indian Moccasins*, 149.

6 E. C. Over to F. Eliason, March 28, 1946, Joseph Lee Phelps Papers (M15), Box 11, "Forestry Commission, 1945–1946 (1)," Provincial Archives of Saskatchewan.

7 Legislative Session, November 10, 1944, Box 6, "Fisheries, 1944–1946 (3)"; Legislative Session, November 19, 1945, Box 28, "Orders-in-Council, 1944–1946 (1)," Provincial Archives of Saskatchewan.

8 Saskatchewan, *Royal Commission on the Fisheries*, 51–52. Since 1930, the United States Food and Drug Division had required that all shipments of whitefish and tullibee to the United States be inspected.

9 Hogg, "Joe Phelps."

10 Phelps, Press Release, October 25, 1944, Joseph Lee Phelps Papers (M15), Box 6, "Fisheries, 1944–1946 (1)"; H. V. Dempsey, Chief Inspector, Federal Department of Fisheries, to Phelps, February 26, 1946, Joseph Lee Phelps Papers (M15), Box 7, "Fish Products (3)," Provincial Archives of Saskatchewan; Saskatchewan, *Journals* (1946), February 27, 1946, 171. The total cost of constructing and equipping the fish filleting plant at Lac la Ronge was $41,692.91.

11 Order-in-Council 1070/45, July 20, 1945, Box 7, "Saskatchewan Fish Products, Minutes," Provincial Archives of Saskatchewan.

12 Commercial Fishing in Saskatchewan, n.d., Box 26, "Speaker's Handbook," Provincial Archives of Saskatchewan. Phelps said that 86 per cent of the fishers who voted favoured such a board. The board paid an initial price to fishers and after it sold the fish and deducted its costs made an additional payment. He maintained that establishing the board had stabilized the income fishers received.

13 *Regina Leader-Post*, February 25, 1946.

14 Ibid., May 27, 1946.

15 "Phelps criticizes fish industry talk," *Regina Leader-Post*, March 29, 1946.

16 "Royal Commission on fish industry," *Regina Leader-Post*, June 4, 1946.

17 Ibid.

18 Phelps to Advisory Representatives, November 13, 1947, Joseph Lee Phelps Papers (M15), Box 7, "Advisors to Fish Board, 1947–1948," Provincial Archives of Saskatchewan.

19 "Close check on fishing," *Regina Leader-Post*, November 15, 1946.

20 Archer, *Saskatchewan*, 272.

21 H. V. Dempsey to Phelps, February 26, 1946, Joseph Lee Phelps Papers (M15), Box 7, "Fish Products, 1944–1946 (3)," Provincial Archives of Saskatchewan. Dempsey, a federal fish inspector, had examined whitefish from the Beaver Lake and Lac la Ronge plants on February 22, 1946, and had found that the infestation of fillets

at these two plants was too high for export. A year later, the situation seemingly improved somewhat, but the filleting process obviously was still unsatisfactory. Phelps indicated in the legislature that because of whitefish inspection regulations, rejections at the United States border had decreased from 200,000 pounds to a few thousand pounds. *Regina Leader-Post*, March 12, 1947, 13.

22 L. J. Waite to Phelps, May 6, 1947, Joseph Lee Phelps Papers (M15), Box 38, "Waite Fisheries Ltd.," Provincial Archives of Saskatchewan. Waite sent Phelps another letter in which he expressed his disappointment that the Fish Marketing Board had rejected his suggestion about reducing the seventy-five-mile radius to fifty miles and voiced his concern about the fishing situation. L. J. Waite to Phelps, May 27, 1947, Joseph Lee Phelps Papers (M15), Box 38, "Waite Fisheries Ltd.," Provincial Archives of Saskatchewan.

23 Commercial Fishing in Saskatchewan, n.d., Joseph Lee Phelps Papers, Box 26, "Speaker's Handbook," Provincial Archives of Saskatchewan.

24 *Regina Commonwealth*, July 21, 1948, 8. In the past, only 10 per cent of the fish caught in the province had been consumed in Saskatchewan—15 per cent had been sent to other provinces, and 75 per cent had been exported to the United States. To try to convince more people in the province to eat fish, the DNR tried canning and smoking fish. *Regina Commonwealth*, February 4, 1948, 2.

25 *Regina Commonwealth*, February 13, 1946, 9. The DNR opened new roads and portages in 1945 that made commercial fishing at Wollaston, Cree, and Foster lakes possible for the first time. The highway from Prince Albert to Lac la Ronge, completed in 1946, also improved transportation.

26 F. Glass to J. L. Phelps, February 27, 1946, Joseph Lee Phelps Papers (M15), Box 18, "Floyd Glass, Northern Supt., 1945–1946"; Don Phelps to J. L. Phelps, February 21, 1946, Joseph Lee Phelps Papers (M15), Box 18, "Fish Marketing Board, 1945–1946," Provincial Archives of Saskatchewan.

27 Dickson to J. F. Gray, September 26, 1947, Joseph Lee Phelps Papers (M15), Box 9, "Saskatchewan Lake and Forest Products Corp., J. F. Gray, 1946–1951," Provincial Archives of Saskatchewan. Dickson showed that air transportation to Wollaston Lake in the summer of 1946 cost $40 per hour or fourteen cents per pound, a price he said was "out of the picture." He suggested they must "get cheaper transportation rates," "carry on only frozen fish operations," or "close the lake."

28 J. L. Phelps, interview by Dobbin, 2.

29 Don Phelps to Phelps, February 10, 1946, Joseph Lee Phelps Papers (M15), Box 7, "Fish Marketing Board, 1945–1946"; Don Phelps to Phelps, February 21, 1946, Joseph Lee Phelps Papers (M15), Box 7, "Fish Marketing Board, 1945–1946," Provincial Archives of Saskatchewan.

30 Various reasons caused markets for Saskatchewan's fish to increase during the war. The German occupation of Norway, Iceland, and Denmark eliminated them as competitors. Shortages of meat products also increased the demand for fish. Saskatchewan, *Debates and Proceedings*, March 11, 1947, 741–743.

31 *Regina Commonwealth*, February 18, 1948, 6–7.

32 Saskatchewan, *Debates and Proceedings*, March 11, 1947, 741–744. H. L. Howell (CCF Meadow Lake) noted that if fish prices in 1939 were considered to be one hundred, they would have climbed to 225 during the war years.

33 Legislative Session, November 10, 1944, Joseph Lee Phelps Papers (M15), Box 6, "Fisheries, 1944–1946 (3)," Provincial Archives of Saskatchewan.

34 *Regina Commonwealth*, February 18, 1948, 5–9.

35 Saskatchewan, *Debates and Proceedings*, March 11, 1947, 753. Phelps alluded to this disagreement when he stated in the House: "Some say the [fishing] industry should fold up. They say what's the use—why bother with the fishing industry, why put money into the fishing industry?" Phelps responded that fish was a healthful food and that the industry was important to the provincial economy.

36 M. Bryce to J. L. Phelps, March 22, 1946, Joseph Lee Phelps Papers (M15), Box 7, "Fish Products, 1944–1946 (3)," Provincial Archives of Saskatchewan. Fishers often misunderstood government policies. They could not understand why the government paid different prices for the same type of fish from "A" and "B" lakes. Frequently, the DNR did not provide sufficient information about the various projects, and communities resented the problems these projects created. For instance, at Lac la Ronge, Murray Bryce observed the existence of "a strong undercurrent of feeling" against the filleting plant and "the government generally." Inhabitants resented the intrusion of outsiders into their town. They worried that waste and sewage would pollute the lake and become a health hazard and that odour from the plant would make conditions unpleasant for the community in the summer.

37 M. Bodner to Lewis, March 8, 1946, Joseph Lee Phelps Papers (M15), Box 7, "Fish Products, 1944–1946 (3)," Provincial Archives of Saskatchewan.

38 Douglas to Tucker, October 19, 1949, T. C. Douglas Papers, VI.105, (6-1-3), Provincial Archives of Saskatchewan. Interestingly, the board removed the seventy-five-mile radius rule in 1949.

39 Richards and Pratt, *Prairie Capitalism*, 121.

40 Michael Howlett, "The Forest Industry on the Prairies: Opportunities and Constraints to Future Development," *Prairie Forum* 14, no. 2 (Fall 1989): 242. Saskatchewan's forest resources are small compared to those of the rest of Canada. They are "about equal to those of Newfoundland and Labrador and are by far the smallest outside of Atlantic Canada." See Howlett, "Forest Industry," 234.

41 *Saskatoon StarPhoenix*, February 19, 1945, 1; Phelps to D. D. Rossenberry, Department of Munitions and Supply, September 14, 1945, Joseph Lee Phelps Papers (M15), Box 11, "Forestry General, 1944–1946," Provincial Archives of Saskatchewan. Even prior to the Royal Commission's report, Phelps indicated that the Forest Branch of the DNR estimated that if cutting proceeded at the current rate, merchantable spruce timber in Saskatchewan would be depleted in five or six years.

42 Phelps had already taken steps to help the forestry industry. By September 21, 1945, he had introduced the Forest Act, subsequently amended it, and established the Saskatchewan Timber Board.

43 E. H. Roberts to Phelps, October 11, 1944, Joseph Lee Phelps Papers (M15), Box 28, "Orders-in-Council, 1944–1946 (1)," Provincial Archives of Saskatchewan. In 1943–1944, Saskatchewan had over four hundred sawmills.

44 Amendment to Forest Act, October 19, 1944, Box 28, "Legislation, 1946," Provincial Archives of Saskatchewan. Regulations were also in effect for other trees that could be cut. For those trees measured 4.5 feet from the ground, the diameters were eleven inches for jack pine, twelve inches for tamarack, and eight inches for poplar. The object of increasing the size of trees that could be cut was to maintain an adequate residual stand of trees to assure a future harvest and encourage the natural regeneration of trees. No evidence exists that these amendments created any great debates in the legislature. However, lumber was very scarce at this time and many lumber companies, foresters, and other individuals who wanted lumber often complained that these new restrictions prevented them from obtaining it. R. T. Cook to Phelps, March 12, 1946, Joseph Lee Phelps Papers (M15), Box 12, "Lumber Marketing, 1944–1946 (3)," Provincial Archives of Saskatchewan.

45 "Reduction in cut of lumber urged," *Regina Leader-Post*, August 8, 1945.

46 Joseph Lee Phelps Papers (M15), Box 28, "Legislation, 1946," Provincial Archives of Saskatchewan.

47 Questionnaire Results, November 6, 1944, Joseph Lee Phelps Papers, Box 11, "Lumber Marketing, 1944–1946," Provincial Archives of Saskatchewan.

48 Williamson to Phelps, February 10, 1945; Phelps to Williamson, February 10, 1945; Williamson to Phelps, February 13, 1945; Phelps to Williamson, February 13, 1945; Howe to Phelps, February 14, 1945, Joseph Lee Phelps Papers, Box 11, "Lumber Marketing, 1944–1946," Provincial Archives of Saskatchewan; *Regina Leader-Post*, February 24, 1945, 17.

49 "Move legal says Howe," *Regina Leader-Post*, September 13, 1945.

50 "Phelps to resurrect timber sales board," *Regina Leader-Post*, September 12, 1945.

51 Order-in-Council, September 20, 1945, Joseph Lee Phelps Papers (M15), Box 29, "Orders-in-Council, 1944–1946 (3)," Provincial Archives of Saskatchewan. The corporation had "the power to operate and carry on in all its branches the business of cutting, logging, sawing and purchasing timber, purchasing and manufacturing timber products of all kinds and selling or otherwise marketing timber products and to carry on and conduct research in connection therewith, together with all powers necessary and incidental thereto." The board would act as a marketing agency, but since it contained no compulsory features, people could use other marketing channels.

52 "Timber Board to sell ties," *Regina Leader-Post*, September 14, 1945.

53 "Phelps joins plea for pulp workers," *Regina Leader-Post*, November 5, 1945.

54 *Saskatchewan Commonwealth*, January 30, 1946, 5.

55 "Forest inquiry contemplated," *Regina Leader-Post*, August 22, 1945.

56 The commission, which was established to investigate all phases of the forest industry, consisted of chairman Frank Eliason, secretary of the UFC (Saskatchewan Section), and members John C. Irwin, Dr. John Mitchell, William Bayliss, and Don Galbraith. It presented three reports: the first interim report, submitted November 12, 1945; the second interim report, submitted March 14, 1946; and a final report,

submitted May 14, 1946. Saskatchewan, *Report of the Royal Commission on Forestry of Saskatchewan* (1946), 3, 5, 10.

57 Saskatchewan, *Royal Commission on Forestry*, 9–10, 23–25.

58 *Regina Leader-Post*, March 12, 1947, 3. The formation of the settlers' fire detection and suppression committees was to be worked out with the Local Improvement District branch of the Department of Municipal Affairs.

59 "New forest fire act now in effect," *Regina Leader-Post*, April 12, 1946; *Regina Leader-Post*, March 12, 1947, 3.

60 "Saskatchewan's forest resources," *Regina Leader-Post*, May 22, 1947.

61 "55 forest fires have caused $25,000 loss," *Regina Leader-Post*, July 22, 1947.

62 Saskatchewan, Department of Natural Resources, *Annual Report*, 1945, 5; 1946, 5; 1947, 5.

63 Saskatchewan, *Royal Commission on Forestry*, 79, 82. In this way, a reduced amount of white spruce saw timber would be available for twenty years and, by that time, some trees now considered immature might be ready to be cut.

64 Saskatchewan, Department of Natural Resources, *Annual Report*, 1947, 9.

65 Saskatchewan, *Royal Commission on Forestry*, 83. The commission had recommended that the government take steps to regain control of these licensed timber berths. Timber berth operators paid a ground rental and fire tax on their berths. After the berth had been cut over, the area reverted to the government. *Regina Commonwealth*, June 5, 1946, 1.

66 *Regina Commonwealth*, February 18, 1948, 2.

67 *Regina Leader-Post*, March 8, 1946, 11.

68 *Regina Commonwealth*, February 18, 1948, 2.

69 Ibid.

60 Saskatchewan, *Royal Commission on Forestry*, 78; Christie to Phelps, May 28, 1948, p. 1a, 13–14, Joseph Lee Phelps Papers (M15), Box 36, "C. R. Christie," Provincial Archives of Saskatchewan. By May 28, 1948, the inventory was completed and found that the volume of green white spruce was 600 million (fbm).

71 Christie to Phelps, May 28, 1948; Christie to Field Officers, November 25, 1948, Joseph Lee Phelps Papers (M15), Box 36, "C. R. Christie," Provincial Archives of Saskatchewan.

72 *Regina Commonwealth*, May 7, 1947, 3.

73 *Regina Leader-Post*, February 13, 1947, 22; Government Business Enterprises, Profits and Losses Before and After Depreciation, Before Interest on Advances, Year Ended March 31, 1947, February 9, 1948, T. C. Douglas Papers (R-33.1) Box 40, IV. 152, "Crown Corporations, January 1946–October 1949," Provincial Archives of Saskatchewan. Johnson noted, "Some ministers...were openly hostile to the limits which the budget and budget control procedures imposed on their freedom. Mr. Phelps, for example, used to insist upon a single appropriation for 'conservation and development resources,' without any breakdown of the activities which were involved. The result was that budget control became virtually impossible, as the Provincial Treasurer and the Opposition in the Legislature repeatedly pointed out." See Johnson, *Dream No Little Dreams*, 275–276.

74 "Veterans get land," *Regina Leader-Post*, December 5, 1945.
75 "Crown land leases held pending study," *Regina Leader Post*, February 28, 1947.
76 Assistant deputy minister C. A. L. Hogg 's report to Phelps, September 1946, Joseph Lee Phelps Papers (M15), Provincial Archives of Saskatchewan.
77 J. L. Phelps, interview by Richards, 17.
78 "Phelps urges natural resources protection," *Regina Leader-Post*, January 28, 1947.

CHAPTER 11

1 J. L. Phelps, interview by Richards, 1.
2 J. L. Phelps, interview by Dobbin, 4.
3 In CCF *Colonialism*, Quiring cites the transcript of the 1976 Phelps interviews to suggest that oral history is not necessarily a valid research tool. He states that since the mine at Beaverlodge was not yet constructed, Phelps could not have visited it. However, further research reveals that while the Beaverlodge Uranium City mine had not yet been developed, a mining camp was in operation at that location. There was also mining activity taking place at Goldfields in the Athabasca region during this time period. Ella Little (in conversation with the author) and Lee Phelps (interview by Larry Shaak, July–August 2001, transcript, private collection) recalled accompanying Joe and Lena Phelps on a trip to a uranium mine site. They are uncertain of the dates, but it was definitely between 1944 and 1948 while Phelps was serving as Cabinet minister.
4 Government of Saskatchewan, Uranium, Mineral and Energy Resources of Saskatchewan, http://er.gov.sk.ca/Default.aspx?DN=de55f2ac-f250-4e6a-a82f-2e22a37c7d25.
5 Robert Bothwell, *Eldorado: Canada's National Uranium Company* (Toronto: University of Toronto Press, 1984), 85.
6 Ibid., 181.
7 Ibid., 281.
8 Ibid., 282.
9 Ibid., 298. From the book jacket of *Eldorado*: "When the cold war accelerated uranium became Canada's largest and most profitable mineral export, but in 1959 the Americans and later the British decided not to renew their Canadian contracts and the bottom dropped out of the uranium market. By the early 1960s the mines were closed. Eldorado turned to the generation of electricity as the market for its products and services."
10 J. L. Phelps, interview by Richards, 3.
11 Ibid., 11.
12 Ibid., 8.
13 "Action to develop deposits is taken," *Regina Leader-Post*, August 14, 1945.
14 J. L. Phelps, interview by Larmour, 8.
15 "No mineral rights to property lost," *Regina Leader-Post*, December 3, 1946.
16 Johnson, *Dream No Little Dreams*, 69.

17 *Regina Leader-Post*, October 31, 1944, 5; *Regina Commonwealth*, November 1, 1944, 1.

18 "Crown gets rights back," *Regina Leader-Post*, January 8, 1946.

19 Brian Banks, "The Political Economy of Petroleum Development in Saskatchewan, 1940–1960" (master's thesis, University of Regina, 1986), 44. Banks notes that the petition contended that the act was *ultra vires* since the legislation was "not direct taxation in order to raise revenue for provincial purposes."

20 "Legislation hits railway leases," *Regina Leader-Post*, February 19, 1947.

21 Ibid.

22 "Injunction hearing goes before court," *Regina Leader-Post*, June 22, 1948; "Phelps halted by injunction," *Regina Leader-Post*, July 6, 1948.

23 *Regina Commonwealth*, January 28, 1948, 1; Barron, *Walking in Indian Moccasins*, 192–193; L. St. Laurent to J. W. Corman, September 21, 1945, 2, Joseph Lee Phelps Papers (M15), Box 5, "Disallowance of Legislation," Provincial Archives of Saskatchewan. The CPR had court summonses served on Corman and Phelps in January 1948.

24 "Province's mineral production for 1947–48 said $32,000,000," *Regina Leader-Post*, December 26, 1947.

25 Hogg, "Joe Phelps."

26 Banks, "The Political Economy," 43.

27 Amendment to Quartz Mining Regulations, June 5, 1945, Joseph Lee Phelps Papers (M15), Box 19, "Orders-in-Council, 1944–1946 (2)," Provincial Archives of Saskatchewan. The old royalty rate, which had been less than 1 per cent, was increased to 5 per cent of the net value received from the sale of the mineral products recovered from such ore, or 10 per cent of the net profits of the mine, whichever was less.

28 *Regina Leader-Post*, August 6, 1945, 3.

29 "$600,000 boost from royalties," *Regina Leader-Post*, May 24, 1945.

30 "High Royalty Is Collected," *Regina Leader-Post*, August 6, 1945.

31 "1,000,000 power plant expansion," *Regina Leader-Post*, December 4, 1946.

32 "150 claims staked," *Regina Leader-Post*, March 25, 1946.

33 "400 foot thick salt bed found in province," *Regina Leader-Post*, July 26, 1946.

34 J. L. Phelps, interview by Richards, 16.

35 Hogg, "Joe Phelps."

36 *Regina Commonwealth*, June 16, 1948, 4; Saskatchewan Minerals—Sodium Sulphate Producers, http://www.saskatchewanminerals.com.

37 Banks, "The Political Economy," 12–13, 15–16, 26–27. The two subsidiaries were Norcanols Oils Ltd. and Northwest Co.

38 "Unity field developing as major gas producer," *Regina Leader Post*, September 27, 1945.

39 Assistant deputy minister C. A. L. Hogg's report to Phelps, September 1946, Joseph Lee Phelps Papers (M15), Provincial Archives of Saskatchewan.

40 Vern Hogg, "Joe Phelps."

41 The regulatory changes put into effect strengthened the government's ability to manage the exploration for and the development of petroleum. The major changes

added to the regulations of the Mineral Resources Act included "reducing the maximum size of an individual exploration permit to 250,000 acres, assigning definite work requirements, ordering drilling equipment to be in place within sixty days of application, requiring companies to report results to the department after ninety days, allowing maximum acreage of seventy-two sections on producing land, and setting aside checkerboard Crown reserves of fifteen per cent of the land in all producing areas." Banks, "The Political Economy," 29.

42 Ibid., 31.

43 Ibid.

44 Ibid., 36.

45 *Regina Leader-Post*, March 17, 1948, 13.

46 *Regina Commonwealth*, January 22, 1947, 1, 12.

47 *Statement of Policy on Oil, Gas, and Mineral Development*, November 29, 1946, T. C. Douglas Papers, IV. 166. (4-28), "Gas Committee Policy, May 1946–July 1961," Provincial Archives of Saskatchewan.

48 *Regina Leader-Post*, November 1, 1944, 19; Saskatchewan, *The Natural Resources of Saskatchewan, 1945* (Regina: King's Printer, 1945), n.p.

49 *Regina Leader-Post*, July 27, 1946, 3.

50 Ibid., February 16, 1948, 3. Later, Phelps indicated he had spoken as "a citizen of the province" about the government's possible involvement in oil exploration.

51 Hogg, "Joe Phelps."

52 Johnson, *Dream No Little Dreams*, 130.

53 "Government oil enterprise seen," *Regina Leader-Post*, July 27, 1946.

54 Johnson, *Dream No Little Dreams*, 69.

55 Johnson, *Dream No Little Dreams*, 156. See also "Road work continuing," *Regina Leader-Post*, August 24, 1946; "Transfer this year," *Regina Leader-Post*, October 12, 1946; "Mineral rights details needed," *Regina Leader-Post*, February 18, 1947; "Research staff is organized," *Regina Leader-Post*, July 5, 1947; "Crown land rulings given clarification," *Regina Leader-Post*, August 6, 1947; "Goldfield is active," *Regina Leader-Post*, September 6, 1947; "Province may join oil hunt," *Regina Leader-Post*, February 16, 1948; "$8,000,000 resources bill up," *Regina Leader-Post*, February 24, 1948; "Northern survey," *Regina Leader-Post*, July 2, 1948.

CHAPTER 12

1 Johnson, *Dream No Little Dreams*, 74.

2 Phelps to Douglas, February 9, 1945, Joseph Lee Phelps Papers (M15), Box 4, "Public Health Department, 1944–1946," Provincial Archives of Saskatchewan.

3 Larry E. Buhr, "An Archeological Survey of Brick Manufacture in Saskatchewan (master's thesis, University of Saskatchewan, 1997), 47.

4 Ibid., 58, 64, 73–76.

5 Ibid., 63.

6 Bowman to Phelps, August 22, 1944, Joseph Lee Phelps Papers (M15), Box 19, "Saskatchewan Development Branch, 1944–1946 (2)," Provincial Archives of Saskatchewan.

7 On February 20, 1946, Hogg was appointed assistant deputy minister of the DNR and Industrial Development Board. In May 1946, he became the DNR's acting deputy minister, and, from October 30, 1946, to April 1, 1953, he was the deputy minister of the DNR.

8 Hogg to Phelps, October 20, 1944, Joseph Lee Phelps Papers (M15), Box 18, "C. A. L. Hogg, 1944–1946," Provincial Archives of Saskatchewan; Banks, "Co-operative Commonwealth Federation," 25–26.

9 Worcester to Phelps, September 19, 1944, Joseph Lee Phelps Papers (M15), Box 19, "Saskatchewan Industrial Development Branch, 1944–1946 (2)"; Worcester to Phelps, November 1944, Joseph Lee Phelps Papers (M15), Box 2, "Saskatchewan Clay Products," Provincial Archives of Saskatchewan; Banks, "Co-operative Commonwealth Federation," 26–27.

10 Richards and Pratt, *Prairie Capitalism*, 109–110. Apparently, the brick plant purchase was one of the "more celebrated incidents in Phelps' stormy relationship with cabinet." In an interview, Phelps related that he had proposed that Cabinet buy the brick plant. In a lengthy discussion, Clarence Fines protested that the lack of adequate economic research did not justify this purchase. The Cabinet agreed. Phelps refused to let the matter drop and finally admitted that the Cabinet had no choice since he had already bought the plant.

11 Worcester to Phelps, September 19, 1944, Joseph Lee Phelps Papers (M15), Box 19, "Saskatchewan Industrial Development Branch, 1944–1946 (2)"; Worcester to Phelps, November 1944, Joseph Lee Phelps Papers (M15), Box 2, "Saskatchewan Clay Products," Provincial Archives of Saskatchewan. Phelps's statement about receiving "three appraisals" is unclear. Evidence indicates that only Hogg and Worcester provided them. Perhaps Worcester gave two, one in September and another in November. However, the letter Worcester wrote Phelps on September 19 must really be considered an opinion rather than an appraisal.

12 Purchase of International Clay Products, May 3, 1945, Joseph Lee Phelps Papers, Box 29, "Orders-in Council, 1944–1945 (2)," Provincial Archives of Saskatchewan.

13 *Regina Leader-Post*, March 27, 1945, 15; *Regina Commonwealth*, September 26, 1945, 4.

14 Saskatchewan Clay Products Minutes, November 16–17, 1945, Crown Corporations Board Minutes, Provincial Archives of Saskatchewan; Hogg to Phelps, October 20, 1944, Joseph Lee Phelps Papers (M15), Box 18, "C. A. L. Hogg, 1944–1946," Provincial Archives of Saskatchewan.

15 *Regina Commonwealth*, June 13, 1945, 1; Cadbury to Phelps, January 28, 1946, 6, Joseph Lee Phelps Papers (M15), Box 5, "Economic Advisory Recommendations, 1945–1946," Provincial Archives of Saskatchewan; *Regina Leader-Post*, April 4, 1946, 15; Cadbury, interview by Larmour, 72.

16 A car tunnel kiln consisted of a long, enclosed passage with a stationary firing zone in the centre. The bricks moved through the tunnel on tracked cars, heating

and cooling gradually before and after passing through the firing zone. Buhr, "An Archeological Survey," 271.

17 Hogg to Phelps, October, 20, 1944, Joseph Lee Phelps Papers (M15), Box 18, "C. A. L. Hogg, 1944–1946," Provincial Archives of Saskatchewan; Saskatchewan, *Journals* (1946), February 19, 1946, 147; Saskatchewan Clay Products Minutes, November 16, 17, 1947, Crown Corporations Board Minutes, Provincial Archives of Saskatchewan; *Regina Leader-Post*, February 13, 1947, 22; February 20, 1946, 1, 8.

18 Pat Rediger, *The Crowns: A History of Public Enterprise in Saskatchewan* (Regina: Canadian Plains Research Center, University of Regina, 2004), 16.

19 Saskatchewan, *Public Enterprise in Saskatchewan* (Regina: Crown Investments Corporation of Saskatchewan, 1981), Appendix A.

20 Saskatchewan, *Reconstruction Council*, Appendix 5, 36.

21 Ibid., 47–48.

22 "Skirting" the fleeces involved placing a sheep's fleece on a flat surface and separating the poorer wool that covered the sheep's legs from the better wool that came from its body.

23 Saskatchewan, *Reconstruction Council*, Appendix 5, 48–49. Custom work meant the conversion of old woollen garments into shoddy or virgin wool that could be made into blankets. "Overcoating" was a heavy cloth material used for making coats that were worn over regular clothing.

24 Ibid., Appendix 5, 50.

25 In 1944, Douglas announced that Monahan had accepted a position in the DNR and had begun to "map out plans for the development of Saskatchewan industries" using agricultural products. Johnson, *Dream No Little Dreams*, 135.

26 Clement to Phelps, October 18, 1944, Joseph Lee Phelps Papers (M15), Box 26, "Woollen Mill, 1944–1946 (2)," Provincial Archives of Saskatchewan. Clement's qualifications were impressive. He had practical experience in all branches of the woollen industry, having served his apprenticeship in Scotland. He had been a general manager and superintendent in three different woollen mills from 1919 to 1941. During that time, he had remodelled each for greater efficiency. He was now a textile consultant, specializing in wool blending, fabric construction, cost, production, and finishing problems. He included six references with his letter.

27 Clement to Phelps, November 22, 1944, Joseph Lee Phelps Papers, Box 26, "Woollen Mill, 1944–1946 (2)," Provincial Archives of Saskatchewan.

28 Monahan to Phelps, November 14, 1944, Joseph Lee Phelps Papers, Box 26, "Woollen Mill, 1944–1946 (2)," Provincial Archives of Saskatchewan.

29 Monahan to Phelps, November 24, 1944, Joseph Lee Phelps Papers, Box 26, "Woollen Mill, 1944–1946 (2)," Provincial Archives of Saskatchewan. Johnson notes that although Monahan and Clement reported favourably upon the venture, the adequacy of their investigation was subsequently to be questioned—range wool was found to be unsatisfactory for the operation, costs were found to be seriously underestimated, and the water supply was found to be inadequate. Johnson, *Dream No Little Dreams*, 196.

30 *Regina Leader-Post*, December 6, 1944, 1, 14.

31 Minutes of the First Meeting of the Saskatchewan Wool Products, June 21, 1945, Joseph Lee Phelps Papers (M15), Box 26, "Woollen Mill Products, Minutes, 1945–1946," Provincial Archives of Saskatchewan.

32 *Regina Commonwealth*, December 13, 1944, 2; Saskatchewan, *Journals* (1946), March 1, 1946, 182. "Coating" was heavy cloth used for making coats and "shirting" was light cloth used for making shirts.

33 Saskatchewan, *Journals* (1946), March 12, 1946, 200; *Regina Leader-Post*, March 2, 1946, 12. Interestingly, on March 1, 1946, Phelps reached under his desk, produced a pair of woollen blankets manufactured at the Moose Jaw mill, and offered them as proof that the mill was producing blankets. Although the mill produced blankets, it never made the other goods Phelps claimed it would.

34 Joseph Lee Phelps Papers (M15), Box 26, "Woollen Mill, 1944–1946, (1)," n.d., Provincial Archives of Saskatchewan. The mill's waste products consisted of wool fat, soap, alkali, mineral oil, bichromate of potash, and sulphuric acid.

35 Wartime Prices and Trade Board to Clement, October 13, 1945, Joseph Lee Phelps Papers (M15), Box 26, "Woollen Mill, 1944–1946, (1)," Provincial Archives of Saskatchewan.

36 No further evidence was available as to Fisher's first name, the nature of the conflict, or the conditions at the plant.

37 Phelps to Clement, November 26, 1945, Joseph Lee Phelps Papers (M15), Box 26, "Woollen Mill, 1944–1946, (1)," Provincial Archives of Saskatchewan. In a letter Clement wrote Phelps the same day, Clement refuted many of the complaints that Phelps had made against him. Clement to Phelps, November 26, 1945, Joseph Lee Phelps Papers (M15), Box 26, "Woollen Mill, 1944–1946, (1)," Provincial Archives of Saskatchewan.

38 Monahan to Phelps, March 21, 1945, Joseph Lee Phelps Papers (M15), Box 22, "Moose Jaw Estimates," Provincial Archives of Saskatchewan.

39 Bevan to Phelps, November 3, 1945, Joseph Lee Phelps Papers (M15), Box 26, "Woollen Mill, 1944–1946, (1)," Provincial Archives of Saskatchewan.

40 Bevan to Phelps, September 10, 1945, Joseph Lee Phelps Papers (M15), Box 26, "Woollen Mill, 1944–1946, (1)," Provincial Archives of Saskatchewan. Bevan stated that $106,325.28 worth of equipment had been purchased and that about $20,000 worth was still to arrive.

41 Minutes of Ninth Meeting of the Saskatchewan Wool Products, April 8, 1946, Joseph Lee Phelps Papers (M15), Box 26, "Woollen Mill, 1944–1946, (1)," Provincial Archives of Saskatchewan.

42 "Wool mill cost so far $393,309," *Regina Leader-Post*, April 5, 1946.

43 "Government blankets now on sale," *Regina Leader-Post*, April 27, 1946.

44 Rediger, *The Crowns*, 18.

45 Richards and Pratt, *Prairie Capitalism*, 116.

46 J. L. Phelps, interview by Larmour.

47 Warren and Carlisle, *On the Side of the People*, 130–133. For over a year and a half the employees of the Prince Albert Box Factory, who were members of the Prince Albert Box Factory Union, had tried unsuccessfully to negotiate a collective

agreement with J. E. Mitchell, president of the company. The union then charged the company with an unfair labour practice and applied to the Labour Relations Board, which found the company guilty. The union then asked the Lieutenant-Governor-in-Council to place a controller in the plant until the company obeyed the order. Douglas asked Mitchell to appear before the Cabinet to submit his case, but Mitchell and his lawyer, C. S. Davis, requested time to prepare a brief. These two then "proceeded to transfer the property of the Company to Mr. Mitchell personally," and they fired all the employees as of November 7, 1945.

48 *Regina Leader-Post*, November 3, 1945, 11; November 7, 1945, 11.

49 T. C. Douglas, interview by Chris Higginbotham, 1958, 262–263, transcript, "T. C. Douglas Recording Series," Provincial Archives of Saskatchewan; *Regina Commonwealth*, November 21, 1945, 5; *Regina Leader-Post*, February 21, 1946, 1, 9.

50 Douglas, interview by Higginbotham, 263.

51 Smith to Board of Directors SLAFPC, July 10, 1947, Joseph Lee Phelps Papers (M15), Box 15, "W. D. Smith, Box Factory, 1946–1948," Provincial Archives of Saskatchewan; Gray to Board of Directors SLAFPC, October 17, 1947, Joseph Lee Phelps Papers (M15), Box 9, "S.L.A.F.P.C., J. F. Gray, 1946–1951 (4)," Provincial Archives of Saskatchewan. On another occasion, Smith indicated that the government and departments treated the box factory as "an illegitimate embarrassing foundling" that "was dumped in the lap of the Department of Natural Resources and Industrial Development" because "no one else had the courage to take it on and that seemed a logical shelf anyway." Smith to Board of Directors SLAFPC, June 1947, Joseph Lee Phelps Papers (M15), Box 15, "W. D. Smith, Box Factory, 1946–1948," Provincial Archives of Saskatchewan.

52 Samletsky to Gray, August 9, 1947, Joseph Lee Phelps Papers (M15), Box 9, "S.L.A.F.P.C., 1946–1949," Provincial Archives of Saskatchewan; W. J. Bague, Resident Director of the SLAFPC, expressed a similar concern when he wrote, "One of the most crippling factors in our present set-up is the lack of space." Bague to Gray, October 20, 1947, Joseph Lee Phelps Papers (M15), Box 9, "S.L.A.F.P.C., 1946–1949," Provincial Archives of Saskatchewan.

53 Smith to Government Finance Office, October 1, 1947, Joseph Lee Phelps Papers (M15), Box 15, "W. Smith, Box Factory, 1946–1948," Provincial Archives of Saskatchewan; Gray to Board of Directors of SLAFPC, October 11, 1947, Joseph Lee Phelps Papers (M15), Box 9, "J. F. Gray, 1946–1951 (4)," Provincial Archives of Saskatchewan; Bague to Gray, October 20, 1947, Joseph Lee Phelps Papers (M15), Box 9, "S.L.A.F.P.C., 1946–1949," Provincial Archives of Saskatchewan.

54 Gray to Board of Directors of SLAFPC, October 11, 1947, Joseph Lee Phelps Papers (M15), Box 9, "S.L.A.F.P.C., J. F. Gray, 1946–1951 (4)," Provincial Archives of Saskatchewan.

55 Ibid.

56 Smith to Board of Directors SLAFPC, May 30, 1947, Joseph Lee Phelps Papers (M15), Box 15, "W. D. Smith, Box Factory, 1946–1948," Provincial Archives of Saskatchewan.

57 Smith to Board of Directors SLAFPC, October 4, 1947, Joseph Lee Phelps Papers (M15), Box 15, "W. D. Smith, Box Factory, 1946–1948," Provincial Archives of

Saskatchewan; *Regina Leader-Post*, August 6, 1947, 11. M. Begley and N. Pollock were the two men dismissed, the former for gross inefficiency, the latter for accepting other employment while on paid sick leave. Seventy out of ninety men at the box factory went out on strike. Concerning his dismissal of the striking employees, Phelps said, "I am the one who issued the dismissal order, and I will do the same thing again under the same circumstances."

58 "Phelps's threat seen as labour act violation," *Prince Albert Daily Herald*, August 5, 1947.

59 *Regina Leader-Post*, August 5, 1947.

60 *Regina Commonwealth*, November 21, 1945, 5. Monahan to Phelps, November 10, 1945, Joseph Lee Phelps Papers (M15), Box 15, "Box Factory, 1945–1946," Provincial Archives of Saskatchewan. Monahan noted that the cost of this agreement could amount to $10,000 to $15,000 per year, and that it might be "enough to break the organization." He felt he could not accept responsibility in same.

61 Harrop to Phelps, n.d., Joseph Lee Phelps Papers (M15), Box 15, "J. J. Harrop, Box Factory, 1947–1951," Provincial Archives of Saskatchewan. The *Saskatchewan dnr Reports* do not provide detailed financial data for fiscal years for the box factory, nor do they provide this information for the brick plant, the woollen mill, and the leather industries.

62 Rediger, *The Crowns*, 54.

63 Saskatchewan, *Public Enterprise*, Appendix A, 117.

64 Saskatchewan, *Reconstruction Council*, Appendix 5, 77–78; Banks, "Co-operative Commonwealth Federation," 33–34.

65 Rediger, *The Crowns*, 20.

66 Counter shoes had a piece of stiff leather forming the back of the shoe or boot around the heel. Toe cap shoes had an extra piece of leather across the shoe's toe to reinforce the front of the shoe.

67 Hogg to Phelps, January 2, 1945, Joseph Lee Phelps Papers (M15), Box 20, "Saskatchewan Leather Products, 1945–1946," Provincial Archives of Saskatchewan.

68 Phelps to Cantor, April 16, 1945, and Phelps to Cantor, April 18, 1945, Joseph Lee Phelps Papers (M15), Box 20, "Saskatchewan Leather Products, 1945–1946," Provincial Archives of Saskatchewan.

69 Saskatchewan, Department of Natural Resources, *Annual Report*, 1946, 96.

70 *Saskatchewan Commonwealth*, June 6, 1945, 5; August 1, 1945, 8; December 5, 1945, 12; Saskatchewan, *Journals* (1946), February 21, 1946, 153; Hogg to Phelps, January 2, 1945, and Auditor's Report, April 24, 1946, Joseph Lee Phelps Papers (M15), Box 20, "Saskatchewan Leather Products, 1945–1946," Provincial Archives of Saskatchewan.

71 Auditor's Report, April 24, 1946, Joseph Lee Phelps Papers (M15), Box 20, "Saskatchewan Leather Products, 1945–1946," Provincial Archives of Saskatchewan; Saskatchewan Leather Products Minutes, July 3, 1945, Crown Corporations Board Minutes, Provincial Archives of Saskatchewan; *Regina Leader-Post*, March 21, 1947, 3.

72 Saskatchewan Leather Products Minutes, September 29, 1945, October 4, 1945, and December 20, 1945, Crown Corporations Board Minutes, Provincial Archives of Saskatchewan. No further evidence was found with respect to Mr. Aldrich's first name or "the labour situation at the Factory."

73 Saskatchewan Leather Products, Interim Report, March 16, 1946, Crown Corporations Board Minutes, Provincial Archives of Saskatchewan.

74 Cadbury, interview by Larmour, 76.

75 Richards and Pratt, *Prairie Capitalism*, 116–117. The factory "produced only a limited range (footwear for 'people on the street, in the home, on the farm and at work…[no] style merchandise' explained Phelps), such an embargo would leave retailers with half-empty shelves." Richards and Pratt, *Prairie Capitalism*, 117.

76 J. L. Phelps, interview by Larmour, 15.

77 Richards and Pratt, *Prairie Capitalism*, 116.

78 McLeod and McLeod, *Tommy Douglas*, 167.

79 Monahan to Phelps, September 15, 1944, Joseph Lee Phelps Papers (M15), Box 19, "Saskatchewan Industrial Development Branch, 1944–1946, (2)," Provincial Archives of Saskatchewan. Phelps should not alone be blamed for trying to undertake so many new ventures. Monahan, who had worked for the Liberal government and whom Douglas had appointed as superintendent of the Industrial Development Branch, gave Phelps a list of twelve projects in which the DNR might become involved. Some of the more unusual ones he listed were canning tomatoes and making tomato juice, processing cheese, manufacturing butylene glycol, growing and processing sugar beets, and making box shooks and excelsior.

80 "Accounting division in government," *Regina Leader-Post*, February 27, 1946.

81 Johnson, *Dream No Little Dreams*, 140.

82 Britnell was the head of the Department of Economics and Political Science; Fowke was a professor in that department; Cronkite was the dean of law. See Shirley Spafford, *No Ordinary Academics: Economics and Political Science at the University of Saskatchewan, 1910–1960* (Toronto: University of Toronto Press, 2000), 131, 133, 134, 136, 157. Thomas McLeod, a political scientist who had studied in Manitoba, acted as its secretary. Banks, "Co-operative Commonwealth Federation," 62.

83 *Regina Leader-Post*, October 31, 1944, 1; Banks, "Co-operative Commonwealth Federation," 22, 62; Richards and Pratt, *Prairie Capitalism*, 108–109.

84 When David Lewis was at Oxford, he had heard about Cadbury and urged Douglas to invite him to Saskatchewan. Cadbury had worked for the family business in England and had graduated in economics from Cambridge when "giants such as Maynard Keynes and Joan and Austin Robinson were generating great intellectual excitement." Besides, he and his wife Barbara "were committed socialists" and "were steeped in the ideas of international socialism." McLeod and McLeod, *Tommy Douglas*, 168.

85 Cadbury, interview by Larmour, 68–69. At this Cabinet meeting, Cadbury had asked about industrial ventures being carried out in Saskatchewan and had specifically inquired about the shoe factory. He recalled, "Having looked at what

facts there were and having considered it I went into the Cabinet Meeting and I said, 'Don't touch it. The man who is running it is a wholesaler for shoes and what he is going to do is have a factory here to make shoes that nobody else will make.'... And I advised them not to do it. Unfortunately the Minister responsible said it was too late. Everything was signed, sealed, and delivered, which lived to haunt us."

86 Marchildon, foreword to *Dream No Little Dreams*, xvi.

87 McLeod and McLeod, *Tommy Douglas*. From the book jacket: "Tommy McLeod was born in Weyburn in 1918 and holds a doctorate in economics and government from Harvard University. He left to a varied career in Canadian universities, overseas development and federal government service, retiring in 1984 as special advisor to the minister of finance."

88 Ibid., 168.

89 Cadbury to Douglas, January 24, 1946, Joseph Lee Phelps Papers (M15), Box 5, "Economic Advisory Committee Recommendations, 1945–1946," Provincial Archives of Saskatchewan.

90 Cadbury, interview by Larmour, 11.

91 Cadbury to T. C. Douglas, January 25, 1946, Joseph Lee Phelps Papers (M15), Box 5, "Economic Advisory Committee Recommendations, 1945–1946," Provincial Archives of Saskatchewan; Box 28, "Orders-in-Council, 1944–1946," January 23 to April 18, 1946, Joseph Lee Phelps Papers (M15), Provincial Archives of Saskatchewan. Between January 23 and April 18, 1946, Cadbury became a director of each industrial project and marketing board, as well as of the Power Commission. He replaced Clement as director of Saskatchewan Wool Products, succeeded Nordal as director of Saskatchewan Clay Products, and joined Hal Berry as director of the Power Commission. He and Murray Bryce replaced K. E. Dickson and Axel Olson on Saskatchewan Fish Products, and he replaced R. McInnis on the Saskatchewan Timber Board.

92 L. C. Paterson had worked with the federal government from 1910 to 1930, then transferred to the provincial government when jurisdiction over natural resources had, and worked for the provincial government until the Liberals were defeated in 1944. In August 1944, he became acting deputy minister of natural resources, a position he held until April 2, 1945, when Henry Lewis became the deputy minister of the DNR. *Saskatchewan Executive and Legislative Directory*, 35.

93 Phelps to Campbell, August 23, 1946, Joseph Lee Phelps Papers (M15), Box 20, "Campbell, A. Shoe Factory, 1946–1947," Provincial Archives of Saskatchewan.

94 Phelps to McKinley, August 23, 1946, Joseph Lee Phelps Papers (M15), Box 20, "McKinley, J. A., Manager, Tannery, 1946–1947"; Phelps to Nordal, August 26, 1946, Joseph Lee Phelps Papers (M15), Box 2, "Clay Products, J. Nordal, Manager, 1944–1946"; Phelps to Moors, August 26, 1946, Joseph Lee Phelps Papers (M15), Box 26, "Moors, J., Manager, Woollen Mill," Provincial Archives of Saskatchewan. Interestingly, J. Moors responded in a letter: "I can honestly say that, during my long business association, I have never found anyone with whom it has been more a pleasure to work." Moors to Phelps, August 28, 1946, Joseph Lee Phelps Papers (M15), Box 26,

"Moors, J., Manager, Woollen Mill, 1946," Provincial Archives of Saskatchewan.

95 Saskatchewan Industries Minutes, August 26, 1946, Crown Corporations Board Minutes, Provincial Archives of Saskatchewan.

96 McLeod and McLeod, *Tommy Douglas*, 167.

97 Baptie, *Joe Phelps*. For contemporary media reaction to the government-owned businesses, see "Accounting division," *Regina Leader-Post*, February 27, 1946; "Wool mill cost so far," *Regina Leader-Post*, April 5, 1946; "Government blankets," *Regina Leader-Post*, April 27, 1946; "Shoe factory appointment," *Regina Leader-Post*, July 13, 1946; "Box factory price told," *Regina Leader-Post*, February 18, 1947; "Irresponsible leadership in box plant union denied," *Prince Albert Daily Herald*, August 8, 1947; "Phelps threat seen as labour violation," *Prince Albert Daily Herald*, August 5, 1947.

CHAPTER 13

1 "Phelps north policy backed," *Regina Leader-Post*, November 1, 1947.

2 *Regina Leader-Post*, November 1, 1947, 5.

3 *Prince Albert Daily Herald*, May 20, 1948, 1; June 21, 1948, 9.

4 *Prince Albert Daily Herald*, May 26, 1948, 2. One of the Liberals' slogans was "What Do You Want Now. Tucker or Tyranny," a reference to their leader Walter Tucker. *Yorkton Enterprise*, May 27, 1948, 13.

5 *Regina Commonwealth*, May 19, 1948, 11; May 26, 1948, 11; June 2, 1948, 11; June 9, 1948, 11; June 16, 1948, 11; *Saltcoats Star*, June 3, 1948, 3; June 16, 1948, 3, 4. Between May 20 and June 19, Phelps made seven radio broadcasts over five different radio stations. His itinerary between May 17 and June 23 included thirty days of campaigning. During this period, he campaigned in several constituencies and spoke at several public meetings in his own riding. These meetings appear to have been well attended: at Esterhazy, "an estimated crowd of 800 overflowed the Community hall." *Esterhazy Observer*, June 24, 1948, 1. Douglas and Phelps addressed an audience of about three hundred at Saltcoats. There, Douglas "lauded the work of Mr. Phelps and his department and urged that people of Saltcoats re-elect him as their representative who was 'at all times looking after the interests of the Saltcoats constituency.'" Phelps also touched "on the work done by his department during the past four years and asked for the continued support of the electors at the polls on June 24." *Saltcoats Star*, June 9, 1948, 1, 4.

6 "Fur market branch has $61,601 in profit," *Regina Leader-Post*, February 20, 1948.

7 "Market boards here to stay," *Regina Leader-Post*, March 3, 1948.

8 Ibid.

9 Ibid.

10 Ibid.

11 "Resources plan set," *Regina Leader-Post*, June 14, 1948.

12 Ibid.

13 "Phelps spoke as citizen," *Regina Leader-Post*, February 20, 1948.

14 "Resources plan set," *Regina Leader-Post*, June 14, 1948.
15 *Saskatchewan Executive and Legislative Directory*, 55–58, 91–158.
16 Archer, *Saskatchewan*, 281.
17 Johnson, "Biography of a Government," 359.
18 *Prince Albert Daily Herald*, May 20, 1948, 1; *Saskatoon StarPhoenix*, June 5, 1948, 12.
19 Phelps to Douglas, August 13, 1948, T. C. Douglas Papers, IV. 152 (4-14), Provincial Archives of Saskatchewan. Phelps seemed bitter. When he was invited to attend a meeting of the SLAFPC on August 16, 1948, he asked the government to accept his resignation as chairman of this Crown orporation immediately. He added, "The objection is not to what is being done but I certainly do object in the strongest possible terms to the methods being employed. If these are to be the future practices of the new government you may also accept this letter as my resignation at your convenience as chairman of Saskatchewan Airways, as well as The Saskatchewan Fur Marketing Service." He added that he wished to be informed of the date at which he would "be relieved of any further responsibility regarding same" and the date he would "be relieved of the necessity of attending any further Board meetings."
20 Phelps attempted to enter politics one more time. In 1962, he became the CCF federal candidate in the Battlefords riding. *Regina Commonwealth*, May 30, 1962, 5. However, Albert R. Horner defeated him. The results were as follows: Albert R. Horner (Progressive Conservative) 11,970; Joe Phelps (CCF) 5,166; and S. Duff Noble (Liberal) 5,045. Saskatchewan, *Directory of Members of Parliament and Federal Elections for the North-West Territories and Saskatchewan, 1887–1966* (Regina and Saskatoon: Saskatchewan Archives Board, 1967), 51.
21 Douglas, interview by Higginbotham, 387.
22 Roy Romanow, interview by Larry Shaak, July–August 2001, transcript, private collection.
23 Kramer to Little, "A Literal Snapshot."
24 Phelps to Florence Barker, August 12, 1944, Joseph Lee Phelps Papers (M15), Box 29, "Saltcoats Constituency, 1945–1946 (2)," Provincial Archives of Saskatchewan. Lena Phelps often responded to complaints or inquiries from Saltcoats constituents and directed their inquiries to various government departments. She also had Phelps's secretary type some of her letters.
25 Phelps to Fish and Game League Executive, June 23, 1945, Joseph Lee Phelps Papers (M15), Box 24, "Saskatchewan Fish and Game League, 1944–1946," Provincial Archives of Saskatchewan.
26 Phelps to Florence Barker, April 29, 1946, Joseph Lee Phelps Papers (M15), Box 29, "Saltcoats Constituency, 1945–1946 (1)," Provincial Archives of Saskatchewan.
27 In a letter dated August 25, 1948, Florence Barker, secretary treasurer for the CCF executive of the Saltcoats constituency, gave a post-mortem of the election results there. One reason she listed for Phelps's defeat was "Devotion of Mr. Phelps to duty of Department caused loss of personal touch with constituents." CCF (Saskatchewan Section), II, Subject Files, 1931–1952, 122, Elections: Provincial Results, 1938–1948, p. 11, 709, Provincial Archives of Saskatchewan.

28 J. L. Phelps, interview by Richards, 15. Ironically, potash, which was at that time "foreign" to the residents of the Saltcoats constituency, now plays a major role there with the opening of two potash mines at Esterhazy in the 1960s.
29 *Regina Leader-Post*, June 9, 1948, 1; June 12, 1948, 1; June 15, 1948, 1; June 16, 1948, 1; June 19, 1948, 1; June 23, 1948, 1. Some of the places where Gardiner spoke were Kindersley, Assiniboia, Fort Qu'Appelle, Punnichy, Foam Lake, and Southey. He maintained, "Canadian farmers got more for their wheat than any farmers in the world except those in the United States and Great Britain." *Regina Leader-Post*, June 15, 1948.
30 *Saskatchewan Executive and Legislative Directory*, 139–140; *Saskatchewan Executive and Legislative Directory Supplement, 1964–1977* (Regina and Saskatoon: Saskatchewan Archives Board, 1978), 71.
31 Chris Hansen, correspondence with the author, July 2012.
32 Saskatchewan, *Journals* (1948), March 25, 1948, 284; Quiring, *CCF Colonialism*, 22.
33 *Regina Leader-Post*, March 22, 1945, 30.
34 Saskatchewan, *Journals* (1948), February 23, 1948, 182–183; Saskatchewan, *Sessional Paper No. 102*, March 28, 1947. Phelps also hired K. E. Dickson, an acquaintance from the Wilkie area, as manager of the Beaver Lake Fish Plant. Quiring, *CCF Colonialism*, 29.
35 Saskatchewan, *Journals* (1947), March 19, 1947, 270. Phelps had given similar responses on March 13 and March 18.
36 *Prince Albert Daily Herald*, May 27, 1947, 2. At the trial, Davis was defending Harry Paul for stealing beaver pelts while he was an employee of the DNR. Responding to Phelps, Davis said, "It is indeed a disgusting spectacle to see a member of His Majesty's Government so debase himself by resorting to such a vile and scurrilous attack."
37 Ibid., May 27, 1947, 2; June 2, 1947, 9.
38 Quiring, *CCF Colonialism*, 22.
39 J. L. Phelps, interview by Richards, 19.
40 *Regina Leader-Post*, July 24, 1948.
41 McLeod and McLeod, *Tommy Douglas*, 160.
42 "Mr. Phelps speaks out," *Regina Leader-Post*, July 28, 1948.
43 *Regina Leader-Post*, July 24, 1948, 8, 13.
44 J. L. Phelps, *As It Happens*, CBC Radio, 1988, interview transcript provided by Phelps family.
45 Lipset, *Agrarian Socialism*, 280.
46 Glen Makahonuk, *Class, State and Power: The Struggle for Trade Union Rights in Saskatchewan, 1905–1997* (Saskatoon: Makahonuk/CUPE, 1997), 21.
47 Baptie, *Joe Phelps*.
48 Dobbin, *One-and-a-Half Men*, 174.
49 Ibid.
50 *Saskatoon StarPhoenix*, July 7, 1948, 3, 5; Quiring, *CCF Colonialism*, 22.
51 Brown, Roberts, and Warnock, *Saskatchewan Politics*, 21.
52 *Regina Leader-Post*, June 25, 1948, 1.
53 "Phelps heading north campaign," *Regina Leader-Post*, July 8, 1948.

54 Carlyle King to T. C. Douglas, July 4, 1948, T. C. Douglas Papers, XVIII. 677, (18-11-2), Provincial Archives of Saskatchewan.
55 *Saskatoon StarPhoenix*, July 7, 1948, 5.
56 "Phelps heading north campaign," *Regina Leader-Post*, July 8, 1948.
57 "Lame duck on the wing," *Prince Albert Daily Herald*, July 12, 1948.
58 Ibid.
59 *Prince Albert Daily Herald*, July 12, 1948, 2. Seeking to offset the dissatisfaction everywhere apparent in Athabasca and Cumberland, Douglas toured the area with Phelps and even suggested that the government might consider the formation of a fisheries co-operative to replace the Saskatchewan Fish Board. He also implied that unless the North elected CCF members, the government might be hard-pressed to justify further expenditures in the North. *Regina Leader-Post*, July 24, 1948, 12.
60 Saskatchewan, *Debates and Proceedings of the Legislative Assembly*, February 10, 1948, Vol. 1, No. 4, 26–28; March 3, 1948, Vol. 1, No. 20, 4.
61 Dobbin, *One-and-a-Half Men*, 168.
62 *Regina Leader-Post*, July 24, 1948, 12; *Estevan Mercury*, July 29, 1948, 3.
63 Barron, *Walking in Indian Moccasins*, 163.
64 Dobbin, *One-and-a-Half Men*, 175.
65 Barron, *Walking in Indian Moccasins*, 140, 143. Barron describes Phelps as being "irascible," and as being known in the Cabinet as a "radical." Barron adds that Phelps ruled "by the seat of his pants" and disregarded "bureaucratic procedure."
66 Ibid., 144–157.
67 Ibid., 143. Phelps knew that the "development of the resources could not be dissociated from the people who used them." He once even referred to himself as "the minister of 'human resources.'"
68 Ibid.
69 Quiring, "Battling Parish Priests, Bootleggers, and Fur Sharks," 5.
70 Radloff, "Cooperative and State Ownership," 73.
71 Dobbin, *One-and-a-Half Men*, 170.
72 Quiring, *CCF Colonialism*, 21.
73 Shackleton, *Tommy Douglas*, 204.
74 Quiring, *CCF Colonialism*, xx.
75 McLeod and McLeod, *Tommy Douglas*, 140.
76 Barron, *Walking in Indian Moccasins*, 203.
77 J. L. Phelps, interview by Larmour, 6.
78 "New post to Phelps," *Regina Leader-Post*, November 26, 1948.
79 J. L. Phelps, interview by White, 13.

CHAPTER 14

1 J. L. Phelps, interview by Richards, 19.
2 "Mr. Phelps speaks out," *Regina Leader-Post*, July 28, 1948.
3 McLeod and McLeod, *Tommy Douglas*, 177–178. "Coop farms comprised of

about 6 families were seen as an ideal way to settle soldiers back from the war and also a means to stop the decline in rural population. By 1949 there were 17 farm cooperatives with 181 members engaged in various types of farming in Saskatchewan. The Matador cooperative operation, specializing in cattle production became an international showpiece. Douglas's planners became even more enthusiastic and recommended expanding the development fund to $1 million. However interest in setting up new farms declined and one by one the existing associations dissolved."

4 Johnson, *Dream No Little Dreams*, 47. The CCF farm security program "promised to stop foreclosure on and eviction from the farm home, introduce legislation to protect farmers from that portion of their crop that is needed to provide for their families, and to use the power of debt moratorium to force the loan or mortgage companies to reduce debts and mortgages to a figure at which they can reasonably be paid at prevailing prices for farm products. The program also promised to declare a moratorium on principal payments and to cancel interest payments in any year when farm income fell below six dollars an acre; to prevent municipalities from collecting on old loans for buying seed grain when the farmers were having difficulty maintaining their families; and to cancel the 1938 Dominion Provincial seed grain loans—the almost colossal debt which had accumulated in providing seed after the 1937 crop failure."

5 Ibid., 48.

6 Several sources use the term "moribund" to refer to the SFU at the time Joe Phelps became president. The earliest source is Fry, "Joe Phelps," n.p. According to Fry, when Phelps was elected president, the UFC had only a few hundred paid-up members and thirty-seven locals. It was in debt $12,000. After his five-year term, the membership rose to "100,000 farm men, women and juniors" and 1,067 locals throughout the province, and the organization was debt-free and had accumulated substantial assets. Other documents show membership at approximately fifty thousand paid members (farm unit members). By 1950, memberships were sold on a "unit" or family basis. The membership fee of $5 for the first quarter and $2 each additional quarter included both husband and wife as senior members, and dependents from twelve to twenty-one years as members in the junior section.

7 Fry, "Joe Phelps," n.p.

8 Lawrence Thoner, "Hell-raising Joe Phelps always eager to challenge establishment," *Saskatoon StarPhoenix*, January 30, 1982.

9 Stuart Thiesson,"Rebuilding the Voluntary Farm Movement." This is a fifteen-page document prepared for the author in 2005, based on Thiesson's forty-one years of service in the farm movement. Thiesson retired in 1992. An unsung hero of the SFU, Thiesson prepared hundreds of papers on topics as varied as the Meech Lake Accord, tax reform, drug patent legislation, child care policy, grain handling and transportation, and free trade, and appeared before the Senate and House of Commons committees on numerous occasions. Thiesson also led National Farmers Union (NFU) delegations to the People's Republic of China in 1972 and 1977, and represented the NFU at an international conference, "For a Triumph

of Peace and Security in the World," in Bulgaria in 1986. On May 24, 2000, the University of Saskatchewan bestowed an honorary doctorate of laws on Thiesson for his many years of service with the SFU.

10 Hoffman, "Entry of the United Farmers," 107, note 1.

11 Jim Wright, *Saskatchewan: The History of a Province* (Toronto: McClelland & Stewart, 1955). Wright noted that the organization had one full-time employee, Ann Gilbertson, listed as secretary, and that it owed some $10,000 to creditors that were pressing for payment.

12 Keith Dryden, "What We Need Is a Protective Organization," *Saskatoon Western Producer*, September 7, 2000. The article is based on the archived notes from the UFC annual meeting in Saskatoon where Phelps was nominated and ran for the presidency of the organization.

13 Ibid., n.p.

14 Ibid., n.p.

15 Thiesson, "Rebuilding the Voluntary Farm Movement."

16 Ibid.

17 J. L. Phelps, "President's Report," *Union Farmer*, September 1950, 1.

18 Chris Hansen, comments on "The Life and Times of Fiery Joe Phelps," manuscript written by Doug Charrett, 2003, private collection.

19 "An Invitation," special supplement of the *Union Farmer*, 1969, 1.

20 James Napier McCrorie, *In Union Is Strength* (Saskatoon: Centre for Community Studies, University of Saskatchewan, 1964).

21 Fry, "Joe Phelps," n.p. Phelps states that "the small farmer—the little man—who is after all most numerous is most apt to be neglected unless some general farm organization is available in which he will have a direct voice, and which is created to protect his interests."

22 Bruce Phelps, interview by Shaak.

23 Lorne Brown, Joseph Roberts, and John Warnock define populism as "a political movement commonly found in rural areas around the world in the late 19th and 20th centuries. It sees a basic antagonism between the people and the 'powerful interests': plutocrats, big corporations, banks and their allies in government. It does not advocate overthrowing the dominant powers but reforming the system through participatory democracy and locally-controlled institutions like cooperatives. Populism has a strong commitment to small private ownership of the means of production. In North America populism has usually been right-wing but in certain localities and periods of history has been left-wing and inclined to make common cause with labour against capital." Brown, Roberts, and Warnock, *Saskatchewan Politics*, 14.

24 Fry, "Joe Phelps," n.p.

25 McCrorie, *In Union Is Strength*, 36.

26 Chris Hansen, correspondence with the author, July 2012.

27 Schulz, *Betrayal*, 49.

28 The *Union Farmer* (May 1950, 2) reported that "three hardworking people registered more than 450 delegates and visitors took in several thousand dollars in SFU memberships."

29 J. L. Phelps, "President's Report," *Union Farmer*, 1950, 1. In each monthly edition of the *Union Farmer*, Phelps submitted a president's report. These reports focused on the immediate problems faced by smaller farmers, and prices, markets, marketing agencies, freight cost, grading of grain, and self-help are recurring themes.

30 Fry, "Joe Phelps," n.p.

31 J. L. Phelps, "My 5 Years as President of the SFU," photocopy of newspaper article (source unknown), 1954, private collection.

32 Fry, "Joe Phelps," n.p. Thoner, "Hell-raising Joe Phelps."

33 Thiesson, "Rebuilding the Voluntary Farm Movement."

34 Alfred P. Gleave, *United We Stand: Prairie Farmers, 1901–1975* (Toronto: Lugus Publications, 1991), 126–127.

35 Stuart Thiesson, correspondence with the author, May 2004.

36 Gleave, *United We Stand*, 126.

37 In Larry Shaak's interviews in 2001, many referred to Phelps's dynamic public speaking ability. For example, Jake Knelson stated, "His speeches were spellbinding." Roy Atkinson said, "He was a powerful speaker. Joe was inspiring.... Learning is like a violin, you need a little tension on the strings to make music...that saying certainly fits for Joe Phelps." Stuart Thiesson noted, "Jo was a very dynamic speaker." Chris Hansen recalled a Farmers' Union rally in Canora in 1952: "The Rainbow Hall in Canora was overflowing with people and so loudspeakers were set up outside for people to hear 'Joe' Phelps and Bernice Norman speak about the problems of the days....I cannot recall what the burning issues of the day were but they must have been important as people stood around in the snow outside to listen. There were three to four hundred farmers in attendance at the meeting which indicates the degree of interest." Wilf Churchman said, "He was a good speaker, spoke clearly. Joe was always sure of himself and that was evident when he spoke publicly." Phelps's niece, Geraldine Wallace, remembered, "He always knew his subject and could inspire people."

38 Olaf (Ollie) Turnbull, interview by Shaak.

39 Charles Hopkins was among a group of students at the College of Agriculture at the University of Saskatchewan that Phelps addressed in the early fifties. He recalled Phelps stressing the importance of farmers speaking with one unified voice and running farming operations efficiently, and remembers Phelps telling a story about a farm boy who had attended college and had come back to the farm: "He looked over the hog enterprise at home rather critically and said to his father, 'Dad we've got to get this hog operation running more efficiently. These hogs should be going to market in five and a half months rather than seven to seven and a half months.' The young man's father was still having trouble accepting his son's advice and not very willing to make changes in the farming operation, and so at this point replied, 'What's time to a hog, son?'" Charles Hopkins, correspondence to Doug Charrett, December 22, 2000.

40 Waiser, *Saskatchewan*, 442. Waiser states, "Always the optimist, Devine was convinced that the situation would turn itself around. 'Don't say whoa in a mudhole,' he fondly counselled."

41 J. L. Phelps, "Address to the Manitoba Farmers Union Annual Convention in December 1951," transcript, Provincial Archives of Saskatchewan. There are very few historic records of Phelps's speeches. According to many in the SFU, Phelps spoke with few notes and, as noted above, was a powerful orator. Self-help was a recurring theme. In an address to the Manitoba Farmers Union, Phelps emphasized the need for farmers to become more actively involved and take action, and told the following story to reinforce his point: "You know that brings to mind the story about the farmer that had three dogs. He called one lawyer, the other doctor and third one farmer. Another farmer asked him, 'Why did you call those dogs by those names?' 'Well,' he said, 'by the way they act and the way they operate.' 'How do you mean?' 'We go out hunting coyotes, and we sight a coyote... take a swing around and get close enough... I pull the door and out they go.' 'What happens then?' 'The lawyer he gets them and the doctor he kills them.' 'Well what does the farmer do?' 'Oh, he sits on his hind end and howls!'"

42 Ibid.

43 Thiesson, "Rebuilding the Voluntary Farm Movement."

44 J. L. Phelps, "President's Report," *Union Farmer*, 1951, 1.

45 In 1954, Phelps defined "parity price" as a price in line with the goods and services we must purchase to continue producing. J. L. Phelps, "President's Report," *Union Farmer*, 1954, 1.

46 Waiser, *Saskatchewan*, 264. Waiser notes that the downside of the Crow Rate was that it discouraged diversification, since it was more expensive to ship other products such as livestock to market, and limited the processing of foodstuffs because it was cheaper to send the raw product out of the region. The railways argued that it was unrealistic to continue the subsidy because it only covered a third of the true cost of hauling the grain. Under the 1984 federal revisions to the agreement, farmers were paid a transportation subsidy. "In 1995 the Liberal government of Jean Chrétien, struggling with the federal debt and wanting to meet its obligations under new international trade agreements, moved to kill the benefit entirely. Farmers stood to lose 300 million annually in freight-rate subsidies." See Waiser, *Saskatchewan*, 433, 470. While opponents of the Crow Rate have argued that it discouraged diversification, many in the farm movement disagree, and the railways' true cost under the Crow remains a matter of debate even now.

47 Thiesson, "Rebuilding the Voluntary Farm Movement."

48 Ibid.

49 Ibid.

50 Phelps, "My 5 Years as President."

51 *Union Farmer*, December 1953. A joint meeting of the IFUC and the CCL was held in Saskatoon, on October 23, 1953, where it was decided to form a coordinating body to include two or three members from each group to find a common basis for agreement. The duties of the committee were to investigate what would be considered an equitable return for agricultural production based on the principle of parity, or using the method of forward pricing, and to follow up the work of the

Toronto Welfare Council to determine a fair wage for labour. Mr. Mosher and Mr. Phelps agreed to act as co-chairmen to make arrangements for future meetings.

52 Theisson, "Rebuilding the Voluntary Farm Movement."

53 J. L. Phelps, *As It Happens*, 8. The fact that Banks carried a revolver was not surprising given the Seafarers International Union's mob connections. The union was imported to Canada to break the communist-controlled Seamans Union in 1949. Eric Geiger, "Hal Banks: From Benefactor to Bully?" *St. Petersburg Times* (Florida), October 27, 1963, https://news.google.com/newspapers?nid=888&dat=19631027&id=c09SAAAAIBAJ&sjid=3nwDAAAAIBAJ&pg=6966,3010510&hl=en.

54 Bruce Dodds, correspondence with the author, January 2007.

55 Schulz, *Betrayal*, 48.

56 Ibid. Dodds worked as an organizer for the National Farmers Union, the OFU's successor, and as an organizer began working with the OFU records. The OFU collection contains numerous letters from Phelps to Cormack, OFU president from 1954 to 1957, as well as Jake Schultz's letters to Cormack and copies of much of Cormack's return correspondence to the western leaders. Dodds also interviewed over 120 farm activists from the 1950s and 1960s, including some from the west.

57 "'Friend of the Farmer' Stuart Thiesson devotes career to improving conditions for farm families," *Saskatoon StarPhoenix*, October 20, 2000.

58 Stuart Thiesson, interview by Larry Shaak, July–August 2001, transcript, private collection.

59 Wendy Roy, "Joe Phelps Rebuilt SFU, 1949–54," *Western People*, supplement in the *Saskatoon Western Producer*, April 29, 1982.

60 "An Invitation," 1.

61 The *Union Farmer* published a detailed obituary in the October 1952 issue.

62 Georgina M. Taylor, "Organized Farm Women in the WGG, UFC, SFU and NFU," *Encyclopedia of Saskatchewan* (Regina: Canadian Plains Research Center, University of Regina, 2005), 673–674.

63 Editorial tribute to Lena Phelps, *Saskatoon StarPhoenix*, September 16, 1952.

64 *Union Farmer*, October 1952.

65 Thiesson, "Rebuilding the Voluntary Farm Movement."

66 Several people interviewed by Shaak noted that Phelps often signed his correspondence "in haste."

67 Schulz, *Betrayal*, 56.

68 Chris Hansen, "Reflections of Joseph Lee Phelps," correspondence to David Goranson, August 1992.

69 Ibid.

70 J. L. Phelps, "President's Report," *Union Farmer*, 1953, 1.

71 Thoner, "Hell-raising Joe Phelps."

72 Warren and Carlisle, *On the Side of the People*, 132.

73 Thiesson, "Rebuilding the Voluntary Farm Movement."

74 Ibid.

75 Phelps, "My 5 Years as President."

76 McCrorie, *In Union Is Strength*, 47–61.

77 Phelps, "My 5 Years as President."
78 Hansen, "Reflections of Joseph Lee Phelps."
79 Roy Atkinson, interview by Larry Shaak, July–August 2001, transcript, private collection; Baptie, *Joe Phelps.*

CHAPTER 15

1 Kramer to Little, "A Literal Snapshot."
2 *Sparks off the Anvil* 23, no. 2, March/April, 1999 (newsletter of the Saskatchewan Western Development Museum).
3 J. L. Phelps, audiotape recording, private collection. Maude Claypool of Saskatoon, a pioneer member of the Women's Auxiliary to the Western Development Museum, who was anxious to have the history recorded, initiated this recording.
4 Leslie Perreaux, "There's a Story in Every Artifact," *Saskatoon StarPhoenix,* April 3, 1999, E1.
5 George LeBeau, *The Story of the Western Development Museum and Pion-Era* (Saskatoon: Western Producer Prairie Books, 1979).
6 Rick Fowler, "The Vision: A History of the Western Development Museum 1947–1954," *Liaison* (Fall 1987): 1–6. Fowler cites SAB Campbell Innes papers, IV Mounted Police and Indian Museum Subject File 40, Phelps, J. L. 1945–50.
7 Ibid. The Western Development Museum fell under the jurisdiction of the Department of Natural Resources and Industrial Development from 1944 to 1948.
8 Fowler, "The Vision." Fowler cites SAB S-W.D.M. Papers Box 11. File 2 General Correspondence, 1952–1954 To Miss H. G. Foster, of the magazine Canadian Business. From M. Porrez. July 22, 1952. The reference to Phelps flying over the North, spotting equipment, has almost become folklore and appears in many sources, including *The Story of the Western Development Museum and Pion-Era* by George LeBeau. Fowler noted that Roy Potter was responsible for going out and investigating the item after Phelps spotted it. In addition, Potter's own leads were mainly responsible for the first couple hundred exhibits. Potter was sometimes called upon by government officials in Washington, DC, to accomplish the "seemingly impossible" restoration of some of these old machines.
9 Fowler, "The Vision."
10 Kaeding, "Reminiscence of a good friend and mentor."
11 Transcription of George LeBeau audiotape, January 2001, private collection.
12 Ibid.
13 *Battlefords News-Optimist*, August 28, 1947, S-W.D.M. Papers, Box 5 File 11 "History—Newspaper Reports," Provincial Archives of Saskatchewan.
14 *50 Years of WDM Achievements*, Western Development Museum 1999–2000 annual report information package, private collection.
15 Fowler, "The Vision."
16 *Annual Report of the Western Development Museum Board*, December 31, 1949, to J. A. Darling, Minister of Public Works, from J. L. Phelps, Chairman, Western Development Museum Board, private collection.

17 *50 Years of WDM Achievements.*
18 Fowler, "The Vision."
19 *50 Years of WDM Achievements.*
20 LeBeau, *Story of the Western Development Museum.*
21 Monique Roy-Sole, "Grass-roots Heritage: Prairie Populism Has Produced a Unique Brand of Museums by the People for the People," *Canadian Geographic*, June/July 1991, 22.
22 LeBeau, *Story of the Western Development Museum.* This booklet includes the letter from WDM Secretary Carl L. McLeod to Phelps, advising that at the annual meeting on April 24, 1963, Phelps was elected honorary chairman of the board of directors by unanimous vote. A portion of the minutes also included read: "The fact that the Western Development Museum now exists as a living reflection of the past, and has magnificent displays in Saskatoon, North Battleford and Yorkton, stands as a lasting monument to Mr. Phelps. More than any other person he may stand up and be counted as the man who built a rich tribute to the people of many lands[,] who came to our country[,] built a province, communities and a way of life. While countless individual acts of generosity and faith have gone into the building of our Museum, it is to Mr. Phelps that we must properly look for having given motivation, drive and the guiding force that brought this Museum to reality."
23 "Phelps Praised at Museum Opening," *Battlefords News-Optimist*, May 1963.
24 Perreaux, "There's a Story in Every Artifact."
25 Roy, "Joe Phelps Rebuilt SFU."
26 As told to the author by Ella Little, 2006.
27 J. L. Phelps, "Put this in your pipe and smoke it," *The Saskatoon Commentator* 3, no. 36 (1971): 1.
28 Bob Little, interview by Larry Shaak, 2001, transcript, private collection.
29 *50 Years of WDM Achievements.*
30 Kramer to Little, "A Literal Snapshot."

CHAPTER 16

1 J. L. Phelps, *Minority Report* (a dissent from certain conclusions and recommendations made in Commission Report 13 on Farm Income) (Regina: Lawrence Amon, Printer to the Queen's Most Excellent Majesty, 1958), Royal Commission on Agriculture and Rural Life, Provincial Archives of Saskatchewan, 1.
2 Paula Ray Rein, "These Changing Times: A Study of the Saskatchewan Royal Commission on Agriculture and Rural Life" (master's thesis, University of Regina, 1999) contains a detailed analysis of the final reports of the Royal Commission on Agriculture and Rural Life. The thesis was an important source for researching this chapter.
3 Province of Saskatchewan, Royal Commission on Agriculture and Rural Life, letter from Phelps to Harding, dated September 6, 1952, Provincial Archives of Saskatchewan.

4 Ibid.
5 Ibid.
6 Ibid.
7 Ibid.
8 William M. Harding, "1952–1957: The Royal Commission on Agriculture & Rural Life," SAB RE 2101, Provincial Archives of Saskatchewan, 20.
9 Ibid., 9.
10 Province of Saskatchewan, Royal Commission on Agriculture and Rural Life, Final Reports, 1958, SAB RE 3945, Provincial Archives of Saskatchewan.
11 Harding, "1952–1957," 12.
12 Rein, "These Changing Times," 168.
13 Ibid., 166.
14 Harding, "1952–1957," 24.
15 Harding, "1952–1957," 20.
16 Rein, "These Changing Times," 169. Forty years later, the Royal Commission's legacy is difficult to assess. In one sense, Saskatchewan in general, and rural Saskatchewan, in particular, have changed dramatically. Yet many of the economic and social issues the Royal Commission discussed continue to dominate public debate in Saskatchewan.
17 Phelps, *Minority Report*, 1, 2.
18 Ibid., 2.
19 CCF, *Regina Manifesto*, 3.
20 Phelps, *Minority Report*, 5.
21 Ibid., 6.
22 Ibid., 9.
23 For example, Chris Hansen left the SFU at the end of his term in 1956 to work as a community consultant for the Centre for Community Studies at the University of Saskatchewan, and, in 1960, worked for the Cooperative Union of Saskatchewan, setting up a provincial education program for local co-operative boards, management, and staff and developing the structure for co-operatives throughout Saskatchewan. He then spent fifteen years with the Saskatchewan Wheat Pool, culminating in the corporate planning position of assistant corporate secretary. He was elected president of the Canadian Cooperative Credit Society, a position he held along with president of the Saskatchewan system and president of Sherwood Credit Union, with the support of the Wheat Pool. His work with the credit union movement took him to Kamloops, British Columbia, to an overseas consulting assignment in Malawi, followed by several years of development projects in southeast Asia, and, later, to the head office of the World Council of Credit Unions in Madison, Wisconsin. Chris Hansen, correspondence with the author, 2012.
24 "An Invitation," special supplement of the *Union Farmer*, 1969, 10.
25 Schulz, *Betrayal*, 124.
26 Ibid., 123.
27 Ibid., 1.

28 Ibid., 120.

29 Ibid., 123.

CHAPTER 17

1 In 1962, Phelps was the CCF federal candidate in the Battlefords riding. *Regina Commonwealth*, May 30, 1962, 5. Before he contested the nomination, a *Battlefords News-Optimist* article stated, "Almost certainly the fighting farmer from Wilkie will win the nomination" (January 10, 1962). He was pictured in front of the new home of the North Battleford branch of the Western Development Museum, and the article stated, "Phelps is president of the Board of Directors of the museum and was a potent force in getting construction started on the museum.... He was the founder of the museum's first branch located at the local airport." He was defeated in the election. The results were as follows: Albert R. Horner (Progressive Conservative), 11,970 votes; Joe Phelps (CCF), 5,166 votes; and S. Duff Noble (Liberal), 5,045 votes. Saskatchewan, *Directory of Members of Parliament and Federal Elections*.

2 "Joe Phelps Vancouver Island Ventures," interviews by Larry Shaak with family and friends of Joe Phelps, including Steve Phelps, Maurice Mitchell, David Hopkins, Larry West, Dem Carrier, Emily Phelps, D. G. Holmwood, Dolly Holmwood, Don Mullet, and Eileen Flintoff, July 2001, transcript, private collection. In July 2001, Joe and Ray Phelps also built a unique, privately owned, sewage treatment plant on the Langford property. Water quality was of concern to residents because bedrock in the area made the use of septic tanks impossible. Eventually, the community of Langford took root as a result, and Phelps Subdivision and Phelps Road were named to recognize the Phelps brothers' role in initiating the Langford development.

3 Ibid.

4 Rick Goranson, interview by Larry Shaak, 2001, transcript, private collection.

5 "Joe Phelps Vancouver Island Ventures," interviews by Shaak.

6 Rick Goranson, interview by Shaak.

7 In January 1967, *The Family Herald: Canada's National Farm Magazine*, ran an article by J. L. Phelps under their *One Man's Opinion* column. In it, Phelps proposed a unique scheme to reorganize the nation's "entire food production, processing and handling facilities," taking control out of the hands of giant food chain corporations and placing it in the hands of the producers:

> I suggest that a general all-Canadian national food producers' organization be established without further delay and that provincial sections of such be organized at once. Among every classification of food producers in Canada a registration or license fee of $10 annually could be charged to each production unit and a levy on production be established by annual deduction from produce marketed. This fund would be used to acquire or construct new structures and facilities for

> shipping, storing, processing, packaging and for administration of a producers' national food marketing board in Canada with provincial sections in each province. These deductions would be included in the final cost of food. Alternatively these facilities could, with justification be financed from the national Treasury and be considered as an essential public service as is the post office system, our roads, or our national defense. The point is an adequate supply of good food is even more important to Canada and the Canadian people than any other item.

He also elaborated on the appointment of a democratic board of directors, the establishment of prices, construction of facilities, necessary legislation, and further administrative suggestions. J. L. Phelps, "Producers Should Get into the Processing Business," *The Family Herald: Canada's National Farm Magazine*, January 5, 1967, 8.

8 Ken Warren, "Exhibit Site Sought: Vintage Machinery of Past B.C. Era Would Be Displayed for Today's Youth," *Victoria Daily Colonist*, August 30, 1968, 21.

9 In 1968, Phelps unloaded railway flatcars of five pieces of machinery to be exhibited at Saanichton Fair Grounds. Additional equipment followed, including several antique steam engines. The artifacts were later moved to the Metchosin Farmers' Institute at the Luxton fairgrounds, where the equipment became a catalyst for growth and development of the institute. "Joe Phelps Vancouver Island Ventures," interviews by Shaak.

10 Ibid.

11 Baptie, *Joe Phelps*, 2. Phelps related this story about his response to a senior who said they were doing all right on their basic pension: "I said, 'Alright, first of all do you own your own home?' She was in a small town…'Oh yes,' she said, 'we've always had our home.' Well, that's a different ball game. Right away quiet. And then I said to her, 'I suppose you're old timers in that district and you had a farm.' 'Oh yeah,' she said, 'we farmed just a half mile up town.'…'and I suppose one of the children have it now.' And she said the oldest son. And then I said, 'well I suppose he brings you in some vegetables once and a while.' She said he pretty well keeps us supplied. And I said, 'in the fall he may bring you in a chunk of meat too.' Yes he does that. And then I said you told me you were living on the pension only…I said, 'listen, you bring your husband down and meet me on second avenue in Saskatoon and bring your cheques with you. We'll look for a place for you to stay for a month, on those cheques only and feed yourself and see how you make out.' 'Oh well,' she said, 'that would be different.' 'Yes,' I said, 'it's different for a lot of people.'"

12 Rosemary Williams, "Challenge always interests Joe Phelps," newspaper clipping, unknown source and date, private collection.

13 Ibid.

14 Baptie, *Joe Phelps*.

15 Saskatchewan, *Debates and Proceedings, Hansard*, Legislative Assembly of Saskatchewan, Second Session, Twentieth Legislature, March 21, 1983.

16 Ibid.

17 Thiesson, eulogy for Joseph Phelps. Joe was survived by his wife Eva; three sons, Lee, of Wilkie, Bruce, of Saskatoon, and Gordon, of Saskatoon; one daughter, Ella Little, of Langley, British Columbia; two stepsons, Bernard Nyholt, of rural North Battleford, and Jon Nyholt, of Calgary, Alberta; one stepdaughter, Marie Campbell; twelve grandchildren; three great-grandchildren; seven step-grandchildren; one sister, Eva Mullett, of Victoria, British Columbia; and one brother, Don, of North Battleford.

18 McLeod and McLeod, *Tommy Douglas*, 308.

EPILOGUE

1 Baptie, *Joe Phelps*.

2 Ella Little, conversation with the author, June 2012. Ella described Joe and Lena as an "original emancipated couple" and noted that they were supportive of each other. Lena supported Joe, but Joe also supported Lena in her own pursuits. Lena loved to entertain and was a wonderful cook.

3 McLeod and McLeod, *Tommy Douglas*, 123–124.

4 *Regina Leader-Post*, February 20, 1946, 1, 8.

5 J. F. C. Wright, quoted in McCrorie, *In Union Is Strength*, 50.

6 T. C. Douglas responding to W. A. Tucker's criticism of the Crown corporations. Douglas to Tucker, October 19, 1949, T. C. Douglas Papers, VI. 105, (6-1-3), Provincial Archives of Saskatchewan.

7 Richards and Pratt, *Prairie Capitalism*, 143.

8 J. L. Phelps, interview by Larmour, 44–45; Baptie, *Joe Phelps*. Phelps said Douglas was receptive but cautious to Phelps's proposals and thought, "We should walk pretty easy." Phelps singled out Oak Valleau as being supportive and Woodrow Lloyd as not being "unsympathetic." J. L. Phelps, interview by Richards.

9 Richards and Pratt, *Prairie Capitalism*, 106.

10 McLeod and McLeod, *Tommy Douglas*, 123–124.

11 A. W. Johnson, "Biography of a Government: Policy Formation in Saskatchewan, 1944–1961" (PhD dissertation, Harvard University, Cambridge, MA, 1963), 198.

12 Richards and Pratt, *Prairie Capitalism*, 109–110.

13 Ibid., 115.

14 Johnson, "Biography of a Government," 184. On November 1, 1944, the government inaugurated the Fur Marketing Service. Phelps to Douglas, February 9, 1945, Joseph Lee Phelps Papers (M15), Box 4, "Public Health Department," Provincial Archives of Saskatchewan.

15 Johnson, "Biography of a Government," 184.

16 Alan Whitehorn, "Regina Manifesto," *Encyclopedia of Saskatchewan* (Regina: Canadian Plains Research Center, University of Regina, 2005), 748.

17 McLeod and McLeod, *Tommy Douglas*, 165.

18 Ibid., 123–124.

19 Radloff, "Cooperative and State Ownership," 41.

20 Seymour Martin Lipset noted that Phelps "entered [the 1944 CCF] government as its most radical member." Lipset, *Agrarian Socialism*, 283.

21 Cadbury, interview by Larmour, n.p.; Baptie, *Joe Phelps*, 8.

22 Richards and Pratt, *Prairie Capitalism*, 142–143.

23 Ibid.

24 M. J. Coldwell, *Left Turn, Canada* (Toronto: Duell, Sloan and Pearce, 1945), 174.

25 Richards and Pratt, *Prairie Capitalism*, 115.

26 Ibid., 115–116.

27 Johnson, "Biography of a Government," 198.

28 Phelps even worked without an actual deputy minister from July 1944 to April 1945. P. W. Doakes was deputy minister, but Phelps shortly demoted him. According to Phelps, Doakes simply became "a figurehead." J. L. Phelps, interview by Larmour, 28. From December 14, 1944, to March 12, 1945, the Joseph Lee Phelps Papers contain at least six letters in which L. C. Paterson refers to himself as the "Acting Deputy Minister," or others, including Phelps, refer to him by that title. On April 2, 1945, Henry Lewis became the official deputy minister. Of course, after Lewis resigned on July 31, 1946, C. A. L. Hogg became the deputy minister on October 15, 1946. *Saskatchewan Executive and Legislative Directory*, 35.

29 As David Quiring points out, one might be surprised that Phelps, an ardent socialist, who so strongly advocated socialism, continued "his own entrepreneurial farming enterprise." Quiring, *CCF Colonialism*, 18. Classical Marxist analysis defines the petit bourgeoisie as an intermediate class that owns and controls their own means of production, including small business owners and farmers.

30 Lipset, *Agrarian Socialism*, 283.

31 Johnson, *Dream No Little Dreams*, 75.

32 Bruce Dodds, correspondence with the author, January 5, 2007. Bruce worked for many years as an agricultural organizer, including for the National Farmers Union. Bruce read an earlier version of this manuscript and sent a detailed critique with many excellent suggestions, including many of the ideas presented in this summary of Phelps's political orientation. He was curator of the museum exhibit *For the Love of the Land: The Story of the Ontario Farmers' Union 1952–1969*, which opened at the Workers Arts and Heritage Centre in Hamilton, Ontario, in September 2006.

33 Ibid.

34 Minutes of UFC Annual Convention, 1931, United Farmer of Canada (Saskatchewan Section) Papers, Provincial Archives of Saskatchewan.

35 James McCrorie identifies four stages in the organizational development of movements. The first is a period of unrest and discontent, the second a stage of collective excitement, the third a stage of organization, and the last a stage of institutionalization. McCrorie, *In Union Is Strength*, 48.

36 Bruce Dodds, correspondence with the author, January 2007.

37 Allan Levine, *The Exchange: 100 Years of Trading Grain in Winnipeg* (Winnipeg: Peguis Publishers Limited, 1987), 238.

38 Ibid., 50.

39 *Saskatoon StarPhoenix*, January 24, 1946, n.p.

40 Bruce Dodds, correspondence with the author, January 2007.

41 Phelps's grandson Greg Phelps noted in his interview with Larry Shaak that Joe Phelps endorsed and supported the Waffle movement when it surfaced provincially. Greg Phelps, interview by Larry Shaak, July–August 2001, transcript, private collection. The Waffle movement emerged within the NDP in the late 1960s, advocating for a move to the left and the return to socialist policies. Brown, Roberts, and Warnock, *Saskatchewan Politics*.

42 Lipset, *Agrarian Socialism*, 286.

43 Bruce Dodds, correspondence with the author, January 2007.

SELECTED BIBLIOGRAPHY

PRIMARY SOURCES

Government Documents

Saskatchewan. *Crown Corporations, Province of Saskatchewan, Annual Report.* 2002.

Saskatchewan. *Debates and Proceedings. Hansard.* Legislative Assembly of Saskatchewan, Second Session, Twentieth Legislature, March 21, 1983.

Saskatchewan. *Directory of Members of Parliament and Federal Elections for the North-West Territories and Saskatchewan, 1887–1966.* Regina and Saskatoon: Saskatchewan Archives Board, 1967.

Saskatchewan Executive and Legislative Directory, 1905–1970. Regina and Saskatoon: Saskatchewan Archives Board, 1971.

Saskatchewan Executive and Legislative Directory Supplement, 1964–1977. Regina and Saskatoon: Saskatchewan Archives Board, 1978.

Saskatchewan. *The Natural Resources of Saskatchewan, 1945.* Regina: King's Printer, 1945.

Saskatchewan. *Public Enterprise in Saskatchewan.* Regina: Crown Investments Corporation of Saskatchewan, 1981.

Saskatchewan. *Report of the Royal Commission on Forestry of Saskatchewan.* 1946.

Saskatchewan. *Report of the Royal Commission on the Fisheries of Saskatchewan.* 1947.

Saskatchewan. *Report of the Saskatchewan Reconstruction Council.* 1944.

Saskatchewan. *Sessional Paper No. 102*, March 28, 1947.

Saskatchewan. *Statutes of Saskatchewan*, 9, George VI (1939), Chapter 9.

Saskatchewan. *Statutes of Saskatchewan*, 8 George VI (1944), Chapter 8.

Saskatchewan. *Wings Beyond Road's End: Airplanes Over Saskatchewan's North.* La Ronge, SK: Saskatchewan Education, Northern Division, 1992.

Manuscript Collections

Co-operative Commonwealth Federation. Papers. Provincial Archives of Saskatchewan.

Douglas, Thomas Clement (T. C.). Papers. Provincial Archives of Saskatchewan.
Farmer-Labour Group 1932–1934. Papers. Provincial Archives of Saskatchewan.
Homestead Records. Provincial Archives of Saskatchewan.
Larmour, Jean. Papers. Provincial Archives of Saskatchewan.
Phelps, Joseph Lee. Papers. Provincial Archives of Saskatchewan.
Saskatchewan Crown Corporations Board Minutes. Provincial Archives of Saskatchewan.
Saskatchewan Royal Commission on Agriculture and Rural Life. Papers. Provincial Archives of Saskatchewan.
United Farmers of Canada (Saskatchewan Section). Papers. Provincial Archives of Saskatchewan.

Interviews

Baptie, Sheila. *Joe Phelps: An Impatient Man*. Winnipeg: Points West, 1981. Video transcript. Provincial Archives of Saskatchewan.
Cadbury, George. Interview by Jean Larmour. June 15, 1981; January 21, 22, 1982. Transcript. Provincial Archives of Saskatchewan.
Douglas, T. C. Interview by Chris Higginbotham. "T. C. Douglas Recording Series." 1958. Provincial Archives of Saskatchewan.
Phelps, J. L. *As It Happens*. CBC Radio. 1988. Interview transcript provided by Phelps family.
Phelps, J. L. Interview by Berry Richards. 1976. Transcript. Provincial Archives of Saskatchewan.
Phelps, J. L. Interview by Clint O. White. January 1975. Transcript. Provincial Archives of Saskatchewan.
Phelps, J. L. Interview by Jean Larmour. June 1, 1982. Transcript. Provincial Archives of Saskatchewan.
Phelps, J. L. Interview by Murray Dobbin. June 1976. Indian History Film Project. Transcript. Provincial Archives of Saskatchewan.
Phelps, J. L. Interview by Saskatchewan Archives Board staff. December 1970. Audiotape. Provincial Archives of Saskatchewan.

SECONDARY SOURCES

Andrews, Ken. "'Progressive' Counterparts of the CCF: Social Credit and the Conservative Party in Saskatchewan, 1935–1938." *Journal of Canadian Studies* 17, no. 3 (Fall 1982): 58–74.
Archer, John H. *Saskatchewan: A History*. Saskatoon: Western Producer Prairie Books, 1980.
Banks, Brian. "The Co-operative Commonwealth Federation Government and Economic Planning in Natural Resources and Industrial Development, 1944–1946." Honours essay, Department of History, University of Regina, 1977.

———. "The Political Economy of Petroleum Development in Saskatchewan, 1940–1960." Master's thesis, University of Regina, 1986.

Barron, F. Laurie. *Walking in Indian Moccasins: The Native Policies of Tommy Douglas and the CCF*. Vancouver: UBC Press, 1997.

Berton, Pierre. *The Promised Land: Settling the West, 1896–1914*. Toronto: McClelland & Stewart, 1984.

Bothwell, Robert. *Eldorado: Canada's National Uranium Company*. Toronto: University of Toronto Press, 1984.

Brennan, J. William. *Regina: An Illustrated History*. Toronto: James Lorimer & Company, 1989.

Brown, Lorne, Joseph Roberts, and John Warnock. *Saskatchewan Politics from Left to Right, '44 to '99*. Regina: Hinterland Publications, 1999.

Buhr, Larry E. "An Archeological Survey of Brick Manufacture in Saskatchewan." Master's thesis, University of Saskatchewan, 1997.

Coldwell, M. J. *Left Turn, Canada*. Toronto: Duell, Sloan and Pearce, 1945.

Co-operative Commonwealth Federation. *Regina Manifesto*. Programme of the Co-operative Commonwealth Federation, adopted at First National Convention held at Regina, Saskatchewan, July 1933. Regina: Service Printing Co., 1933.

Dobbin, Murray. *The One-and-a-Half Men: The Story of Jim Brady and Malcolm Norris, Métis Patriots of the 20th Century*. Vancouver: New Star Books, 1981.

Douglas, T. C. "Reflections of a Hard-headed Dreamer." *Reader's Digest*, 1979.

Duffin, Jacalyn. "The Guru and the Godfather: Henry Sigerist, Hugh MacLean, and the Politics of Health Care Reform in 1940s Canada." *CBMH/BCHM* 9 (1992): 191–218.

The Eighty Year History Society. *A Harvest of Memories: A History of Rural Wilkie*. Battleford, SK: Turner-Warwick Printers, 1984.

Fairbairn, Garry. *From Prairie Roots: The Remarkable Story of the Saskatchewan Wheat Pool*. Saskatoon: Western Producer Prairie Books, 1984.

Forrieter, Eileen. "Joseph Lee Phelps: An Impulsive Radical." Master's thesis, University of Regina, 2005.

Fowler, Rick. "The Vision: A History of the Western Development Museum 1947–1954." *Liaison* (Fall 1987): 1–6.

Fry, H. S. "Joe Phelps, President, Saskatchewan Farmers Union." *Country Guide*. November 1, 1950.

Gleave, Alfred P. *United We Stand: Prairie Farmers, 1901–1975*. Toronto: Lugus Publications, 1991.

Gulig, Anthony, G. "In Whose Interest? Government Indian Relations in Northern Saskatchewan and Wisconsin, 1900–1940." PhD dissertation, University of Saskatchewan, 1997.

———. "Sizing up the Catch: Native-Newcomer Resource Competition and the Early Years of Saskatchewan's Northern Commercial Fishery." *Saskatchewan History* 47, no. 3 (Fall 1995): 3–11.

Higginbotham, C. H. *Off the Record: The CCF in Saskatchewan*. Toronto: McClelland & Stewart, 1968.

Hoffman, George. "Eliason, Frank." *Encyclopedia of Saskatchewan*. Regina: Canadian Plains Research Center, University of Regina, 2005.

———. "The Entry of the United Farmers of Canada, Saskatchewan Section into Politics: A Reassessment." *Saskatchewan History* 30, no. 3 (1977): 99–109.

———. "The Saskatchewan Farmer-Labour Party, 1932–1934: How Radical Was its Origin?" In *Pages from the Past: Essays on Saskatchewan History*, edited by D. H. Bocking, 211–224. Saskatoon: Western Producer Prairie Books, 1979.

———. "The Saskatchewan Provincial Election of 1934: Its Political, Economic, and Social Background." Master's thesis, University of Saskatchewan, Regina Campus, 1973.

Howlett, Michael. "The Forest Industry on the Prairies: Opportunities and Constraints to Future Development." *Prairie Forum* 14, no. 2 (Fall 1989): 233–257.

Johnson, A. W. "Biography of a Government: Policy Formation in Saskatchewan, 1944–1961." PhD dissertation, Harvard University, Cambridge, MA, 1963.

———. *Dream No Little Dreams: A Biography of the Douglas Government of Saskatchewan, 1944–1961*. Toronto: University of Toronto Press, 2004.

LeBeau, George. *The Story of the Western Development Museum and Pion-Era*. Saskatoon: Western Producer Prairie Books, 1979.

Levine, Allan. *The Exchange: 100 Years of Trading Grain in Winnipeg*. Winnipeg: Peguis Publishers Limited, 1987.

Lipset, S. M. *Agrarian Socialism: The Cooperative Commonwealth Federation in Saskatchewan: A Study in Political Sociology*. Berkeley: University of California Press, 1967.

Makahonuk, Glen. *Class, State and Power: The Struggle for Trade Union Rights in Saskatchewan, 1905–1997*. Saskatoon: Makahonuk/CUPE, 1997.

Marchildon, Gregory. Foreword to *Dream No Little Dreams: A Biography of the Douglas Government of Saskatchewan, 1944–1961* by A. W. Johnson, xv–xxxi. Toronto: University of Toronto Press, 2004.

McCrorie, James Napier. *In Union Is Strength*. Saskatoon: Centre for Community Studies, University of Saskatchewan, 1964.

McLeod, Thomas H., and Ian McLeod. *Tommy Douglas: The Road to Jerusalem*. Edmonton: Hurtig Publishers, 1987.

Milnor, Andrew Jackson. "Agrarian Protest in Saskatchewan, 1929–1948: A Study in Ethnic Politics." PhD dissertation, Duke University, Durham, NC, 1962.

Phelps, J. L. "Producers Should Get into the Processing Business." *The Family Herald: Canada's National Farm Magazine*. January 5, 1967.

Pitsula, James M. "The Saskatchewan CCF Government and Treaty Indians, 1944–64." *Canadian Historical Review* 75, no. 1 (March 1994): 21–52.

Potyondi, Barry. *In Palliser's Triangle: Living in the Grasslands, 1850–1930.* Saskatoon: Purich Publishing, 1995.

Quiring, David M. "Battling Parish Priests, Bootleggers, and Fur Sharks: CCF Colonialism in Northern Saskatchewan." PhD dissertation, University of Saskatchewan, 2002.

———. *CCF Colonialism in Northern Saskatchewan: Battling Parish Priests, Bootleggers, and Fur Sharks.* Vancouver: UBC Press, 2004.

Radloff, Karla. "Cooperative and State Ownership in Northern Saskatchewan under the CCF Government." Master's thesis, University of Saskatchewan, 2004.

Rediger, Pat. *The Crowns: A History of Public Enterprise in Saskatchewan.* Regina: Canadian Plains Research Center, University of Regina, 2004.

Rein, Paula Ray. "These Changing Times: A Study of the Saskatchewan Royal Commission on Agriculture and Rural Life." Master's thesis, University of Regina, 1999.

Richards, John, and Larry Pratt. *Prairie Capitalism: Power and Influence in the New West.* Toronto: McClelland & Stewart, 1979.

Roy-Sole, Monique. "Grass-roots Heritage: Prairie Populism Has Produced a Unique Brand of Museums by the People for the People." *Canadian Geographic.* June/July 1991.

Schulz, Herbert. *Betrayal: Agricultural Politics in the Fifties.* Calgary: University of Calgary Press, 2004.

Shackleton, Doris French. *Tommy Douglas.* Toronto: McClelland & Stewart, 1975.

Sherdahl, Raymond Merle. "The Saskatchewan General Election of 1944." Master's thesis, University of Saskatchewan, 1966.

Sinclair, Peter R. "The Saskatchewan CCF: Ascent to Power and the Decline of Socialism." *Canadian Historical Review* 54, no. 4 (December 1973): 419–433.

Smith, David E. *Prairie Liberalism: The Liberal Party in Saskatchewan, 1905–1971.* Toronto: University of Toronto Press, 1975.

Spafford, Duff. "The Origin of the Farmers' Union of Canada." *Saskatchewan History* 18, no. 3 (Autumn 1965): 89–98.

Spafford, Shirley. *No Ordinary Academics: Economics and Political Science at the University of Saskatchewan, 1910–1960.* Toronto: University of Toronto Press, 2000.

Steininger, Friedrich. "George H. Williams: Agrarian Socialist." Master's thesis, University of Regina, 1976.

Swerhone, Elise. *Tommy Douglas: Keeper of the Flame.* Montreal: National Film Board of Canada, 1986. Film, 58 min.

Taylor, Georgina M. "Organized Farm Women in the WGG, UFC, SFU and NFU." *Encyclopedia of Saskatchewan.* Regina: Canadian Plains Research Center, University of Regina, 2005.

Thiesson, Stuart A. "Farm Movement (1901–49)." *Encyclopedia of Saskatchewan.* Regina: Canadian Plains Research Center, University of Regina, 2005.

Thomas, Lewis H. "The CCF Victory in Saskatchewan, 1944." *Saskatchewan History* 34, no. 1 (Winter 1981): 1–16.

Waiser, Bill. *Saskatchewan: A New History.* Calgary: Fitzhenry & Whiteside, 2005.

Warren, Jim, and Kathleen Carlisle. *On the Side of the People: A History of Labour in Saskatchewan.* Regina: Coteau Books, 2005.

White, Clinton O. *Power for a Province: A History of Saskatchewan Power.* Regina: Canadian Plains Research Center, University of Regina, 1976.

Whitehorn, Alan. "Regina Manifesto." *Encyclopedia of Saskatchewan.* Regina: Canadian Plains Research Center, University of Regina, 2005.

Winkel, James. *Northern Saskatchewan: A Transformation.* Regina: Saskatchewan Northern Affairs, 2002.

Wright, Jim. *Saskatchewan: The History of a Province.* Toronto: McClelland & Stewart, 1955.

Young, Walter D. *The Anatomy of a Party: The National CCF, 1932–61.* Toronto: University of Toronto Press, 1969.

———. "M. J. Coldwell, The Making of a Social Democrat." *Journal of Canadian Studies* 9, no. 3 (August 1974): 50–60.

INDEX

Q

R

S